On the Edge

THE U.S. SINCE 1945

DAVID A. HOROWITZ
Portland State University

PETER N. CARROLL
Stanford University

WADSWORTH

THOMSON LEARNING

Australia • Canada • Mexico • Singapore • Spain • United Kingdom • United States

WADSWORTH

─────✳─────™

THOMSON LEARNING

Editorial Director: Clark G. Baxter
Senior Development Editor: Sue Gleason
Assistant Editor: Jennifer Ellis
Editorial Assistant: Jonathan Katz
Executive Marketing Manager:
Diane McOscar
Marketing Assistant: Kasia Zagorski
Project Manager: Dianne Jensis Toop
Print Buyer: Robert King
Permissions Editor: Joohee Lee
Production Service: Hal Lockwood,
Penmarin Books
Photo Researcher: Connie Hathaway

Copy Editor: Betty Berenson
Cover Designer: Lisa Devenish
Cover Images: Clockwise from top left:
Kennedy, AP/Wide World Photos;
Hiroshima, AP/Wide World Photos; war
protester, © Bettmann/CORBIS; President
and Mrs. Clinton, AP/Wide World Photos;
Kent State shooting, John Filo/Archive
Photos; Nixon, © Liaison Agency
Cover Printer: Maple-Vail (NY)
Compositor: Thompson Type
Printer: Maple-Vail (NY)

Printed in the United States of America
1 2 3 4 5 6 7 05 04 03 02 01

For permission to use material from this text, contact us by:
Web: http://www.thomsonrights.com   **Fax:** 1-800-730-2215   **Phone:** 1-800-730-2214

Wadsworth/Thomson Learning
10 Davis Drive
Belmont, CA 94002-3098
USA

For information about our products,
contact us:
Thomson Learning Academic
Resource Center
1-800-423-0563
http:/www.wadsworth.com

International Headquarters
Thomson Learning
International Division
290 Harbor Drive, 2nd Floor
Stamford, CT 06902-7477
USA

UK/Europe/Middle East/South Africa
Thomson Learning
Berkshire House
168-173 High Holborn
London WC1V 7AA
United Kingdom

Asia
Thomson Learning
60 Albert Street, #15-01
Albert Complex
Singapore 189969

Canada
Nelson Thomson Learning
1120 Birchmount Road
Toronto, Ontario M1K 5G4
Canada

Library of Congress Cataloging-in-Publication Data

Horowitz, David A.
On the edge : the U.S. since 1945 / David A. Horowitz, Peter N. Carroll—3rd ed.
p. cm.
Includes bibliographical references and index.
ISBN 0-534-57187-5
1. United States—History—1945– 2. United States—Politics and government—1945–1989.
3. United States—Politics and government—1989– I. Carroll, Peter N. II. Title.
E741 .H68 2001
973.92—dc21   2001026297

For

DAVID W. NOBLE

and to the memory of

LOIS NOBLE

Contents

of individuals to illuminate important themes of the period. Chapter reading lists describe four recommended titles found in most college libraries, followed by an annotated list of additional sources. We have further simplified graphs, charts, and tables for quick reference and easy comprehension. Monetary figures are conveyed in current dollars—the actual value for the period under discussion. A separate volume, *On the Edge: The U.S. in the 20th Century*, is also available from this publisher.

David Horowitz extends appreciation for the aid, comfort, and sustenance of Gloria Myers Horowitz. Peter Carroll acknowledges the counsel and support of Jeannette Ferrary. The authors offer special thanks to Editorial Director Clark G. Baxter and Developmental Editor Sue Gleason.

DAVID A. HOROWITZ and PETER N. CARROLL

Preface

On the Edge: The U.S. Since 1945 is an interpretive history that describes the challenges and dilemmas that have confronted the nation since the end of World War II. The book follows two major themes. First, it traces the expansion of national economic and political power at home and abroad. Second, it provides an account of the domestic conflicts and controversies precipitated by such growth.

On the Edge seeks a balanced perspective by providing equitable coverage to elites and out-groups, liberals and conservatives, modernists and traditionalists, and politicians and cultural figures. The text goes beyond the narration of conflict among powerful institutional leaders to portray the significant historical roles played by nominally powerless people—ranging from the working class and poor to be the beleaguered middle class to women in all classes and to the nation's racial, ethnic, and cultural minorities. It also explores how technology, popular culture, and social innovation have affected mainstream life and institutions.

Our intention is to stimulate the critical perspective of instructors and students by combining narrative and analytic history in jargon-free prose. Three major revisions characterize the current edition. First, the narrative now commences in 1945, a starting point for many courses in recent U.S. history. Second, political and cultural developments have been combined in chapters covering briefer time spans. Third, each chapter includes a popular culture insert that highlights a U.S. film with particular social significance.

Although chapters follow a general chronological outline, they are divided into thematic sections to encourage conceptualization and provocative discussion. Each chapter also includes several biographical sketches that use the lives

THE SEARCH FOR SECURITY, 1945–1949

On August 6, 1945, President Harry S Truman, successor to the late Franklin D. Roosevelt, announced that the United States had just exploded a new weapon—an atomic bomb—over the Japanese city of Hiroshima. After another atomic weapon incinerated the city of Nagasaki, Japan agreed to surrender, ending World War II, the most devastating war in human history, on August 14 (V-J Day). The defeated Axis countries—Germany and Japan—lay in ruins. The victorious Allies had also suffered huge casualties, including 25 million Russians who perished. Nazi German concentration camps had killed about 10 million people, including 6 million Jews, in an unprecedented human holocaust. American casualties were relatively low: 405,000 U.S. soldiers had died; 800,000 more were wounded. The war had not even touched North America.

"Ours is the supreme position," exulted a New York newspaper as the war came to an end. "The Great Republic has come into its own; it stands first among the peoples of the earth." The nation's massive wartime production had provided the materials for victory and proven the immense power of its economic system. The formation of the World Bank and the International Monetary Fund in 1944 promised to bring stability to overseas economic relations and reduce the national rivalries that had led to military aggression. Political leaders looked to an interrelated international marketplace to prevent the conditions that had caused the Great Depression of the 1930s. The United States also tried to implement democratic principles of self-government in other countries, although international agreements and global power relations would limit success. Nevertheless, the founding of the United Nations in 1945 suggested that international cooperation would protect the national interests of member nations and prevent another world war.

The Allies also determined to establish international rules of justice that would discourage, or at least punish, the crimes committed by German militarists. In 1945 the Allies convened the International Military Tribunal at Nuremberg, Germany, to bring Nazi war criminals to trial. In convicting twenty-two

Germans of war crimes, the tribunal upheld basic principles of warfare: wars of aggression and inhuman acts constituted war crimes; individuals accused of crimes were entitled to judicial trials; and individuals remained accountable for their actions even though they were following orders of superiors. These legal principles endeavored to create a postwar world of peace and justice.

American optimism was tempered, however, by new realities of global power. Six days after the atomic bombing of Hiroshima, radio commentator Edward R. Murrow observed, "Seldom, if ever, has a war ended leaving the victors with such a sense of uncertainty and fear, with such a realization that the future is obscure and that survival is not assured." Just as the war against fascism had obliged the United States to develop awesome military and industrial power, the crisis had taught American leaders that they could never again retreat into the shell of isolationism that had limited U.S. involvement in world affairs during the 1930s. Recognizing that the nation's security depended on worldwide military, economic, and political interests, Presidents Roosevelt and Truman—and most of the public—expected the United States to become a major factor in postwar international relations. Yet despite such expectations, serious disagreements among the Allies, especially with the Soviet Union, left many unsolved problems to threaten the peace. Within two years of victory, the nation faced another global war—the "Cold War"—that altered the scope of government activity and changed political life on the home front.

Harry Truman stood at the center of the postwar puzzle. The Missouri-born politician had served two full terms as senator but just five weeks as vice president before becoming president when Franklin Roosevelt died suddenly. Anyone who succeeded the charismatic Roosevelt would have suffered by comparison, but Truman's blunt style and the unusual crises he faced created the appearance of presidential ineptness. His popularity ratings, which began at 87 percent when he took office in April 1945, dropped to 50 percent a year later and slid to 32 percent by the November 1946 congressional elections. Yet as the Cold War intensified in 1947, his bold—some would say acerbic—leadership restored his image and reputation. In 1948 his presidential campaign defied the public opinion odds and his election surprised almost everyone but Truman himself. As president, he realized that the decisions he made often had grave and dangerous consequences—as a sign in his White House office said, "The Buck Stops Here." His sheer determination set the tone of the postwar presidency.

REBUILDING CIVILIAN SOCIETY

The sudden end of World War II accentuated the difficulties of restoring civilian society. Although Roosevelt's New Deal programs of the 1930s had enlarged government responsibility for economic policy and social welfare,

Washington had failed to resolve the problems of massive unemployment until the nation began to mobilize for war. The abrupt termination of wartime contracts in August 1945, together with the demobilization of 12 million soldiers, raised fears of another economic depression.

Anticipating such problems, Congress had passed the Servicemen's Readjustment Act of 1944 (known as the GI Bill of Rights) which allowed veterans a year's unemployment benefits, education scholarships, insurance, and home loans. Such assistance, limited to military veterans, was as far as Congress was willing to go toward guaranteeing social welfare benefits for postwar society. The measure served to reintegrate veterans into civilian life and increased their purchasing power to support the economy. To provide work for returning veterans, moreover, the government joined business leaders and labor unions in forcing women to surrender their wartime jobs for domestic roles. "Nobody's job is safe," a woman salesclerk learned in Hollywood's classic 1946 film, *The Best Years of Our Lives.*

Truman addressed the public's fears of depression in a twenty-one point program presented to Congress in September 1945. "The ultimate duty of government," he said, "is to prevent prolonged unemployment." The president proceeded to ask Congress to enact full-employment legislation, which would guarantee jobs in times of unemployment as well as a package of liberal measures, such as a permanent Fair Employment Practices Commission (FEPC), public housing, higher minimum wages, and urban redevelopment. This ambitious program soon collided with a conservative Congress led by southern Democrats and northern Republicans opposed to government intervention in the economy. "It is just a case of out–New Dealing the New Deal," complained one Republican leader of Truman's agenda. Fearing "creeping socialism," Congress instead passed the Employment Act of 1946 that promised "maximum" rather than "full" employment. Yet even that measure offered few benefits. Although the law committed the federal government to maximize employment—and created the Council of Economic Advisors—neither Truman nor his successors supported the creation of government jobs to ease unemployment. The abrupt layoff of women workers brought no government response.

Truman's economic choices were also limited by earlier decisions. Wartime government had relied on the expertise of corporate leaders—"dollar-a-year" men—who remained on the payrolls of their private corporations while making economic policy for the nation. Their primary commitment to big business triggered a bitter debate about the reconversion to a civilian economy. As the need for war materials declined in 1944, the War Production Board recommended that small businesses that were losing war contracts reconvert to peacetime production while larger corporations would continue to meet military needs. Corporate leaders vigorously resisted this proposal because they did not want small firms to gain advantages in the transition to civilian production. Unwilling to slacken war manufacturing, military leaders backed the

The Best Years of Our Lives (1946)

"I feel like I was going in to hit a beach," says the battle-toughened sergeant as he returns from World War II to meet his family and resume his desk job at the Cornbelt Trust Company. The Best Years of Our Lives, which gathered nine Academy Award Oscars including best picture, addressed the issues of homecoming and adjustment to civilian life. Director William Wyler personalized the issues by focusing on three veterans—an infantryman/banker (Frederic March); a bombardier/soda jerk (Dana Andrews); and a sailor who lost his hands/ex-football star (Harold Russell). The choices of characters who were rich, middle class, and poor allowed the movie to explore a mix of social and psychological pressures (nightmares, alcoholism, handicaps, gender identity) and the practical problems of finding jobs, starting families, and accepting normal life. Best Years thus portrayed a world not of triumph but uncertainty.

As the former warriors struggle to create a male identity in peacetime, their journeys illuminate family tensions caused by the war's disruption. One veteran reluctantly resumes his patriarchal role as family breadwinner while another

RKO/Archive Photos

grapples with his wife's infidelity. Such dilemmas explained the nation's soaring divorce rate in 1946. Meanwhile, the unmarried handicapped sailor agonizes about marrying anyone. Although the Veterans Administration would ensure an adequate income for life, he receives no training for a job, nor advice about his relationship with the devoted girl next door. "All I want to be is treated like everybody else," he says, sweeping aside the turmoil that later war veterans would call posttraumatic stress disorder. Although the final wedding scene affirmed traditional virtues of chastity and marriage, the film depicted the uneasiness of family life.

The mood of the film evoked feelings of cautious optimism. Reflecting widespread fears that the end of wartime government spending would bring another depression, the movie's recommended job of choice for the veterans is selling insurance. Here Hollywood had its finger on the national pulse, for insurance became one of the growth industries of the postwar era. Hollywood's version of readjustment also embraced the search for security through hard work and the loving support of a dutiful wife. One veteran dreams of owning a nice house with a white fence in the country, a fantasy that the GI Bill of 1944 appeared to offer to millions of ex-serviceman. Yet housing and employment remained a pervasive problem for returning soldiers.

Equally disturbing for movie audiences was the uncertain political atmosphere. One of the movie's heroes has seen the ruins of Hiroshima but professes to know less about radiation than his high school son. "Things will settle down nicely," remarks another civilian, "unless we have another war and then we'll all be blown to bits the first day." Despite the fear of atomic bombs, this extremely popular movie specifically disavowed a coming conflict with the Soviet Union. When Best Years *premiered in November 1946, the Cold War had not yet begun. In more subtle ways, the movie illuminated other social issues. There are no African Americans with speaking roles; white ethnics with Slavic names appear as heroes, entitled to full postwar benefits. The labor shortage had claimed the rich family's maid, and the women have compensated by learning "domestic science." A big chain store has taken over the neighborhood pharmacy.* Best Years *thus acknowledged the changes of World War II on the home front but suggested that after a period of adjustment, traditional values and the resources of ordinary Americans would restore prosperity and security.*

major war contractors. This alliance delayed economic reconversion until 1945, thereby protecting the wartime expansion of big business but also extending shortages of civilian goods when the war ended.

Slighting the problems of small business, the War Production Board lifted wartime regulations as soon as hostilities ended. The abrupt termination of government control over scarce resources benefited larger corporations that had stockpiled such materials. Because they were unable to obtain basic manufacturing resources, many small producers folded or sold out to bigger firms. Large corporations took advantage of Washington's generous reconversion sales and bought government-built plants and resources at a fraction of their cost. Such subsidies ensured that the biggest companies would continue to dominate the economy. The Federal Trade Commission (FTC) reported in 1947 that 2,450 independent mining and manufacturing firms had disappeared since 1940 because of mergers and acquisitions. Congress eventually responded to small business pressure by creating the Small Business Administration in 1953, but most government contracts still went to the largest corporations.

Truman's efforts to maintain wartime price controls to prevent runaway inflation also provoked wide opposition. After four years of government regulation, consumers resented continued shortages. But the lifting of some price controls in 1945 prompted huge jumps in prices, which offended consumers even more. In addition, price controls contained substantial loopholes that aggravated shortages. Because companies made greater profits from expensive goods than from cheaper ones (for example, gowns rather than house dresses), manufacturers preferred to produce high-priced goods.

The resulting shortage of necessities led to skyrocketing prices and an illegal black market. Nearly half the nation's lumber sales in 1946 occurred illegally. Yet lifting controls on building materials stimulated construction of profitable industrial plants without alleviating residential housing shortages. Builders and real estate brokers made enormous profits as house prices soared overnight. Shortages and inflation emerged as the major political issues during the 1946 elections as congressional conservatives opposed extension of wartime regulations and Truman demanded consumer protection. Yet despite soaring prices, voters that year rejected government controls. As a result, most price controls ended by 1947, and the consumer price index increased 30 percent between mid-1946 and 1948.

EXHIBIT **1-1   GROSS NATIONAL PRODUCT, 1946–1950**
(IN ROUNDED BILLIONS OF DOLLARS)

1946	212
1950	288

Source: *Economic Report of the President* (1988).

LABOR UNIONS AND ECONOMIC STABILITY

Rising prices stimulated worker unrest. During the war, labor unions had adopted a no-strike pledge and members benefited by improved wages and overtime pay. But the war's end reduced weekly take-home pay at the same time that price inflation undermined purchasing power. By the fall of 1946, average weekly wages in real dollars had dropped to Depression levels. Such sacrifices contrasted with the immense profits made by businesses during the war. In 1945, Philip Murray, head of the steelworkers' union, pointed out that steel company stockholders had received more than $700 million in dividends during the war. "Contrast this," he said, "with the financial position of America's 475,000 steelworkers."

Labor tensions exploded with a wave of strikes even before the Japanese surrender. During the summer of 1945, 5 million workers called some 4,600 stoppages that amounted to nearly 120 million days of lost labor. Labor strikes quickly spread to the nation's basic industries, such as oil, automobiles, steel, and coal. Some labor protests became "general strikes," involving communities that sympathized with the unions. The strikes brought workers substantial increases, including the new cost-of-living adjustments (COLA) that keyed wages to inflation. But the result contributed to inflationary trends. A 15 percent wage increase for steelworkers led to a $45-per-ton hike in steel prices. Meanwhile, consumers expressed outrage at the inconveniences caused by the strikes.

Truman decided to draw the line. When railroad workers voted to strike in May 1946, effectively paralyzing the nation's transportation, the president seized the railroads. Then he asked Congress for legislation to authorize court injunctions to keep workers on the job, to allow the army to operate the trains, and to permit the drafting of strikers into the military to force them to work. Although the walkout ended before Congress could act, the proposal brought wide criticism. "In his angry determination to get the trains running on time again," protested the liberal *Nation*, "Truman took . . . a leaf from the book of another man who made railroad history, Benito Mussolini." Nonetheless, Congress approved the use of court injunctions to stop certain strikes.

Truman soon used government power to end a coal strike by John L. Lewis's United Mine Workers (UMW). Several times during the war, this union had broken labor's no-strike pledge. When Lewis called another strike in 1946, Truman seized the mines and ended the walkout by accepting an inflationary settlement. Six months later, the UMW defied the government again by calling a strike. Unlike Roosevelt, who in wartime had met Lewis's demands, Truman obtained an injunction and a $3.5 million judgment against the union (and another $10,000 judgment against Lewis), which forced the UMW to surrender. According to a Gallup poll, the president's antiunion stand increased his popularity.

Economic quarrels continued to undermine Truman's position as the 1946 elections approached. Liberals scorned the failure to maintain price controls and his hostility to unions; Republicans criticized him for promoting big government, for administrative ineptness, and for laxity in protecting federal agencies from communist influence. "The choice which confronts Americans," advised the Republican national chairman, "is between Communism and Republicanism." New Republican candidates, such as Joseph R. McCarthy of Wisconsin and Richard M. Nixon of California, appealed to popular fears of communist subversion.

Widespread disapproval of strikes, inflation, and bureaucracy fueled mounting criticism of Democratic leadership. Organized labor, the backbone of the New Deal, resented Truman's lack of support; African Americans, who had recently aligned with Democrats, saw little to praise when the president failed to address a wave of violence against black veterans in the South. Both groups avoided the polls in 1946. And with the simple campaign slogan "Had Enough?" Republicans won in a landslide, gaining a congressional majority in both houses for the first time since 1928. McCarthy and Nixon stood among the victors.

Once in control of the Eightieth Congress, Republicans established a working alliance with southern Democrats to thwart civil rights legislation and to block Truman's other liberal measures, such as public housing, federal aid to education, higher Social Security payments, and certain farm benefits. Ohio Senator Robert Taft, a leader of the conservative Old Guard, told Republicans "to cast out a great many chapters of the New Deal, if not the whole book." But divisions between Republican moderates and conservatives undermined the party's strength. Truman vetoed seventy-five bills, and Congress managed to override only five.

One of those exceptions was the controversial Taft-Hartley Act of 1947, which limited labor union activities. To reduce the number of strikes, the law allowed government to seek injunctions against strike action and provided for a sixty-day "cooling-off" period during which federal mediators would try to settle disputes. To weaken the unions, Taft-Hartley also prohibited "closed" shops (which forced employers to hire only union members) but permitted "union" shops (in which all employees had to join a union after being hired). Taft-Hartley responded to community-wide general strikes by prohibiting secondary boycotts, jurisdictional strikes, and certain "unfair labor practices." The law also required union leaders to certify that they were not members of the Communist Party or other "subversive" groups. Truman, seeking to restore his support among labor unions, criticized the law as "vindictive" and vetoed the bill; but in a show of conservative muscle, Congress easily overrode the veto. Truman's opposition, however, helped him regain the support of organized labor.

Taft-Hartley established the legal framework of labor-management relations for the remainder of the century. On the state level, federal legislation encouraged passage of "right-to-work" laws, which permitted "open" shops, in which workers did not have to join a union. The enforced cooling-off period and the threat of government injunctions (used seventeen times by President Truman and his successor, President Dwight Eisenhower) forced unions and businesses to seek negotiated settlements that would ensure economic stability. Thus union and business leaders increasingly negotiated long-term, industry-wide contracts that included cost-of-living increases and other welfare benefits. "We need the union to ensure enforcement of the contract we have signed," explained one business executive, "to settle grievances, to counsel employees in giving a fair day's work, . . . to help increase productivity." By the early 1950s, union membership reached the highest level in U.S. history. At the same time, 80 percent of Americans described themselves as middle class. Indeed, economists attributed the rapid increase in manufacturing productivity to peaceful labor-management relations and the decline of class conflict.

The emphasis on industry-wide stability sometimes led union leaders to ignore the local problems of rank-and-file workers, and unauthorized ("wildcat") strikes targeted both employers and unresponsive union leaders. Worker participation in union elections declined from 82 percent before World War II to 58 percent in 1958, a trend that continued in the next decades. While critics complained about labor leaders' "passion for respectability," congressional investigation unearthed widespread corruption in managing union funds. The Landrum-Griffin Act of 1959 required unions to file economic statements with the Department of Labor.

Union leaders often neglected the problems of unorganized workers, especially in the new white-collar jobs. Many unions ignored women workers, who were seen as competition for male jobs, and all-white local unions opposed opening membership to racial minorities. Instead, the rival American Federation of Labor (AFL) and Congress of Industrial Organizations (CIO) unions debated jurisdictional issues and raided each other's membership. Although union membership increased from nearly 15 million in 1945 to 18 million a decade later, the proportion of unionized workers declined 14 percent by 1960. The desire for worker stability began to minimize the differences between the AFL and the CIO. In 1955 the two unions merged into the AFL-CIO. Yet five years later organized labor accounted for less than one-third of all nonfarm workers; by 2000, the ratio had fallen to one-sixth.

FARMS AND FOOD

Although political leaders agreed to restrain the independence of labor unions, divisions between liberal Democrats and conservatives of both parties limited government programs for other constituencies. Southern and western farmers, who were among the poorest Americans during the 1930s, had benefited from federal assistance under the New Deal but generally held conservative views about social policy. As a former farm boy, Truman well understood the problems of small farmers. His liberal agenda proposed a soil conservation program, subsidies for school lunches, farm tenant loans, and crop insurance. But congressional conservatives attacked this extension of government services and reduced or cut the administration's program. Later, Truman would tell North Carolina farmers, "You stand for the Democratic farm program or you stand for the Republican wrecking crew." However, federal agricultural programs generally benefited large corporate agribusinesses more than family farmers.

Such results reflected basic changes in postwar farming. During the war, food producers recognized the profitability of mechanization and land consolidation. By investing in farm machinery and hybrid crops that could be handled by machines, farmers needed fewer workers. Farmers also increased their use of chemical fertilizers, pesticides, additives, and antibiotics. This type of farming was expensive—poorer farmers could not compete; and wealthier farmers acquired ever-larger holdings. Between 1949 and 1959, farm production increased 6 percent per year as the farm population declined and the number of farms dwindled.

Government assistance to corporate farming encouraged these patterns. In the early postwar years, federal loans to war-torn Europe subsidized the export of farm surpluses. After European farming recovered, the Agricultural Acts of 1948 and 1949 established government price supports for sales of basic crops. In 1956 Congress authorized payment for not planting certain crops, and the Soil Bank Act of 1956 provided reimbursements for converting crop land into noncommercial conservation acreage. Larger farms gained most. "The majority of farm people derive little or no benefit from our agricultural price support legislation," stated a presidential economic report; "those with the higher incomes are the main beneficiaries." Meanwhile, the reduction in government rice allotments and the replacement of sharecroppers with hired labor and tractors stimulated an exodus of millions of poor whites and blacks from the rural South.

Technological agriculture encouraged consumption of mass-produced food. As consumers bought more processed and frozen foods, food processors such as Birdseye dictated which crop strains would be planted, leading to a decline in the number of available seed and food varieties. Franchise restaurant chains, which also proliferated in this period, preferred standardized menus, which created another vast market for single strains of produce. Meanwhile, average per capita consumption of dairy products, fresh fruits, and fresh vegetables declined. Since processed food needed nutritional additives and preservatives to maintain the food's value, each edible pound cost as much as 30 percent more than naturally grown food. Corporate consolidation similarly affected beverage consumption. In the beer industry the number of breweries steadily declined. Such changes encouraged the homogenization of eating and drinking habits in all regions.

THE TECHNOLOGICAL FRONTIER

Wartime engineering and scientific research provided the model for postwar technological development. The introduction of radar and jet propulsion, the use of pesticides such as DDT, the effectiveness of "miracle drugs" such as penicillin, and the emergence of synthetic compounds as substitutes for scarce resources such as rubber all testified to the importance of research for social progress. In popular wartime imagery the scientist and the engineer appeared as heroic figures.

The atomic bomb dwarfed these technological accomplishments. Although the bomb appeared to prove U.S. invincibility in war, the use of nuclear weapons raised profound questions about uncontrolled scientific investigation. During the war the government had classified atomic energy research (the "Manhattan Project") as top secret, although physicists around the world understood the theoretical basis of the bomb. In 1945 U.S. scientists predicted that other countries could develop similar weapons in three to five years. However, President Truman preferred to believe the opinion of military leaders who claimed that the United States could monopolize atomic bombs for at least twenty years. The president therefore rejected recommendations to share atomic research with the Soviet Union. Both Congress and public opinion supported this position. The Atomic Energy Act of 1946 established the Atomic Energy Commission (AEC) and placed control of nuclear research and development in civilian hands.

J. Robert Oppenheimer, the head of the Los Alamos research team that developed the atomic bomb, expressed widely held anxieties about the future of scientific research: "In some sense, which no vulgarity, no humor, no overstatement can quite extinguish," he said, "the physicists have known sin; and this is a knowledge which they cannot lose." The realization that atomic science could bring human annihilation spread through the popular culture. Hardly a Hollywood movie of the postwar era lacked some reference to the bomb and its potential destructiveness. Indeed, a new film genre—later named *film noir* (dark film)—now celebrated a different type of hero who inhabited a world of moral ambiguity, uncertainty, and fear. Movies such as *Force of Evil* (1948), *They Live By Night* (1949), and *D.O.A.* (1950) depicted characters trapped by pressures they scarcely understood. Such themes also appeared in postwar science fiction, which enjoyed a remarkable revival. Authors such as Isaac Asimov and Ray Bradbury wrote futuristic stories involving human beings seeking to avert ultimate catastrophe.

The serious scientist now appeared as an ambivalent character, simultaneously capable of bringing salvation or annihilation. "To the average civilized man of 1950," wrote the editor of *Scientific American*, "science no longer means primarily the promise of a more abundant life; it means the atomic bomb." Although nearly all nuclear research involved military work, the AEC launched a public relations division in 1947 to counter public fears. With private contractors such as General Electric and Westinghouse, the agency sponsored public programs suggesting that atomic energy would be used for social betterment and minimized the harmful effects of testing and radiation.

Despite pervasive anxieties about atomic research, the public generally welcomed technological innovations for domestic consumption. Rayon, nylon, and Dacron increasingly replaced cotton and wool. In home furnishings, plastics supplanted wood and leather. Artificial flavors, colors, and preservatives became staples of the U.S. diet. (Most synthetics, however, were derivatives of petroleum products and depleted nonrenewable resources and left non-biodegradable waste.) Another innovation was the fluoridation of water, which reduced tooth decay. When given the choice of voting for fluoridation, nearly all local communities initially rejected the proposals, but by 1963, 50 million people—25 percent of the population—were drinking fluoridated water. During the postwar decade, the United States replaced Europe as the prime manufacturer of precision scientific instruments. New medical technologies included kidney dialysis machines (1945), artificial heart valves (1953), and electronic heart pacemakers (1957). Meanwhile, new antibiotics such as streptomycin and aureomycin helped to control infectious diseases. Most dramatically, the introduction of Dr. Jonas Salk's poliomyelitis vaccine in 1955 effectively eliminated a dreaded disease that had claimed 55,000 victims each year.

Advances in technology reinforced public optimism about unlimited progress. A few ecologists, such as William Vogt and Fairfield Osborn, warned about the limits of available resources, but the public accepted corporate assurances that applied science would solve such technological problems. Consumers supported both the automobile industry's high-horsepower engines and the petroleum industry's high-octane gasoline, although with added auto body weight, automobile fuel efficiency fell as low as 10 miles per gallon.

Jet aircraft and missiles, electronic transistors, and computers testified to the expanding technological frontiers of the postwar era. Committed to national security and military preparedness, the federal government spent billions of dollars in research and development (R&D), some of it financing university research. Aircraft manufacturing, one of the leading growth industries, drew 80 percent of its business from military contracts. The government also backed electronics, which grew 15 percent per year, making it the fifth largest industry by 1960. Secret military programs for nuclear weapons, missiles, and cryptography demanded complicated mathematical calculations that sparked the computer industry. The first World War II–era computers occupied 15,000 square feet and used 18,000 radio tubes. The introduction of the transistor by Bell Laboratories in 1947 paved the way for miniaturization. Although the federal government purchased most electronics for military programs, computers entered the industrial marketplace in 1951.

Military needs also justified generous government help for the petroleum industry. Accepting the industry's argument that security depended on preserving domestic reserves while exploiting foreign oil, the government waived antitrust regulations to permit development of Middle Eastern oil and devised generous tax credits to subsidize private contracts with Saudi Arabia. Under the Truman administration's Marshall Plan of 1947 (see The Truman Doctrine below), the United States refinanced a major shift in western European energy consumption from coal to petroleum. This step provided a $384 million subsidy to U.S. oil companies and made the Western Allies dependent on imports. In addition, Congress enacted mandatory petroleum import quotas in 1950, which kept cheap foreign oil from lowering domestic prices. In supporting the oil industry, government agencies continued the World War II practice of awarding contracts to the largest corporations. Only 4 percent of R&D funds reached small businesses. Although convenient for government administrators, dealing with big business did not reduce costs. Without competitive bidding, federal budgets routinely had to absorb business cost overruns.

PEACE AND PLENTY

While government leaders struggled to rebuild the postwar economy, most citizens focused on personal concerns of security and prosperity. For the generation that came of age during the Depression and World War II, however, government assistance provided considerable support. Most important was the GI Bill of Rights, which allowed veterans to obtain private homes through government-insured mortgages that required small down payments and allowed extended periods for repayment. In addition, government-funded scholarships gave veterans unprecedented opportunities for educational advancement. Between 1945 and 1950, 6 million veterans (half the nation's total) used nearly $13 billion of government money to enroll in colleges, universities, and vocational training programs. Postwar surveys found that about 20 percent of college-bound veterans would not have returned to school without federal aid.

Women also entered colleges in high numbers, but without veterans' benefits they formed a smaller percentage of college students than they did before the war. Still, the influx of students encouraged colleges to expand facilities, open branch campuses, offer evening instruction, and adjust their curricula to accommodate older students, many of whom held jobs and supported families. By underwriting tuition bills, federal funds boosted the expansion of academia and established a precedent for later support of education. In addition, the appearance of more ethnically diverse students eroded the homogeneity that had dominated elite campuses.

King Hiram ("Hank") Williams (1923–1953)

"Don't worry," country singer Hank Williams once confided to a concert crowd, "nothing's gonna turn out right no how." Williams grew up in small Alabama towns during the Depression. He was raised by a strong-willed mother who introduced him to the hymns and gospel tunes of the funda-

mentalist Baptist Church. As a boy, Williams sold peanuts and newspapers and shined shoes. He formed his own "hillbilly" band when he was fourteen years old, combining the influence of black street musicians and the commercial sound of prominent country stars. After Williams won an amateur-night contest in Montgomery in 1937, he formed the Drifting Cowboys band and played the "blood buckets"—the rough southern Alabama honky-tonk clubs.

After working in the shipyards during World War II, Williams traveled to Nashville to become a songwriter. As the war relocated southern blacks and whites to defense plants and military bases, and as jukeboxes spread across the country, rhythm and blues and country music became national phenomena. Fusing gospel, blues, and honky-tonk, Williams won a recording contract in 1947 and produced his first hit, "Move It On Over," an up-tempo tune that influenced the structure of early rock and roll. The next year he joined the *Louisiana Hayride,* a country music radio show from Shreveport, Louisiana, which appealed to workers in the booming regional oil and gas industry.

THE BIRTH OF THE SUBURBAN BOOM

Ex-servicemen and their wives produced the most remarkable population explosion in U.S. history. Taking their cue from a popular 1945 song "Gotta Make Up for Lost Time," veterans rushed to get married and settle down with their families. The national birth rate had begun to rise as prosperity returned in 1940, but in May 1946, nine months after the war ended, the number of births soared and remained high until 1957. Demographers found that the "baby boom" resulted from couples marrying younger, thereby increasing the years

Following his smash hit, "Lovesick Blues," Williams reached the top of his profession in 1949 and made regular guest appearances on Nashville's *Grand Ole Opry*. He sold 11 million records between 1949 and 1953, using his unpolished, light voice to master blues techniques such as falsetto singing and call-and-response. He won the devotion of working-class fans because he appeared to "live" his music. "When a hillbilly sings a crazy song," he once explained, "he feels crazy . . . He sings more sincere than most entertainers because the hillbilly was raised rougher. . . . You got to have smelt a lot of manure before you can sing like a hillbilly."

Williams bonded with audiences by sharing the sense of betrayal and abandonment often inflicted by romance. By conveying emotions of loneliness and despair, love songs such as "Your Cheating Heart" and "Cold Cold Heart" relieved listeners of postwar insistence on domestic bliss. Williams expressed another form of release through drinking songs such as "Jambalaya," which celebrated immediate pleasure over the rigors of delayed gratification and middle-class propriety.

Although the singer poured out his personal problems in music, he was unable to stop a descent into alcoholism. On New Year's Day 1953, eight months before his thirtieth birthday, Hank Williams suffered a fatal heart attack. A biracial crowd of more than 20,000 gathered in Montgomery as leading country music stars conducted a gospel tribute to the fallen performer. By portraying pain and joy as the common denominators of life, Williams became a legendary figure in working-class culture and had an enormous impact on all forms of popular music.

of marital fertility and producing more third and fourth babies. Yet the number of families with five or more children declined, which suggested a greater willingness to use birth control. Pushed by the baby boom, the nation's population grew from 140 million in 1945 to 152 million in 1950. Such growth also reflected the slightly declining death rate, which resulted from medical advances that extended longevity.

The burst of population accelerated long-term patterns of geographic mobility. Attracted by industrial expansion during World War II, workers and their families had flocked to the southwestern and western states. In Texas the growth of the petrochemical industry, stimulated by the increased use of oil

EXHIBIT **1-2   BIRTH RATES, 1940–1950**

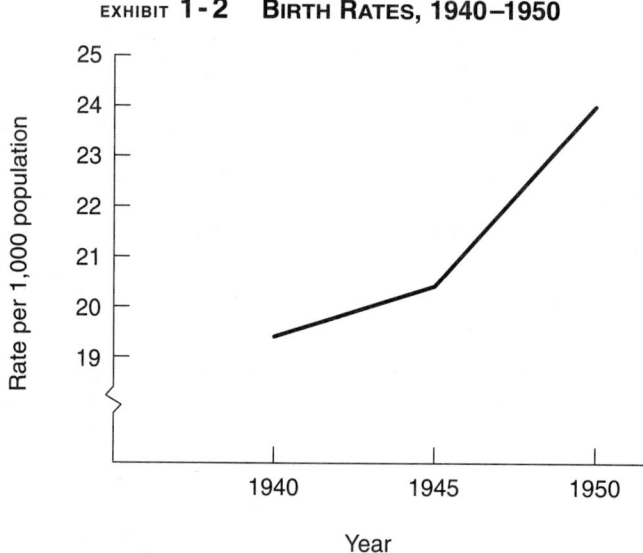

and natural gas, encouraged a 30 percent population growth. In Arizona, Tucson and Phoenix mushroomed into sizable cities, selling the advantages of a warm, sunny climate. Yet when asked in 1956, "Which city would you most like to live in?" more Americans responded: "Los Angeles." California, home of the prospering aircraft and electronics industries, attracted more than 5 million people between 1940 and 1960, doubled in size, and surpassed New York as the most populous state in 1963.

The baby boom soon underscored what many considered the nation's most serious domestic problem: a shortage of housing. Since the Depression, residential construction had virtually ended, and by 1945 the nation's housing was worth 7 percent less than in 1929. Returning veterans often had to share dwellings with other families, camp out in public facilities, or accept substandard rooms in converted chicken coops or Quonset huts. Postwar shortages of building materials and the inflation of real estate prices accentuated the shortage. Responding to the crisis, congressional liberals joined Republican Robert Taft in proposing federal support of public housing. But a coalition of antigovernment conservatives, including Senator Joseph McCarthy, and private builders, such as William Levitt, challenged public housing as a socialist or communist scheme. Instead, these conservatives argued that private enterprise could solve the housing shortage, with federal assistance under the Federal Housing Authority (FHA) or Veterans Administration.

Private builders like Levitt stepped into the breach. Levitt purchased large tracts of land in the suburban fringes of big cities, such as New York's Long Island, and drew on his experience as a war contractor to develop a system of mass producing standardized housing at affordable prices. He used special-ized work crews, interchangeable designs, prefabricated materials, and pack-age deals that included interior appliances, landscaping, and legal fees to pro-duce four-and-a-half room, Cape Cod–style houses for $8,000 in 1949. Many were financed by veterans' loans, which required minimal down payments and offered government-protected finance charges. To keep prices low, the de-signs eliminated dining rooms, basements, and attics as well as unnecessary trim. Efficient production methods enabled the builder to erect one four-room house every sixteen minutes!

Between 1947 and 1951 Levitt built more than 17,000 dwellings in Levit-town, Long Island, and converted a potato field into a community of 75,000 residents. When critics complained that the structures were monotonously repetitious, the developer offered different exterior paint, curved streets, and homes placed at slightly different angles. Such housing, imitated by builders around the nation, benefited from new standardization within the appliance and home-furnishing industries.

This postwar suburban boom rested on government financing of housing loans, highways, and sewer systems. Federal tax deductions for mortgage inter-est—what was, in effect, a tax break for middle-class housing—annually ex-ceeded $1 billion. The mixture of private enterprise and government policy en-abled most of the nation's families to own their residences for the first time in U.S. history. Although some social critics lamented the bland uniformity of sub-urban lifestyles, promoters stressed the value of individual home ownership. "No man who owns his own house and lot can be a Communist," Levitt declared.

The distance from downtown areas made the use of automobiles a subur-ban necessity. Auto registration jumped from 26 million in 1945 to 40 million in 1950, a trend that continued for decades. The increase in driving encour-aged the spread of fast-food restaurants, drive-in theaters, shopping centers, motels, mobile home parks, and gasoline service stations. Although fuel prices remained low (about 25 cents per gallon), automobiles brought other costs such as increased national dependence on foreign oil and worsening air pol-lution. In 1947 journalist John Gunther boasted that Los Angeles used elec-tricity to produce "clean industry" and uncontaminated air. Yet within one decade the city's auto exhaust had added a new and permanent aspect to the local environment—smog that was deemed a hazard to public health.

In suburbia, mobility became more valued than community attachments. As families grew, suburbanites readily moved to larger homes. Residential change often mirrored the interchangeability of jobs in an increasingly white-collar service economy. The proliferation of chain stores reflected this trend. As chains increased their share of total food sales from 29 percent to 44 per-cent in the ten years after 1948, nearly 100,000 independent groceries disap-peared. Corporate managers, Gunther noted, never become "a real ingredi-ent in the life of a community."

NEW ISSUES OF GENDER AND SEXUALITY

The baby boom and the rise of suburban living reflected a renewed emphasis on the role of women as wives, mothers, and homemakers. Although women had readily accepted paid labor during the war, most surrendered their jobs, willingly or not, to returning veterans in 1945–1946. Popular magazines and movies insisted that a woman's proper place was in the home. In the film *Mildred Pierce* (1945), for example, the ambitious, self-employed working mother proves to be a failure as a parent, while in the supposedly sensitive picture *The Snake Pit* (1949), rebellion against domesticity appears as a form of mental illness. A popular psychology book of 1947, *Modern Woman: The Lost Sex*, explained that "a mature woman without children is the psychological equivalent of a man without the male organ." Such statements had a practical effect. Surveys of women college students found that most enrolled not for careers but to find husbands. Two-thirds of postwar college women quit school before obtaining their B.A.'s.

Despite such pressure, however, female employment began to rise sharply in 1947 and returned to World War II levels by 1950, establishing a trend that would continue through the century. The increasing proportion of working women reflected new social patterns. Although women traditionally had worked until marriage and then left the work force, the new female workers were married and had children who were attending school (and so needed less supervision). Increasingly, households included two working parents. Before World War II, working wives and mothers usually came from the poorest classes of society, but in the postwar period an increasing number of middle-class women found jobs even when their husbands earned substantial incomes.

Working women emphasized financial necessity as a motive for their employment. Despite the emphasis on women's domesticity, the national divorce rate had spiked in 1946, as hasty wartime marriages collapsed, and remained substantially higher than prewar divorce rates. Widows, unmarried mothers, and women who were divorced, separated, or deserted headed about 7 percent of U.S. households in 1950. Most worked as secretaries, salesclerks, or semiskilled workers—occupations that labor unions usually ignored—and earned lower salaries than men did for similar tasks. Women-headed households were among the poorest in the nation. Moreover, because postwar real wages remained lower than wartime earnings until 1955, families needed additional incomes to acquire goods and services. In middle-class households the demand for luxury items or a private home encouraged two-income families.

Dissatisfaction with traditional marriage also reflected a conflict between sexual values and sexual behavior. In 1948 Alfred Kinsey of Indiana University published a major research study, *Sexual Behavior in the Human Male*, followed five years later by a similar study of women. Both became best-sellers.

Kinsey tilted his research sample to support the unconventional conclusions he wished to dramatize. Yet at a time when traditional morality advocated pre-marital virginity, Kinsey's statistical data showed that most men and nearly 50 percent of the women interviewed had experienced premarital intercourse. Fully 95 percent of the study's adult white males claimed to have committed at least one "illegal" sexual activity. Half the men and 26 percent of the women reported that they had experienced extramarital sexual relations. Kinsey con-cluded that two-thirds of the marriages studied had serious sexual problems, and he speculated that sexual incompatibility caused 75 percent of divorces.

The Kinsey report also pointed to surprising patterns of homosexual be-havior: 37 percent of the men and 13 percent of the women interviewed said they had participated in at least one postadolescent homosexual encounter. Such figures reflected the growth of homosexual communities in most major cities after World War II. Yet the proliferation of gay lifestyles did not pro-duce greater tolerance of homosexuals. Police raids and blackmail plagued the gay population, and the federal government viewed homosexuals in the military and government as susceptible to compromise by foreign agents. Thousands of homosexuals lost government jobs during the 1940s and 1950s. Although homosexuals would form self-protective groups, such as the Matta-chine Society (1951) and the Daughters of Bilitis (1955), fear of exposure prevented them from effectively defending their rights.

Free expression of sexuality among youth prompted social conservatives to warn about the collapse of traditional morality and a new national malaise—juvenile delinquency. Newspapers luridly described teenage crimes, most of which involved underage drinking, premarital sex, and driving with-out a license. Critics such as FBI Director J. Edgar Hoover blamed juvenile delinquency on working mothers and warned that youth crime would increase unless society strengthened the family, home, church, and local community. President Truman joined a chorus of politicians who urged working mothers to end the crime wave by returning to the home. In fact, however, New York City arrest rates for children under the age of sixteen lagged far behind those reported in the first two decades of the century. Sociologists insisted that poverty caused juvenile crime and advocated slum clearance and social wel-fare programs as solutions. In addition, Dr. Kinsey said that teenage sexuality appeared normal and healthy and called for greater tolerance from parents and law enforcement authorities.

Kinsey's advice reinforced the message adults received from the most pop-ular pediatrician of the postwar era, Dr. Benjamin Spock, whose book, *Baby and Child Care*, first published in 1946, has sold more than 22 million copies. "Trust yourself," Spock told anxious parents. "Don't be overawed by what the experts say. Don't be afraid to trust your common sense." Although earlier government child-rearing pamphlets had recommended strict regimens, Spock called for flexibility. His respect for children led critics to denounce his "permissiveness" although Spock advocated firm parental control based on love and understanding.

POSTWAR GLOBALISM

Although the postwar years saw more Americans entering the middle class and focusing on personal problems of family life, the country's political leaders increasingly worried about the difficulty of stabilizing global affairs and assuring national security. Indeed, some scholars have speculated that the emphasis on domesticity on the home front reflected the extreme uncertainty of the global arena. For politicians and private citizens alike, the new world of atomic bombs introduced fearful prospects of mass death. And the promise of a lasting peace gradually and frustratingly gave way to endless conflicts with the nation's former wartime ally, the Soviet Union. By the end of the decade, the American people found themselves waging a "cold war" to preserve their way of life.

Despite widespread approval of participation in the United Nations, public demands for rapid demobilization and military budget cuts in 1946 showed a limited commitment to global involvement. Such pressure forced Truman to reduce the size of the armed forces from 12 million to 3 million within a few months. The president's failure to reach postwar agreements with the Soviet Union contributed to his loss of popularity, but public suspicion of world communism enabled him to develop an increasingly militant and internationalist position. His primary postwar goal was to secure the nation from foreign threat—militarily or economically. "We must face the fact that peace must be built on power," Truman said in 1945, "as well as upon good will and good deeds." Such power depended on military strength as well as on a stable economic environment. The huge expenditure of natural resources during the war underscored the importance of protecting the nation's access to raw materials.

"Our foreign relations inevitably affect employment in the United States," explained Secretary of State James F. Byrnes in 1945. "Prosperity and depression in the United States just as inevitably affect our relations with other nations of the world." To ensure access to markets and resources and to prevent economic stagnation at home, postwar leaders advocated a worldwide system of free trade that would include the Soviet Union. "Peace, freedom, and world trade are indivisible," Truman remarked. "We must not go through the thirties again."

This economic approach to foreign affairs partially reflected the social background of many of the nation's policymakers in the postwar period. Leading State Department officials such as Dean Acheson and John Foster Dulles often had personal ties to the nation's largest corporations and held powerful positions as corporate lawyers, financiers, or big-business executives. For example, the names of five of the six secretaries of state between 1945 and 1960 and of five of the six secretaries of defense between 1947 and 1960 appear in the *Social Register* of the nation's richest families. Such men, appointed by both Democratic and Republican presidents, formulated a foreign policy that expressed and protected the values of the corporate elite. "I am an advocate of business," conceded Secretary of Defense James Forrestal in 1947. "Calvin Coolidge was ridiculed for saying . . . 'The chief business of the United States is business,' but that is a fact."

Although foreign trade comprised only 6 percent of the gross national product in 1945, State Department planners hoped to use U.S. economic power to persuade Great Britain, France, and the Soviet Union to open their trading blocs to U.S. businesses. When these nations applied for U.S. loans in 1945 to replace the wartime assistance, negotiators delayed action to win trading concessions. Nearly bankrupted by the war, Britain reluctantly accepted U.S. conditions; so did France. But the Soviet Union, although devastated by the war, refused to agree.

While Soviet leaders continued to advocate the Marxist-Leninist doctrine of worldwide communist revolution, Josef Stalin rejected trade deals with Western capitalists and decided to rebuild his war-ravaged country with German reparations. Stalin also demanded "friendly governments" in eastern Europe to prevent another invasion of his country and rejected free elections in some areas occupied by Soviet troops. In Poland, the Red Army repressed political freedom to promote a pro-Soviet regime. During the war, Roosevelt had minimized the problem of Soviet expansion in eastern Europe, largely because he could do nothing about it and needed to preserve the Grand Alliance against Hitler. Although he remained suspicious of Stalin and refused to share information about the atomic bomb, the president tried to treat the Soviet Union as a "normal" state that was only protecting its national interests.

But Roosevelt failed to attract public support for this approach. Fearful of a resurgence of isolationism, he hesitated to move ahead of public opinion. Nor did he challenge the popular view that the United Nations, like the League of Nations, would be based on President Woodrow Wilson's principle of equal representation for all nations. Yet Roosevelt believed that the U.N. could succeed where the League had failed only if the Big Powers dominated international diplomacy. He assumed that the Big Four (Britain, China, the United States, and the Soviet Union) would use their veto power in the U.N.'s Security Council to protect their national interests. At the 1945 Yalta Conference, Roosevelt and Churchill acknowledged Soviet dominance in eastern Europe, the British claimed special privileges in the Mediterranean, and the United States sought to maintain power in Latin America. Roosevelt accepted these realities because he understood the special interests of each Allied nation.

At Roosevelt's death, Truman knew little about these foreign policy assumptions. Instead, the new president viewed the Soviet presence in eastern Europe as an infringement of the principle of national self-determination and a violation of the Yalta agreements. In a foreshadowing of future conflicts, Truman clashed angrily with Soviet Foreign Minister V. M. Molotov in 1945 about the undemocratic character of the Polish government and decided to withhold U.S. economic aid until Stalin retreated.

The new administration also shifted U.S. policy toward the British, Dutch, and French empires, most significantly in French Indochina. Roosevelt was opposed to French imperialism and had proposed that Indochina be placed under international trusteeship until the French colony achieved independence. When the leader of the Indochinese national liberation movement, Ho Chi Minh, drafted a declaration of independence in 1945, however, British pressure forced Roosevelt to accept the return of French troops—although with the goal of ultimately granting Indochina independence. Truman dropped that essential qualification. Instead, he agreed to return Indochina to France. Ho's sympathy toward communism had alarmed State Department officials. Equally important, Truman wished to retain French support in Europe, where France could be an ally against the Soviet Union. In 1945 the United States helped to transport French troops back to Indochina. Thereafter, the State Department ignored Ho Chi Minh's appeals for support.

While restoring French colonialism in Southeast Asia, Truman proceeded with prewar plans to grant independence to the Philippine Islands, first seized from Spain in 1898. Yet before departing from that strategic region, Washington negotiated long-term treaties providing for military bases and the stationing of U.S. troops in the Philippines. Besides ensuring military security, the treaty protected U.S. economic investments and reinforced the rule of its entrenched allies. Similar arrangements brought the United States a string of military bases in Iceland, in North Africa, in Okinawa (an island near Japan), and the Azores (a group of islands in the Atlantic Ocean). In Spain, Truman legitimized the fascist dictator Francisco Franco as a defender against socialist revolution and Soviet influence.

THE COLD WAR BEGINS

After the defeat of Germany, the three major Allies met in Potsdam in July 1945 but failed to resolve their differences about a peace settlement in Europe. Stalin continued to demand German reparations and expressed no interest in reducing Soviet influence in eastern Europe. Truman, emboldened by the first successful atomic bomb test that month, rejected such a Soviet sphere of influence. He proposed smaller reparations from Germany in hopes of maintaining Soviet dependence on U.S. exports. Since they failed to reach agreement, the Big Three postponed these issues until a subsequent Foreign Ministers Conference in London. Frustrated by Soviet stubbornness, Truman decided to exclude the Soviet Union from participation in the eventual occupation of Japan.

Despite basic disagreements, the Big Three—(left to right) Prime Minister Winston Churchill, President Truman, and Premier Josef Stalin—pose amicably at the Potsdam Conference in 1945. Days later, Churchill's defeat at the polls forced his replacement by Clement Atlee.

The atomic bombings of Japan in August 1945 reinforced Truman's confidence but aroused Soviet suspicions. At the London conference, the Soviets offered minor concessions on elections in Bulgaria and Hungary, but Washington demanded Western-style elections. Again, the diplomats could not agree. This failure showed the futility of atomic bomb diplomacy. When Molotov asked jokingly whether Secretary of State Byrnes had an atomic bomb in his pocket, Byrnes replied, "If you don't cut out all this stalling . . . I am going to pull an atomic bomb out of my hip pocket and let you have it!" To the surprise of U.S. negotiators, the Soviet Union would not be coerced into accepting Truman's demands. Secretary of War Henry Stimson, who had once viewed the bomb as a diplomatic lever, now saw an opportunity to ease tensions by sharing atomic secrets with the Soviets. "If we fail to approach them now and merely continue to negotiate with them, having this weapon rather ostentatiously on our hip," he warned, "their suspicions and their distrust . . . will increase." Yet after a high-level policy debate, the president chose to maintain the atomic monopoly.

Despite doubts about further negotiations, Secretary of State Byrnes met with Stalin in Moscow in December 1945. The meeting produced tentative agreements about portions of eastern Europe, Korea, and a United Nations Atomic Energy Commission. Yet pressure from congressional conservatives, who opposed any concessions to Stalin, forced Truman to adopt a more rigid position, and he abruptly disavowed Byrnes's agreements. "Unless Russia is

EXHIBIT **1-3**   **ORIGINS OF THE COLD WAR, 1945–1949**

Year	Event
1945	Yalta Conference V-E Day: Germany surrenders Potsdam Conference Atomic bombing of Japan. Japan surrenders (V-J Day)
1946	Kennan telegram Churchill's "Iron Curtain" speech Soviet occupation of northern Iran Acheson-Lilienthal plans for atomic energy Atomic Energy Act (creates AEC—Atomic Energy Commission)
1947	Truman Doctrine Federal Employee Loyalty Program National Security Act
1948	Communist coup in Czechoslovakia Marshall Plan—European Recovery Program Berlin airlift
1949	NATO Soviet A-bomb detonated Communist victory over Chinese Nationalists

faced with an iron fist and strong language, another war is in the making," he declared. "I'm tired of babying the Soviets." Meanwhile, Stalin rejected participation in the International Monetary Fund, asserting the Soviet desire to maintain economic independence.

Truman's firmness won support within the State Department from George F. Kennan, a longtime analyst of Soviet affairs, who insisted that it was not possible to gain concessions from Stalin through negotiation. "We have here," Kennan cabled from Moscow in February 1946, "a political force committed fanatically to the belief that . . . it is desirable and necessary that the internal harmony of our society be disrupted, our traditional way of life destroyed, the international authority of our state be broken if Soviet power is to be secure." Kennan's "long telegram" confirmed the president's belief that there could be no compromise with communist nations. One month later, Truman accompanied Winston Churchill to Fulton, Missouri, where the former prime minister attacked the Soviet Union for drawing an "iron curtain" around eastern Europe. The speech, approved by Truman, brought wide editorial criticism but publicized the change in foreign policy.

The United States also challenged the Soviet Union within the United Nations. The first major crisis involved Soviet occupation of northern Iran in 1946. The problem was oil. During the war, the Soviets, the British, and the Americans had occupied Iran jointly, but the Soviets hesitated to leave until they received oil concessions similar to those won by the British. Fearing a

Soviet attempt to control vital oil resources, the White House supported Iran in the Security Council, where the United States controlled a preponderance of votes. Such diplomatic pressure forced Iran and the Soviet Union to negotiate oil concessions in exchange for a Soviet withdrawal. Afterward, Iran repudiated the agreement. Using U.N. institutions, the United States had thwarted Soviet expansion.

The United Nations also sanctioned the U.S. decision to maintain a monopoly on atomic weapons. In 1946, to ease public fear of atomic war, the Truman administration announced the Acheson-Lilienthal plan, which proposed that atomic energy become an internationally shared technology. The United States would relinquish control of atomic weapons in stages. During the transition, the United States would maintain a monopoly, and other countries would be required to allow international inspection. The United States "should not under any circumstances throw away our gun until we are sure the rest of the world cannot arm against us," said Truman. In presenting the program to the United Nations, Truman's advisor, financier Bernard Baruch, added other conditions, including the surrender of the U.N. Security Council veto on atomic energy issues and the imposition of "condign punishments" against violators of the plan by a majority vote (which was controlled by U.S. allies). Although fearful of the U.S. atomic monopoly, the Soviet Union was rushing to build its own atomic bombs and rejected the Baruch plan. Instead, the Soviets suggested immediate nuclear disarmament and sharing of atomic secrets. Truman considered the Soviet alternative unacceptable.

Frustrated by Soviet negotiators, U.S. leaders believed that Stalin could not be trusted. The Soviet leader's ruthless killing of his domestic rivals (as well as millions of innocent citizens), his cynicism in signing a nonaggression pact with Nazi Germany in 1939, and his determination to extend Soviet influence as far as possible—all reinforced fears of a communist plan to undermine U.S. national security. Defining Soviet communism as "red fascism," U.S. leaders were determined to avoid a repetition of the "appeasement" that had allowed Germany to control Europe in the 1930s. "The language of military power is the only language which disciples of power politics understand," presidential adviser Clark Clifford assured Truman in 1946. Moreover, in identifying the Soviet Union with Nazi Germany, Truman broadened support for his policy. Under the principle of "bipartisanship," Republicans, led by Senator Arthur Vandenberg and foreign policy expert John Foster Dulles, supported Truman's diplomacy, at least in Europe.

As a Cold War consensus crystallized in Washington, one former New Dealer emerged as a major critic—Henry A. Wallace, secretary of agriculture during the 1930s, Roosevelt's third-term vice president, and now Truman's secretary of commerce. In September 1946, after gaining Truman's approval, Wallace spoke publicly at Madison Square Garden in New York City, arguing that the United States had "no more business in the political affairs of Eastern Europe than Russia had in the political affairs of Latin America, Western Europe, and the United States." Yet when other members of the administration protested the speech, Truman abruptly fired Wallace. "The Reds, phonies, and the 'parlor pinks,'" Truman wrote, "seem to be banded together and are becoming a national danger."

Fear of communist influence permeated the nation. Preparing for a Soviet attack, FBI Director J. Edgar Hoover developed a Custodial Detention Program and compiled lists of suspected subversives who would be arrested at the outbreak of war. When the White House tried to minimize the communist threat, Hoover aligned with more militant anticommunists in Congress. "Communism," Hoover told the House Committee on Un-American Activities (HUAC), "is . . . an evil and malignant way of life." Persuaded by such testimony, Congress voted to provide more funds for FBI investigations of government workers. These political pressures pushed Truman toward a more militant anticommunist position.

The dismissal of Wallace revealed the administration's growing intolerance of positions that had seemed acceptable only a year before. After conservative Republican victories in the 1946 elections, some liberals deserted Truman and formed a coalition group, Progressive Citizens of America (PCA). The PCA complained that the Democratic Party had departed from Roosevelt's New Deal and urged a return to liberal principles or the creation of a third party. Although the PCA did not discriminate against members of the Communist Party, most liberals opposed communism and especially resented conservative accusations that liberals were tools of Soviet foreign policy. In January 1947 these anticommunist liberals formed Americans for Democratic Action (ADA). Like the PCA, the ADA endorsed expansion of the New Deal, the United Nations, and civil rights, but the ADA explicitly rejected any association with communists.

THE TRUMAN DOCTRINE

Early in 1947 U.S. intelligence detected a relaxation of Soviet policy, but the State Department concluded that such changes were deliberately deceptive. This mistrust was reinforced by growing concern about the slow pace of economic recovery in Europe. Washington feared that economic unrest would encourage political instability and communist expansion and undermine U.S. interests. Matters climaxed in February 1947 when Britain announced it could no longer provide aid to Greece, a client state it had supported since World War II in a civil war against communist guerrillas. Truman welcomed the opportunity to replace Britain in the area, but U.S. intervention required congressional approval at a time when conservatives sought to cut government expenses. Moreover, the public appeared uninterested in Greek affairs. Truman decided, as Vandenberg put it, to "scare hell out of the American people."

EXHIBIT **1-4** **GREECE, TURKEY, AND THE MEDITERRANEAN, 1947**

In an impassioned speech, the president personally presented the "Truman Doctrine" to a special session of Congress in March 1947, requesting $400 million in economic and military assistance for Greece and Turkey. Condemning a communist system based on "terror and oppression, a controlled press and radio, fixed elections and the suppression of political freedoms," Truman depicted an emergency situation that forced the United States to "support free peoples who are resisting attempted subjugation by armed minorities or by outside pressures."

The Truman Doctrine represented a major turning point in foreign policy, announcing that threatened communist expansion obliged the United States to initiate unilateral action without consulting the United Nations. The new policy was later called "containment." Truman now abandoned the idea of effecting changes within the Soviet sphere of influence and stressed instead the importance of containing Soviet expansion. The doctrine, in effect, drew a line, dividing the globe into areas of "freedom" and zones of "terror and oppression." Such language allowed no room for compromise: all communists were dangerous; all communist threats became equally critical. The Truman Doctrine expanded the definition of "national security" to encompass conflicts anywhere in the world. "Wherever aggression, direct or indirect, threatened the peace," Truman later explained, "the security of the United States was involved."

George Catlett Marshall (1880–1959)

When Indiana Senator William Jenner opposed George Marshall's nomination as secretary of defense in 1950 by dismissing the general as a "living lie . . . a front man for traitors," it was as if someone had attacked the integrity of George Washington. Described by President Truman as "the

The Granger Collection

greatest living American," Marshall had designed and coordinated World War II's Normandy invasion. He served as secretary of state from 1947 to 1949 and headed the Defense Department from 1950 to 1951. He was the key architect of the European Recovery Program, known as the Marshall Plan, and in 1953 he became the first career soldier to win the Nobel Peace Prize.

"We are now concerned with the peace of the world," Marshall declared as World War II ended. One day after the general resigned from the military, Truman appointed him special presidential emissary to China with orders to seek an accord between warring Nationalists and Maoist communists. American officials worried that a victory by Maoists would strengthen Soviet influence in Asia. Marshall arrived in China in 1946 and used the lever of U.S. aid to compel the Nationalist government of Chiang Kai-shek to institute democratic reforms. Meanwhile, he tried to convince the communists to agree to a coalition government and unified army under Chiang's leadership.

Truman's belief that communism represented a monolithic threat placed the United States on the side of authoritarian governments in Greece and Turkey. Since he viewed Greek communists as minions of Moscow, Truman supported a conservative monarchy that had little popular support. In Turkey, the United States backed a repressive regime that had cooperated with the Germans during World War II and continued to crush internal dissent. The administration justified these alliances by articulating what later became known as the "domino" theory: "If Greece and then Turkey succumb," one State Department official advised, "the whole Middle East will be lost. France

Aware that political pressures in the United States precluded a complete cessation of U.S. aid to an anticommunist ally, Chiang ignored Marshall's pleadings and launched a major military offensive. Perceiving that negotiations had "reached an impasse," Marshall warned Washington that "the Communists have lost cities and towns but they have not lost their armies." After more than 300 meetings with the disputing parties, Marshall returned home in 1947, citing "complete, almost overwhelming" mutual suspicion as "the greatest obstacle to peace."

The failure of the China mission underscored Marshall's conviction that military effectiveness was limited by political and social conditions. Believing that armed strategy should serve policy, not drive it, he recommended the firing of Korean War commander General Douglas MacArthur in 1951. Months later, Senator Joseph McCarthy denounced Marshall as an accessory to the 1949 victory of the Chinese Maoists and a coconspirator in the communist quest for world domination.

"God bless democracy," Marshall once had exclaimed. "I approve of it highly but suffer from it extremely." The general had popularized the Marshall Plan as a fight against the enemies of "hunger, poverty, desperation, and chaos." Yet the "fall" of China challenged U.S. plans for global peace, prosperity, and democracy, and the principal architect of the postwar world became the centerpiece of recriminating debates that tore at the Cold War consensus.

may then capitulate to the communists. As France goes, all Western Europe and North Africa will go."

Truman's commitment to interventionism on a global scale alarmed conservatives and liberals alike. Republican Senator Taft protested that Truman had made fundamental policy choices without adequately consulting Congress. Meanwhile, the liberal Wallace broadcast a scathing critique: "There is no regime too reactionary" to receive U.S. aid, he said, "provided it stands in Russia's expansionist path." Despite such criticism, the announcement of the Truman Doctrine rapidly boosted the president's approval ratings. Yet U.S. aid neither suppressed the Greek rebellion nor made the monarchy less oppressive. "There is no use pretending . . . that for $400 million we have bought peace," admitted Vandenberg. "It is merely a down payment."

Meanwhile, the slowness of European economic recovery disturbed U.S. leaders concerned about the lack of markets and the potential for social unrest. Secretary of State George C. Marshall, seeking to end economic shortages in Europe, stabilize economic growth, and stimulate U.S. trade, unveiled the administration's innovative European Recovery Program in a highly publicized speech at the Harvard University commencement in June 1947. Marshall described severe economic problems in Europe and called for a massive program of economic aid that offered assistance to all European nations, including communist governments. "Our policy is directed not against any country or doctrine," he stated, "but against hunger, poverty, desperation, and chaos." However, the Marshall Plan's purportedly unselfish offer of aid to the Soviets was deceptive because the plan threatened the independence of the Soviet economy. In addition, the program attempted to return to the prewar conditions that had left eastern Europe less industrialized than the West. Instead of receiving reparations, the Soviet Union might have to contribute food to other countries. Finally, the plan would rebuild the German economy and hasten German integration with western trade.

The State Department correctly predicted that the Soviet Union would reject participation in what came to be known as the Marshall Plan and would force its satellite states in eastern Europe to do the same. But sixteen nations drafted a four-year program of economic recovery and gladly accepted $17 billion in U.S. aid. This economic power allowed Washington to persuade political leaders in Italy and France to exclude the Communist Party from participation in their coalition governments.

Despite the anticommunist aspects of the Marshall Plan, the conservative majority in Congress remained suspicious of executive power, foreign aid, and potential benefits to large exporters rather than domestically oriented small firms. Moreover, as late as November 1947, 40 percent of the public had never heard of the Marshall Plan. But as economic conditions in Western Europe continued to deteriorate and Communist parties throughout Europe organized protests, street demonstrations, and strikes, the White House moved quickly to arouse domestic opinion, launching a major lobby effort in Congress.

"We'll either have to provide a program of interim aid relief until the Marshall program gets going," Truman warned congressional leaders, "or the governments of France and Italy will fall, Austria too, and for all practical purposes, Europe will be Communist." Drawing on his personal standing among Republican leaders, Marshall sold Congress on the program. The idea that Europe would be saved from communism undermined conservative scruples about government spending abroad. Truman summoned a special session of Congress, played down the economic basis of the plan, and returned to the militant anticommunist rhetoric of the Truman Doctrine. The strategy worked, and Congress passed an interim aid measure. By 1950 the program had delivered $35 billion in government grants and loans to European countries and was credited with restoring morale and revitalizing political moderates.

THE RED SCARE

Anticommunist foreign policy paralleled an anticommunist crusade at home. Washington not only viewed the Soviet Union as a hostile and expansionist foreign power but also viewed the U.S. Communist Party as Stalin's domestic agent. Indeed, since the 1930s, various American Communists had provided information to the Soviet state, including aspects of atomic bomb research. Some evidence of Soviet espionage had surfaced in two highly publicized scandals: the discovery in 1945 of stolen secret documents in the offices of *Amerasia*, a left-wing diplomatic journal, and the capture of Soviet spies in Canada in 1946. Republican candidates, such as Richard Nixon and Joseph McCarthy, had exploited this issue in winning election to Congress.

After the Republican victories in 1946, Truman attempted to defuse the explosive issue of communist influence in government by creating a Temporary Commission on Employee Loyalty. Nine days after enunciating the Truman Doctrine, the president created a permanent Federal Employee Loyalty program to eliminate subversives from government. The announcement reflected continuing pressures from congressional conservatives as well as anticommunist attitudes within the administration. In 1947 the House Committee on Un-American Activities (HUAC) opened new investigations of communist infiltration of government, Hollywood, education, and labor unions. HUAC's inquiry into the movie industry resulted in contempt charges against the "Hollywood Ten," a group of writers and directors who refused on First Amendment grounds to answer questions about their political activities. After the Supreme Court refused to hear their appeals, the Hollywood Ten went to prison.

Truman attempted to preempt similar investigations of government employees by issuing an executive order that mandated loyalty investigations of all federal workers and job applicants. The president also ordered dismissal of workers for whom "reasonable grounds" for suspicion of disloyalty existed. He instructed Attorney General Tom Clark to publicize a list of "subversive" organizations, and ninety-one groups were so designated in 1947. The Justice Department contended that these groups were "fronts" for the Communist Party. Federal investigators would treat membership in such organizations as grounds for further inquiries of individuals thus suspected of disloyalty. "There are many Communists in America," the attorney general declared. "They are everywhere—in factories, offices, butcher shops, on street corners, in private businesses—and each carries with him the germs of death for society." Perhaps it was no coincidence that 1947 witnessed the first UFO scare as Americans in thirty-five states and in Canada reported seeing flying saucers or "unidentified flying objects." In any case, the belief in a pervasive conspiracy allowed the administration to ignore due process protections in stigmatizing opponents of government policy and members of so-called subversive groups.

"What," asked a HUAC pamphlet, "is the difference in fact between a Communist and a Fascist? Answer: None worth noticing." In 1947 J. Edgar Hoover published a widely circulated article, "Red Fascism in the United States Today," warning of the imminent danger of communist subversion. To obtain judicial sanction for further surveillance and detention programs, Hoover pressed the Justice Department to prosecute leaders of the Communist Party for violating the Smith Act of 1940. That law made it a crime to advocate the overthrow of government by force or to belong to a group with such a goal. In 1948 the Justice Department charged twelve leading Communists with violations of the Smith Act, winning convictions and stiff prison sentences.

Even though cases of espionage by U.S. Communists and sympathizers certainly occurred before 1945, the political danger of domestic communism appeared minimal. At its peak strength during World War II, the U.S. Communist Party could claim fewer than 100,000 members. Most of them had no interest in subversive activities or the overthrow of the U.S. government. They did, however, hold political positions outside the prevailing consensus. The Communist Party had strenuously opposed racist policies in the South; and the party itself was one of the few racially integrated political organizations in the country. Communists demanded government support of social welfare programs, such as unemployment and health insurance, and preached of a more equitable economic order that gave incentives not for profit but for social benefit.

Although politicians warned about communist subversion, espionage, and other illegal activities, the core of anticommunism lay in public perceptions of its ideology. A wave of novels, movies, essays, and newspaper stories portrayed communism as the epitome of heartless atheism, deadening bureaucracy, and ruthless totalitarianism. Many eastern European ethnic groups hated the Soviets for invading their homelands and destroying Christian churches. Many Americans believed that communism jeopardized traditional values of religion, family, individual liberty, and personal initiative. "Communism is secularism on the march," J. Edgar Hoover told a Methodist gathering. "It is a moral foe of Christianity."

Ironically, the growth of government bureaucracy, big corporations, and impersonal, homogenized communities already threatened traditional values. "Our problem is not outside ourselves," admitted Republican presidential candidate Thomas E. Dewey in 1948. "Our problem is within ourselves." Anticommunist spokesmen such as Joseph McCarthy, J. Edgar Hoover, and Richard Nixon saw themselves as defending individualism, religion, and free enterprise. Their wrath focused not so much on actual Communists as on the sophisticated, cosmopolitan leadership that they saw tolerating communists in government

and accommodating the Soviet Union. "I look at that fellow," Senator Hugh
Butler of Nebraska remarked about Secretary of State Dean Acheson. "I watch
his smart-aleck manner and his British clothes and that New Dealism, everlast-
ing New Dealism in everything he says and does, and I want to shout, 'Get out,
Get out. You stand for everything that has been wrong with the United States.'"

Conservative Republicans such as Nixon and McCarthy exploited anticommunist feelings to attack Democrats and the New Deal tradition. Public
distrust of elites who were not accountable to voters—government bureaucrats, intellectuals, scientists, media and entertainment leaders—encouraged
loyalty oaths, "naming names" of alleged communist associates, blacklists, and
legal persecution. Mickey Spillane's detective novel *One Lonely Night* (1951),
which sold 7 million copies, advocated another method to eliminate communists: "Don't arrest them, don't treat them with the dignity of the democratic
process of courts of law . . . do the same thing that they'd do to you! Treat 'em
to the inglorious taste of sudden death."

Thus backed by public opinion and the courts, law enforcement officials
and anticommunist activists faced few obstacles in purging "red" elements from
American life. As the FBI budget increased from $35 million in 1947 to $53 million in 1950, the agency's watchdogs processed nearly 5 million loyalty forms between 1947 and 1954. Under Truman, more than 7,000 federal government
employees lost their jobs; thousands more were never hired in the first place.
State and municipal governments adopted similar programs barring "subversives" from public employment. Workers and managers in private industry cooperated to harass suspected employees. Teachers, union leaders, even factory
workers were forced to sign loyalty oaths—refusal usually meant dismissal. New
York City high school students had to sign loyalty oaths to collect their diplomas. And the U.S. Post Office intercepted and opened mail from certain communist countries. "If ignorant people read it," said one censor, "they might
begin to believe it."

Such excesses might have been checked by an independent judiciary, but
Truman's appointments to the Supreme Court, including Attorney General
Clark, consistently voted against civil liberties. In the *Dennis* case (1951) the
Court upheld the convictions of eleven Communist Party leaders, ruling that
"communist speech" was not protected by constitutional guarantees because
communists participated in an international movement. As a result of 141 in-
dictments and other harassment, many Communist Party leaders went "underground," and the party lost half its membership.

THE MILITARY CRISIS

The sense of national emergency stimulated the reorganization of the military
services. The National Security Act of 1947 unified command over the armed

services within the new Department of Defense, formalized the Joint Chiefs of Staff, and created an independent air force. The law also established the National Security Council (NSC) and the Central Intelligence Agency (CIA) as secret bureaus responsible only to the president. The NSC would coordinate and refine foreign policy for the White House and act as the president's liaison to the security bureaucracy. The CIA would preside over the gathering of intelligence information. The agency's congressional charter also provided for "such other functions as the Director of Central Intelligence shall, from time to time, deem appropriate." This loophole allowed the agency to develop secret military and political projects overseas. Amendments to the charter in 1949 exempted the CIA from budgetary accounting requirements, thereby releasing the agency from strict congressional oversight.

The National Security Act consolidated the power of the executive branch. Foreign policy decisions increasingly became insulated from external scrutiny. In a critical choice of military strategy, Truman opted in 1948 for an "air-atomic" plan that made strategic bombing, including nuclear weapons, the primary military force. Yet the United States possessed few atomic bombs or technicians capable of assembling more. To the budget-conscious president, air-atomic technology seemed an inexpensive way to build an unassailable defense. The plan had the additional advantage of reducing the need for a large army.

The decision to rebuild U.S. military strength faced opposition from both conservatives and liberals. Wallace, who announced his presidential candidacy as leader of the new Progressive Party, chastised Truman for ignoring the United Nations and provoking the Soviet Union. More powerful opposition came from Republicans such as Taft, who denounced the swollen federal budget and argued that the war with communism was ultimately a contest of ideas, not military might. When the president requested funds for the air-atomic plan in 1948, Congress seemed uninterested. "The outlook for greatly increased aviation budgets is not bright," the trade journal *Aviation Week* lamented early in 1948.

Congress abruptly snapped to attention, however, when communists seized power in Soviet-occupied Czechoslovakia in February 1948. Although the State Department had treated Czechoslovakia as part of the Soviet bloc, news of the communist coup shocked the public, confirming fears of Soviet aggression through internal subversion. Truman resolved not to repeat the Munich sellout of Czechoslovakia of 1938, when British and French "appeasement" had permitted Hitler to occupy Czech territory.

Speaking to a joint session of Congress in March 1948, the president warned that the United States was on the verge of war. The Soviet Union had "destroyed the independence and democratic character of a whole series of nations," said Truman, and so revealed "the clear design" to conquer "the remaining free nations of Europe." "There is some risk involved in action— there always is," he admitted, "but there is far more risk in failure to act." The

EXHIBIT **1-5**   **BERLIN BLOCKADE, 1948**

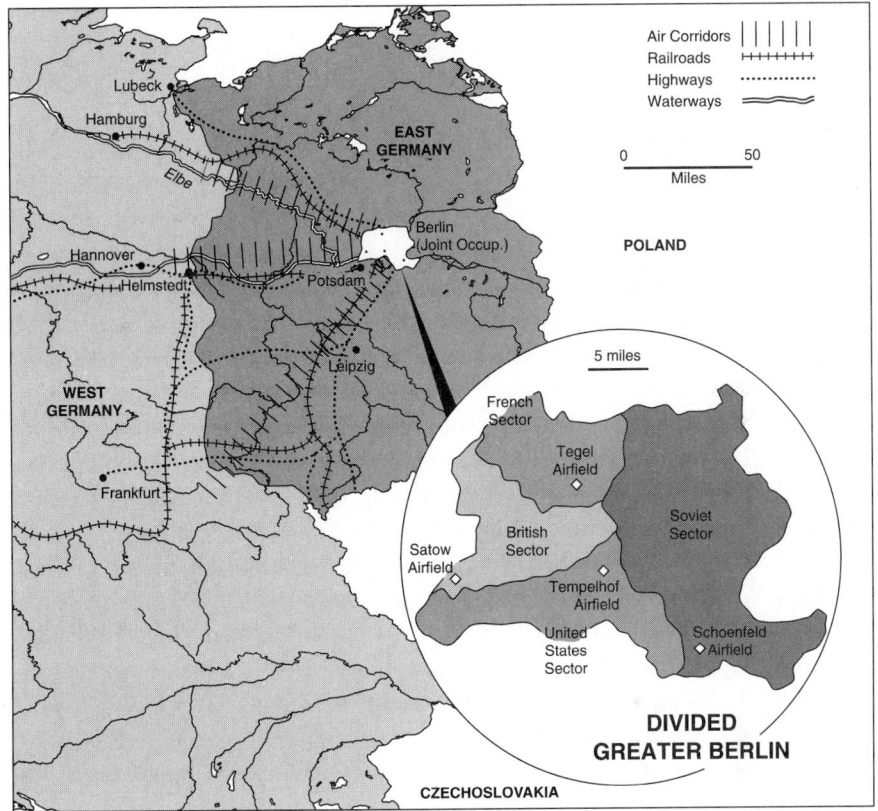

somber speech persuaded Congress to approve the Marshall Plan and to reestablish the military draft. Conservatives managed to defeat a proposal for universal military training, but Congress allocated $3.5 billion for military purposes, 25 percent more than the White House had requested.

Military confrontation came one step closer when the Soviet Union blockaded Berlin in June 1948. Since the end of the war, the great powers had failed to sign a final peace settlement. While Truman and Stalin argued about German reparations, the former enemy remained divided into occupied zones. Since the United States and Britain planned to merge their occupied zones into a single unit, Stalin realized that the Western powers were hastening German independence to bring Germany into the Western alliance. In response the Soviets blocked access to Berlin through East Germany.

Truman saw war on the horizon. Determined to support Berlin, the president ordered a massive airlift of food and supplies that lasted eleven months. Stalin was unwilling to go to war and had to accept U.S. plans for West Germany. Yet the crisis escalated the level of conflict. In July 1948 Truman ordered

B-29 bombers to England. These were the only planes capable of dropping atomic bombs in Europe, although (unknown to the Soviets) they were not modified for such work until 1949. For the first time, atomic weapons had become an explicit instrument of foreign policy.

The Cold War crisis enabled Congress to reverse Truman's policies in Asia. In China, the corruption of Chiang Kai-shek's Nationalist regime and the success of Mao Zedong's communists had persuaded the president to allow the Chinese civil war to run its course. However, the Truman Doctrine suggested that any communist expansion threatened U.S. interests. Influenced by a well-funded pressure group known as the China Lobby, congressional conservatives insisted on a literal interpretation of the Truman Doctrine. Contrary to White House intentions, Congress proceeded to appropriate funds to support Chiang's regime, committing the United States to a repressive but noncommunist government and influencing subsequent foreign policy in Asia for three decades. Meanwhile, Truman's decision to abandon Chiang accelerated accommodation with Japan, a noncommunist ally. In 1947 Truman extended economic assistance to Japan and strengthened U.S. military forces there.

Washington also solidified its sphere of influence in Latin America. The Rio Pact of 1947 provided for collective self-defense of the Western Hemisphere. In 1948 the Bogota Treaty created the Organization of American States to coordinate policy, and the United States disavowed intervention in the affairs of other states. In creating this alliance, Washington avoided economic commitments, preferring to support private development. Yet in a series of bilateral agreements, the administration offered military assistance, including the training of Latin American armies. Such support stabilized military and landed elites throughout the region and increased dependence on U.S. trade.

THE ELECTION OF 1948

With the nation facing a series of foreign policy crises, political pundits questioned Truman's leadership. A March 1948 Gallup poll showed that the Democrats would lose the presidential election to any one of several Republican challengers: New York Governor Thomas E. Dewey, Vandenberg, former Minnesota Governor Harold Stassen, or General Douglas MacArthur. Meanwhile, Henry Wallace announced an independent candidacy. "There is no real fight between a Truman and a Republican," said Wallace. "Both stand for a policy which opens the door to war in our lifetime and makes war certain for our children." Yet military mobilization against Soviet communism worked to the president's advantage. By identifying Wallace as procommunist, the president kept most liberals in the Democratic Party.

Truman also moved to rebuild the New Deal coalition. Despite inherent conflicts between white southern Democrats and northern black voters, he opted to endorse civil rights, issuing an executive order to desegregate the military. The choice strengthened his appeal among both African Americans and northern liberals who might have backed Wallace. His veto of Taft-Hartley restored his support among organized workers. Truman also improved his standing among Jews by recognizing the new state of Israel in 1948.

The Wallace insurgency emboldened Republicans. They nominated Dewey for president and adopted a moderate platform that called for federal support of housing, farm payments, abolition of poll taxes, a permanent Fair Employment Practices Commission (FEPC), and increases in Social Security benefits. Confident of an election victory, Republicans deliberately excluded foreign policy issues from debate, which freed Truman from having to defend his positions. The president then undermined the Republicans by calling the Eightieth Congress into special session and daring the Republican majority to enact their party platform.

Truman also confronted divisions within the Democratic Party. At the Democratic National Convention, liberals, led by Minneapolis Mayor Hubert Humphrey, demanded a commitment to civil rights legislation. "The time has arrived for the Democratic Party to get out of the shadow of states rights," Humphrey declared, "and walk forthrightly into the bright sunshine of human rights." Democrats responded by backing a strong civil rights plank. Angry southern delegates who opposed this plank left the convention. Three days later, these Dixiecrats met in Birmingham, Alabama, formed the States' Rights Party, and nominated South Carolina's Strom Thurmond for president. Other southern Democrats stayed in the party, but ignored the party platform. Lyndon B. Johnson, running in Texas for the Senate, attacked the FEPC ("because if a man can tell you whom you must hire, he can tell you whom you cannot employ"), and opposed proposals to end the discriminatory poll tax or enact federal antilynching laws.

Supporters of Henry Wallace proceeded to organize the Progressive Party and launched another independent campaign. Although communists held important positions in the party, the platform primarily reflected liberal principles. The Progressives challenged Truman's Cold War and Dewey's bipartisanship by arguing that "ending the tragic prospect of war is a joint responsibility of the Soviet Union and the United States." Yet the Progressives could never overcome their association with communism. "Politicians of both major parties have tried to pin the Communist tag on the followers of . . . Wallace," observed pollster George Gallup. "Apparently their efforts have succeeded." The Wallace campaign encountered harassment, mob violence, and denial of public meeting places, particularly in southern states that refused to permit racially mixed gatherings.

EXHIBIT 1-6   THE ELECTION OF 1948

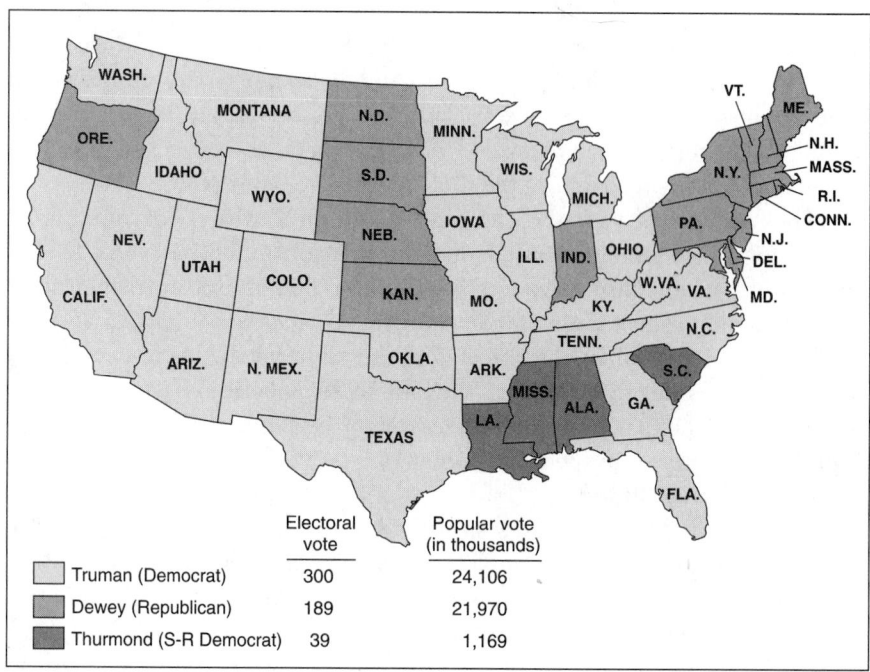

	Electoral vote	Popular vote (in thousands)
Truman (Democrat)	300	24,106
Dewey (Republican)	189	21,970
Thurmond (S-R Democrat)	39	1,169

While Dixiecrats and Progressives attacked Truman, the special session of the Eightieth Congress convened. If Republicans enacted their platform, Truman would get credit for goading them to act; if not, they would appear hypocritical. After much discussion, Congress adjourned without passing significant legislation. The decision gave Truman campaign ammunition against "do-nothing" Republicans. Preelection polls forecast a Republican victory, but Truman launched a personal "whistle-stop" campaign that covered more than 20,000 miles. "Give 'em hell, Harry!" became a rallying cry as Truman appealed to anxious farmers about Republican threats to the price support program and became the first president to campaign for the African American vote in Harlem.

The results brought a surprise Democratic victory in November when Truman topped Dewey by more than 2 million votes. "The publishers' press is a very small part of our population," gloated Truman. The electoral college gave Truman 304 votes, Dewey 189, Thurmond 34 (all in the South), and Wallace none. Each third-party candidate attracted slightly more than 1 million votes, but Truman did best among farmers, organized labor, and blacks, all groups that supported Roosevelt's New Deal.

THE FAIR DEAL

"Every segment of our population and every individual," Truman told the Eighty-first Congress, "has a right to expect from our Government a fair deal." With a Democratic majority again in Congress, the president called for increased Social Security benefits and minimum wages, civil rights legislation, federal aid to education, national health insurance, and repeal of the Taft-Hartley Act. However, White House proposals soon met resistance from the true majority in Congress—a conservative coalition of southern Democrats and midwestern Republicans. By controlling the congressional committee system, these groups prevented consideration of Truman's program. Although Congress passed the Housing Act of 1949, providing for slum clearance and low-income housing, insufficient appropriations limited the program. In addition, civil rights legislation died in committee. Truman, choosing to avoid a hopeless skirmish, did not push for its passage.

Truman's support of civil rights appeared ambiguous. Despite the president's 1948 order to desegregate the armed services, the military evaded enforcement. In Truman's inauguration parade of 1949, black soldiers marched with whites, but the army blocked full integration by segregating platoons. Truman's Department of Justice supported civil rights suits, but the Federal Housing Authority continued to accept residential segregation, even after the Supreme Court outlawed restrictive covenants in 1948. As for equal employment opportunity, the president hesitated to reestablish the FEPC, then failed to halt discrimination in war industries. Nonetheless, African Americans praised Truman's moral support. "No occupant of the White House since the nation was born," wrote black leader Walter White, "has taken so frontal or constant a stand against racial discrimination as has Harry S Truman."

The limitations of Truman's Fair Deal reflected changes in liberal thinking. After Wallace's defeat, liberals repudiated associations with communism and moved away from radical positions. Anticommunist liberals, including theologian Reinhold Niebuhr and historian Arthur M. Schlesinger Jr., argued that the search for a perfect society such as a communist utopia was naïve, self-deceptive, and led to totalitarian excesses. At a time when more middle-class citizens were enjoying personal prosperity, creating the baby boom, and celebrating conformity, U.S. liberalism understandably supported the status quo.

LIMITED BIPARTISANSHIP

Although political disagreement eventually undermined the foreign policy consensus, a bipartisan spirit prevailed on European issues. In June 1948 the Senate passed the Vandenberg Resolution, which permitted participation in a

Arthur H. Vandenberg *(1884–1951)*

"The Old Guard dies but never surrenders," wrote journalist Milton S. Mayer of the last-ditch noninterventionists in 1940; "Vandenberg surrenders, but never dies." Michigan Senator Arthur H. Vandenberg blazed the trail for those conservative Americans who made the transition from prewar anti-interventionism to postwar internationalism.

Although staunch Old Guard Republicans such as Robert Taft of Ohio refused to compromise their "America-first" principles, Vandenberg believed that national security required a new internationalist commitment. He insisted that the Soviet Union constituted a threat to U.S. interests around the world and worked with the Truman administration to build a national consensus in support of the Cold War.

Born in Grand Rapids, Michigan, Vandenberg embraced the traditionalist middle-class and midwestern values of his surroundings. Yet Pearl Harbor and the requirements of World War II prompted him to embrace internationalism, leading to the senator's support for a postwar United Nations. To win Republican backing of the postwar settlement, Truman chose

peacetime military alliance with the nations of western Europe. The next year, the United States signed the North Atlantic Treaty, a pact that provided for a collective defense against the Soviets by forming the North Atlantic Treaty Organization (NATO). The administration also moved to create a new West German state, and in 1949 the Federal Republic of Germany joined the Western alliance. Although the treaty obligated the United States to send military assistance to European allies, its purposes appeared less military than political. First, NATO served as a deterrent to Soviet expansion. Second, the alliance ensured U.S. domination of western Europe by obliging its members to adopt a united, U.S.–influenced approach to the region's security. Third, the pact linked German industrial and military power with the rest of western Europe to avoid old rivalries. Taft, who was opposed to permanent military commitments, led the fight against the treaty's ratification in the senate, but could not overcome the president's supporters. The House, however, hesi-

Vandenberg to attend the first United Nations conference in San Francisco in 1945, where the delegate persuaded his colleagues to adopt Article 51 of the U.N. Charter, providing for regional alliances. Intended to protect U.S. influence in Latin America, this proviso later provided the basis for NATO and other regional pacts.

As the leading internationalist in the Republican Party, Vandenberg demanded a voice in foreign policy in exchange for bipartisan support of the Cold War. Criticizing any sign of "appeasement" of the Soviet Union, he denounced negotiations to internationalize atomic energy in 1946. His vanity, though, made him easily subject to flattery and pressure. Using the principle of bipartisanship, the administration won his support of the Truman Doctrine, Marshall Plan, and NATO. Vandenberg also intervened with Republican leaders to prevent any serious debate of foreign policy during the 1948 presidential election.

Unlike Taft, Vandenberg did not question the high cost of the Cold War or the growth of a national security state. Taft's opposition to the military state prevented him from winning the Republican nomination in 1948 and 1952. Yet Vandenberg, whose foreign policy position seemed more popular, failed to win the respect of his colleagues and never became a party leader.

tated to allocate funds to implement the treaty's provisions. Then, in September 1949 the president announced that the Soviet Union had exploded an atomic bomb. Within a week, the House provided the NATO funding.

Perceiving the Soviet Union as a relentless enemy that now possessed devastating weapons of destruction, Republicans and Democrats alike felt increasingly vulnerable to attack both at home and abroad. Although Soviet spies accelerated the development of a Soviet atomic bomb (probably by fewer than two years), fears of domestic subversion assumed nightmarish proportions. Allegations that government "traitors" such as former State Department official Alger Hiss had passed secret documents to communist agents reinforced the climate of suspicion. Yet Washington recognized that the Soviet Union lacked the military capacity to launch an atomic attack. Even so, Truman opted to strengthen U.S. military power. During the fall of 1949, top administration advisors debated whether the country should proceed to build a "superbomb."

EXHIBIT **1-7**   **THE NORTH ATLANTIC TREATY ORGANIZATION (NATO)**

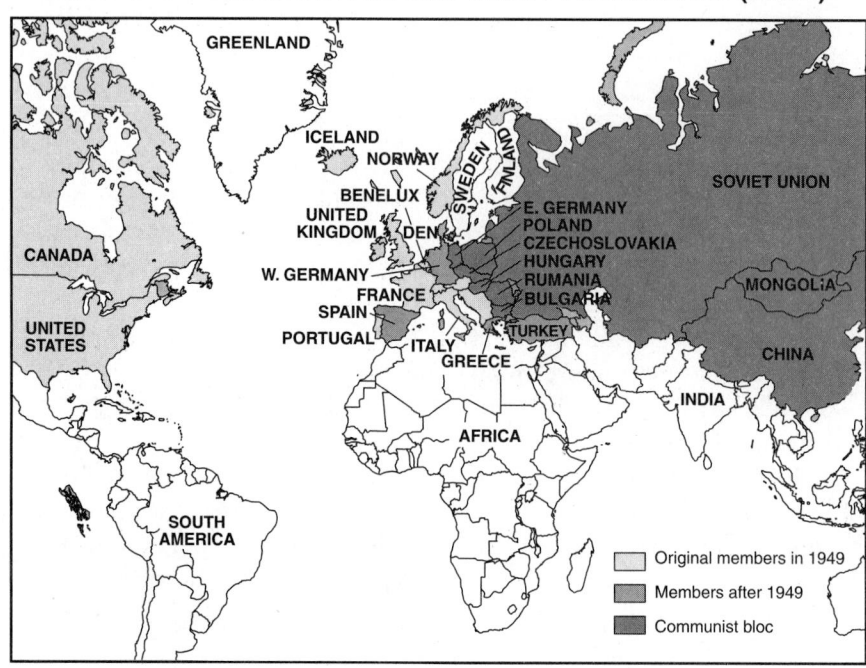

Despite unanimous objections by scientists and civilians on the Atomic Energy Commission's General Advisory Council, commission head Lewis Strauss,
backed by physicist Edward Teller, urged the development of the new hydrogen weapon. In January 1950 Truman ended the debate by ordering development of the bomb. By the end of the next year the United States successfully
tested the new weapon; within two years the Soviet Union did the same.

Truman continued to face Republican criticism for neglecting China's
Chiang Kai-shek. Despite appropriations exceeding $1 billion for the Chinese
Nationalists, communist armies steadily destroyed Chiang's crumbling forces.
By August 1949 the State Department predicted a communist victory and
halted further assistance. "The only alternative open to the United States,"
asserted a State Department white paper, "was full-scale intervention in behalf of a government which had lost the confidence of its own troops and its
own people." Yet, although it conceded the inevitability of a communist victory, the administration rejected accommodation with the Chinese insurgents.
Four months later Mao Zedong's communist forces swept into power, forcing
Chiang to abandon the mainland and flee to the island of Taiwan (Formosa).

Given the logic of containment, the communist victory in China could
only be seen as a defeat of U.S. policy, especially after Mao signed a mutual

assistance pact with the Soviet Union in 1950. The China Lobby, which included leading Republican senators, attacked the administration for failing to support an anticommunist ally. Such criticism reinforced Truman's reluctance to negotiate with the Chinese communists. Instead, the United States adopted a policy of nonrecognition that lasted for more than two decades.

The so-called "loss" of China, the explosion of a Soviet atomic bomb, allegations of communists in government—all disturbed the search for security that had followed World War II. Two days after Truman announced the first Soviet atomic test in September 1949, a young evangelical Baptist named Billy Graham opened a tent revival meeting in Los Angeles and addressed the most pressing question of the age. "Time is desperately short," he warned; "prepare to meet thy God." Worried citizens had to wonder how the country had moved so rapidly from the optimism of peace in 1945 to the perils of atomic warfare with the Soviet anti-Christ.

INFOTRAC COLLEGE EDITION

Using Keywords, enter the following search terms:

Cold War
Harry Truman
George Marshall
George Kennan
J. Edgar Hoover

RECOMMENDED READING

Gary A. Donaldson, *Truman Defeats Dewey* (1999). A study of postwar election politics, this book describes Truman's success at rebuilding the New Deal coalition in 1948.

Rosalyn Baxandall and Elizabeth Ewen, *Picture Windows: How the Suburbs Happened* (2000). The authors place postwar suburban growth in a century-long context of housing issues and public policy.

Melvyn P. Leffler, *A Preponderance of Power: National Security, the Truman Administration, and the Cold War* (1992). A thorough and balanced analysis of postwar foreign policy, this volume explains U.S. motivations in the emerging Cold War.

William Graebner, *The Age of Doubt: American Thought and Culture in the 1940s* (1991). This book explores wartime and postwar cultural expression, including media, literature, and the arts, emphasizing the underlying anxieties caused by political events.

Additional Readings

The major issues of the Truman years are explored in Alonzo L. Hamby, *Beyond the New Deal: Harry S. Truman and American Liberalism* (1973). Two good biographies are Robert H. Ferrell, *Harry S Truman: A Life* (1994), and Alonzo L. Hamby, *Man of the People: A Life of Harry S Truman* (1995). Also useful as an introduction to the period is an anthology, Barton J. Bernstein, ed., *Politics and Policies of the Truman Administration* (1970). A convenient collection of primary sources is Barton J. Bernstein and Allen Matusow, eds. *The Truman Administration* (1966). See also Gary W. Reichard, *Politics as Usual: The Age of Truman and Eisenhower* (1988).

The postwar relationship between government and business is illuminated in Elizabeth A. Fones-Wolf, *Selling Free Enterprise: The Business Assault on Labor and Liberalism, 1945–1960* (1994). For a fine study of the relationship between technology and industrial development, see David F. Noble, *Forces of Production: A Social History of Industrial Automation* (1986). Government support of science and technology is the major theme of three valuable studies: Walter A. McDougall, *The Heavens and the Earth: A Political History of the Space Age* (1985); Richard Rhodes, *Dark Sun: The Making of the Hydrogen Bomb* (1995); and Kenneth Flamm, *Creating the Computer: Government, Industry, and High Technology* (1988). For the impact of the atomic bomb on U.S. society, see Paul Boyer, *By the Bomb's Early Light: American Thought and Culture at the Dawn of the Atomic Age* (1985), and Spencer R. Weart, *Nuclear Fear: A History of Images* (1988). For Truman's farm policies, see Allen Matusow, *Farm Policies and Politics in the Truman Years* (1967); for labor, see R. Alton Lee, *Truman and Taft-Hartley* (1966).

The consequences of the high postwar birthrate are described in Landon Y. Jones, *America and the Baby Boom Generation* (1980). For the influence of pediatrician Benjamin Spock, see Julia Grant, *Raising Baby by the Book: The Education of American Mothers* (1998). The broader problems of economic class and wealth are well analyzed in George Lipsitz, *Rainbow at Midnight: Labor and Culture in the 1940s* (1994). A survey of women's history can be found in Elaine Tyler May's *Homeward Bound: American Families in the Cold War Era* (1988), which can be supplemented with Rochelle Gatlin, *American Women Since 1945* (1987).

The literature on the Cold War is vast. A sensible and readable introduction is Walter Lafeber, *America, Russia, and the Cold War* (1985), as is Bernard Weisberger, *Cold War, Cold Peace* (1984). John Lewis Gaddis's *Now We Know: Rethinking Cold War History* (1997) places Soviet-American conflict in a longer perspective. An excellent analysis of the creation of the new national defense policies is Michael Hogan, *A Cross of Iron: Harry S Truman and the Origins of the National Security State* (1998). See also Daniel Yergin, *Shattered Peace: The Origins of the Cold War and the National Security State*

(1977). The importance of the atomic bomb in foreign policy and military planning is analyzed carefully in Gregg Harken, *The Winning Weapon: The Atomic Bomb in the Cold War, 1945–1950* (1980). For the sources of economic conflict, see Robert A. Pollard, *Economic Security and the Origins of the Cold War, 1945–1950* (1985). The close relationship between domestic anticommunism and foreign policy is presented in Richard M. Freeland, *The Truman Doctrine and the Origins of McCarthyism* (1972).

The impact of the Red Scare is thoroughly documented in David Caute, *The Great Fear: The Anti-Communist Purge Under Truman and Eisenhower* (1978). Also illuminating is Les Adler, *The Red Image: American Attitudes Toward Communism in the Cold War Era* (1991). A series of recent volumes, based on declassified but often ambiguous evidence, depicts Soviet espionage activities: see Harvey Klehr and Ronald Radosh, *The Amerasia Spy Case: Prelude to McCarthyism* (1996); John Earl Haynes and Harvey Klehr, *Venona: Recoding Soviet Espionage in America* (1999); and Allen Weinstein and Alexander Vassiliev, *The Haunted Wood: Soviet Espionage in America—the Stalin Era* (1999).

The political consequences of anticommunism are explored in Francis H. Thompson, *The Frustration of Politics: Truman, Congress, and the Loyalty Drive, 1945–1953* (1979); in Athan Theoharis, *Seeds of Repression: Harry S Truman and the Origins of McCarthyism* (1971); and in Alan D. Harper, *The Politics of Loyalty* (1969). The investigations of Hollywood are detailed in Larry Ceplair and Steven Englund, *The Inquisition in Hollywood: Politics in the Film Community, 1930–1960* (1980), and in Victor Navasky, *Naming Names* (1980). For the effect of the new political climate on the movie industry, see Lary May, *The Big Tomorrow: Hollywood and the Politics of the American Way* (2000). An oral history exploring these issues can be found in Griffin Fariello, *Red Scare: Memories of the American Inquisition* (1995).

The Wallace candidacy of 1948 is described in Richard J. Walton, *Henry Wallace, Harry Truman, and the Cold War* (1976), which contains many primary sources, and in Norman D. Markowitz, *The Rise and Fall of the People's Century: Henry A. Wallace and American Liberalism* (1973). James T. Patterson's *Mr. Republican: A Biography of Robert A. Taft* (1972) examines the career of the leading conservative. For the early career of Lyndon B. Johnson, see the second volume of Robert Caro's *The Years of Lyndon Johnson: Means of Ascent* (1990).

The role of key personalities in policymaking emerges in Robert L. Messer, *The End of an Alliance: James F. Byrnes, Roosevelt, Truman, and the Origins of the Cold War* (1982). See also Michael J. Hogan, *The Marshall Plan: America, Britain, and the Reconstruction of Western Europe* (1987). The persistence of isolationism is the subject of Justus D. Doenecke, *Not to the Swift: The Old Isolationists in the Cold War* (1979). A useful anthology on the dissenters from Truman's policies is Thomas G. Paterson, ed., *Cold War Critics* (1971).

The Cold War in Asia is described in Robert M. Blum, *Drawing the Line: The Origin of the American Containment Policy in East Asia* (1982); in William Whitney Stueck Jr., *The Road to Confrontation: American Policy Toward China and Korea, 1947–1950* (1981); and in Nancy Tucker, *Patterns in the Dust: Chinese-American Relations and the Recognition Controversy, 1949–1950* (1983). A good analysis of postwar Asian policy can be found in Gordon H. Chang, *Friends and Enemies: The United States, China, and the Soviet Union, 1948–1972* (1990). For U.S. policy in Indochina, see the relevant chapters of Lloyd C. Gardner, *Approaching Vietnam: From World War II Through Dienbienphu, 1941–1954* (1988).

American policy in the Middle East is presented in Aaron David Miller, *The Search for Security: Saudi Arabian Oil and American Foreign Policy, 1939–1949* (1980); in Barry Rubin, *Paved with Good Intentions: American Experience in Iran* (1980); and in Zvi Ganin, *Truman, American Jewry, and Israel, 1945–1948* (1979). For international economic affairs, see Fred L. Block, *The Origins of International Economic Disorder* (1977). Also insightful is Ernest R. May, *"Lessons" of the Past: The Use and Misuse of History in American Foreign Policy* (1973).

REPUBLICAN LEADERSHIP AND THE ANTICOMMUNIST CRUSADE, 1950–1954

The 1950s began ominously, accentuating public anxieties about the Soviet atom bomb and the communist victory in China. In January a jury waded through hours of allegations and denial and found former State Department official Alger Hiss guilty of perjury for denying that he had passed classified documents to erstwhile Communist Whittaker Chambers in the 1930s. The sensational case confirmed conservative fears that a link existed between Hiss's New Deal liberalism and communist influence in government. The case further embarrassed Democrats because President Harry Truman had labeled the congressional investigation of Hiss "a red herring" and had issued a 1948 executive order barring Congress from access to government loyalty files without presidential approval.

The Hiss case solidified the Cold War suspicion that association with the U.S. Communist Party was equivalent to service for the Soviet state. Indeed, recent revelations from Soviet archives show that the Russians had found willing agents among some U.S. Communist Party members, although the nature of their activities remains unclear. However, most U.S. communists attempted to affect policy through more conventional political activities, such as participation in labor groups, elections, or public events. Nonetheless, Richard Nixon, who had sparked the Hiss investigation for the House Committee on Un-American Activities (HUAC), denounced "high officials" for concealing a larger subversive "conspiracy." Hereafter, anticommunist liberals would disassociate themselves from political activities that might prove embarrassing.

Truman, in any case, had no intention of relaxing the nation's defenses. In January 1950, the commander in chief rebuffed the objections of some civilian scientists and ordered the Atomic Energy Commission to proceed with the development of a thermonuclear or hydrogen bomb, a thousand times more powerful than atomic weapons. In February the Soviet Union and the People's Republic of China signed a treaty of friendship, alliance, and mutual assistance and both communist states extended recognition to Indochina's rebels, the Viet Minh. That month, British authorities arrested physicist Klaus Fuchs on suspicion of passing atomic secrets to the Soviet Union during World War II. The Fuchs case set off a string of arrests that netted other accused atomic spies, including U.S. citizens Julius and Ethel Rosenberg. Meanwhile, the National Security Council (NSC) began to put the finishing touches on a secret comprehensive plan of global defense labeled NSC-68, which warned that the public was suffering from "a false sense of security."

In this climate of mounting global tension, Wisconsin Senator Joseph R. McCarthy presented a Lincoln Day address to the Women's Republican Club in Wheeling, West Virginia, which stunned the nation. "Five years after a world war has been won, men's hearts should anticipate a long peace," he said, "and men's minds should be free from the heavy weight that comes with war." Instead, he declared, the country was engaged in a frightening Cold War between "communistic atheism and Christianity." In defining the conflict with Soviet communism as a religious crusade, McCarthy offered a secularized version of total war between good and evil in which the outcome remained uncertain.

Now, however, the Wisconsin senator presented a startling revelation about the cause of the country's unexpected and dangerous predicament. According to McCarthy, America's crisis resulted from a secret diabolical conspiracy against the U.S. government. "I have in my hands," said McCarthy, "a list of 205 [government employees] that were made known to the secretary of state as being members of the Communist Party and who nevertheless are still working and shaping policy in the State Department." In later versions of his speech, McCarthy changed the specific number of alleged communists—facts, to McCarthy, were slippery items—but he vigorously affirmed the charge that subversives permeated the federal bureaucracy.

McCarthy's attacks on communism stamped his name indelibly on the era. Of course, the anticommunist crusade had preceded his election to Congress in 1946, and other conservative leaders, such as California's Richard Nixon and South Dakota's Karl Mundt, had warned about communist subversion of government. President Truman had created a loyalty security program to identify and purge spies and subversives (see Chapter 1). But McCarthy's rhetorical style—his claims of possessing evidence and proof of conspiracy—added to the sense of emergency. Moreover, McCarthy disdained the legal steps of due process associated with government investigations. A contentious, tough-talking ex-Marine, the Wisconsin senator often drank to excess, insulted witnesses, swore at his critics, and assaulted a Washington journalist who challenged his conspiratorial claims. Such behavior would ultimately prove McCarthy's undoing. But between 1950 and 1954, he hurled innumerable charges of communism at upstanding citizens and created a climate of persecution that his critics compared to a witch hunt.

THE RED SCARE

McCarthy's success reflected the national mood. In June 1950 the arrest of Julius and Ethel Rosenberg, who were charged with transmitting atomic bomb secrets to the Soviet Union during World War II, underscored the domestic threat. That month, the "Hollywood Ten" who had refused to testify to HUAC about their political associations began to serve one-year prison sentences for "contempt" of Congress. By then, the movie industry had established a blacklist, refusing to employ alleged communists in films. A new movie, *The Flying Saucer,* claimed that UFOs were Soviet airplanes "designed for one purpose— to carry an atomic bomb," while the science fiction thriller *Destination Moon* had U.S. business leaders racing to beat the Russians to the uranium-rich lunar surface. "I cannot tell you when or where the attack will come," admitted President Truman as he announced the first national civil defense program. "I can only remind you that we must be ready when it does come."

The belief in a pervasive communist conspiracy prompted efforts to identify and control all communist activities. In 1950 Nevada's Democratic Senator Patrick McCarran introduced the Internal Security Act, which banned communists from employment in defense industries, established a Subversive Activities Control Board to monitor communist organizations, required communists to register with the attorney general, and barred communists from obtaining passports. Senate liberals, hoping to defeat the measure, offered an alternative bill that authorized the president to declare an "internal security emergency" and to detain suspected dissidents. But then the Senate combined and passed both proposals. Truman vetoed the bill "because any governmental stifling of the free expression of opinion is a long step toward totalitarianism." Congress overrode the veto by an overwhelming margin. Terrified by the prospect of an atomic war with the Soviet Union, the public supported such anticommunist measures.

McCarthy's accusations concerning communists in government won the support of most conservative Republicans, who, despite occasional misgivings about his tactics, endorsed attacks on the Truman administration. One exception was Maine Republican Margaret Chase Smith, the only woman in the Senate. Responding to the climate of "fear and frustration," she drafted a "Declaration of Conscience" that denounced her party's support of "fear, ignorance, bigotry and smear." In 1950 a Senate investigating committee chaired by Maryland Democrat Millard Tydings found no evidence to support McCarthy's charges and concluded that the allegations were "a fraud and a hoax." Yet the Senate responded to the report along strict party lines. Such party loyalty enabled McCarthy to remain a presence if not a decisive factor in the 1950 congressional elections. In Maryland, McCarthy smeared Tydings as a procommunist and contributed to Tydings's defeat. In California, Nixon defeated liberal Democrat Helen Gahagan Douglas, whom he dubbed the "Pink Lady," to win election to the Senate.

After the 1950 elections, McCarran's Senate Internal Security subcommittee focused on communist influence at the United Nations, and HUAC resumed investigations of Hollywood figures in 1951. Meanwhile, McCarthy's accusations that communists were employed in the State Department gained wide public attention. Truman called McCarthy a liar. Yet the administration reacted to the charges not by defending the civil liberties of the accused but by affirming its own anticommunist credentials. In April 1951 Truman issued an executive order introducing a new standard for ferreting out subversives: a federal employee could be fired not when there were "reasonable grounds" but rather when there was "reasonable doubt" about the person's loyalty. The burden of proof thus shifted from the accuser to the accused.

In 1952 Congress endeavored to protect U.S. borders by establishing new rules for immigration. The McCarran-Walter Immigration Act, passed over Truman's veto, gave the president power to exclude any foreigner deemed "detrimental" to the national interest. The law continued previous immigration policies by favoring immigrants from northern and western European countries and sharply limiting immigrants from the colonies of those countries. The act slightly increased Asian immigration quotas and permitted wider immigration from Latin America but reduced immigration from the West Indies and Africa. Consistent with the anticommunist crusade, the McCarran-Walter Act also limited immigration from countries under communist control and facilitated expulsion of "undesirable" aliens and naturalized citizens.

THE WAR IN KOREA

By the spring of 1950 the National Security Council had completed the secret analysis of U.S. foreign policy, NSC-68. Asserting that "the Soviet Union . . . is animated by a new fanatic faith . . . and seeks to impose its absolute authority over the rest of the world," the report emphasized the possibility of immediate war and recommended that the United States be prepared to halt Soviet expansion throughout the world. Such a goal demanded a global defense system that included hydrogen bombs, expansion of conventional military forces, and a network of international alliances. To finance this policy, NSC-68 recommended quadrupling the $13 billion national defense budget. This costly plan faced considerable opposition in Congress, particularly because the Soviet Union had avoided any overt action since 1948 that justified U.S. military intervention. Meanwhile, in secret meetings, the administration debated plans to defend Taiwan from invasion by Chinese communists.

The tense peace was shattered on June 25, 1950, when North Korean troops suddenly invaded South Korea. Six months earlier, Secretary of State

EXHIBIT **2-1**   **THE KOREAN WAR**

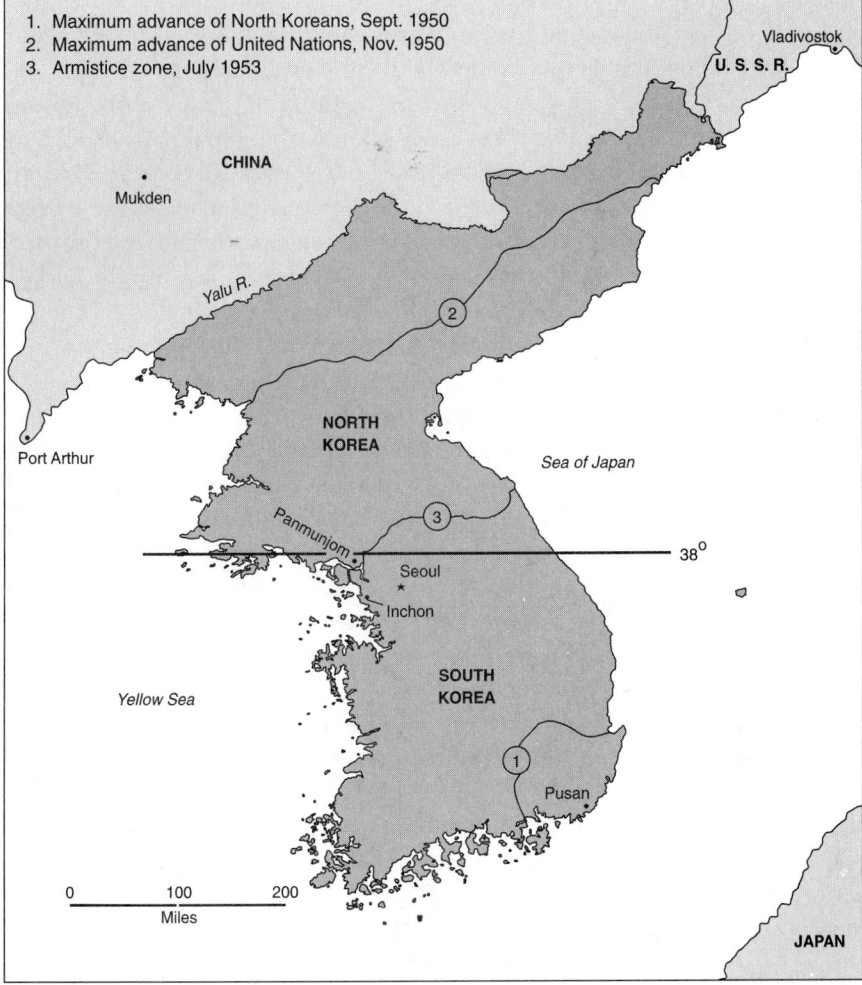

1. Maximum advance of North Koreans, Sept. 1950
2. Maximum advance of United Nations, Nov. 1950
3. Armistice zone, July 1953

Dean Acheson had remarked in a speech to the National Press Club that Korea and Taiwan lay beyond the U.S. "defense perimeter" in the Pacific. The statement, though challenged by Republican conservatives, had justified a reduction of aid to the Chinese Nationalist regime of Chiang Kai-shek. But as North Korean armies advanced quickly, Truman ordered military assistance to South Korea and directed the Seventh Fleet to sail between mainland China and Taiwan to prevent an invasion of the Nationalist-held island. The next day the White House called an emergency session of the U.N. Security Council, which branded North Korea an aggressor. (The Soviet delegation, boycotting the Security Council because of U.S. refusal to discuss the admission of communist China, missed the critical vote.)

As the South Korean army collapsed, Truman saw the North Korean invasion as equivalent to the 1941 attack on Pearl Harbor and ordered U.S. troops into action. "The attack upon Korea," he declared, "makes it plain beyond all doubt that communism has passed beyond the use of subversion to conquer independent nations." The United Nations later approved Truman's action, giving international sanction to U.S. policy. Sixteen nations eventually participated in the war, but the United States provided most of the resources and leadership.

Intervention in Korea stemmed from the conviction that the United States had to "draw the line" against communist aggression and demonstrate its willingness to fight the Soviets anywhere in the world. As with the earlier decisions of challenging the Berlin blockade and developing hydrogen bombs, the president bypassed consultation with congressional leaders, thereby setting important precedents for successors. Although Senator Robert A. Taft denounced Truman's "complete usurpation . . . of authority to use the armed forces," public opinion supported the president's action. Indeed, Truman's claim to be enforcing U.N. policy won favor among liberals, even though the U.S. military commander, General Douglas MacArthur, took orders directly and exclusively from Washington.

American troops landed in Korea just in time to stop a complete North Korean victory. After hard fighting near the southern port of Pusan, the Allied armies forced the enemy to retreat. At the start of the war, the administration insisted that fighting was "solely for the purpose of restoring the Republic of Korea to its status prior to the invasion." In September 1950, however, Truman authorized a military advance north of the thirty-eighth parallel, the border between North and South Korea, in an effort to liberate North Korea from communism before the U.S. congressional elections. General MacArthur promised victory by Christmas. In October Truman conferred with MacArthur at Wake Island and agreed to allow U.N. troops to proceed to the Yalu River, which bordered China. This advance aroused Chinese concerns about U.S. intentions, and China decided to protect North Korea. By November Chinese "volunteers" were fighting in Korea. The U.N. advance soon stalled, and the combined communist armies proceeded to drive the U.N. forces into a retreat south of the thirty-eighth parallel.

The confrontation with Chinese troops raised the possibility of another world war, which might include the use of nuclear weapons. Truman, however, exercised his power as commander in chief to restrain MacArthur and prevent an attack on China. By 1951, battle lines again stabilized around the thirty-eighth parallel, but MacArthur criticized the limits of U.S. involvement. "There is no substitute for victory," he declared. Unfamiliar with the concept of limited war, public opinion appeared ambivalent, showing both strong support for the use of atomic bombs and a desire to withdraw from the war altogether. When Truman announced a stalemated cease-fire, MacArthur, harboring his own presidential ambitions, publicly criticized the president's "no-win" policy.

Harry S Truman Library

General Douglas MacArthur greets President Truman at Wake Island in the Pacific to discuss Korean War strategy in 1950. It was the only time the two met. Truman fired the general the next year.

Exasperated by MacArthur's insubordination, Truman fired the general in 1951. The decision infuriated Republican leaders, who spoke of impeaching the president and welcomed MacArthur home with parades and a unique address to a joint session of Congress. The general took the opportunity to condemn the idea of limited war. Yet the removal of MacArthur facilitated the opening of truce negotiations, which began in 1951. These talks lasted for two years, while the fighting continued under the command of General Matthew Ridgeway. (Truman's refusal to repatriate communist prisoners of war who declined to return to their homelands stalled the negotiations.) The impasse ended only after the inauguration of the next administration in 1953. In the end, the limited war cost 34,000 U.S. lives.

The Korean crisis nevertheless justified the military buildup envisioned in NSC-68. Wartime appropriations expanded the armed forces and nuclear arsenal and increased the number of overseas bases. Funding for aircraft research and development escalated from $1.8 billion to $3.1 billion. Furthermore, the CIA expanded in size and scope of operations and increased its staff from fewer than 5,000 in 1950 to 15,000 by 1955. The war led the president to hold regular meetings with the NSC, setting a precedent for Truman's successors. On the home front, Congress gave Truman authority to establish wage, price, and rent controls. In December 1950 the president declared a "national emergency" and implemented those economic powers, stabilizing the cost of living index for the remainder of the war. When steelworkers went on strike in 1952, Truman seized operations of the steel industry, but the Supreme Court later ruled the act unconstitutional.

The Korean War also prompted the administration to proceed with plans to rearm Germany. When France objected, Truman offered to station U.S. troops in Europe to ensure stability. Congressional conservatives, worried that waging the Cold War would create a "garrison state" at home, protested these unprecedented peacetime military commitments. In the "Great Debate" of 1951, Republicans ended the bipartisan foreign policy that had characterized Cold War politics since 1947. Attacking the limited war in Korea and expressing frustration that Chiang Kai-shek had not been permitted to enter the fray, Republicans focused on Truman's unilateral military decisions and insisted that Congress have a role in foreign policy. Republicans then sponsored a Senate resolution that blocked U.S. troops from being sent to Europe without approval from Congress. Although testimony from NATO's supreme commander, General Dwight D. Eisenhower, blunted some of the Republicans' criticism, Congress passed a compromise version of the resolution that limited troop deployments to four divisions.

The Korean War also stimulated a more aggressive U.S. policy in Asia. Although the administration had been prepared to accept a communist Chinese invasion of Taiwan in early 1950, the Korean conflict provided an excuse to send the Seventh Fleet to protect the besieged island. Truman also deepened U.S. involvement in Indochina. When Ho Chi Minh, leader of the anti-French liberation movement, accepted support from China and the Soviet Union, the United States increased aid to France. After the Korean War began, Truman permitted U.S. military personnel to assist French forces. "If Indochina went," explained a State Department official in 1951, "the fall of Burma and the fall of Thailand would be absolutely inevitable." These would be followed by communist victories in Malaysia and India. Such assumptions led to increasing commitments in Southeast Asia that culminated in the Vietnam War.

Investment in the French empire contrasted with lack of support for colonized peoples. In his 1949 inauguration address, Truman introduced the Point Four program, asserting that the United States had a responsibility to spread "the benefits of our scientific advances and industrial progress" to the "underdeveloped areas" of the world. Yet Point Four foreign aid offered no alternatives to existing economic relations: "underdeveloped areas" were seen only as suppliers of raw materials and consumers of industrial goods. Rather than a humanitarian program, Point Four funded economic studies to facilitate private business investment. Even so, the administration could not persuade Congress to appropriate more than a token $27 million in 1950.

Such priorities reflected the overwhelming emphasis on using procapitalist countries as allies in the Cold War. After Japan accepted a new constitution in 1947 that disavowed war, the United States brought Japan's rebuilt economy into an Asian anticommunist network, which included South Korea, Taiwan, and Indochina, to stabilize relations in the Pacific. A new treaty of 1951 restored Japanese control of their home islands but allowed U.S. occupation of Okinawa and the stationing of troops on Japanese territory. To overcome objections from Japan's former enemies in the Pacific, the United States promised to protect Australia and New Zealand from attack, an agreement formalized in the ANZUS treaty of 1951. With such alliances, Washington established an anticommunist barrier against Chinese and Soviet expansion in the Pacific.

Alliances with former enemies included support of Italy and Spain. In 1951 the Western Allies lifted military restrictions imposed on Italy at the end of World War II. At the same time, Truman entered negotiations with Franco's Spain, which culminated in a 1953 treaty that allowed U.S. military bases in Spain in exchange for economic and military assistance. (Meanwhile, on the home front, the attorney general placed Veterans of the Abraham Lincoln Brigade, whose members had fought against Franco in the Spanish Civil War, on a list of subversive organizations.) In supporting Spain, Italy, Germany, and Japan against China and the Soviet Union, Truman had ironically reversed the Grand Alliance of World War II.

By 1952 the Cold War had undermined Truman's initial foreign and domestic policies. The commitment to Soviet containment had ended earlier State Department hopes for expanded international trade; U.S. exports to eastern Europe and China remained minimal. Even worse, containment had bogged down in the "limited" Korean War, which promised neither victory nor an early end. High military expenditures, in turn, weakened the president's Fair Deal agenda of social legislation at home. Congressional conservatives worried that high budgets and big government bureaucracies would stifle the very freedoms for which the country was fighting overseas. Meanwhile, McCarthy continued a campaign to expose alleged communists in government. Revelations of corruption by administration officials compounded Truman's difficulties. Republican leaders expected to change government policy by capturing the White House in 1952.

THE ELECTION OF 1952

The Republican campaign slogan of 1952 summarized the troubles of the incumbent administration—"K1C2": Korea, Communism, Corruption. The phrase offered a convenient formula for tapping voter dissatisfaction. According to opinion polls, the limited war in Korea remained the primary public concern. As part of the Cold War, moreover, the Korean conflict intensified fear of atomic war. Congress appropriated $3 billion for bomb shelters, but officials admitted that less than 1 percent of the population would be protected from an atomic strike. In New York and San Francisco, public schools routinely issued dog tags to pupils to help identify victims of nuclear war. The Hollywood science fiction film *The Thing* (1951) ended by advising audiences to "Watch the skies!"

Republicans expected to benefit from this climate of fear. The party's front-runner, Senator Taft of Ohio, appealed to conservatives by demanding a retreat from expensive international commitments and a reduction in the size and scope of government programs. "The greatest enemy of liberty," he declared, "is the concentration of power in Washington." Taft's conservatism attracted midwestern and western Republicans, but his strident hostility to big government alarmed more liberal eastern Republicans, particularly big-business leaders. These "corporate liberals" preferred an internationalist foreign policy to stabilize world trade and recognized that New Deal programs such as Social Security bolstered purchasing power and helped to prevent social unrest at home.

Fearing that Taft's conservatism would doom the party at the polls, eastern Republicans led by Massachusetts Senator Henry Cabot Lodge Jr. and former Governor Thomas Dewey of New York turned to a candidate who claimed to have no interest in presidential politics: General Dwight David "Ike" Eisenhower. As supreme commander of NATO forces in Europe, Eisenhower's political views appeared sufficiently ambiguous for Truman to hint at giving him the Democratic nomination. Eisenhower, however, was too conservative to run as a Democrat. Yet, unlike Taft, the general believed in the importance of the U.S. military presence in Europe. After a series of successful primary showings, including a surprise victory in New Hampshire, Eisenhower came home from Europe in June 1952 to seek the Republican presidential nomination. Benefiting from his immense popularity and some astute maneuvering at the convention by Lodge, the general captured a first-ballot nomination. As a concession to conservatives, Eisenhower chose Richard Nixon as his running mate.

While Eisenhower promised "to lead a great crusade . . . for freedom," K1C2 dictated the Republican platform. "There are no Communists in the Republican Party," it boasted, whereas Democrats "shielded Traitors . . . in high places." Denouncing Truman's containment policy as "negative, futile, and immoral," Republicans vowed to bring "genuine independence" to the "captive peoples" of eastern Europe, a promise that appealed to eastern European ethnics, who usually voted for Democrats. The platform showed the Republicans' conservative position on civil rights by insisting that state governments had primary responsibility in that area.

The Democratic spotlight flashed briefly on Tennessee's Senator Estes Kefauver, who won a series of primary contests. But Democratic leaders feared that Kefauver's televised investigations of organized crime would hurt the party in the cities and preferred Governor Adlai Stevenson of Illinois. A cultivated liberal, Stevenson presented himself as a voice of reason. He criticized McCarthyism ("we want no shackles on the mind . . . no iron conformity," he said) and promised to "talk sense to the American people." To balance the ticket in the South, Stevenson chose Alabama Senator John Sparkman as his running mate.

Despite the Democratic candidate's efforts to distance himself from the Truman administration, Stevenson stood for a continuity of principles and policies. He defended the Korean War as "a long step toward building a security system in Asia" and echoed the White House attack on domestic communism. But unlike Truman, Stevenson took a quiet position on civil rights by emphasizing the importance of state sovereignty. Only after intense criticism from liberals did he endorse a permanent Fair Employment Practices Commission (FEPC). This belated gesture cost Stevenson support among African Americans while offending southern whites. Stevenson further angered Gulf Coast Democrats by opposing state control of offshore oil wells. The candidate's hesitancy to attack the Taft-Hartley labor law also alienated the traditional Democratic labor constituency.

Eisenhower, meanwhile, stood as a candidate above parties, a middle-of-the-road moderate with leadership experience that reflected caution, restraint, and common sense. After making peace with Taft, the general scrupulously avoided antagonizing Old Guard Republicans. Although personally insulted by McCarthy's rhetorical attack on former Secretary of State George Marshall, Eisenhower's wartime superior officer, the nominee quietly deleted a defense of Marshall when speaking in McCarthy's home state of Wisconsin. The candidate also played up allegations of Democratic corruption. "Let's clean up the mess in Washington!" said Ike, in the first political advertising to appear on television in 1952. Coached by Hollywood actor Robert Montgomery and a leading advertising agency, Eisenhower's campaign proved the political value of the new media. Usually Eisenhower left the partisan oratory to Nixon, who denounced "Adlai the appeaser . . . who got a Ph.D. from Dean Acheson's College of Cowardly Communist Containment."

Nixon's verbal ammunition exploded when newspapers reported that the vice presidential candidate had a secret "millionaire's" fund to defray his political expenses. When Democrats used the issue to reply to Republican accusations about the "mess in Washington," Eisenhower's advisers urged him to drop Nixon from the ticket. Nixon responded by buying television time to defend his personal honesty. Emphasizing that his family had not profited from politics, Nixon said his wife still wore a "plain Republican cloth coat" and that despite criticism he would not return a gift his daughter had received, a cocker spaniel named Checkers.

The sentimental performance proved effective. As public support for Nixon increased, Eisenhower kept him on the ticket. For the first time, political pundits saw the immense influence of television. This recognition highlighted the importance of a candidate's image and suggested that a politician could effectively appeal to the voters over the heads of party leaders. As for Nixon, the

Billy Graham (1918–   )

The most famous religious figures of the 1950s were two southerners in the Baptist tradition, Billy Graham and Martin Luther King Jr., but whereas King challenged U.S. society with a stinging moral critique on behalf of the dispossessed, Graham won access to the rich and powerful with a message palatable with social conventions.

Handsome, charismatic, and committed, Graham threw himself into evangelism early in life, honing his skills while traveling the country after World War II for a fledgling fundamentalist group, Youth for Christ. His big break came during the fourth week of a 1949 Los Angeles revival, when the powerful newspaper publisher William Randolph Hearst sent a blunt telegram to the editors of his newspapers: "Puff Graham." Attracted to the anticommunist themes of Graham's sermons, Hearst was the first of many powerful figures eager to use the preacher's sincerity and popularity to advance their own agendas. Within a year, Graham had been the subject of feature articles in the major magazines; within a decade, he was the most popular religious figure in the country.

Like evangelists before him, Graham blended familiar hymns and an altar call with a dynamic and polished pulpit style. Cutting through the ap-

speech gave him confidence in the power of television. In later years he returned to the small screen to win vindication of other aspects of his career, although seldom with the success of his 1952 effort.

Since he supported the basic premises of Truman's Cold War, Eisenhower avoided the militant rhetoric of the Republican platform on matters of foreign policy. He approved of Truman's intervention in Korea but opposed General MacArthur's call for all-out war. When Stevenson argued that the only "answer" to Korea was to "keep it up as long as we have to," Eisenhower hinted at alternative policies. His military experience enabled him to speak with authority. In a late campaign speech, Eisenhower suggested that ending the war required his personal attention. "I shall go to Korea," he declared. Eisenhower's promise ignited the hopes of a war-weary nation.

parent complexities of the "age of anxiety," he called on listeners to heal their lives through a personal commitment to Jesus. To a nation that had survived depression and war only to find itself in the midst of the nuclear age, the simplicity and directness of Graham's message had enormous appeal. Although Graham traveled constantly, conducting six major crusades a year, he and his associates soon realized that print, films, radio, and television offered enormous opportunities to broaden their ministry even further. His direct-mail techniques were so sophisticated that representatives of both political parties visited his headquarters to study them. This pioneering work in marketing and media techniques paved the way for the televangelists of later years.

Although Graham has declared himself to be "completely neutral in politics," his fundamentalist, eschatological theology made him a particular favorite of conservative Republicans. Called by some a "Gabriel in gabardine," Graham spent much of his career preaching a gospel that upheld traditional values while calling for domestic consensus against overseas communist expansion. Even though he insisted that his crusade audiences be integrated even before the Supreme Court's *Brown* decision, Graham typically emphasized otherworldly solutions to social problems. "My message is so intensely personal," he explained, "that people miss the overwhelming social content."

Eisenhower achieved a stunning victory. He captured nearly 34 million votes (55 percent) to Stevenson's 27 million (44 percent) and swept the electoral college 442–89. The Republican ticket carried four southern states, breaking the Democrats' "solid South" for the first time since Al Smith's defeat in 1928. Eisenhower attracted traditional Democrats in the big cities— African Americans, Catholics, and white ethnics. His coattails pulled a Republican majority into both houses of Congress for the first time since the Great Depression.

Republicans exulted in the destruction of the New Deal coalition. The reelection of conservatives like McCarthy and the defeat of several of McCarthy's critics seemed to vindicate the anticommunist crusade. However, statistics also showed that Eisenhower ran far ahead of other Republicans, including

EXHIBIT **2-2   THE ELECTION OF 1952**

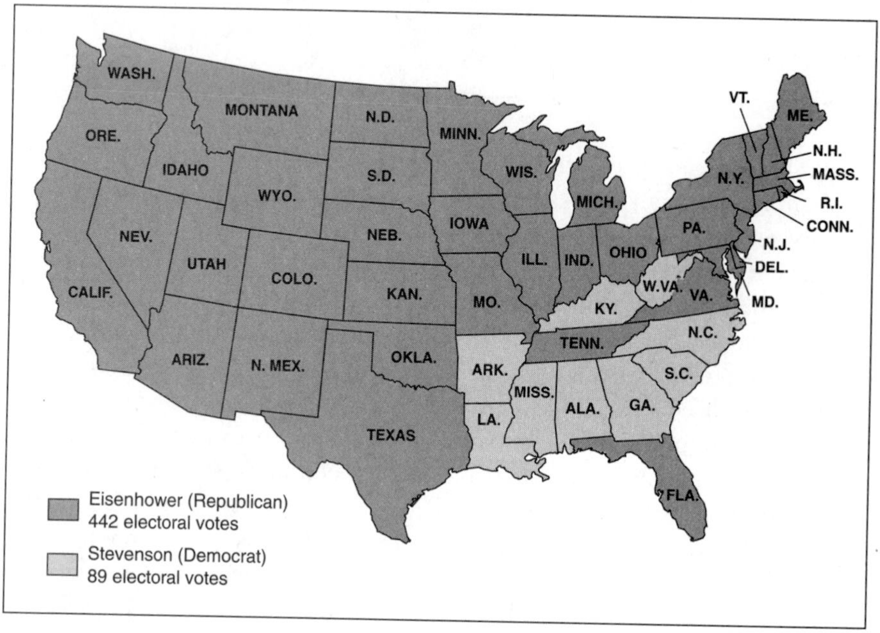

Eisenhower (Republican)
442 electoral votes

Stevenson (Democrat)
89 electoral votes

McCarthy. The election of 1952 was an Eisenhower victory, not a Republican landslide, and the party controlled the House by only eight seats, the Senate by one. During the 1950s voters seemed less interested in political ideology and appeared more sensitive to short-term issues or party affiliation. Yet Eisenhower managed to attract independent voters and Democrats, including a well-funded "Democrats for Eisenhower" organization headed by Hollywood actor Ronald Reagan. The breadth of Eisenhower's support reflected not only his personal popularity but also a political consensus based on internationalism abroad and minimum social welfare at home.

THE GENERAL TAKES COMMAND

Eisenhower's success among Democrats reinforced his political philosophy of consensus. As a career military officer, the former general represented the new managerial middle class of the twentieth century. In a world dominated by large corporate bureaucracies he emphasized the importance of voluntary cooperation between government and business. Nearly all the members of his cabinet—including Secretary of State John Foster Dulles, Secretary of Defense Charles E. Wilson, Secretary of the Treasury George M. Humphrey, and Attorney General Herbert Brownell Jr.—came from the highest ranks of corporate management and law. (The exception was Secretary of Labor Martin Durkin, a plumber, who soon resigned and was replaced by a department store personnel manager.) Eisenhower believed these leaders could apply conservative principles to the management of government without turning back the clock or canceling promises of social justice.

To streamline administration, Eisenhower relied more heavily than Truman on the National Security Council (NSC), but the president frequently overrode the advice of the Joint Chiefs of Staff. Eisenhower distrusted special interests, partisan conflicts, and mass movements. Contrary to the wishes of Old Guard Republicans, he preserved the New Deal and even established a cabinet-level Department of Health, Education, and Welfare in 1953. However, the president initiated no social welfare legislation because he believed that expansion of government services would stultify a free, capitalist society. "We cannot risk living all our lifetime under emergency measures," he said in ending economic controls established by Truman during the Korean War.

Eisenhower envisioned a world order based on free trade and protected by restrained military power. On many occasions, he resisted pressure to increase the Pentagon budget or to rush rashly into war. "I just don't believe you can buy 100 percent security in every little corner of the world," the president said in 1954. Yet Eisenhower permitted the nuclear arsenal to expand from hundreds to thousands of weapons and ordered the deployment of nuclear weapons overseas. He also relied increasingly on covert operations by the CIA, headed by Allen Dulles, brother of the secretary of state. Always the cold warrior, Eisenhower assumed that the United States should maintain military superiority over communist nations. "Forces of good and evil are massed and armed and opposed as rarely before in history," he explained in his inaugural address. "Freedom is pitted against slavery; lightness against the dark. . . . In the final choice, a soldier's pack is not so heavy a burden as a prisoner's chains."

These metaphors of morality and struggle reflected the new administration's approach to foreign policy. Determined to take the initiative in the Cold War, Eisenhower and Secretary of State Dulles replaced the Democratic strategy of containment with a new doctrine of "massive retaliation." Dulles argued that neither public opinion nor the nation's economy could sustain a series of limited conventional wars like the Korean War. Instead, he echoed conservative policy by calling for reliance upon air and naval superiority, a position Eisenhower supported.

The nations of the "free world," the president proclaimed, would be prepared "to retaliate instantly" against the Soviet Union "by means and at places of our own choosing." Nuclear weapons aimed at the Kremlin—not at some border area—would deter further communist expansion. In military terms, massive retaliation reaffirmed the air-atomic strategy approved by Truman and updated his policy of containment with the doctrine of nuclear deterrence. Eisenhower never intended to go to war to overturn communist control of "captive nations" in eastern Europe. However, his administration hoped to use the nuclear arsenal as a symbolic weapon—and an ever-present threat—in the political crusade for anticommunist liberation.

A policy of massive retaliation had distinct domestic advantages. Conservative Republicans led by Taft had long opposed soaring military budgets. Eisenhower shared these sentiments, although he believed that cost-cutting should not compromise the nation's strength. Air power and nuclear weapons provided a cheaper solution. Eisenhower's "new look" in military policy enabled the Pentagon to reduce the size of conventional forces. This policy cut $7 billion from Truman's projected budget. Subsequent opinion polls found wide support for these reductions.

Eisenhower's enormous prestige and electoral popularity enabled him to accomplish in Korea what Truman had been reluctant to suggest. After fulfilling his campaign promise to visit Korea, the new president recognized that a continuation of the ground war would only bleed the army and the federal budget. Secretary Dulles joined conservative senators such as Styles Bridges and William Knowland in advocating complete victory. Yet Eisenhower, primarily concerned with reaching a political settlement, rejected the use of atomic weapons. The president instead used a show of force to persuade the enemy to negotiate. In his inaugural address Eisenhower announced the removal of the Seventh Fleet from the area separating Taiwan from the Chinese mainland and hinted that he might "unleash" Chiang Kai-shek against the communist enemy. The White House also used diplomatic channels to notify China that the United States might use nuclear weapons if negotiations failed. The death of Josef Stalin in March 1953 added to China's uncertainties about Soviet support.

Both China and Eisenhower understood and accepted the limits of military struggle in Korea. The main stumbling block now involved the return of prisoners of war. Hoping to discourage communist China's future reliance on its troops, the United States refused to require the repatriation of communist prisoners who did not wish to go home. After Washington made additional threats to use atomic weapons, China accepted the idea of voluntary repatriation of prisoners of war. At the last minute, South Korea's dictator, Syngman Rhee, nearly thwarted the truce by suddenly releasing 27,000 prisoners, who promptly disappeared into the countryside. The move violated the armistice agreement, but Eisenhower ignored Rhee's action, and the United States signed a truce in July 1953. "We have won an armistice on a single battlefield—not peace in the world," Eisenhower reminded the nation. "We may not now relax our guard nor cease our quest."

The end of the Korean War brought not a sense of celebration but plain relief. Nearly 34,000 U.S. soldiers had died to defend an area that in 1950 Secretary of State Dean Acheson had acknowledged lay beyond the nation's strategic defense perimeter. Sensitive to criticism from conservatives about selling out Korea to the communists, the White House reiterated the possibility of massive retaliation against any further aggression. The retention of U.S. military bases in South Korea added credibility to those threats. Eisenhower also approved a multibillion-dollar program of economic and military assistance to bolster South Korea. The Korean armistice, then, actually formalized Truman's policy of communist containment in Asia.

Frustrated by the Korean compromise, nationalist Republicans criticized Eisenhower's version of containment. In 1951 Republican Senator John Bricker of Ohio had introduced a constitutional amendment requiring congressional approval of all international agreements. Through this partisan move, Bricker had sought to limit Truman's executive independence, but the measure never came to the Senate floor. The 1952 Republican Party platform kept the issue alive by promising to "repudiate all commitments contained in secret understandings." This position reflected strong congressional opposition to presidential control of foreign policy. In 1954 Bricker reintroduced his constitutional amendment. Eisenhower strongly opposed the proposal. Yet because the president believed in a rigid separation of powers, he exercised minimal leadership in the Senate debates. Democrats led by Lyndon Johnson saved the president from his own party's militants. Although the Bricker amendment won a 60–31 majority, it fell one vote short of the necessary two-thirds required for the passage of constitutional amendments. The White House, not Congress, would continue to control foreign policy.

Eisenhower's European policies revealed basic continuities with those of Truman. Although the new administration talked about liberating eastern Europe, the principles of massive retaliation appeared too inflexible to respond effectively to minor crises. When East German workers staged anticommunist protests in June 1953, Dulles could offer only moral encouragement and $15 million in food.

Eisenhower also made gestures to reduce Cold War tensions, but they were more symbolic than real. In 1953 the president addressed the U.N. General Assembly, presenting a dramatic "atoms for peace" proposal that urged international control of atomic weapons. In offering to join the Soviet Union in pooling nuclear resources for peaceful purposes, the president hoped to overcome the mutual hostility that set the two powers on a deadly course. Yet Eisenhower knew, as did the Soviets, that his proposal would preserve U.S. nuclear superiority. When the Soviet Union reacted unfavorably, the president settled for the propaganda advantages and made no counteroffer. Eisenhower had no intention of reducing the nation's military preparedness.

Like Truman, Eisenhower worked instead to strengthen U.S. allies in western Europe. When the Soviet Union proposed a treaty that would make Germany a neutral country, Eisenhower saw the plan as a ruse to divide the Western Alliance and rejected the Soviet overture. More concerned with bringing Germany into the West's political camp, the administration urged the formation of a European Defense Community. When France objected to rearming Germany, however, the president chose an alternative policy that enabled Germany to rearm under NATO. "These agreements are founded upon the profound yearning for peace which is shared by all the Atlantic peoples," Eisenhower declared. "The agreements endanger no nation." Yet the entry of West Germany into NATO assured a long-term division of central Europe. In 1955 the Soviet Union created the Warsaw Pact, a military alliance that attempted to balance the power of NATO.

Secret Foreign Policy

While exercising restraint in Korea and Europe, Eisenhower pursued an aggressive but secret foreign policy beyond the scrutiny of Congress and the public. Under the Central Intelligence Agency Act of 1949, the CIA had a multibillion-dollar, top-secret budget that was exempt from congressional accountability and control. Initially intended to obtain and assess intelligence, the CIA under Eisenhower became an interventionist force as well. In one secret mission, the agency built an underground tunnel beneath East Berlin and used wiretaps and recording devices to obtain an intelligence windfall. Besides establishing spy networks around the world, the CIA performed secret, illegal operations that promoted the State Department's formal policy. For example, the CIA regularly supported disruptive raids launched from Taiwan onto the Chinese mainland. When such activities were discovered, the United States denied all allegations and used the episodes to denounce its enemies. In 1955 Democratic Senator Mike Mansfield proposed the creation of a congressional intelligence oversight committee, but the White House effectively blocked such interference with foreign policy management by the executive branch.

The intervention of the CIA proved especially effective on the new battlefronts of the Cold War in the developing ("third") world. In 1953 the United States instigated a coup d'etat in Iran, then denied complicity in the affair. Two years earlier, the premier of Iran, Dr. Mohammed Mossadegh, had attempted to end British exploitation by nationalizing Iran's oil wells. Western-owned companies retaliated by boycotting Iranian oil. Mossadegh appealed to Eisenhower for assistance, but the president rebuffed him, stating, "It would not be fair to American taxpayers." Mossadegh then turned to the Soviet Union.

Eisenhower responded by ordering the CIA to intervene in Iran's internal affairs. In August 1953 U.S. agents provided crucial military support that enabled the hereditary shah to topple the Mossadegh regime and return to power. In the ensuing negotiations, Iran agreed to replace the nationalized oil wells with an international consortium in which U.S.–owned companies held a 40 percent interest. The Western oil companies then agreed to limit Iranian oil production to maximize their profits at the expense of Iran. By overthrowing

Mossadegh, the United States not only broke the British oil monopoly but also placed Iran safely in the noncommunist camp. Continued economic and military aid to the shah strengthened this realignment. Yet the CIA never acknowledged its role in the coup; even today, the relevant documents remain classified.

The CIA also implemented Eisenhower's foreign policy in Guatemala in 1954. As in Iran, a popular leader, Colonel Jacobo Arbenz, attempted to improve economic conditions by enacting land reform and nationalizing the holdings of the U.S. United Fruit Company. Arbenz offered compensation for the expropriated property, but United Fruit, backed by the State Department, rejected the sum. The administration then began planning the overthrow of Arbenz with the help of a CIA invasion army trained in Nicaragua and Honduras.

To justify this new version of dollar diplomacy, the United States described Arbenz as a front man for "international communism," someone who imperiled the entire hemisphere. In 1954 Washington sponsored a resolution at the Tenth Inter-American Conference, declaring that communist control of "any American State" endangered "the peace of America." Guatemala alone voted against resolution. Two months later, Arbenz received a shipment of arms from Czechoslovakia, which confirmed administration fears. The next month a CIA-backed rebel army and mercenary force invaded and bombed Guatemala and defeated Arbenz. The invasion won bipartisan approval at home. "There is no question here of United States interference in the domestic affairs of any American State," insisted Senator Lyndon Johnson.

Claiming to have saved Guatemala from an international conspiracy, the administration supported the regime of Colonel Carlos Armas with $90 million in economic and military aid. Armas returned the nationalized land to United Fruit, provided tax benefits for the corporation, crushed the labor union movement, and disenfranchised illiterate people, who constituted 70 percent of the population. Restoring conditions favorable to U.S. investment, the administration then supported military government in Central America.

BUILDING A CORPORATE COMMONWEALTH

Like Truman, Eisenhower believed in preserving a balanced budget; and like his predecessor he accepted the necessity of high military expenditures to wage the Cold War. But where Truman preferred more spending for social welfare programs, such as health insurance, Eisenhower had little interest in liberal policies. Yet Eisenhower did not oppose modest domestic programs. Rather, he believed that government should be used to moderate economic conflict and sustain growth without threatening private enterprise or becoming too burdensome, and he attempted to steer a middle course between unregulated capitalism and an activist government.

Hank Walker/*Life* magazine © Time Warner, Inc.

Charles E. Wilson, shown with models of some of the Pentagon's best toys, went from being head of General Motors to a job that seemed much the same—head of the Defense Department.

Eisenhower saw the government's role as a mediator among society's interests and hoped that cooperation and consensus, not coercion, would direct the nation toward social harmony. Instead of prosecuting violations of antitrust laws, for example, the administration preferred negotiated settlements between government and business. The president also resolved to reduce the scope of federal government activities and supported Secretary of the Treasury George Humphrey's efforts to balance the federal budget by reducing expenses. However, Eisenhower would not agree to drop basic New Deal programs such as Social Security and the minimum wage. To balance the budget, therefore, the White House reluctantly delayed a tax cut. Despite Humphrey's efforts to promote frugality and the sharp criticism of conservative Republicans, government expenditures remained a basic prop of the economy.

Although Eisenhower joined "corporate liberals" in retaining New Deal regulations and social welfare nets, he sided with conservatives in defending the petroleum industry against federal regulation. The president believed that a prosperous oil industry reinforced national defense. For more than a decade, the federal government had contested the claim of several coastal states, particularly Texas, Louisiana, and California, to jurisdiction over offshore oil. Because the major petroleum companies expected beneficial legislation from state governments, they supported the state claims. Conservative Republicans opposed federal control of private business and also supported the states' claims. So did southern Democrats, who saw state control of oil as not only in their economic interests but also as a defense of states' rights. In 1946 and again in 1952 Congress passed legislation giving control of offshore oil to the states. Truman vetoed both measures and before leaving office reserved offshore oil for the navy. Eisenhower reversed his predecessor's position. In 1953 Republicans cooperated with southern Democrats to pass a measure giving control of offshore oil to the states.

The White House also opposed public control of electric power projects. In 1954 Eisenhower recommended a revision of the Atomic Energy Act to allow private manufacture and operation of atomic reactors. This legislation led to the first privately run nuclear power plants. The administration's decision to bypass the Tennessee Valley Authority (TVA) in providing electricity for the Atomic Energy Commission (AEC) facilities proved more controversial. By ignoring the TVA, long a symbol of New Deal liberalism, the policy attacked federal support of public power. Hints of political corruption weakened the president's position, and a compromise ended the controversy. The administration did succeed in blocking public power projects in other parts of the country, such as Hell's Canyon on the Snake River.

Despite his military background—or because of it—Eisenhower strove to strengthen civilian control over military decisions. Following precedents established by Truman, the administration relied on a presidential Science Advisory Committee to obtain expert opinion about technological issues and questions of research and development. Such counsel gave Eisenhower independent information to respond to proposals made by the armed services. Thus while military leaders urged the expansion of the nation's offensive weapons for massive retaliation, science advisors advocated greater continental defense against Soviet attack. Such discussions culminated in the 1954 agreement between the United States and Canada to construct a distant early warning (DEW) line of radar installations across North America. The president's science advisors would later play an important role in negotiating nuclear test restrictions with the Soviet Union.

THE ANTICOMMUNIST CRUSADE

Although Eisenhower, the hero of World War II, appeared as the consummate cold warrior, his personal popularity could not shield him from criticism of militant anticommunists who alleged that communists continued to influence the government. Indeed, the president's efforts to stand above controversy strengthened the most fervent congressional anticommunists, particularly Joseph McCarthy. Yet the administration had hardly ignored the problem. Soon after taking office in 1953, the president agreed to appoint Scott McLeod, a McCarthy supporter, to head the State Department's personnel program, accelerating the dismissal of alleged subversives. Eisenhower also revised Truman's loyalty program, issuing Executive Order 10450, which established new standards for dismissal of government employees. Although Truman had required evidence of disloyalty or subversion, Eisenhower authorized dismissal on the grounds that an individual's employment "may not be clearly consistent with the interests of national security." Under the new guidelines, Eisenhower removed 2,200 "security risks" in his first year in office. Few were actually charged with disloyalty.

The administration's definition of security risks revealed the underlying cultural assumptions within the Cold War consensus. Besides obvious cases of negligence, criminality, and insanity, Eisenhower's criteria for dismissal included "notoriously disgraceful conduct, habitual use of intoxicants to excess, drug addiction, or sexual perversion." Persons practicing such acts were considered risks because they were vulnerable to blackmail, and government loyalty boards frequently dismissed homosexuals from their jobs (making such people *more* vulnerable to blackmail). Ironically, to protect themselves from government reprisals, the homosexual activists who organized the Mattachine Society in Los Angeles deliberately adopted the structure of the Communist Party to avoid entrapment.

The insistence on ideological conformity also demanded the suppression of political dissent. Shortly after moving into the State Department, Dulles fired several career diplomats, including prestigious China experts such as John Carter Vincent and John Paton Davies, who had predicted Mao's victory in China in 1949. Dulles also encouraged the departure of George Kennan, viewed as the architect of containment. To replace Kennan as ambassador to the Soviet Union, the administration supported Charles E. Bohlen. However, rigid anticommunists questioned the nomination, pointing out that Bohlen had acted as a translator for President Franklin D. Roosevelt at international conferences with the Russians. Rumors of the nominee's homosexuality also surfaced. Unwilling to drop one of his first appointees, Eisenhower accepted a compromise, permitting two senators to examine Bohlen's confidential FBI file. Their favorable report led to senatorial confirmation. Nonetheless, Taft warned the president: "No more Bohlens."

J. Robert Oppenheimer, the celebrated physicist who had directed the development of the atomic bomb, also fell victim to the loyalty controversy. Fearing that Oppenheimer's moral doubts about the hydrogen bomb might influence other scientists, Eisenhower supported the AEC's decision to lift the scientist's security clearance. In yet another controversial case, the president refused to provide clemency to the convicted atomic spies Julius and Ethel Rosenberg, exaggerating their activities by claiming that the couple "may have condemned to death tens of million of innocent people all over the world." Despite ambiguous evidence about Ethel Rosenberg's espionage activities, the unrepentant couple was electrocuted in 1953.

"In America," protested the playwright Arthur Miller in *The Crucible*, a 1953 version of the Salem witch trials, "any man who is not reactionary in his views is open to the charge of alliance with the Red hell." The next year, Congress underscored the religious stakes by adding to the Pledge of Allegiance the words "under God." Meanwhile, church membership in all denominations in the United States increased—from 64 million in 1940 to 115 million in 1960, or from 50 percent to 63 percent of the population. The Cold War remained a struggle between the godly and the damned.

Through the first years of the Eisenhower presidency, the nation's foremost witch hunter remained Senator McCarthy, a crude, intemperate inquisitor who disregarded courtesy and due process in his quest for communist sympathizers. Even after Eisenhower's inauguration, McCarthy continued to attack communist influence in government. As chairman of a Senate subcommittee on government operations, McCarthy held public hearings in 1953 about the Voice of America, the government's overseas radio stations, and claimed that the State Department's propaganda organ served as a front for communists.

With the tacit consent of Secretary Dulles, McCarthy meddled in other State Department affairs. Two members of McCarthy's staff, Roy Cohn and G. David Schine, embarked on a chaotic investigation of the United States Information Agency (USIA) in Europe. Their scrutiny of USIA libraries unearthed many "subversive" works by authors such as novelist Theodore Dreiser and historian Arthur M. Schlesinger Jr. Fearing McCarthy's wrath, the agency removed several thousand volumes from library shelves.

"I will not get into the gutter with that guy," said Eisenhower, avoiding direct confrontation with the vitriolic senator. Wishing to prevent a split in Republican ranks, the president hoped that if he ignored McCarthy the senator would recede from the limelight. Instead, McCarthy felt emboldened to attack the administration. In September 1953 he launched an investigation of army security procedures at Fort Monmouth, New Jersey. Concerned about the routine promotion of a Communist dentist, McCarthy clashed publicly

J. Robert Oppenheimer (1904–1967)

The security status of one of the nation's leading atomic physicists provoked a dramatic closed-door clash in 1954 between traditional freedom of scientific inquiry and Cold War demands for absolute conformity. The ensuing top-secret hearings into the matter of J. Robert Oppenheimer revealed  both changing standards of political propriety and a growing concern about "national security" in an age of fundamental anxiety.

Oppenheimer was a secular Jew who had studied quantum mechanics at Harvard, Cambridge, and the University of Gottenburg. He helped to make the University of California at Berkeley the global center of theoretical physics in the 1930s. Yet the Depression-era poverty of his students and anti-Semitism in Nazi Germany encouraged the affluent bachelor to support progressive social causes promoted by the Communist Party.

Appointed head of the wartime Los Alamos Laboratory charged with developing the atom bomb, Oppenheimer became a postwar advocate of international control of nuclear energy. As chief advisor to the Atomic Energy Commission, he led efforts to oppose research on the hydrogen fusion bomb, which he regarded as a "weapon of genocide." He called for the use of tactical nuclear weapons for continental defense instead of the massive strategic bombing preferred by the air force. He also insisted that it was technically premature to build nuclear-powered aircraft and opposed construction of atomic submarines.

with military leaders, chastising one officer for defending "Communist conspirators." The army responded by releasing documents showing that McCarthy sought special privileges for Cohn's coworker, Private David Schine. McCarthy then ordered a full investigation of the army, including Eisenhower's Secretary of the Army Robert Stevens.

The president now entered the conflict, refusing to cooperate with the Senate investigation. "In opposing Communism," he told a March 1954 press conference, "we are defeating ourselves if we use methods that do not conform to the American sense of justice." Although Attorney General Brownell

The AEC gave Oppenheimer security clearance in 1947, but six years later a former congressional staffer sent the FBI a detailed list of accusations against the physicist. A subsequent report prompted President Eisenhower to demand that a "blank wall" be erected between Oppenheimer and sensitive information. Eisenhower feared that the highly respected scientist might persuade other researchers to abandon the superbomb project. The president also wished to head off potentially embarrassing investigations by McCarthy. Consequently, the White House asked the AEC to initiate hearings on Oppenheimer's security clearance.

Although Oppenheimer apologized to the inquiry for naïve associations with "fellow travelers" and for occasional lapses of candor, colleague Edward Teller testified that the physicist lacked the "wisdom and judgment" for a security clearance. This finding was upheld by the AEC, which ruled that the father of the atomic bomb had "placed himself outside the rules that govern others" and "exhibited a willful disregard of the normal and proper obligations of society."

By focusing on Oppenheimer's character, the AEC rejected the view that scientists should be judged differently than military and government personnel. By 1954, many Americans distrusted intellectual cosmopolitans such as Oppenheimer and believed that loyalty to the struggle against communism was the most important qualification for public service. Deprived of a security clearance, Oppenheimer returned to teaching at Princeton University and never again worked for the government.

could find no legal precedents for denying subpoenaed documents, Eisenhower invoked the right of executive privilege to block McCarthy's access to his staff. Eisenhower was concerned that McCarthy's indiscriminate investigations would uncover the continuing Oppenheimer controversy and disturb scientific work on the hydrogen bomb. "We've got to handle this so that all our scientists are not made out to be Reds," Eisenhower remarked. "That goddamn McCarthy is just likely to try such a thing." To Eisenhower's alarm, McCarthy was threatening to penetrate the secrets of the national security state.

McCarthy also showed disdain for the Democratic leadership. "Those who wear the label—Democrat," he said, "wear it with the stain of an historic betrayal." Yet precisely because of such charges, Democrats hesitated to attack McCarthy directly. In 1954 a Senate appropriations committee voted nearly unanimously to continue funding McCarthy's subcommittee. Indeed, some liberal Democrats attempted to deflect McCarthy's rhetoric by demonstrating their own anticommunist credentials. Minnesota liberal Hubert Humphrey introduced the Communist Control Act in 1954 to make membership in the Communist Party illegal. Democrat Paul Douglas of Illinois supported the measure, explaining that "we liberals must destroy the Communists if this dirty game is to stop."

As McCarthy pursued the investigation of army security procedures and the army made accusations against him, Senate leaders looked for an opportunity to weaken McCarthy's power. To show the public the extent of McCarthy's malice, Minority Leader Lyndon Johnson demanded that the public hearings be televised. Beginning in March 1954 the three major television networks broadcast the much-heralded Army-McCarthy hearings. The spectacle once again demonstrated the new medium's power to influence public opinion. For thirty-six days viewers witnessed McCarthy's erratic, stormy behavior.

As the senator attacked colleagues, threatened witnesses, and ignored legal procedures, his favorable public opinion ratings declined from 50 percent to 34 percent. The hearings climaxed when McCarthy chastised a young army lawyer for once belonging to the National Lawyers Guild, which was, in McCarthy's words, "the legal bulwark of the Communist Party." Chief Army Counsel Joseph Welch used the episode to strike back at McCarthy. "Little did I dream you could be so reckless and so cruel," Welch berated McCarthy before the cameras. "Have you no sense of decency, sir, at long last? Have you left no sense of decency?"

When McCarthy amended his denunciation of "twenty years of treason" to "twenty-*one* years," thus implicating the Eisenhower presidency in a cover-up of communism, his reach exceeded his grasp. "Were the junior Senator from Wisconsin in the pay of Communists," Republican Senator Ralph Flanders of Vermont declared, "he could not have done a better job for them." In July 1954 Flanders introduced a resolution that called for McCarthy's censure by the Senate.

In a carefully orchestrated proceeding, a panel of conservative senators, chaired by Republican Arthur Watkins of Utah, recommended censure for conduct that "tended to bring the Senate into dishonor and disrepute." McCarthy continued to rage against his adversaries, accusing the Senate of serving the communists, but half the Republicans joined the unanimous Democrats to censure McCarthy by a vote of 67–22. Vice President Nixon, presiding in the Senate, deleted the word *censure* from the final document. It was a formality that made no difference. McCarthy had lost his power. He remained in the Senate, politically ineffective, until his death, attributed to alcoholism, in 1957.

McCarthy's fall created an illusion that communist witch hunts had ended, but the attack on communism extended beyond Congress and assumed the power of a national obsession. Libraries removed controversial books; school boards and universities fired radical teachers; industries established blacklists to prevent employment of suspected communists. Many high school students had to sign loyalty oaths to receive their diplomas. And the Hollywood blacklist continued. In 1954 the winner of eight Oscars, including Best Picture, was Elia Kazan's *On the Waterfront,* a movie that celebrated "naming names" to government investigators.

Encouraged by the anticommunist consensus, FBI Director J. Edgar Hoover stepped up his attacks on the Communist Party. Because the Communist Control Act stated that the Communist Party was "not entitled to any of the rights, privileges, and immunities . . . [of] legal bodies," Hoover moved to disrupt the organization with a Counterintelligence Program (COINTELPRO) introduced in 1956. Using informants, infiltrators, wiretaps, and a variety of "dirty tricks" (forged letters, anonymous telephone calls, police harassment), the FBI doggedly attacked the dwindling communist movement. This harassment, together with revelations of Stalin's totalitarianism and Soviet aggression in eastern Europe, drastically reduced the party's membership. From a peak membership of 75,000 during World War II, the party dwindled to fewer than 3,500 members by the end of 1957.

A SHAKY CONSENSUS

The political demise of Senator McCarthy contributed to a mood of consensus. Republican leaders expected the anticommunist crusade to remain an effective campaign weapon in the 1954 congressional elections. True to his dispassionate style of leadership, Eisenhower avoided the emotionally charged issue. Nixon repeated his performance of 1952 and attacked the Democrats for tolerating communists in government. Yet neither Eisenhower's prestige nor Nixon's rhetoric could overcome the political effects of the economic recession that followed the Korean War. Although Eisenhower could attract independent voters, other Republicans were linked with traditional party labels. In the end, Democrats gained small majorities in both houses of Congress.

Instead of creating partisan conflict between the branches of government, the Democratic congressional victories actually encouraged cooperation. Senate Majority Leader Johnson and House Speaker Sam Rayburn, both of Texas, accepted a political consensus and a balance of power between the parties. Because congressional committee assignments depended on seniority, southerners, who came from a one-party region, enjoyed advantages. Patterns of congressional representation also strengthened conservative groups. Urban areas, which usually supported liberals, were underrepresented in Congress because state

Salt of the Earth (1953)

When the House Committee on Un-American Activities (HUAC) began to investigate the communist presence in the motion picture industry, studio owners agreed to fire and blacklist politically undesirable employees. As the Hollywood Ten went to federal prison for refusing to testify about their political associations and hundreds more lost their jobs, producers scrutinized films for signs of embarrassing political content and avoided social issues.

Fighting for their livelihoods, some blacklisted moviemakers moved to Europe or looked for roles in theatrical productions or on television; others, who did not appear before the cameras, adopted pseudonyms and sold their scripts through friendly agents, known as "fronts." A rare few attempted to challenge the blacklist by making independent movies about social problems.

"We were agreed that our films must be based in actuality," explained producer Paul Jarrico and director Herbert Biberman about their efforts to

Photograph courtesy Second Line Search

skirt the blacklist. Together with exiled screenwriter Michael Wilson, the Hollywood outcasts decided to make a movie about a long and bitter labor strike that had occurred in the early 1950s among Mexican American miners of the Mine, Mill and Smelters Union in New Mexico. To save money, bypass actor boycotts, and add authenticity to the film, the producers asked the miners and their families to play themselves. They also allowed the workers' community to edit the script under the principle: "No Hollywood shenanigans."

The result was Salt of the Earth, a black-and-white film that depicted the troubled relationship of Esperanza and Ramon Quintero, a young hardworking couple with two children who are drawn reluctantly into the community labor action. Mine safety is the triggering issue as the mining company places Mexican employees in more dangerous situations than Anglo workers. Meanwhile, the miners' wives complain about the lack of decent plumbing in the company-owned housing.

As the miners go on strike, the company imports strikebreakers and encourages local police to provoke violent confrontations and make arbitrary arrests. When the strikers maintain their solidarity, the company obtains a strike injunction under the Taft-Hartley Act, requiring the miners to abandon the picket line. Just as the union faces legal defeat, however, the miners' wives take the initiative, observing that the court injunction does not apply to a women's picket line. Overcoming the men's objections to this role reversal, the women replace the striking men and stand up to the corrupt police, eventually forcing the mine company to negotiate a settlement.

Salt thus presented several radical themes. First, it showed that unions were democratic institutions and did not depend on foreign agitators to raise grievances. Second, it illuminated racial discrimination in the workplace and depicted salutary cooperation between Mexican and Anglo miners. Third, the movie put women at the center of political action. "Why must you say to me, 'Stay in your place,'" Esperanza protests to her husband. "I want to rise. And push everything up with me as I go."

During the shooting, movie companies refused to provide processing and other services to the blacklisted filmmakers, and the federal government deported the film's only professional Mexican actress. Besides these problems, the completed movie encountered a nearly total boycott by distributors and theaters. In the end, this passionate protest against political, racial, and gender discrimination played in only thirteen locations.

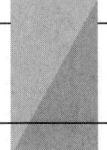

J. Edgar Hoover (1895–1972)

Without question, J. Edgar Hoover was the most successful bureaucrat in U.S. history. Raised a few blocks from the Capitol, Hoover graduated from George Washington University, took a clerical job with the Department of Justice, and assumed the directorship of the agency that became

Stock Montage

the Federal Bureau of Investigation in 1924, a post he held for the rest of his life. Energetic and capable, Hoover professionalized the bureau and cultivated a positive image through well-publicized and successful manhunts for celebrated gangsters.

During World War II, the FBI broke up Nazi spy rings in the United States and South America. As the Cold War ensued, Hoover turned the bureau's attention to alleged Soviet espionage and perceived threats of "red fascism." Critics charged that the director ignored the spread of organized crime and white-collar felonies to pursue conspiratorial notions of communist subversion at the expense of individual civil liberties. Yet Hoover insisted that an ever-broadening front of alien radicals was seeking to transform the United States into a land of class struggle, that communism embraced a materialistic religion that inflamed its adherents with destructive fanaticism.

legislatures divided voting districts to suit local needs and felt no obligation to provide representation based on population. (Not until 1962 did the Supreme Court uphold the principle of equal representation in the case of *Baker v. Carr.*)

Eisenhower did not identify with the conservative wing of the Republican Party that held strong antigovernment views. In a 1953 speech to the nation's newspaper editors, he warned that the costly arms race would rob society of other valuable assets. He lamented that the cost of one heavy bomber deprived the country of "a modern brick school in more than thirty cities" and that funds for one fighter plane could buy half a million bushels of wheat. He also acknowledged that the federal government "must do its part to advance human welfare and encourage economic growth with constructive actions."

As public opinion hardened against government controls, domestic labor unrest, and Soviet expansionism in the years following World War II, Hoover assumed a prominent role in the coalition of political activists, government prosecutors, congressional staffers, and conservative clergy who comprised the anticommunist lobby. Members of the group depicted communism as a menace to U.S. security, democratic freedoms, individual privacy, and religious values. Hoover liked to say that Soviet agents were corrupting society through covert propaganda and confidence tricks.

Acting on these principles, Hoover pushed the FBI into full participation in the postwar Red Scare. The bureau maintained thousands of files on domestic dissidents, did the field work for government employee loyalty investigations, provided intelligence on high-profile defendants such as Alger Hiss and the Rosenbergs, and leaked information to friendly politicians and the press when it served the director's interests.

The culmination of Hoover's anticommunist activities came in the 1950s when the bureau adopted a variety of counterintelligence techniques and "dirty tricks" designed to disrupt the Communist Party. The director's covert methods, racial paranoia, and tendency to associate domestic political groups with subversion would come under heavy criticism in subsequent years. But at the height of the Cold War, Hoover's reputation was virtually untarnished as a protector of the "American Way of Life."

The administration thus continued to subsidize farm prices, even though Secretary of Agriculture Ezra Taft Benson persuaded Congress to lower the level of supports. The president also backed a slight expansion of Social Security to include self-employed workers and approved modest housing legislation. Using the justification of "national security," Eisenhower signed legislation in 1954 to build the St. Lawrence Seaway to connect the Great Lakes to ocean ports.

Committed to such "modern Republicanism," Eisenhower presided over a national consensus that unified moderates in both political parties through vigorous pursuit of the Cold War. Democrats and Republicans alike shared a belief in the communist menace and agreed to seek military superiority. The correlation between military expenditures and economic prosperity also assured minimal resistance to administration requests for large Pentagon budgets.

Even as the Army-McCarthy hearings focused public attention on the communist threat in the spring of 1954, however, two other issues of immense potential revealed the shaky foundations of the national consensus. The first occurred in distant Indochina when Vietminh guerrillas surrounded the French garrison at Dien Bien Phu, threatening France's colonial domination and forcing Eisenhower to face the choice of U.S. intervention in that remote part of the world. The second occurred in Washington, D.C., on May 17, 1954, when the U.S. Supreme Court ruled in the case *Brown v. Board of Education of Topeka* that racial segregation in public schools was unconstitutional. Each situation raised questions that existed outside the Cold War consensus and each forced the American people to confront unexpected conflicts within the nation's identity.

INFOTRAC COLLEGE EDITION

Using Keywords, enter the following search terms:

Dwight D. Eisenhower
Korean War
Alger Hiss
CIA, History
J. Robert Oppenheimer
Elections: 1952

RECOMMENDED READINGS

Ellen Schrecker, *Many Are the Crimes: McCarthyism in America* (1998). This study of the anticommunist crusade examines the major political issues, weighing the conflict between national security and civil liberty.

Greg Mitchell, *Tricky Dick and the Pink Lady: Richard Nixon vs. Helen Gahagan Douglas—Sexual Politics and the Red Scare, 1950* (1998). Focusing on the 1950 California Senate race, the author describes the increasing importance of communism as the primary domestic issue.

Victor Navasky, *Naming Names* (1980). The author presents a sensitive analysis of the moral, psychological, and ideological dimensions of anticommunism in the entertainment industry.

Richard Whelen, *Drawing the Line: The Korean War, 1950–1953* (1990). This book provides a clear, balanced account of the global issues and military dimension of the conflict.

Additional Readings

The domestic anticommunist crusade is described by Richard M. Fried, *Nightmare in Red: The McCarthy Era in Perspective* (1990). For Joseph McCarthy, the best starting point is David M. Oshinsky, *A Conspiracy So Immense: The World of Joe McCarthy* (1983), but see also Thomas C. Reeves, *The Life and Times of Joe McCarthy* (1981); Mark Landis, *Joseph McCarthy: The Politics of Chaos* (1987); and Robert Griffith, *The Politics of Fear: Joseph R. McCarthy and the Senate* (1988). McCarthy's attack on one State Department official is told in Robert P. Newman, *Owen Lattimore and the "Loss" of China* (1992).

For the impact of McCarthyism in academia, see Ellen W. Schrecker, *No Ivory Tower: McCarthyism and the Universities* (1986). An interesting collection of case studies appears in Bud Schultz and Ruth Schultz, eds., *It Did Happen Here: Recollections of Political Repression in America* (1989). Also helpful in understanding McCarthy's support are Michael Paul Rogin, *The Intellectuals and McCarthy* (1967), and David M. Oshinsky, *Senator Joseph McCarthy and the American Labor Movement* (1976). A recent effort to rehabilitate McCarthy's reputation can be found in Arthur Herman, *Joseph McCarthy: Reexamining the Life and Legacy of America's Most Hated Senator* (2000).

There are numerous books about the dramatic political trials of the era. A good background to such trials is Stanley Kutler, *The American Inquisition: Justice and Injustice in the Cold War* (1982). Also see Allan Weinstein, *Perjury: The Hiss-Chambers Case* (1978); Ronald Radosh and Joyce Milton, *The Rosenberg File* (1987), which asserts the guilt of Julius Rosenberg (not Ethel Rosenberg). For the harassment of U.S. Spanish Civil War veterans, see Peter N. Carroll, *The Odyssey of the Abraham Lincoln Brigade: Americans in the Spanish Civil War* (1994). More sympathetic to the anticommunist crusade is Richard Gid Powers, *Not Without Honor: The History of American Anticommunism* (1995). The role of the FBI is detailed in Richard Gid Powers, *Secrecy and Power: The Life of J. Edgar Hoover* (1987), and in Athan G. Theoharis and John Stuart Cox, *The Boss: J. Edgar Hoover and the Great American Inquisition* (1988).

The background of the Korean War is best studied in James Irving Matray, *The Reluctant Crusade: American Foreign Policy in Korea, 1941–1950* (1985); in Jian Chen, *China's Road to the Korean War: The Making of the Sino-American Confrontation* (1994); and in William Whitney Stueck Jr., *The Korean War: An International History* (1995), which may be supplemented by Bruce Cumings's two-volume study, *The Origins of the Korean War* (1981–1990), and Rosemary Foot's *The Wrong War: American Policy and the Dimensions of the Korean Conflict, 1950–1953* (1985). Still valuable is Ronald Caridi, *The Korean War and American Politics* (1968). One wartime legal case dealing with the relation between government and business is the subject of Maeva Marcus, *Truman and the Steel Seizure Case* (1977).

The traditional view of Eisenhower as a laissez-faire president can be found in Peter Lyon, *Eisenhower: Portrait of a Hero* (1974). This view has been challenged persuasively in Blanche Wiesen Cook, *The Declassified Eisenhower: A Divided Legacy* (1981), and Fred Greenstein, *The Hidden Hand Presidency: Eisenhower as Leader* (1982). A detailed collection of primary sources can be found in Robert L. Branyan and Lawrence H. Larsen, *The Eisenhower Administration*, two volumes (1971).

Numerous biographies offer insight into the domestic issues of the 1950s. For the workings of congressional power, see Rowland Evans and Robert Novak, *Lyndon B. Johnson: The Exercise of Power* (1966). Good studies of the leading Democrat include Jeff Broadwater, *Adlai Stevenson and American Politics: The Odyssey of a Cold War Liberal* (1994), and John Bartlow Martin's more detailed two-volume *The Life of Adlai Stevenson* (1976–1977). For the vice president's career, see Stephen E. Ambrose's biography, *Nixon: The Education of a Politician* (1987), as well as the superb analysis by Garry Wills, *Nixon Agonistes* (1970). The liberal perspective emerges in Carl Solberg's, *Hubert Humphrey: A Biography* (1984). Voting behavior in the 1950s is explained in Norman H. Nie et al., *The Changing American Voter* (1976).

A good introduction to Eisenhower's foreign policy is Walter Lafeber, *America, Russia, and the Cold War* (1985). A more favorable account is Robert A. Divine, *Eisenhower and the Cold War* (1981). These works should be supplemented by the suggestive articles in Richard A. Melanson and David Mayers, eds., *Reevaluating Eisenhower: American Foreign Policy in the 1950s* (1987). Eisenhower's economic foreign policy is the subject of Burton I. Kaufman's *Trade and Aid: Eisenhower's Foreign Economic Policy, 1953–61* (1982). U.S. interest in Iran and oil is analyzed in Mary Ann Heiss, *Empire and Nationhood: The United States, Great Britain, and Iranian Oil, 1950–1954* (1997).

U.S. intervention in Central America is best described in Piero Gleijeses, *Shattered Hope: The Guatemalan Revolution and the United States, 1944–1954* (1991); see also R.H. Immerman, *The CIA in Guatemala: The Foreign Policy of Intervention* (1982), and Stephen C. Schlesinger and Stephen Kinzer, *Bitter Fruit: The Untold Story of the American Coup in Guatemala* (1982).

White House anticommunism is the theme of Jeff Broadwater's *Eisenhower and the Anti-Communist Crusade* (1992). For the Oppenheimer case, see Peter J. Goodchild, *J. Robert Oppenheimer: Shatterer of Worlds* (1981). For the impact of Cold War anticommunism on popular culture, see Margot A. Henriksen, *Dr. Strangelove's America: Society and Culture in the Atomic Age* (1997).

EISENHOWER'S TROUBLED CONSENSUS, 1954–1960

By the middle of the 1950s, the United States stood as the most powerful and prosperous nation on earth. Although its inhabitants constituted just 6 percent of the world's population in 1955, they made two-thirds of the world's manufactured goods. In addition to this industrial strength, the number of jobs in the service sector of the economy—sales, clerical, and other white-collar occupations—exceeded the number of manufacturing occupations for the first time in 1956, heralding a new postindustrial society based on technological innovation and labor productivity. But although economists such as John Kenneth Galbraith depicted "the affluent society," deep pockets of poverty remained untouched by technological progress and economic growth. Persistent disparities of wealth between the elderly and the young, between racial minorities and whites, between city dwellers and suburbanites stimulated concerns about social inequities.

Foreign policy issues appeared equally problematic. The anticommunist crusade had effectively silenced dissent against mounting government expenditures for national security or the preoccupation with political loyalty. But although President Dwight D. Eisenhower endorsed the expansion of a vast military arsenal, the Cold War with the Soviet Union remained unresolved, and crises erupted continually around the world—in Southeast Asia, Taiwan, the Middle East, Berlin, and Latin America. Fear of nuclear warfare permeated the land, prompting increased concern about civil defense, but also the high cost of domestic security. Eisenhower himself lamented the growth of a "military-industrial complex" that threatened to swamp traditional freedoms and the entrepreneurial spirit. The Cold War consensus thus rested on a shaky foundation, both at home and abroad.

CRISIS RELATIONS IN ASIA

In the spring of 1954—at the same time that Senator Joseph McCarthy presided over televised investigations of the U.S. Army and Eisenhower quietly canceled the security clearance of physicist J. Robert Oppenheimer—a Vietnamese guerrilla force was surrounding the French garrison at Dien Bien Phu in Vietnam. Facing military disaster that would doom the French empire in the region, France appealed to Eisenhower for U.S. military intervention. Since the outbreak of the Korean War, the United States had provided major support for French attempts to suppress the Vietminh rebels led by Ho Chi Minh. By 1954 Washington had spent $1.2 billion on military assistance and was financing nearly 80 percent of France's total war costs. These expenses included several hundred "technical" advisers. The administration justified intervention on the grounds that Vietnam provided valuable raw materials such as tin and rubber and remained a vital strategic link in the attempt to halt communist expansion. Yet, although Washington supported the French in Southeast Asia, administration leaders repeatedly expressed frustration at France's failure to develop support among noncommunist Vietnamese.

Despite U.S. aid, the French position worsened. As a new crisis loomed in 1954, Eisenhower faced critical choices. Sensitive to the limited success in Korea, he hesitated to commit U.S. military forces unilaterally. Although the Central Intelligence Agency (CIA) flew relief missions to the embattled garrison and conducted reconnaissance flights, the doctrine of massive retaliation—by which the United States threatened nuclear reprisals against communist enemies—had limited use in jungle warfare in Indochina. Tactical air strikes, perhaps with atomic weapons, alarmed British allies, who worried that all-out war in Indochina would trigger Chinese intervention, particularly against Hong Kong and Malaysia. The British also feared Soviet retaliation and an atomic war. Without British support, moreover, congressional Democrats led by Senator Richard Russell refused to sanction military action. Democratic Majority Leader Lyndon Johnson told Secretary of State John Foster Dulles, "No more Koreas with the United States furnishing 90 percent of the manpower."

For Eisenhower, Vietnam held the future of Asia. And in 1954 a special National Security Council (NSC) committee called for military victory "to provide tangible evidence of Western strength and determination to defeat Communism." At a press conference that year the president buttressed this position with the "falling domino" theory: "You have a row of dominos set up, you knock over the first one, and what will happen to the last one is the certainty that it will go over very quickly." The fall of Vietnam would mean that "many human beings pass under a dictatorship that is inimical to the free world." It would interfere with the acquisition of precious resources, imperil Japanese trade, and force that ally "toward the Communist areas in order to live."

EXHIBIT **3-1**   **INDOCHINA AFTER THE GENEVA ACCORDS OF 1954**

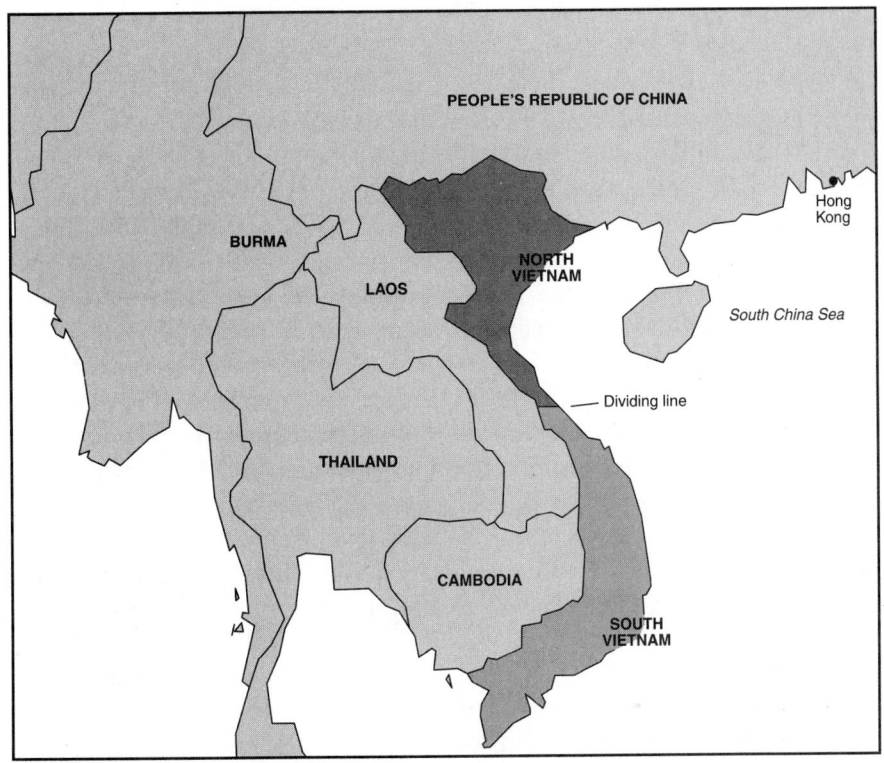

Source: Thomas A. Bailey, *A Diplomatic History of the American People* (Prentice Hall, rev. ed., 1980).

Eisenhower never wavered from the belief that the Vietminh were not an anticolonial force but part of an international communist conspiracy. But the commander in chief had learned from the Korean experience. Without British support and explicit approval from Congress, Eisenhower refused to commit ground forces to another war in Asia. Yet when the French finally surrendered to the Vietminh in May 1954, Senator Johnson criticized the White House's failure to act. "American foreign policy had never in all its history suffered such a stunning reversal," he declared.

The French defeat made a diplomatic settlement imperative. In July 1954 France signed the Geneva Accords and ended eight years of war by accepting the independence of Vietnam, Laos, and Cambodia. The agreement divided Vietnam militarily at the seventeenth parallel, but this temporary line did not imply a political separation. The agreement called for national elections, supervised by an international commission, to be held within two years. By acknowledging a Vietminh government, if only in North Vietnam, the Geneva settlement represented a defeat of Eisenhower's anticommunist foreign policy.

The United States announced it would respect the Geneva Accords, but the administration refused to sign the document, and Secretary of State John Foster Dulles referred to South Vietnam as a "country."

The United States soon began to violate the Geneva agreement by continuing a secret war against the Vietminh. Instead of accepting a communist Vietnam, Washington worked to build an anticommunist nationalist movement in South Vietnam led by Ngo Dinh Diem, a U.S.–educated Catholic. Installed as premier of the French-controlled portion of the country, Diem welcomed a U.S. military mission, which organized a South Vietnamese army and launched acts of sabotage and a propaganda campaign against the Vietminh in the north. Meanwhile, the CIA distributed $12 million to bribe Diem's rivals into neutrality.

Eisenhower also moved to replace France's influence in Vietnam. Washington bypassed French officials and transmitted aid directly to Diem, thus avoiding the appearance of supporting French colonialism. Such policies led France to withdraw from Vietnam before the 1956 election deadline. Quickly stepping into the power vacuum, U.S. advisers began to train a large South Vietnamese army "to deter Vietminh aggression." Acknowledging that Ho Chi Minh would win national elections, the administration worked to stop national unification under the terms of the Geneva Accords. Diem made these policies explicit in 1955 by announcing his rejection of national elections. Unlike France and Britain, Eisenhower backed Diem and welcomed him in Washington, where the two leaders reaffirmed the struggle against "continuing Communist subversive capabilities."

During the next five years, when Vietnam seldom attracted attention in the U.S. media, Washington sent nearly $1.5 billion in economic and military aid to South Vietnam to finance most of Diem's government expenses. Such support enabled the dictator to suppress his political rivals by arresting both communist and noncommunist opponents. Diem also subverted land reform begun by the Vietminh. By 1959 these repressive policies triggered another guerrilla revolt. Although the United States urged Diem to allow political and social reforms, the South Vietnamese leader refused, prompting the U.S. ambassador to suggest "it may become necessary . . . to begin consideration of alternative courses of actions and leaders." Eisenhower passed this unresolved predicament to the next U.S. presidential administration in 1961.

While adopting unilateral action in Vietnam, Eisenhower instituted collective security plans to prevent the spread of communism in Asia. In 1954 Dulles signed a Southeast Asia Treaty Organization (SEATO) pact with Britain, France, Australia, New Zealand, Thailand, Pakistan, and the Philippines. This accord provided for mutual defense against armed attack, subversion, or indirect aggression. "An attack on the treaty area would occasion a reaction so united, so strong, and so well placed," said Dulles, "that the

EXHIBIT **3-2**   **TAIWAN AND THE PEOPLE'S REPUBLIC OF CHINA**

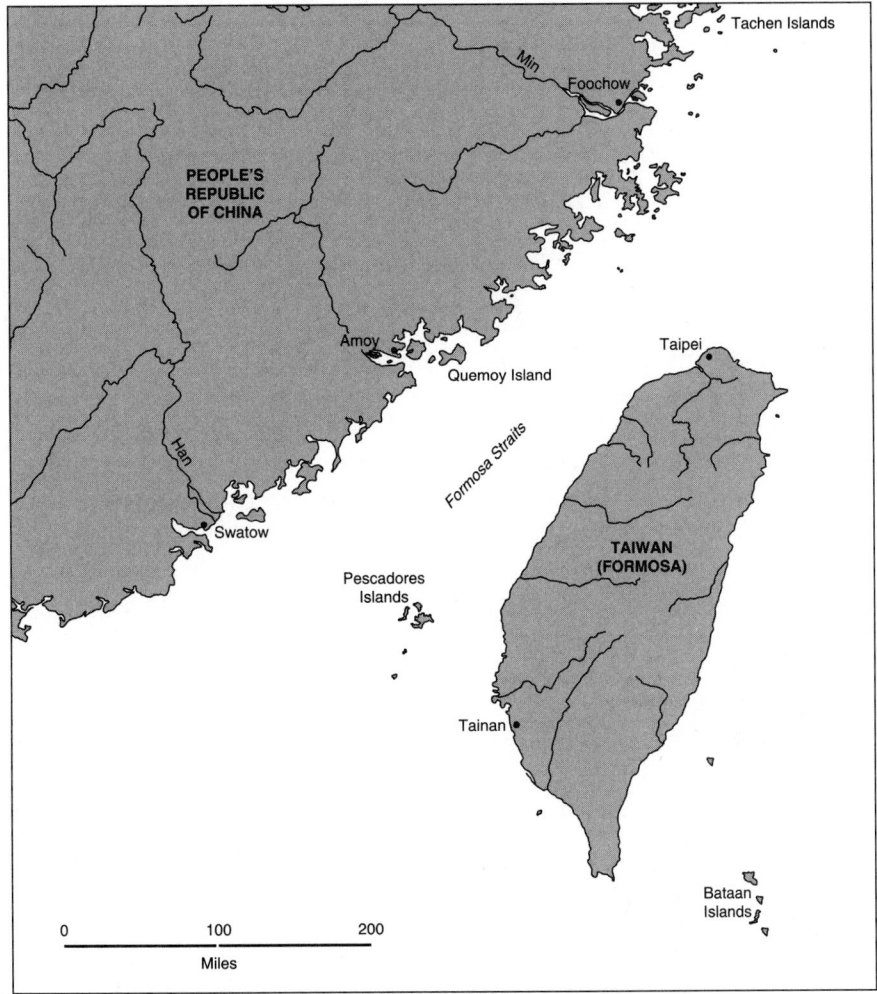

aggressor would lose more than it could hope to gain." Yet the SEATO agreement had inherent limitations, including the refusal of neutral India to participate and the difficulty of using massive retaliation against subversion. The Senate ratified the treaty with little dissent, but the military provisions were never invoked, and the treaty ended in 1977.

Even as Dulles was flying to Manila to negotiate the SEATO pact in 1954, the weaknesses of the treaty became apparent. Without warning or obvious provocation, Chinese artillery suddenly began to bombard Quemoy, one of the small islands (along with Matsu and the Tachen Islands) between China and

Taiwan. The attacks moved Washington to prepare for war, including considering atomic bombing of China. Although Eisenhower recognized that the islands were not crucial to the defense of Taiwan, he defined the Taiwan regime as part of the "backbone" of international security. The government of China began to prepare for an atomic attack. As war fever rose, Dulles negotiated a mutual defense pact with Taiwan but made no mention of the disputed islands.

When China captured one of the Tachen Islands, Eisenhower asked Congress for authority to use armed forces to defend Taiwan and the nearby islands. Approved by nearly unanimous votes of both houses of Congress in 1955, the so-called Formosa Resolution gave the president discretionary power to declare war, a virtual blank check for future presidential foreign policy. As China continued to bomb the islands, Eisenhower indirectly reiterated the threat of atomic attack. At the same time, however, the Soviet Union was seeking a relaxation of global tensions and hoping for an arms control agreement in Europe. Soviet pressure, combined with Eisenhower's threats, persuaded China to break the deadlock. As abruptly as it began, the crisis passed.

Eisenhower's threats to use atomic bombs moved the People's Republic of China to develop its own nuclear capacities. Meanwhile, the Taiwanese government proceeded to strengthen fortifications on the disputed offshore islands. Tensions between the two Chinas kept the world on edge. Then, in 1958, the People's Republic abruptly reopened the crisis by launching a steady bombardment of Quemoy. This time, as the administration rushed military aid to Taiwan, Eisenhower avoided reference to nuclear weapons. By then both the United States and the Soviet Union were discussing an arms control agreement, and scientists meeting in Geneva had announced "a workable and effective control system for the detection of violations." The refusal of the Soviet Union to support China's attack intensified the rift between the communist allies. Yet neither the United States nor the Soviet Union could abandon their rival Chinese clients. The result was the preservation of the two-China status quo. Eisenhower and Dulles had accomplished no more than Truman's policy of containment.

A VIGILANT THAW

The Cold War climate of mutual suspicion made negotiations with the Soviet Union difficult and unrewarding. During his first years in office, Eisenhower avoided presidential diplomacy, preferring Dulles to handle direct talks. But by 1955, Democrats in Congress urged the president to make some gesture of reconciliation to ease world tensions. As a precondition to meeting with other leaders, Eisenhower insisted that the Allies of World War II first sign a peace treaty with Austria. When the Soviets agreed in 1955, Eisenhower flew to a summit meeting in Geneva with British, French, and Soviet leaders. The international press heralded the meeting as a "thaw" in the Cold War.

The main topics on the global agenda—the status of Germany and disarmament—could not be settled. Hoping to break the stalemate of suspicion, Eisenhower introduced a new plan, known as the "open-skies" proposal, which would permit aircraft to fly freely over foreign countries to inspect military installations and thus avert the risk of a surprise attack. Yet the plan clearly offered advantages to the less-secretive United States, and the Soviet Union rejected the scheme. After the conference ended, Eisenhower proceeded with plans to use a new secret spy plane (the U-2) to achieve the goal that the open-skies plan had intended. Both superpowers continued to test hydrogen bombs and intercontinental missiles, but the Geneva meeting did ease world tensions. "Communist tactics against the free nations have shifted," observed Eisenhower in 1956, "from reliance on violence to reliance on division."

The "thaw" in the Cold War had obvious limits. When Poland and then Hungary tried to establish more liberal communist governments in 1956, Americans celebrated what appeared to be a collapse of the Soviet empire. However, when Soviet tanks crushed the uprising in Budapest, massive retaliation proved worthless. Although the U.S. government's Radio Free Europe broadcast moral support to the Hungarian rebels, Eisenhower could only condemn Soviet aggression and allow 20,000 Hungarian refugees to enter the country. Both sides remained vigilant and mistrustful.

The arms race continued, leading the federal government to invest heavily in military technology, such as jet aircraft, missiles, electronic transistors, and computers. Between 1950 and 1959, the federal government sponsored $12 billion in research and development (R&D), including $300 million per year for university research. Aircraft manufacturing, one of the leading growth industries, drew 80 percent of its business from military contracts. The government also backed electronics, which grew 15 percent per year, making it the fifth largest industry by 1960. Secret military programs for nuclear weapons, missiles, and cryptography also demanded complicated mathematical calculations that boosted the computer industry.

Among the most sophisticated R&D programs was the plan to launch an artificial satellite that would orbit the earth in 1958. Indeed, it was the prospect of this technological breakthrough that had inspired Eisenhower to make the "open-skies" proposal. But before U.S. scientists could achieve a satellite launch, the Soviet Union surprised the world in October 1957 by sending the 184-pound *Sputnik* satellite into space. The event sent psychological shock waves across the nation, suggesting both a technological defeat for U.S. science and a military threat in the Cold War.

"The time has clearly come," said one Republican critic, "to be less concerned with the depth of pile on the new broadloom rug or the height of the tail fin on the car and to be more prepared to shed blood, sweat, and tears if this country and the Free World are to survive." "The Soviets have beaten us at our own game," declared Senator Johnson, "daring scientific advances in the

Invasion of the Body Snatchers (1956)

In a world of monstrous atomic explosions, imminent global warfare, and fear of subversive infiltration, director Don Siegel's adaptation of Jack Finney's magazine story, "The Body Snatchers," evoked the terror of creatures from another world taking over small-town America. Yet unlike most science fiction films that depicted alien enemies at the doorstep, Invasion of the Body Snatchers suggested the existence of home-grown problems that were causing mutations in the national character.

The story begins when Dr. Miles Bennell (played by Kevin McCarthy) returns from a medical convention to find his patients complaining of vague psychological symptoms. One boy says his mother really isn't his mother; another claims "Uncle Ira isn't Uncle Ira." Goaded by curiosity and intuition, Bennell realizes that mysterious vegetable pods have developed the capacity to repro-

Archive Photos

atomic age." Besides the philosophic shock caused by the triumph over the earth's gravitation, *Sputnik* aroused fear that the communist enemy could deliver intercontinental ballistic missiles armed with nuclear weapons before the United States could muster sufficient retaliatory power. This belief in a missile gap fed widespread fear of nuclear annihilation. Best-selling books such as Nevil

duce by inhabiting the bodies of human beings. "They're taking us over, cell by cell," he exclaims, attributing the phenomenon to radiation. "It's a malignant disease spreading through the whole country." Such phrases mirrored a belief that communism, too, was a "disease," as Adlai Stevenson put it in 1952, seeking "total conquest, not merely of the earth, but of the human mind."

The symptoms of the pod victims revealed other anxieties of the 1950s. Family members, instead of protecting each other, become instruments of betrayal and subversion. Both leading characters are divorced. Unlike normal people, moreover, the mutants are incapable of expressing emotion; "everything else is the same," observes one character, "but not the feeling." To avoid entrapment, Bennell conceals facial expressions or spontaneous conversation. Like the mutants, he appears robotic. And it is this lack of emotional display that constitutes the film's critique of contemporary society.

"In my practice I see how people have allowed their humanity to drain away," the doctor says, "only it happens slowly instead of all at once. . . . We harden our hearts . . . grow callous . . . only when we have to fight to stay human do we realize how precious it is." Like many dissidents of the 1950s, Bennell resists such dehumanization. He refuses to capitulate, finally escaping to a nearby highway where he tries, futilely, to attract help. "You're next," he cries, as passing motorists ignore his pleas. "You're next."

When preview audiences in California saw the film, however, they hated the pessimistic ending. Producer Walter Wanger then ordered additional shooting to show Bennell telling his story as a flashback to a psychiatrist. The new version ended in "Hollywood style" with the doctor reaching for the telephone: "Operator, get me the Federal Bureau of Investigation! Yes, it's an emergency."

Instead of ending with despair at the life-deadening prospects of mass conformity, Invasion thus promised rescue by traditional government institutions. Twenty-two years later, a remake of the movie by Philip Kaufman restored the grim ending. In that post-Watergate climate of opinion, U.S. audiences no longer shared Miles Bennell's faith in small-town values of individualism and the goodness of their government.

Shute's On the Beach (1957) and Walt Miller's A Canticle for Leibowitz (1959) dramatized the imminence of holocaust.

Although military intelligence understood that U.S. rocketry remained competitive with the Soviet achievement, public fears stimulated greater government support for scientific research. In 1958 Congress created the National

Aeronautics and Space Administration (NASA), a civilian space program, and increased appropriations for missile and satellite research. Government expenditures for R&D jumped from $6.2 billion in 1955 to $14.3 billion six years later, a 131 percent increase.

Throughout the *Sputnik* crisis, Eisenhower denied U.S. military weakness and rejected plans to build fallout shelters around the country. In any case, the country was soon prepared to match the Soviet achievement. After a few highly publicized failures, the army lofted the *Explorer* satellite into orbit in 1958. The president also created a White House Science Advisory Committee headed by the Massachusetts Institute of Technology's James Killian. By bringing scientists into the administration, Eisenhower for the first time had access to authoritative opinions about a range of technological issues. These scientists would later contradict the advice of the Atomic Energy Commission (AEC) and the Pentagon and suggest that the nuclear arms race could be controlled, paving the way for negotiations about restricting nuclear testing.

The administration also proceeded with a program to explore outer space. In 1959 NASA unveiled Project Mercury, a program for manned space flight, and introduced the first seven astronauts to the public. In the international "space race," U.S. rocketry at first lagged behind Soviet successes. Early Soviet missiles carried more than a ton of cargo (and even a dog), whereas the first U.S. satellite weighed only 30 pounds. However, in the next decade, electronic miniaturization and the development of intercontinental ballistic missiles (ICBMs) brought primacy to U.S. rocketry. The space program thus benefited from military defense research.

CRISES IN THE MIDDLE EAST

Huge expenditures for military aircraft and transportation underscored the importance of petroleum resources for waging the Cold War and reinforced the strategic role of Middle East countries. Although the United States had supported the independence of Israel in 1948, Presidents Truman and Eisenhower encouraged U.S. oil companies to provide Arab states with subsidies, which were tacitly repaid by the federal government in the form of tax deductions. Eisenhower also backed British influence in the Middle East to check Soviet expansion and supported a British plan for regional cooperation through the Baghdad Pact of 1955.

This anticommunist alliance alarmed Egyptian leader Gamal Abdel Nasser, a nationalist who needed economic and military assistance to strengthen his country. As Nasser negotiated with communist Czechoslovakia to purchase arms, Washington offered to finance the Aswan Dam, a giant hydroelectric project that promised to modernize Egypt. But when Nasser announced his recognition of the People's Republic of China in 1956, U.S. coop-

EXHIBIT **3-3**   **THE MIDDLE EAST, 1956–1958**

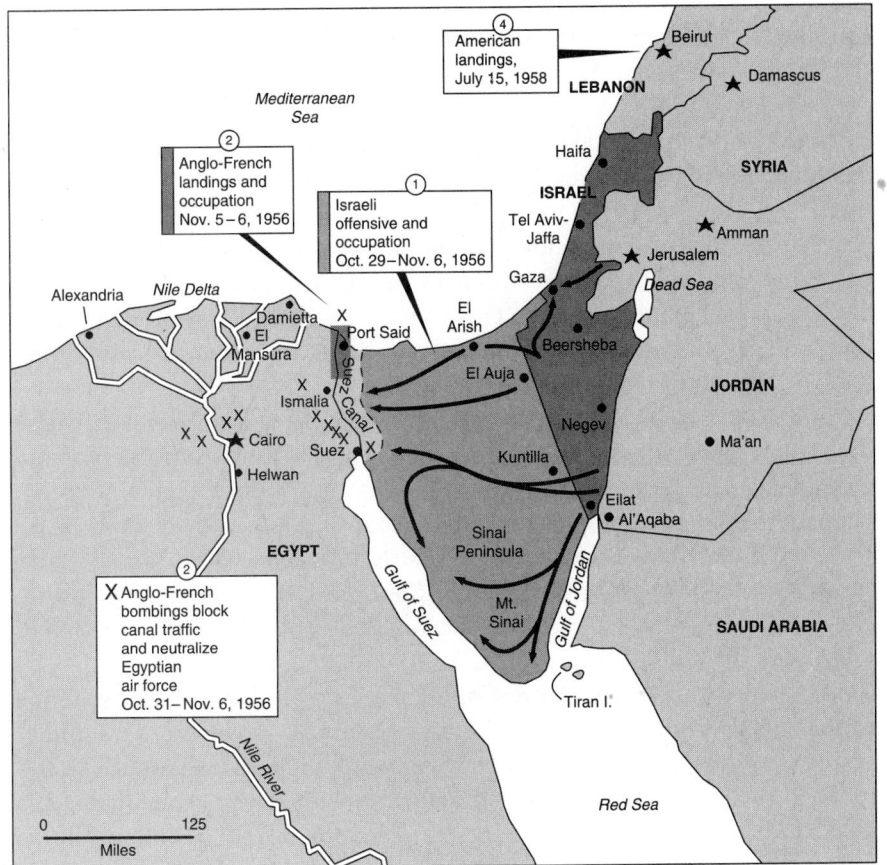

eration ceased. "Do nations which play both sides get better treatment than nations which are stalwart and work with us?" asked Dulles angrily. Eisenhower promptly withdrew the offer to build the dam. The reversal humiliated Nasser. One week later, the Egyptian leader nationalized the Suez Canal, thereby jeopardizing western Europe's access to oil and Israel's shipping rights.

Although Britain and France threatened military reprisal, Eisenhower opposed a reassertion of colonialism. The two countries then resolved to take action without U.S. participation, using Israel as an instigator. In October 1956 the Israelis launched a surprise attack on Egypt, which provided Britain and France with an excuse to intervene to protect the canal. The invasion coincided with the Soviet suppression of the Hungarian uprising. Faced with a double crisis, Eisenhower demanded the withdrawal of troops from Egypt. So did Premier Nikita Khrushchev, who warned the Western nations of a retaliatory attack and expressed interest in a Soviet presence in the Middle East. To prevent such Soviet expansion, Eisenhower increased pressure on the allies by halting oil shipments to western Europe. The embargo forced the British and French to remove their forces from the Middle East by the end of the year.

To fill the resulting power vacuum in the Middle East, Eisenhower presented a plan, known as the Eisenhower Doctrine, in 1957. The president asked Congress to approve unspecified economic and military assistance and also requested a resolution announcing that "overt armed aggression from any nation controlled by international Communism" would be met by U.S. military force. Congress agreed. Once again, the United States would police the world against communist influence, confusing Arab nationalism with communist expansion.

The Eisenhower Doctrine nonetheless gave the White House extensive authority to intervene in the Middle East. In 1957 Jordan's King Hussein claimed that a nationalist rebellion in his country constituted a communist attack. Although Eisenhower understood the king's duplicity, he sent the Sixth Fleet to protect the political status quo. In 1958 a similar distortion of events led the president to order the marines into Lebanon. This dramatic gesture served notice to Arab nationalists that the United States was determined to protect access to Middle Eastern oil.

"What makes the Soviet threat unique in history," the president stated in 1958, "is its all-inclusiveness. . . . Trade, economic development, military power, arts, science, education, the whole world of ideas—all are harnessed to the same chariot of expansion." Fear of Soviet influence in economically underdeveloped countries stimulated a reappraisal of U.S. economic foreign policy. As a proponent of free enterprise, Eisenhower hoped that foreign trade and private investment would assure U.S. influence without adding to government expenditures. Foreign aid remained largely military and was justified on grounds of national security.

But increased Soviet competition persuaded the president to endorse foreign aid as a way of accelerating the economic development of other countries and linking their interests to the West. In 1957 Congress established the Development Loan Fund and two years later created the Inter-American Loan Bank for Latin America. Both projects provided relatively small sums and emphasized private investment. Eisenhower defined such assistance not as an attempt to reduce poverty but rather as a defense of national security in the fight against communism. Moreover, foreign military aid far exceeded economic assistance and caused a severe imbalance in international payments that weakened the dollar abroad. Yet Eisenhower's commitment to foreign economic development provided a precedent for later administrations.

The Politics of Moderation

Surveying the political spectrum in 1956, Democratic contender Adlai Stevenson concluded that "moderation is the spirit of the times." Although liberals such as Hubert Humphrey and Paul Douglas spoke eloquently about social reform, Democrats worked closely with Eisenhower's "modern" Republicans to enact minimal social legislation, such as raising the minimum wage slightly and constructing limited public housing.

The grandfatherly Eisenhower remained extremely popular. Although the president's 1955 heart attack shook public confidence, he recovered rapidly and resolved to seek a second term. After slight hesitation, Ike agreed to keep Vice President Richard Nixon on the Republican ticket. Democratic chances seemed slim. Stevenson won a first-ballot nomination and then, in a dramatic moment, opened the vice-presidential choice to the whole Democratic National Convention. In the exciting floor fight, Tennessee Senator Estes Kefauver managed to defeat Senator John F. Kennedy of Massachusetts.

The Democrats then adopted a moderate platform. Hoping to regain the southern white voters, the party waffled on the issue of racial segregation. The party also echoed Eisenhower's Cold War principles. Stevenson did introduce two controversial proposals by calling for an end to the military draft and suggesting a moratorium on hydrogen bomb testing. However, both issues played to Eisenhower's reputation as an experienced military leader. "The butchers of the Kremlin," said Nixon, "would make mincemeat of Stevenson over a conference table."

Eisenhower's 1956 margin of victory exceeded the totals of his first election. He captured 58 percent of the popular vote and carried all but seven states. Other Republican candidates ran far behind, and Democrats strengthened their control of both houses of Congress. This anomalous situation reflected the persistence of party voting habits. With 50 percent more registered Democrats than Republicans, congressional Democrats coasted to victory in 1956. But unlike congressional candidates, Eisenhower could attract voters from all parts of the political spectrum because specific issues appeared relatively unimportant. One exception to the rule was the African American vote. In 1956, 40 percent of black voters, including Martin Luther King Jr., supported the Republican Party against Democratic racists who controlled southern politics.

Emboldened by their success in the congressional elections, Democrats moved to clarify their political position and define their differences with the Republican agenda. Eisenhower's success in the black neighborhoods of northern cities goaded congressional liberals into action. "I don't think a party should run on 'trouble,' on economic difficulty," declared Hubert Humphrey. "We

Estes Kefauver (1903–1963)

In an era of political consensus and corporate expansion, Tennessee's Senator Estes Kefauver flourished as a maverick politician and a champion of the ordinary citizen against big business and political corruption. Running for the Senate in 1948, he broke with Tennessee's political machine and

Stock Montage

adopted a coonskin cap as a symbol of his frontier independence. The folksy style became his political trademark. Kefauver's image as a populist, enhanced by televised broadcasts of his Senate hearings on organized crime in 1950 and 1951, catapulted him to national fame and made the senator a strong Democratic presidential contender. Yet his individualism created many enemies. In the end, he was deemed too much a southerner for liberals, too much a liberal for southerners.

Born in eastern Tennessee, Kefauver studied law at Yale and worked as a corporate lawyer before being elected to Congress in 1939. He supported small business interests against corporate concentration, advocated congressional reform, and coauthored the book *A Twentieth Century Congress* (1947). Although Kefauver was sensitive to civil liberties issues, he placated his southern constitutents by opposing a federal Fair Employment Practices Commission and antilynching legislation. But, unlike most racial opportunists, he urged repeal of poll taxes because they disenfranchised the poor of both races, and he opposed the use of the filibuster to kill civil rights legislation. Indeed, after the Supreme Court overturned school segregation in 1954, he readily accepted the idea of racial integration.

must design a new liberal program." Led by Humphrey and Douglas, liberal senators presented a sixteen-point "Democratic Declaration" that advocated civil rights legislation, public housing, unemployment compensation, and other reforms. Meanwhile, Democratic leaders organized a Democratic Advisory Council distinct from the cautious congressional leadership of Lyndon Johnson and Sam Rayburn to press for a liberal agenda.

Kefauver's investigation of organized crime in the first televised Senate hearings created a national sensation in 1950. Exposure of national crime networks and widespread political graft underscored an abiding fear in the Cold War era that secret forces—"government-within-a-government," as he put it—were threatening national values. For Kefauver, it was crime and corruption, not communism, which were the prime menace. Significantly, he opposed provisions of the 1954 communist control bill that made Communist Party membership a felony. Kefauver's crime hearings also showed the political power of television. In his book, *Crime in America* (1951), the senator estimated that more than 20 million people watched the hearings. As a result, Kefauver suddenly became a nationally known politician.

Capitalizing on this popularity, Kefauver donned his coonskin cap in 1952 and entered a series of Democratic presidential primaries as the first major candidate to recognize the potential of grassroots support. He surprised the country by defeating President Truman in New Hampshire, but his unorthodox style did not allow him to build a national organization. Kefauver's nonpartisan investigations of organized crime also alarmed the Democratic leadership, which feared a loss of party strength in the cities. Meanwhile, his spotty record on civil rights weakened his support among liberals, and his opposition to filibusters cut into his southern base.

Twice defeated for the presidential nomination by Adlai Stevenson, Kefauver staged a dramatic floor rally in 1956 to win the vice presidential slot over Massachusetts Senator John F. Kennedy. After the presidential loss, Kefauver returned to the Senate. In 1963 he collapsed during a floor speech in 1963 and died a few days later.

The revitalization of Democratic liberals produced greater conflict with the Republican administration. The first controversy erupted when the president presented a $73.3 billion budget request, the highest appropriation ever requested in peacetime, for fiscal year 1958. Committed to a balanced budget, Treasury Secretary George Humphrey predicted that such expenditures would cause a depression. Eisenhower complicated the situation by inviting Congress to reduce government expenditures. The result was a bitter legislative "battle of the budget" as Congress picked apart the president's entire program, shaving the budget by $4 billion. For Eisenhower, the outcome was an embarrassing personal defeat.

Instead of boosting the economy, however, the reduction of government expenditures slowed economic growth. By mid-1957, industrial production had dropped and unemployment had increased. Eisenhower remained skeptical about the ability of government spending to stimulate the economy. But the Democratic Congress had fewer reservations. Increased appropriations, including public works projects, added more than $8 billion to the budget and halted the recession. Yet continued government spending resulted in large budget deficits.

THE CULTURE OF CONSUMPTION

The debates about government spending underscored the role of big business in shaping society and culture during the 1950s. In supporting what Eisenhower called the military-industrial complex, government agencies awarded most contracts to the country's largest corporations. Only 4 percent of R&D funds reached small businesses. Although convenient for government administrators, support of big business did not reduce costs. Without competitive bidding, federal budgets routinely absorbed business cost overruns. Nothing better showed the marriage between the federal government and big business than the Interstate Highway Act of 1956, which facilitated the integration of national roadways in the name of national defense. The law committed the federal government to spend more than $30 billion to develop a continental freeway system. Not coincidentally national automobile registration increased from 40 million in 1950 to 62 million in 1960. There was little irony, then, when Eisenhower's secretary of defense, Charles E. Wilson, the former president of General Motors, said: "For years I thought what was good for the country was good for General Motors, and vice versa."

Spurred by the baby boom, suburban growth, and the expansion of white-collar jobs, corporate prosperity increased and stimulated tremendous confidence in the economic future. "Not only do the younger people accept the beneficent society as normal," observed author William H. Whyte Jr., "they accept improvement, considerable and constant, as normal too." Peaceful labor-management relations had brought unprecedented prosperity to the nation's workers. Between 1955 and 1960, average hourly earnings rose more than 22 percent, twice the rate of inflation. Long-term union contracts assured blue-collar employees regular cost-of-living wage hikes as well as paid vacations.

Although economic recessions occurred three times after the war—in 1948–1949, 1953–1954, and 1957–1958—private consumption steadily in-

EXHIBIT **3-4**   **GROSS NATIONAL PRODUCT, 1954–1958**
(IN ROUNDED BILLIONS OF DOLLARS)

1954	372
1958	457

Source: *Economic Report of the President* (1988).

creased each year. In the immediate postwar years consumers exhausted their savings to buy durable household goods such as appliances, furniture, and automobiles—some 21 million cars, 20 million refrigerators, 5 million stoves, and 12 million TVs. Then they relied on borrowed money to purchase disposable goods and services such as insurance, entertainment, and travel. In 1950 Diner's Club introduced the personal credit card to allow businessmen to charge their meals. By the end of the decade Carte Blanche, American Express, and Bankamericard extended easy credit to predominantly male members. (Most married women could not obtain personal credit until the 1970s.) Installment credit soared from $4 billion in 1954 to $43 billion in 1960.

Some consumer spending reflected the age-specific demands of the baby boom: children's clothing, toys, "family-size" products. In 1956 for the first time the airline industry attracted as many passengers as did railroads; in 1958 the Boeing 707 brought jet speed to commercial aviation. Planned obsolescence made consumption appear to be an end in itself. Men's clothing styles began following women's fashions by undergoing annual changes that made serviceable wardrobes outmoded. By emphasizing cosmetic innovations such as fender "fins," annual changes in automobile models encouraged frequent trade-ins.

Advertising, not coincidentally, became one of the major growth industries of the postwar period. Although best-selling books such as Vance Packard's *The Hidden Persuaders* (1957) publicized the psychological techniques of advertising, market research found that consumers remained more responsive to emotional appeals than to product substance. As advertising touted consumer disposables and luxuries such as tobacco, beverages, drugs, amusements, and extra home furnishings, annual advertising expenditures exceeded $10 billion by 1960. Postwar advertising relied increasingly on national media, such as network television and mass circulation magazines rather than local radio stations or newspapers. The new outlets facilitated product recognition for a population that increasingly migrated around the country. Advertisers also geared their pitches to market segments identified by demographic factors such as age, income, education, and lifestyle. And in 1952, Eisenhower became the first presidential candidate to film televised commercials.

The growth of advertising paralleled the expansion of all service industries. Each year consumers spent ever-larger sums for insurance, automobile repairs, medical care, and travel. These expanding service industries also had a major impact on the nature of work. As part of a long historical trend, technological innovation increased individual worker productivity, which in turn reduced the proportion of blue-collar jobs. Meanwhile, the growth of corporations created new managerial jobs for employees who administered business activities rather than producing commodities. In 1956 the number of people employed in service industries exceeded the number of producers for the first time, which heralded the postindustrial society. Government bureaucracies also swelled on all levels. State and local government increased by 2 million employees during the 1950s, an increase of 52 percent. By 1960, nearly 8.5 million employees drew government paychecks, largely for white-collar employment.

Skilled work now took another form. In the growing corporate and government bureaucracies, managerial expertise focused on increasing the productivity of white-collar workers and touted new values such as teamwork and administrative efficiency. The requirements of the corporate workplace contributed to an emphasis on consensus in postwar society. College students appeared greatly concerned about the need to conform and to "get along." Dubbed the "silent generation," many young people preferred courses in business administration and education to those in the liberal arts.

In the social sciences, William Whyte observed a "bias against conflict" among scholars who viewed terms such as "disharmony, disequilibrium, maladjustment, disorganization" as "bad things." Sociologists and political scientists stressed social "pluralism," a belief that a diversity of interest groups competed on an equal basis and adjusted their differences through reason and compromise. Liberal theory held that democracy was unworkable if people maintained loyalties to social classes, ethnic groups, or ideologies. Indeed, sociologist Daniel Bell declared that ideology was "dead." Historians Louis Hartz, Richard Hofstadter, and Daniel Boorstin described the national past in terms of a homogenized culture that succeeded because it avoided major social conflicts.

Postwar consensus was also reflected in the resurgence of church membership in all denominations—from 64 million in 1940 to 115 million in 1960, or from 50 percent to 63 percent of the population. This interest in spiritual security partly demonstrated the underlying anxieties of a rootless society and the search for identity in new communities. Religious leaders of the 1950s offered less a promise of salvation than a sense of secular reassurance and solace. "Believe in yourself!" the Reverend Norman Vincent Peale proclaimed in the popular tract, *The Power of Positive Thinking* (1952). "Have faith in your abilities! Without a humble but reasonable confidence in your own powers you cannot succeed." Worshippers spent $1 billion building churches in 1960 alone.

The postwar consensus also influenced the values of young people. "I would like to be able to fly if everybody else did," a twelve-year-old girl told sociologist David Riesman, "but it would be kind of conspicuous." Critics contended that conformity had worked its way into the public schools through a perversion of John Dewey's philosophy of progressive education. Instead of encouraging students to question social values, as Dewey had urged, teachers typically stressed the values of social adjustment. Yet, ironically, progressive education became the target of further attacks when the Soviet *Sputnik* launch of 1957 abruptly challenged the pedagogical status quo. Shocked by this Cold War "defeat," educational reformers scurried to improve academic standards. Congress quickly passed the National Defense Education Act of 1958, the first major federal aid to education, to encourage the study of science, mathematics, and foreign languages. This government support, which later included such subjects vital to the "national defense" as U.S. history, financed the vast expansion of higher education in the next decade.

MASS CULTURE AND THE YOUTH CULT

Rising personal consumption brought larger postwar recreation expenditures, which jumped from $11 billion in 1950 to more than $18 billion in 1959. Professional baseball truly became the national pastime in 1958 when major-league teams moved to San Francisco and Los Angeles. Television proved to be the major innovation in postwar entertainment. In 1947 ten TV broadcasting stations reached about 20,000 TV sets. The next year TV sales suddenly skyrocketed. By 1957 U.S. households owned 40 million TV sets and could select programs from as many as seven broadcasting channels at a time. Television quickly became part of family life—seen by promoters as a modern "hearth" to encourage "togetherness" and by critics as an omnipresent salesman's foot in the door.

Although a new industry, television was controlled by the same corporations that dominated radio. Advertising rather than programming content determined the broadcast schedule. In 1951 the first coaxial cable linked the East and West Coasts and enabled national audiences to see the same thing at the same time. That year TV commercial sales surpassed radio advertising revenue for the first time. Although a host of young writers and performers produced brilliant examples of live drama and spontaneous comedy, the pressure to increase network ratings mostly generated formulaic series, variety programs, and quiz shows.

Television nonetheless eclipsed the other popular media such as radio, newspapers, magazines, and motion pictures. During the immediate postwar years, Hollywood had examined such controversial subjects as racism (*Home of the Brave*, 1948); anti-Semitism (*Crossfire*, 1947; *Gentlemen's Agreement*, 1947); and mental illness (*The Snake Pit*, 1949). Yet the investigation of Hollywood for communist subversion sent a chill through the industry and discouraged social criticism. Hollywood also suffered from declining movie attendance.

By 1953 ticket sales were a scant half of their 1946 record highs. The postwar baby boom, which tended to keep young adults at home, contributed to the drop. However, enthusiasm for TV—by 1953 more than 43 percent of U.S. families owned a set—simply swamped the old entertainment. Hoping to recapture audiences, Hollywood introduced production innovations, such as 3-D, wide screens, and more color, which were unavailable on TV, but as movie mogul Sam Goldwyn predicted in 1949, people were "unwilling to pay to see poor pictures when they can stay at home and see something which is, at least, no worse."

Hollywood's recourse was to concentrate on psychological themes, daring sex, and films geared to the youth culture. Television's family audiences limited sexual content to vague double-meanings or slapstick comedy. Although the motion picture industry still prohibited nudity or explicit sexuality, movies exploited the sexuality of stars like Marilyn Monroe, who combined provocative costumes with an uncanny sense of humor. Although many of Monroe's films portrayed sexual pleasure as a reward of affluence, the actress was a complex figure. A working-class woman who had escaped the dreariness of Los Angeles factory life, Monroe resented being judged by appearances even as she mastered the art of cinematic seduction.

Hollywood achieved greater success in exploiting a growing youth culture with sensitive young actors such as James Dean, Montgomery Clift, and Marlon Brando. "What are you rebelling against?" a teenage waitress asks a motorcycle tough in the Hollywood epic, *The Wild One* (1954). "What do ya got?" replies Brando. Popular movies about youth culture, such as *Rebel Without a Cause* (1955), portrayed a young generation that rejected the materialistic values of its parents. These films also expressed a lack of confidence in the older generation's ability to guide the young. "No longer is it thought to be the child's job to understand the adult world as the adult sees it," complained David Riesman in his classic study, *The Lonely Crowd* (1950).

Searching for peer approval and a sense of belonging, many adolescents turned to clubs, cliques, and gangs and experimented with cigarettes, alcohol, and sex. The antiauthoritarian *Mad* magazine, scoffing at mainstream culture, politicians, teachers, and parents, emerged as an instant hit among high school and college students. However, the primary form of social rebellion among postwar youth involved rock and roll music, a derivative of black rhythm and blues that was introduced to wider audiences by Cleveland disc jockey Allan Freed. Records by African American performers such as Chuck Berry and Little Richard often contained themes that rejected adult authority and assumed knowledge of sexual matters. By 1956 Elvis Presley, a sideburned white southerner whose music was based on the country rockabilly tradition, had achieved cult status by blatantly mixing pelvic thrusts with raunchy blues shouts. The introduction of a new dance, the Twist, by Chubby Checker in

In the 1955 film *Rebel Without a Cause,* teenage delinquents in leather jackets seemed more concerned with social conformity than alternative lifestyles.

1959 turned suggestive body expression into a national fad and hinted at the social integration of blacks and whites in postwar society.

Clergy and moral authorities professed shock at the frankness of rock and roll and its roots in the working-class cultures of blacks and southerners. In Boston police banned a live show staged by Freed and claimed that the loud and heavy beat excited teenagers to violence and delinquency. Yet for all its symbolic rebellion, rock and roll served more as a collective ritual for adolescents experiencing the traumas of puberty. Even "delinquents" in black leather jackets and motorcycle boots emulated the adult world by participating in consumer culture. And, after *The Blackboard Jungle* (1955) used Bill Haley's "Rock Around the Clock" in its soundtrack, Hollywood began to tailor its products to the burgeoning youth market. Other youth-oriented commodities included clothing, records, jewelry, cosmetics, soft drinks, and automobiles. Meanwhile, the music of white country legends such as Hank Williams, Patsy Cline, and Bob Wills and the Texas Playboys continued to express the joys and hardships of sexual love for working-class audiences. By 1955 annual record sales in the United States reached $225 million.

Economic abundance thus appeared in the 1950s as the epitome of national virtue. When Vice President Nixon visited Moscow in 1959 to accompany a traveling exhibition of U.S. home furnishings, he engaged in a highly publicized "kitchen debate" with Premier Khrushchev about the superiority of the U.S. way of life. While communists clung to a belief in a class revolution that would offer equality to all workers, Nixon pointed to the products of U.S. abundance—"44 million families with their 56 million cars, 50 million televisions and 143 million radios"—which showed the triumph of a truly "classless society." The superiority of the United States, said Nixon, could be seen in the multitude of its conveniences and its beautiful housewives.

Such political rhetoric disguised two enduring problems that would soon shatter the political consensus at home. The first concerned a growing realization that the fruits of U.S. capitalism did not reach all people equally. The second involved criticism from cultural outsiders who lamented corporate conformity and the homogenization of middle-class social roles and values.

RACE, POVERTY, AND THE URBAN CRISIS

"The saving grace of the American social system," boasted *Life* magazine in 1949, "is . . . the phenomenon of social 'mobility'—the opportunity to move rapidly upward through the levels of society." Indeed, the postwar period saw an era of unprecedented prosperity as family earnings among all recipients of income increased by at least 2.4 percent per year until 1973. Yet even in the prosperous 1950s unemployment rates remained between 3 and 8 percent, and unemployment insurance reimbursed only 20 percent of lost income. While touting middle-class success, social commentators typically ignored what author Michael Harrington called "the other America"—the numerous subcultures of poverty.

Among the poorest people were those older than sixty-five. A 1960 Senate report found that "at least one-half of the aged—approximately 8 million people—cannot afford today decent housing, proper nutrition, adequate medical care, preventive or acute, or necessary recreation." Mandatory retirement programs drove many able-bodied workers into poverty. During the 1950s the number of people entitled to Social Security benefits increased fivefold to 9.6 million, but government assistance filled a small fraction of their needs. More than half of the households headed by people older than sixty-five had incomes less than $3,000 a year in 1960.

Another pocket of poverty consisted of migrant farmworkers. On Thanksgiving Day 1960 Edward R. Murrow's TV broadcast, "Harvest of Shame," stunned the nation by revealing the poverty of rural workers. At the end of the 1950s, 1.5 million farmworkers, five-sixths of them white, had net incomes less than $3,000. Most lived in the South in dilapidated housing without elec-

Indian Health Service, Public Health Service, Dept. of Health and Human Services

Many Native Americans, like this man in a remote village in Alaska, still obtained water from unsafe or contaminated sources in the 1950s, despite the increasing affluence of other social groups.

tricity and plumbing. Migrant farmworkers of every nationality had virtually no protection from illegal labor practices that kept them poor and dependent.

Minority workers—Puerto Ricans, Mexican Americans, Native Americans, and Asian Americans—also earned extremely low incomes in occupations unprotected by minimum wage laws. Eighty percent of New York City's Puerto Rican families earned less than the government's estimated minimum levels for "modest but adequate" living standards. In California the average income of Japanese and Chinese American families in 1959 was a lowly $3,000, but even that was higher than the income of Spanish-speaking workers. Native Americans appeared poorest of all nonwhites and lived in such squalor that their death rate was three times the national average.

American Indian peoples continued to struggle with problems of poverty and assimilation. Stimulated by wartime migrations, the urban Native American population more than doubled during the 1940s and reached 56,000 by 1950, but many faced severe economic hardships and discriminatory policies. In two southwestern states, Native American citizens were denied the vote until 1948, and officials routinely prevented them from receiving veterans' benefits and from making other civil claims.

Hoping to end Native American dependence on government, Congress passed the Indian Claims Commission Act of 1946, which allowed tribes to bring legal action against the federal government for violations of previous treaties. The Bureau of Indian Affairs (BIA) and congressional conservatives saw the measure primarily as an opportunity to terminate government responsibility for native peoples. Although many assimilated American Indians welcomed the opportunity to claim compensation for past wrongs, traditionalist leaders warned that termination would leave native peoples vulnerable to economic problems and cultural isolation. Yet Congress embraced detribalization by passing a series of termination laws in 1954 to dissolve tribal structures, disburse tribal assets, and end federal assistance. For the Menominee of Wisconsin and the Klamath of Oregon as well as 100 smaller groups, the policy created severe economic and social dislocation.

Unemployment rates on reservations were staggering—more than 70 percent among the Blackfeet of Montana and the Hopi of New Mexico and more than 86 percent among the Choctaw of Mississippi. Many job-seekers moved to nearby cities, where they lived in poverty. Off the reservations, traditional tribal rituals became less important, and the number of spoken Native American languages declined. Yet Indian peoples also mobilized resistance to white culture. Thus the postwar period also saw a revitalization of Native American religion and identity, particularly among the young. Assertions of American Indian pride helped block the termination program in the 1960s.

The economic situation among African Americans was more complex. As middle-class whites assumed new lifestyles in the suburbs between 1940 and 1970, 5 million blacks left southern farms for the North and West. By 1960 half the nation's African Americans lived in central cities. Migration to industrial areas helped to increase their incomes. Although less than 17 percent of the nation's blacks were in the middle-income category in 1940, nearly 47 percent were middle-income earners by 1970. Black social mobility was symbolized by the eradication of the color barrier in organized sports. In 1947 Jackie Robinson signed a contract with the Brooklyn Dodgers, becoming the first African American to play major league baseball in more than sixty years. By 1960 professional basketball and football had become racially integrated sports followed by millions of television viewers.

Despite such dramatic gains, black migrants to the cities often faced limited job opportunities. As technological advances reduced the number of blue-collar jobs, white-collar opportunities were shifting to the suburbs. Moreover, racial policies created disparities of salaries. African American women earned less as factory workers than white women and continued to be relegated to unskilled or semiskilled jobs such as housekeeping, waitressing, and practical nursing. Similarly, black men earned a fraction of the wages paid to white men.

African American urban dwellers also confronted severe problems in acquiring satisfactory housing. Although Congress passed the Housing Act of

1949, authorizing slum clearance and construction of low-rent housing, the federal program was undermined by budget cutbacks and by uncooperative real estate interests, which blocked loan programs in inner cities. City planners found loopholes in the law that permitted the destruction of old buildings without replacement by low-cost rentals. One million postwar residential units faced the wrecking ball, but fewer than 350,000 took their place. Urban renewal programs worsened the situation. Such programs replaced old residential neighborhoods with convention centers, office buildings, parking lots, and other nonresidential units. During the postwar period every large city had a skid row with from 5,000 to 10,000 homeless people.

Urban newcomers also encountered patterns of racial discrimination supported by government policy. Through "restrictive covenants," white property owners and real estate agents adopted legal agreements to avoid selling or renting dwellings to minorities. "If a neighborhood is to retain stability," advised one federal guideline, "it is necessary that properties shall continue to be occupied by the same social and racial classes." In a practice known as redlining, the Federal Housing Authority (FHA) denied insurance coverage to racially integrated housing projects and discouraged loans to residents of older, racially mixed neighborhoods.

In 1948 the Supreme Court responded to a lawsuit, sponsored by the National Association for the Advancement of Colored People (NAACP)—*Shelley v. Kraemer*—by ruling that restrictive covenants were illegal. However, residential segregation persisted and affected African Americans and other minorities. Levittown, for example, did not accept African Americans until 1960. Of the nearly 1 million Puerto Ricans residing in New York City in 1960, 40 percent lived in inadequate dwellings, yet rent absorbed as much as one-third of their incomes. In higher income brackets, residential segregation affected such groups as Jews, Chinese Americans, and Japanese Americans, who tended to cluster in homogeneous communities.

City dwellers also found that the suburbanization of middle-class taxpayers shrank the urban tax base and curtailed municipal services. Because of the increased use of automobiles, mass transit deteriorated for want of passengers. In cities such as Los Angeles, St. Louis, Philadelphia, and Salt Lake City, municipal officials accepted bribes from General Motors to replace inexpensive electric trolley cars with the company's gas-consuming buses. The resulting traffic congestion could not be eased even by the construction of new freeways in most major cities.

African Americans in southern states faced far harsher conditions than their northern counterparts. Under the 1896 *Plessy* doctrine of "separate but equal," seventeen states required segregated public school facilities in 1951. Southern boards of education typically spent twice as much to teach white children as black children, and whites were four times as likely as blacks to finish high school. During the postwar era, civil rights groups led by NAACP

Earl Warren *(1891–1974)*

Of his eight years in the White House, President Eisenhower later said that the nomination of Earl Warren as Chief Justice of the Supreme Court in 1953 was "the biggest damnfool decision I ever made." Warren produced a number of constitutional surprises for the Republican White

House. In making the choice, Eisenhower had fulfilled a political debt. As the three-term governor of California, Warren represented the liberal wing of the Republican Party. He had run for vice president (with Thomas Dewey) in 1948 and remained an important "dark horse" candidate four years later.

Warren's political background had offered few clues to his subsequent career. As a California district attorney and state attorney general, he earned a reputation as a tough law enforcement officer. During World War II he advocated the confinement of all Japanese Americans regardless of their political beliefs. His position reflected an undisguised racism that viewed "Orientals" as essentially unassimilable. Elected governor in 1942, Warren supported liberal legislation in such areas as health insurance and prison reform.

Warren's appointment to the Supreme Court led to dramatic reversals of legal precedent. In his first major decision, *Brown v. Board of*

lawyer Thurgood Marshall initiated legal suits to end academic discrimination. Benefiting from postwar criticism of racism, Marshall won legal victories against segregated law schools and graduate schools by arguing that the alternative black institutions were unequal in quality to white schools. Emboldened by these legal victories, the NAACP attacked public school segregation by denying that educational systems could be racially separate and still equal.

Using psychological evidence to argue that "prejudice and segregation have definitely detrimental effects on the personality development of the Negro child," Marshall persuaded the Supreme Court to reconsider the *Plessy* doctrine. In a historic ruling delivered in May 1954 in *Brown v. Board of Education of Topeka*, the Supreme Court declared that segregating children "because of their race generates a feeling of inferiority . . . that may affect their

Education (1954), the Chief Justice dismantled the doctrine of "separate but equal" and paved the way for fundamental changes in race relations. Eight years later he carried the principle of democracy further by mandating the reapportionment of all legislative districts according to the principle of one person, one vote in *Baker v. Carr.* As in the *Brown* ruling, the decision attacked traditional political structures—in this case, state legislatures—that had enabled rural interests to ignore numeric majorities.

The California jurist also emerged as a strong defender of individual civil liberties. In the *Yates* decision (1957), he concurred in reversing the conviction of leading communists by differentiating between the theory of subversion and its actual practice. This position led to the eventual overthrow of certain loyalty oaths and state laws against communists. Under the principle of due process of law, he defended the rights of criminals to legal counsel (*Escobedo,* 1964) and to fair treatment by police (*Miranda,* 1966). The Warren-led court tightened the interpretation of obscenity to protect the rights of free speech and freedom of the press from censorship. In 1962 the Court supported a rigid separation of church and state by denying prayer and Bible reading in public schools. Such opinions earned Warren the hatred of right-wing groups such as the John Birch Society, which called for his impeachment and stimulated the rise of populist conservatism after the 1960s.

hearts and minds in a way unlikely ever to be undone." In public education, the Court concluded, "'separate, but equal' has no place. Separate educational facilities are inherently unequal."

THE BIRTH OF A NEW CIVIL RIGHTS MOVEMENT

The *Brown* ruling landed like a bombshell on the political scene, forcing complacent politicians to rethink the goals of U.S. education and heralding a new era of civil rights protest. African Americans and southern whites alike perceived a new political force emerging to topple the old social order based on race and discrimination. Black leaders such as Thurgood Marshall believed that by attacking race prejudice in schools, the youngest Americans would learn the lesson that discrimination was undemocratic; other segregated institutions would soon disappear. The Council of Negro Education placed the ruling in the context of the Cold War against totalitarian communism. "We hail the decision, because it dramatically distinguishes our way of life in a democracy . . . Here in the United States great social wrongs can be and are righted without bloodshed and without revolutionary means."

While African Americans and liberals expected the end of racial segregation in all aspects of social life, however, conservatives warned about the dangers of rapid upheaval. Responding to concern about implementing the *Brown* decision, the Supreme Court issued a second decree in 1955 ordering compliance with desegregation not immediately but "with all deliberate speed" and gave the responsibility for desegregation to federal district courts, which were dominated by traditional segregationist judges. The ruling opened a broad loophole for local defiance. "You are not required to obey any court which passes out such a ruling," advised Mississippi Senator James Eastland. "In fact, you are obligated to defy it." Some southerners opposed any alteration of traditional race relations; others resented the expansion of federal power over states' rights. Either way, segregationists endorsed "massive resistance" to public school integration.

As southern leaders defended segregation, African Americans took the initiative by organizing a grassroots civil rights movement that changed the face of U.S. life. The crusade began on a public transit bus in Montgomery, Alabama, in December 1955, when Rosa Parks, a local NAACP worker, refused to obey a law requiring segregated seating. Overnight, her arrest produced a carefully orchestrated citywide bus boycott led by Baptist minister Martin Luther King Jr. "We have known humiliation, we have known abusive language, we have been plunged into the abyss of oppression," King declared from the pulpit of the Dexter Avenue Baptist Church. "And we decided to rise up only with the weapon of protest. It is one of the greatest glories of America that we have the right to protest." The year-long boycott unified the African American community, but the Supreme Court had to intervene before municipal officials accepted bus desegregation. Montgomery showed the power of organized black protest and inaugurated the mass actions of the civil rights movement.

As African Americans adopted direct action protests against racial discrimination, southern resistance increased. State legislatures passed new laws making voter registration more difficult, harassed civil rights organizations (the NAACP was outlawed in several states), and sanctioned police violations of legal rights. Whites also created local citizens councils, which implemented economic reprisals against blacks who attempted to exercise their rights to vote or register their children in integrated schools. The rejuvenated Ku Klux Klan responded with acts of violence and a rash of bombings that targeted integrated schools, black churches, and Jewish synagogues. In 1955, fourteen-year-old

Emmett Till, a Chicago youth visiting relatives in Mississippi, was murdered for whistling at a white woman. The acquittal of his accused killers showed that local law enforcement had failed. But the Eisenhower administration refused to intervene.

Affirming this policy of massive resistance, 101 defiant southern congressmen issued a "Declaration of Constitutional Principles" in 1956 that denied the power of the federal government to order desegregation in the states. Eisenhower, who personally opposed the *Brown* ruling, declared, "The final battle against intolerance is to be fought—not in the chambers of any legislature—but in the hearts of men." The president firmly rebuffed suggestions that he take a stand supporting the desegregation of public schools. But in response to appeals from Harlem Congressman Adam Clayton Powell, the White House ordered the desegregation of employment in southern navy yards and worked quietly to desegregate public facilities such as movie theaters in the District of Columbia. In 1956 Attorney General Herbert Brownell proposed legislation to protect African Americans' voting rights, but the measure died in a southern-controlled committee in the Senate. In the absence of clear support from the federal government, violence and coercion reduced the number of registered black voters in some southern states.

"Give us the ballot," declared Martin Luther King, "and we will no longer have to worry the federal government about our basic rights." On the third anniversary of the *Brown* ruling in 1957, African American leaders organized a Prayer Pilgrimage to Washington that attracted 30,000 protesters against racial discrimination. That year Eisenhower again requested legislation to protect the right to vote. This time the proposal won support from Senate Majority Leader Lyndon Johnson, who sought to broaden his national political appeal. Working behind the scenes, Johnson persuaded southern leaders to drop the filibuster in exchange for a mild bill. The new law called for a weak Civil Rights Commission and authorized the attorney general to seek injunctions for violations of voting rights. The measure was the first civil rights legislation since Reconstruction. However, in 1960 only 25 percent of eligible African Americans could exercise the right to vote.

Direct action by blacks soon forced the president to support desegregation. In September 1957 Governor Orval Faubus of Arkansas mobilized the National Guard to prevent the integration of Central High School in Little Rock, an action that violated a federal court order. While armed soldiers prevented nine black students from attending the school, Eisenhower remained aloof. Yet Faubus's defiance of federal authority threatened the constitutional system of government, and national protests aroused Eisenhower to action. "Law cannot be flaunted with impunity by any individual or mob of extremists," he conceded. The president then federalized the National Guard and ordered paratroopers to enforce the court decision. Despite continuing mob violence, black

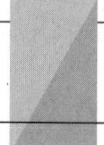

Richard B. Russell Jr. *(1897–1971)*

One of the great barons of the U.S. Senate at mid-century was Richard Russell. Styled as the "boy wonder" of Georgia politics, he was elected governor in 1930 at the age of thirty-three. Two years later he won a seat in the Senate, where he remained for the rest of his life. A bachelor who

had spartan habits, Russell devoted himself completely to the Senate, and over the years as his seniority and his shrewdness grew, he became one of its most powerful members. Always mindful of details, he read every line of the *Congressional Record* daily and was an acknowledged master of parliamentary maneuver. Although he rejected an opportunity to become majority leader in 1953, Russell functioned as "dean of the Senate establishment," presiding over the informal inner club that largely dominated its affairs.

Russell's career illustrated both the power and the frustration of ambitious southern politicians in an era of segregation. The systematic disenfranchisement of blacks, poor whites, and city dwellers produced a political system that generally did not challenge entrenched leadership.

students began attending the school under federal military protection. Faubus managed to close the school the next year, but a court order ended Little Rock school segregation in 1959. Elsewhere in the South, school desegregation continued to provoke violence. By 1960 less than 1 percent of African American children attended integrated schools in southern states. In the North the Supreme Court decision did not address de facto segregation.

Despite southern white resistance, black activists kept the issue of segregation alive. In 1957 black religious leaders, including Martin Luther King, formed a coalition group, the Southern Christian Leadership Conference (SCLC). Committed to nonviolent civil disobedience, the group emphasized the spiritual righteousness of the cause and endeavored to touch the conscience of whites. A new generation of African Americans educated after World War II

Once elected, members of Congress could expect a long tenure. Consequently, Russell, like many other southerners, steadily accumulated great power in a legislative branch that stressed seniority of membership. When the system assured them chairs of major committees, they could channel federal dollars to their constituents. An advocate of military preparedness almost from his earliest days in Congress, Russell became chair of the Senate Armed Services Committee in 1951. By 1960, Georgia had some fifteen military installations employing 40,000 people and was home to the major defense contractor Lockheed Aircraft.

Although the southern political system was an important element in Russell's power, it ultimately thwarted his broader ambitions by making him unacceptable to a national Democratic constituency. He tried to move the party away from reforms that would threaten states' rights by seeking the presidential nomination in 1952, but he was resoundingly defeated. A disappointed man, Russell increasingly devoted his energy and talents to opposing civil rights legislation. If the integrationists "overwhelm us," he declared, "you will find me in the last ditch." Tragically, both for his region and his own career, too much of Russell's talent and energy went into a misguided defense of what he considered to be "the Southern way of life."

rejected compromise with racial injustice and demanded the full rights of citizens. Many were encouraged by the emergence of the new nations of black Africa in the late 1950s, which inspired hopes of freedom at home.

"All of Africa will be free," exclaimed novelist James Baldwin, "before we can get a lousy cup of coffee." Such anger and frustration provoked a series of disciplined nonviolent sit-in protests by African American college students at the lunch counters of Greensboro, North Carolina, in February 1960. The idea spread like wildfire through the southern states. Instead of waiting for legislative or judicial sanction, young blacks simply violated segregation laws and went to jail. These actions won support among white liberals, who joined African Americans in a national crusade for civil rights. During the next decade, these protests would alter forever the nation's political and cultural landscape.

CRITICIZING MASS CULTURE

The emergence of the black civil rights movement demonstrated deep cracks within the national consensus. But even middle-class beneficiaries of corporate capitalism raised questions about the moral tone and social values of postwar society. Although most agreed that U.S. business could provide superior economic satisfaction, many questioned the poverty of the nation's spiritual life. "The religion that actually prevails among Americans today has lost much of its authentic . . . content," observed Will Herberg, author of the popular *Protestant Catholic Jew* (1956).

The blandness of spirituality reflected a larger problem of alienation. "When white-collar people get jobs," cautioned sociologist C. Wright Mills in *White Collar* (1951), "they sell not only their time and energy but their personalities as well." Similar warnings came from such works as David Riesman's *The Lonely Crowd* (1950), Herbert Marcuse's *Eros and Civilization* (1955), and William Whyte's *The Organization Man* (1957). These books attacked the prevalence of social conformity, the decline in individual initiative, and the obsession with security in business and private life.

While critics of U.S. conformity lamented the loss of older male values of danger, risk, and virility, more and more middle-class women rejected the ideals of domesticity that endeavored to separate women from the male world of work. Despite the postwar baby boom, women curtailed childbearing at a relatively young age (slightly above thirty), leaving many years for active careers. Indeed, during the 1950s middle-class women—particularly married women with school-age children—entered the workforce in unprecedented numbers. Their private decisions added up to a mass movement of women's employment that would become a typical pattern in the next decade. Meanwhile, individual women decried the price of idealizing domesticity. The young poet Sylvia Plath put it succinctly by describing herself as living inside a "bell jar" of conformity.

Alternative voices also emerged in art, music, and comedy. Although the public preferred the representational painting of Thomas Hart Benton, Grant Wood, and Grandma Moses, a new group, abstract expressionists, turned New York City into an international center of nonrepresentational action painting. Jackson Pollock, Willem de Kooning, and Mark Rothko painted with vigorous line and color that compelled viewers to find meaning in the work on their own. Abstract painters also celebrated traditional national subjects, but suggested that surfaces could be deceiving. Larry Rivers's blurry, tongue-in-cheek version of *Washington Crossing the Delaware* (1953), for example, or Jasper Johns's numerous depictions of the American flag hinted at unease with patriotic subjects. In music, teenagers danced to rock and roll while their parents worked and shopped to Muzak. The bebop sound of Charlie Parker and Dizzy Gillespie brought new vitality to jazz by offering hard-driving rhythms and complex, non-linear harmonies. Nightclubs featured a new breed of "sick" comedians—Mort Sahl, Lenny Bruce, Dick Gregory—who derided social convention.

The strongest voices of protest came from a group of poets and writers who congregated in New York and San Francisco—the Beats. Jack Kerouac, William Burroughs, Lawrence Ferlinghetti, and Gary Snyder condemned the alienating effects of bureaucratic culture and called for a new spiritualism that would merge the body and the spirit. The Beats emphasized the spoken word and celebrated the human voice as an alternative to mass media. Most eloquent was poet Allen Ginsberg. In *Howl,* read aloud in 1955 and published the next year, he indicted a sterile society that watched "the best minds of my generation destroyed by madness." Strong, rolling cadences condemned "scholars of war" with their "demonic industries" and "monstrous bombs." Ginsberg pleaded with America to "end the human war." Here, in the cultural underground, lay the roots of protest and transcendence that would puncture middle-class illusions of stability and security in the 1960s.

THE END OF AN ERA

The emergence of dissident voices, the reawakening of the civil rights movement, the appearance of a youth culture, the shock of *Sputnik,* an economic recession in 1958, and the continuing Cold War with the Soviet Union—all fed a growing frustration with Eisenhower and the Republican leadership. In 1958 Democrats achieved landslide election victories and shifted the congressional leadership in a liberal direction. Since they now controlled the House by seventy votes and the Senate by thirty, the Democrats rejected the president's fiscal austerity and promptly voted to increase the military budget. Congress also admitted Alaska and Hawaii into the union in 1959 but carefully reversed the administration's priorities by welcoming the Democratic Alaska first. For the first time since 1925 the Senate rejected a White House cabinet nominee, Lewis Strauss, Eisenhower's choice to head the Department of Commerce, because of political disagreements. Despite these disputes, however, the administration worked with Congress to enact the National Defense Education Act of 1958 and the Landrum-Griffin labor law.

EXHIBIT **3-5**   **U.S. NATIONAL DEFENSE AND VETERANS OUTLAYS, 1955–1960 (IN BILLIONS OF DOLLARS)**

1955	47.4
1960	53.5

Source: *Statistical Abstract of the United States* (1987).

Lenny Bruce (1926–1966)

Lenny Bruce, a stand-up nightclub performer, emerged as the most controversial comedian of the postwar era. Using a jazz soloist's style, Bruce blended plain street talk with Yiddish and black idiom to satirize and demystify social conventions. His most scathing routines focused on reli-

gious hypocrisy, the artificiality of traditional sexual relationships, and racial prejudice. Because of his brutal honesty, the established media labeled Bruce and his colleague Mort Sahl "sick" comedians. "I'm not a comedian," Bruce retorted. "And I'm not sick. The world is sick and I'm the doctor. I'm a surgeon with a scalpel for false values. I don't have an act. I just talk." Even the title of his autobiography— *How to Talk Dirty and Influence People*— made fun of the popular homilies for success.

Born Leonard Schneider in New York, he joined the navy at the age of sixteen and saw active service in the Mediterranean. After the war Bruce hustled as a con-artist for phony charities before drifting into comedy work in sleazy nightclubs and dance halls. But, by the mid-1950s, his brand of comedy captured national attention. He appeared on network television, made popular records, and captivated audiences at top nightclubs across the country.

Bruce's comic routines illuminated the anxieties and unspoken assumptions of postwar society. Although middle-class ethnic groups embraced homogenized suburban values (including, as in Bruce's case, the

After the death of Secretary of State Dulles in 1959, Eisenhower engaged more openly in personal diplomacy. In 1958 he sent Nixon on a goodwill tour of Latin America, but hostile crowds vigorously protested U.S. economic and political exploitation. The administration dismissed these demonstrations as examples of communist propaganda. Democrats disagreed. "It is foolish . . . to attribute anti-Americanism just to Communist agitation," explained Adlai Stevenson after a trip to Latin America in 1960. Rather, the Eisenhower administration "has been basically concerned with making Latin America safe

changing of ethnic names), the comedian's sketches reaffirmed the vitality of ethnic, religious, and racial identity. While middle-class media celebrated traditional monogamous marriage despite a soaring divorce rate, Bruce spoke about alternative, premarital, extramarital, and homosexual relationships. He attacked middle-class consumption patterns, raged against bureaucracy and organized religion, and noted the absurdity of a Christian country waging endless war.

"All my humor is based on destruction and despair," he admitted. "If the whole world were tranquil, without disease and violence, I'd be standing on the breadline right in back of J. Edgar Hoover and . . . Dr. Jonas Salk." Bruce's insistence on creative freedom led him to attack legal censorship of free speech. "What's wrong with appealing to the prurient interest?" he wanted to know. "We appeal to the killing interest." His use of explicit language brought police reprisals, and he endured a series of arrests and court trials in several cities on charges of obscenity. He was also accused of using illegal drugs. The endless litigation drained his energy, and the subject of legal harassment came to dominate his nightclub act. "The halls of justice," quipped Bruce. "That's the only place you see the justice . . . in the halls."

As police departments worked with municipal courts to silence the irreverent comedian, Bruce died of a heroin overdose. His obscenity conviction, however, was overturned posthumously. Bruce's quarrel with censorship and his ability to merge humor about sex, race, and politics foreshadowed the radical and counterculture sensibilities that would impact U.S society after his death.

for American business, not for democracy," especially by supporting "hated dictators."

Attention soon focused on Cuba. After backing dictator Fulgencio Batista since 1952, Eisenhower reacted cautiously to the revolutionary government established by Fidel Castro in 1959. Although the United States offered Castro economic aid, the administration opposed Castro's agrarian reform laws because they nationalized private U.S. holdings. Eisenhower cut aid to Cuba and demanded immediate compensation. As relations between the two nations worsened in 1960, Castro announced the sale of sugar to the Soviet Union in exchange for economic and military assistance.

Eisenhower responded with a two-pronged attack. In 1960 the president ordered the CIA "to organize the training of Cuban exiles mainly in Guatemala against a possible future day when they might return to their homeland." Meanwhile, the president exerted economic pressure by decreasing purchases of Cuban sugar. Castro protested that the reduction in U.S. sugar imports was a prelude to an invasion, and Soviet leader Khrushchev announced that his country would protect the Cuban government. Frustrated by Castro's audacity, Eisenhower severed diplomatic relations with Cuba in January 1961 and left the problem for his successor.

Eisenhower attempted nonetheless to reduce conflict with the Soviet Union. Since his "atoms for peace" proposal of 1953, the president had emphasized inspection and control as a precondition for disarmament. In 1956 he had sneered at Stevenson's call for a halt in nuclear testing, but a diplomatic conference among scientists in Geneva in 1958 indicated that controls could be implemented. Domestic science advisors also warned Eisenhower that strontium 90, an element of radioactive fallout from atomic testing, was threatening to poison the nation's food chain. Consequently, the president announced in 1958 that the United States was ending further nuclear testing. The Soviet Union performed a final series of tests before it too halted such explosions.

Despite these accommodations, Eisenhower vigorously resisted Khrushchev's demands that Allied forces depart from Berlin. "Any sign of Western weakness at this forward position," he declared in 1958, "could be misinterpreted with grievous consequences." Both powers now spoke about World War III, but in the next year tensions abated when Khrushchev and Eisenhower agreed to engage in personal diplomacy. In 1959 the Soviet leader toured the United States and met amicably with the president at Camp David. Although substantive issues remained unresolved, the two powers were close to agreement about nuclear arms.

The loss of a U-2 airplane destroyed those hopes. In May 1960, on the eve of a summit conference to discuss arms control, Khrushchev announced that the Soviet Union had shot down a U.S. spy plane. The administration immediately denied the charge and claimed that a "weather plane" had merely strayed off course. To Eisenhower's embarrassment, Khrushchev produced the CIA pilot, Francis Gary Powers, which revealed the president's lie. While the whole world watched anxiously, the State Department acknowledged the U-2 mission and justified such flights with the open-skies reasoning that the Soviets had rejected in 1955.

Eisenhower still hoped to salvage the summit conference. By claiming ignorance of the U-2 program, the president attempted to avoid complicity in the spy flight. Yet Eisenhower's disavowal of knowledge of the mission implied that subordinates were controlling crucial foreign policy decisions. The situation threatened the president's credibility as a political leader. Reluctantly, Eisenhower acknowledged his involvement. "It is a distasteful but vital necessity," he declared, reminding the public of the lessons of Pearl Harbor. Eisenhower's admission destroyed the summit meeting. At the Paris session, Khrushchev denounced the president and refused to negotiate.

The intensification of the Cold War had a profound effect on public opinion. Democratic politicians criticized the president's clumsy diplomacy. More fundamentally, the U-2 affair shocked the public by revealing the government's dishonesty. Eisenhower, who strove to rise above parties, had lied not only to Khrushchev but to his own citizens. The notion of a credibility gap between the people and their government would haunt politicians for the next two decades. Together with the new voices of dissidence and the larger frustrations of corporate capitalism, some Americans would demand fresh answers to abiding social issues.

InfoTrac College Edition

Using Keywords, enter the following search terms:

Ho Chi Minh
Montgomery Bus Boycott
Cuban Revolution
John Kenneth Galbraith
Southeast Asia Treaty Organization
Sputnik
Martin Luther King Jr.

Recommended Reading

Stephen E. Ambrose, *Eisenhower* (1984). The second volume of a large biography of the president, this study provides a thorough and sympathetic account of administration policies at home and abroad.

Taylor Branch, *Parting the Waters: America in the King Years, 1954–1963* (1988). This detailed narrative of the civil rights crusade places the protest movement in historical context and underscores the great human effort involved in seeking change.

Jessica Weiss, *To Have and To Hold: Marriage, the Baby Boom, and Social Change* (2000). Placing marriage and family patterns of the 1950s in a longer historical perspective, this study stresses the innovative roles of postwar women in pursuing careers.

Daniel Belgrad, *The Culture of Spontaneity: Improvisation and the Arts in Postwar America* (1998). This book explores new styles of expression in art, poetry, music, and dance as a response to the values of corporate conformity.

Additional Reading

Eisenhower's response to the Vietnam crisis is described in James R. Arnold, *The First Domino: Eisenhower, the Military, and America's Intervention in Vietnam* (1991); in Melanie Billings-Yun, *Decision Against War: Eisenhower and Dien Bien Phu, 1954* (1988); and in the relevant chapters of Lloyd Gardner, *Approaching Vietnam* (1990). For China and the offshore islands issue, see Gordon H. Chang, *Friends and Enemies* (1990). The origin of the space race is analyzed in Walter A. McDougall, *The Heavens and the Earth: A Political History of the Space Age* (1985), as well as in Robert A. Divine, *Sputnik Challenge* (1993). For the disarmament question, see Robert A. Divine, *Blowing on the Wind: The Nuclear Test Ban Debate, 1954–1960* (1978). African American views about international affairs are discussed in Brenda Gayle Plummer, *Rising Wind: Black Americans and U.S. Foreign Affairs, 1935–1960* (1996).

For surveys of the postwar civil rights movement, see Harvard Sitkoff, *The Struggle for Black Equality: 1954–1980* (1981), and Manning Marable, *Race, Reform, and Rebellion: The Second Reconstruction in Black America, 1945–1982* (1991). The legal struggle to end racial discrimination is brilliantly described in Richard Kluger, *Simple Justice: The History of Brown v. Board of Education and Black America's Struggle for Equality* (1976). Also valuable are the first four volumes of *The Papers of Martin Luther King, Jr.*, edited by Clayborne Carson (1992–1999). An excellent study of the relationship between sports and race can be found in Jules Tygiel, *Baseball's Great Experiment: Jackie Robinson and His Legacy* (1983).

African American voting is treated in two books by Steven F. Lawson: *Black Ballots: Voting Rights in the South, 1944–1969* (1976) and *Running for Freedom: Civil Rights and Black Politics in America Since 1941* (1991). Federal jurisdiction is analyzed in Michael R. Belknap's *Federal Law and Southern Order: Racial Violence and Constitutional Conflict in the Post Brown South* (1987). Other studies include William Chafe, *Civilities and Civil Rights: Greensboro, North Carolina, and the Black Struggle for Freedom* (1980); Robert F. Burk, *The Eisenhower Administration and Black Civil Rights* (1980); and Juan Williams, *Eyes on the Prize: America's Civil Rights Years, 1954–1965* (1987). For an excellent single-state study, see John Dittmer, *Local People: The Struggle for Civil Rights in Mississippi* (1994). For the origins of the Southern Christian Leadership Conference, see Adam Fairclough, *To Redeem the Soul of America: The Southern Christian Leadership Conference and Martin Luther King, Jr.* (1987). Changes in southern society are described in Pete Daniel, *Lost Revolutions: The South in the 1950s* (2000); see also Jack Bass and Walter DeVries, *The Transformation of Southern Politics: Social Change and Political Consequence Since 1945* (1976).

For the Warren Court, see the relevant chapters of Paul L. Murphy, *The Constitution in Crisis Times: 1918–1969* (1972), and two fine biographies: G. Edward White, *Earl Warren: A Public Life* (1982), and Bernard Schwartz, *Super Chief: Earl Warren and His Supreme Court: A Judicial Biography* (1983).

Government policy toward Native Americans is described in Donald L. Fixico, *Termination and Relocation: Federal Indian Policy, 1945–1960* (1986); in Vine Deloria Jr., *Custer Died for Your Sins: An Indian Manifesto* (1969); and in the relevant chapters of Richard Drinnon, *Keeper of Concentration Camps: Dillon S. Myer and American Racism* (1987). The emergence of homosexual communities is well treated in John D'Emilio, *Sexual Politics, Sexual Communities: The Making of a Homosexual Minority in the United States, 1940–1970* (1983) and in Marc Stein, *City of Sisterly and Brotherly Loves: Lesbian and Gay Philadelphia, 1945-1972* (2000). See also Stephanie Coontz, *The Way We Never Were: American Families and the Nostalgia Trap* (1992).

The problems of youth are described in James Gilbert, *A Cycle of Outrage: America's Reaction to the Juvenile Delinquent in the 1950s* (1986). For the history of early rock and roll, see James M. Salem, *The Late Great Johnny Ace and the Transition from R&B to Rock'n'Roll* (1999); Charlie Gillett, *The Sound of the City: The Rise of Rock and Roll* (1983); and Nelson George, *The Death of Rhythm and Blues* (1988). An examination of TV's impact on postwar society can be found in Lynn Spigel, *Make Room for TV: Television and the Family Ideal in Postwar America* (1992). Erik Barnouw's *The Image Empire* (1970) describes the television industry. Also interesting is Jeff Kisseloff's *The Box: An Oral History of Television, 1920–1961* (1995). For the movies, see Peter Biskind, *Seeing Is Believing: How Hollywood Taught Us to Stop Worrying and Love the Fifties* (1983) and Thomas Doherty, *Teenagers and Teenpics: The Juvenilization of American Movies in the 1950s* (1988). James Gunn's *Alternative Worlds: The Illustrated History of Science Fiction* (1975) surveys the genre. For the bebop revolt and social attitudes of black musicians, see the relevant chapters of Ben Sidran, *Black Talk* (1981). The fine arts are the subject of two excellent books: Serge Guilbaut, *How New York Stole the Idea of Modern Art: Abstract Expressionism, Freedom, and the Cold War* (1983) and Sidra Stich, *Made in USA: An Americanization in Modern Art, the '50s and '60s* (1987).

For a survey of dissident intellectuals, see Andrew Jamison and Ron Eyerman, *Seeds of the Sixties* (1994). Postwar novels and novelists are discussed in Josephine Hendin's, *Vulnerable People: A View of American Fiction Since 1945* (1978). For the Beat writers, see Lawrence Lipton, *The Holy Barbarians* (1959); John Tytell, *Naked Angels* (1976); Dennis McNally, *Desolate Angels* (1979); and Michael Davidson, *The San Francisco Renaissance: Poetics and Community at Mid-Century* (1989).

THE AGE OF LIBERAL ACTIVISM, 1960–1965

"Somehow the wind is beginning to change," wrote liberal historian Arthur M. Schlesinger Jr. in the first month of 1960. "People—not everyone by a long way, but enough to disturb the prevailing mood—seem to seek a renewal of conviction, a new sense of national purpose." Writing in *Esquire* magazine, Schlesinger proposed a liberal agenda that ranged from education reform to equal rights for minorities, from more foreign aid to improved weapons. "Thus," he predicted, "the Sixties will probably be spirited, articulate, inventive, incoherent, turbulent, with energy shooting off wildly in all directions. Above all, there will be a sense of motion, of leadership and of hope."

Few historians have been so prophetic. Indeed, the 1960s introduced a new era of liberal activism. Rejecting Dwight Eisenhower's belief in limited government, Democratic Presidents John F. Kennedy and Lyndon B. Johnson advocated an active federal government to achieve economic and social progress. As African Americans and other minorities pleaded for political equality, liberal programs brought greater government benefits to disadvantaged groups. Such policies improved the rights and roles of minorities, but also accentuated conflicts between competing interests.

Kennedy and Johnson also pursued an assertive Cold War foreign policy that intensified global conflicts. Accepting the notion of a monolithic international communist conspiracy aimed at overthrowing capitalist democracies, the Democratic administrations focused attention not only on the Soviet menace but also on the status of smaller countries in the so-called third world. Prepared to defend such nations from communist infiltration, Washington boldly intervened overseas in Cuba and Southeast Asia. But in the new climate of the 1960s, such policies also provoked criticism and opposition at home, triggering a militant antiwar movement. By the end of the decade, the Cold War consensus had been replaced by bitter strife about the proper use of U.S. power at home and abroad.

THE ELECTION OF 1960

"The American people are tired of the drift in our national course," said Massachusetts Senator John Kennedy in launching his run for the presidency in 1960. For eight years Eisenhower had extolled the warrior virtues of strength and power. Yet the grandfatherly Ike, then the oldest man to serve as president, seemed helpless against Soviet Premier Nikita Khrushchev's indignation, the eruption of liberation movements in Asia and Africa, and anti–U.S. protests in Latin America and Japan. At home, voters blamed the administration for the recession of 1957–1958. "Wind up the Eisenhower doll," ran a popular joke, "and it does nothing for eight years."

Kennedy, at forty-two, was youthful in appearance (and concealing serious chronic illnesses), and he symbolized strength, vigor, and energy. In the Senate, he attacked the administration for creating a "missile gap" between Soviet and U.S. arsenals. "This is not a call of despair," he stated. "It is a call for action."

Kennedy's ambition benefited from great personal wealth, but his Roman Catholic religion remained a major handicap. Only one Catholic, Al Smith, had run for president, and he had suffered a devastating defeat in 1928. Kennedy challenged religious prejudices directly, entering a series of primaries against his major rival, Minnesota Senator Hubert H. Humphrey. Kennedy won their first contest in Wisconsin, but voting analysis showed that he carried Catholic districts, whereas Humphrey attracted Protestants. The race moved to West Virginia, an impoverished state with a 95 percent Protestant population. Humphrey shamelessly used the theme song, "Give Me That Old-Time Religion." Kennedy responded with an expensive campaign that emphasized his commitment to New Deal liberalism. A decisive victory over Humphrey overcame the issue of religion, and Kennedy went on to win a first-ballot nomination for the presidency. To balance the Democratic ticket in the South, he chose as his running mate Senate Majority Leader Lyndon Johnson of Texas.

Kennedy's Catholicism remained a controversial issue in the campaign against Vice President Richard M. Nixon. "I am not a Catholic candidate," Kennedy insisted. "I am the Democratic Party's candidate, . . . who happens also to be a Catholic." Vowing to maintain the separation of church and state, the nominee expressed disbelief that 40 million citizens "lost their chance of being president on the day they were baptized." Although since 1945 white ethnics had been accepted in many educational, business, and social organizations, religious prejudices still influenced political behavior. In the election, Kennedy won a high proportion of Catholic supporters but lost among Protestants. One exception was Kennedy's appeal to black evangelical Protestants. When civil rights activist Martin Luther King Jr. was sentenced to prison for trespassing in a segregated restaurant in Georgia, a much-publicized telephone call from Kennedy to King's family revealed the candidate's genuine compassion as well as his astute political calculation. By appealing both to African Americans and white ethnics, Kennedy restored the New Deal coalition, but subsequent voting analysis suggested that the issue of religion probably cost him more votes than it won for him.

Religion seemed important in 1960 because the differences between Kennedy and Nixon remained small. Four nationally televised debates, which attracted more than 100 million viewers, spotlighted their similarities. Both candidates were cold warriors who vowed to end communist expansion and disagreed only about whether to defend the islands between mainland China and Taiwan. Both stressed the importance of economic growth. Both used the phrase "new frontiers" to evoke a spirit of opportunity and expansion. "Mr. Nixon says, 'We never had it so good,'" Kennedy stated in a typical remark. "I say we can do better."

Despite these common assumptions, television illuminated not the candidates' words but their manner of presentation. Radio listeners, who were not distracted by visual appearances, reacted favorably to Nixon's speeches, but the television cameras accentuated the vice president's shadowy face and dripping makeup. In contrast, Kennedy projected self-confidence. Polls indicated that the debates may have swayed 4 million voters, three-quarters of whom supported Kennedy.

Such intangible factors had immense significance because the balloting was extremely close. Kennedy's popular majority was only 118,000—a margin of one-tenth of 1 percent. The electoral college vote was 303–219, but these

John F. Kennedy responds to opponent Richard M. Nixon at their televised debate during the 1960 presidential contest.

EXHIBIT **4-1**   **THE ELECTION OF 1960**

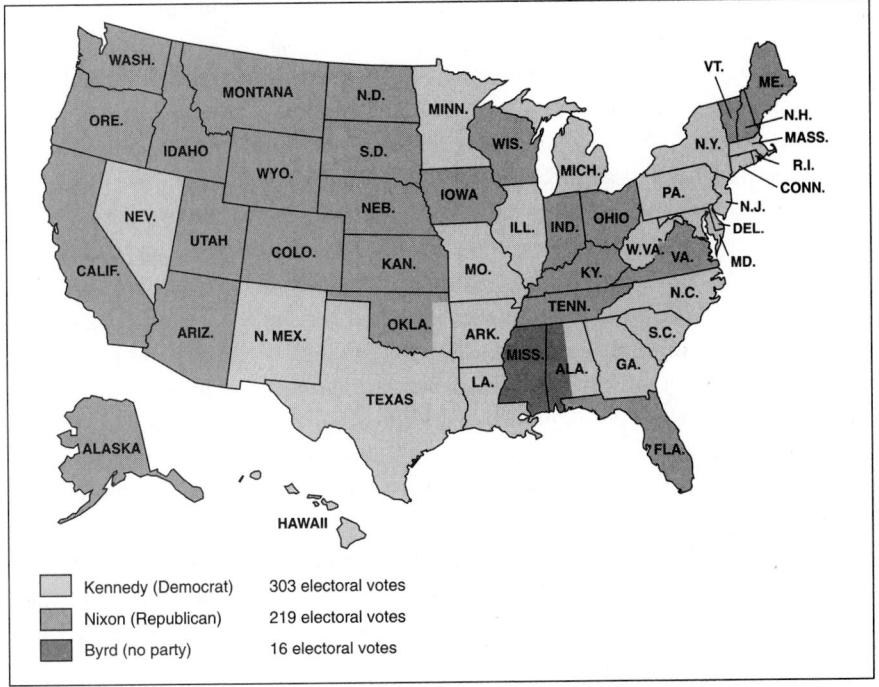

	Kennedy (Democrat)	303 electoral votes
	Nixon (Republican)	219 electoral votes
	Byrd (no party)	16 electoral votes

figures concealed paper-thin majorities and probable fraud in such key states as Illinois and Texas. Kennedy also trailed behind Democratic congressional candidates. Although the Democrats held control of both houses of Congress, most of the sixty-three new legislators subsequently voted against the White House on important issues. Because southern Democrats frequently aligned with Republicans, Kennedy lacked a working majority in Congress.

LAUNCHING THE NEW FRONTIER

Kennedy labeled his program the "New Frontier." "Let the word go forth that the torch has been passed to a new generation of Americans," he declared. With his slender majority, Kennedy's inaugural speech avoided domestic topics and focused exclusively on the international peril. Indeed, he exaggerated the Soviet threat. Although Khrushchev had recently advocated wars of national liberation, the Soviet leader was addressing criticism from his more radical Chinese ally rather than the United States. To Kennedy, however, Khrushchev's speech had brought the nation to "its hour of maximum danger," and he stressed the "burden" of "relentless struggle." Said Kennedy:

"Ask not what your country can do for you—ask what you can do for your country," but despite his dynamic language, he lacked a political base to initiate bold policy departures.

Kennedy's leadership reflected the era's distrust of emotionalism and ideology and extolled the virtues of scientific management and cold reason. "Most of the problems . . . that we now face are technical problems, are administrative problems," he said in 1962. "They are very sophisticated judgments which do not lend themselves to the great sort of 'passionate movements' which have stirred this country so often in the past." Matters of foreign policy, the president suggested, "are so sophisticated and so technical that people who are not intimately involved week after week, month after month, reach judgments which are based on emotion rather than knowledge of the real alternatives."

Secretary of Defense Robert S. McNamara typified the liberal leadership. Taking charge of the Pentagon, the former head of the Ford Motor Company initiated a program of rigorous cost-benefit accounting to determine military priorities. In place of Eisenhower's "massive retaliation," the new administration preferred flexibility, conventional arms for "brushfire" wars, and the elite Special Forces (Green Berets) for guerrilla warfare. Unlike Eisenhower, Kennedy rejected the use of nuclear weapons outside the strategic struggle with the Soviet Union. However, he did demand additional nuclear missiles even after learning that no "missile gap" existed. Within a month of the inauguration, the White House requested funds for missiles, warheads, and electronic support systems such as computer databases and orbiting communications and spy satellites. This emphasis on technological developments in turn encouraged a managerial revolution within the Pentagon. Under McNamara, the Defense Department centralized research and development and created a Defense Intelligence Agency to coordinate information.

Enthusiasm for technical management flourished in the space program. Five months after taking office, Kennedy used the continuing rivalry with the Soviets to call for a human landing on the moon by the end of the decade. "No single space project," he said, "will be more impressive to mankind." Vice President Johnson, author of the 1958 legislation that established the National Aeronautics and Space Administration (NASA), now served as chair of the National Aeronautics and Space Council and shared Kennedy's zeal. To Secretary McNamara, the space program promised to compensate the aerospace industry for cuts in military contracting demanded by cost-benefit analysis. Concerned about winning support from big business, Kennedy and Johnson endorsed private ownership of a communications satellite corporation and worked vigorously to overcome a 1962 Senate filibuster led by Tennessee's Estes Kefauver to block this federally supported private monopoly.

A carefully orchestrated public relations program reinforced popular support for space exploration. The media portrayed the first astronauts as all-American pioneers and heralded John Glenn's 1962 flight around earth as a

Cold War victory. As NASA planned Project Mercury (the circumnavigation of Earth by single astronauts, 1962); Project Gemini (multimanned flights, rendezvous in space, and spacewalks, 1964–1965); and Project Apollo (moon landing, 1969), the space budget leaped fivefold by 1964 and accounted for 78 percent of all U.S. research and development. Although the White House emphasized the prestige of space exploration, expenditures served essential military functions involving ballistic missiles, communications, and intelligence gathering. For national security reasons, this aspect of the space program remained secret. Moreover, although the Outer Space Treaty, signed by sixty-two nations in 1967, would prohibit nuclear weapons in space and declare the moon a demilitarized zone, the defense strategy of both superpowers depended on continuing military operations in space.

THE POLITICS OF ECONOMIC GROWTH

As Kennedy took office in 1961, a Gallup poll found that 42 percent of the public hoped the president would pursue moderate policies; 24 percent hoped he would be conservative; and 23 percent desired a liberal position. This middle-of-the-road climate reinforced the cautious congressional leadership. Despite growing public concern about poverty, especially after the publication of Michael Harrington's influential book, *The Other America* in 1962, Congress thwarted social reform. Although legislators responded favorably to Kennedy's request in 1961 for an Area Development Agency to stimulate industrial development in economically depressed areas such as Appalachia, Congress never provided sufficient funds to implement the program of road construction or encourage business relocation. By 1963 the entire state of West Virginia had gained only 350 jobs. Similarly, public housing legislation in 1961 permitted the razing of slums but failed to mandate adequate replacements. By 1967 some 400,000 buildings had been demolished, which resulted in more than 1.4 million displaced residents. Kennedy lacked enough political support even to introduce legislation providing hospital insurance for the elderly.

During the presidential campaign, Kennedy promised to produce a 5 percent annual rate of economic growth. This goal seemed especially relevant because the unemployment rate was 7.7 percent in January 1961. White House economic advisors, particularly the liberal Walter Heller, urged more vigorous federal spending. However, except for military appropriations, the president declined to request additional programs. Instead, Kennedy proposed a tax credit to encourage business investment in new plant equipment. By stimulating capital investment, he believed the measure would simultaneously attack unemployment and stimulate long-term growth. To compensate for the loss of tax revenue, Kennedy requested the elimination of corporate tax loopholes such as expense accounts and tax-exempt foreign income. But

John H. Glenn, Jr. *(1921–   )*

"We have stressed the team effort in Project Mercury," said the nation's newest hero three days after becoming the first American to circumnavigate the Earth from outer space on February 20, 1962. "It goes across the board . . . sort of a crosscut of Americana, of industry and military

and civil service, government workers, contractors—a crosscut of American effort in the technical field." At this moment of awesome technological achievement, however, astronaut John Glenn also symbolized the vitality of traditional earthbound virtues: love of family, religion, and patriotism.

Born and raised in small-town Ohio in the 1920s and 1930s, Glenn left home to become a Marine aviator during World War II and remained in the military as a combat flyer in

Korea and later as a test pilot of jet aircraft. In 1957 he set the coast-to-coast speed record in a plane that required three midair refuelings with high-flying tankers. Such technical proficiency and iron-willed self-discipline qualified Glenn to become one of the seven original astronauts.

Glenn deliberately blended his enthusiasm for modern technology with old-fashioned "Manifest Destiny." "I take my religion very seriously," the Presbyterian stated at the first Project Mercury press conference in 1959. "We are placed here with certain talents and capabilities. . . . I think we would be most remiss in our duty if we didn't make the full use of our

these reforms adversely affected influential corporate leaders, and Congress delayed action until 1962. Meanwhile, large military expenditures boosted the sagging economy.

Concern about recession was soon supplanted by fear of inflation. In 1962 the president's Council of Economic Advisers announced wage-price "guideposts" to discourage inflationary increases. However, corporate leaders resisted efforts to regulate business costs and profits. The disagreement climaxed in a major clash between the White House and the nation's largest industry—steel—in 1962. When the U.S. Steel company led other producers in increasing prices 3.5 percent, an amount the administration considered inflationary,

talents in volunteering for something . . . as important as this is to our country and to the world in general right now."

Framed by the Cold War with the Soviet Union, the "space race" pitted free-enterprise capitalism against state-supported technological planning. The U.S. astronauts were the human side of the competition. To the public's dismay, however, the nation appeared to be running second. Soviet cosmonaut Yuri Gagarin circumnavigated the globe in April 1961, a month before Project Mercury's first suborbital flight. Thus, despite serious technological malfunctions aboard Glenn's *Friendship 7* capsule, the mission restored national confidence in the space program. "This is the new ocean," declared Kennedy moments after Glenn splashed down in the Atlantic, "and I believe the United States must sail on it and be . . . second to none."

The public spontaneously embraced the sunny-faced astronaut. "I still get a hard-to-define feeling inside when the flag goes by," Glenn told a joint session of Congress, which interrupted his patriotic remarks twenty-five times with applause. Four million people—equivalent to half the population of New York City—lined the streets of lower Manhattan to form the largest ticker-tape parade crowd in history. During the next year Glenn received more than half a million letters of encouragement from around the country, was named Father of the Year, and was saluted for his patriotism by the Daughters of the American Revolution. Treated as a prophet of the space age, Glenn set his eyes on a Senate seat from Ohio, which he eventually won in 1974.

the president responded by using the government's economic power to force the industry to retreat. McNamara instructed the Department of Defense to purchase steel only from noninflationary companies, and Attorney General Robert F. Kennedy ordered investigations of price-fixing. These pressures led one company to reject the price increase, a retreat that spread throughout the industry. Kennedy had effectively defended his economic strategy.

Although lower steel prices reduced costs for other manufacturers, business leaders bitterly resented this show of government economic power. A slumping stock market intensified their anger. In May 1962 Wall Street prices reached their lowest point since the Crash of 1929. The downturn reflected the belated impact of the 1960–1961 recession, which had reduced corporate earnings. However, the president's stand on steel prices disheartened elements of the business community, which blamed the administration for the slump. Kennedy responded by emphasizing his support of business, and the administration moved quickly to support corporate prosperity. The Treasury Department liberalized depreciation allowances for business equipment, thereby encouraging the replacement of older machinery. Congress finally enacted the proposed tax credit for new investments as well as tax reforms that gave business specific benefits. Kennedy endorsed new legislation favorable to the drug industry and lobbied Congress to permit private control of space communications.

This commitment to business culminated in the president's support of foreign trade. Since the late 1950s the economy had suffered imbalances of foreign payments, largely because of heavy spending for military bases abroad. In 1961 Kennedy created a new position in the Pentagon to encourage sales of U.S. arms to foreign nations. By 1962 the White House persuaded Congress to pass a foreign trade expansion bill.

Departing from the tradition of strict balanced budgets, Kennedy also embraced the "new economics" of John Maynard Keynes, who advocated deficit spending to stimulate the economy. Taking the advice of Keynes's disciples on the Council of Economic Advisers, Kennedy came to accept the theory that a tax cut would increase consumer spending and increase the rate of economic growth. In 1963 the president submitted a bill calling for a $13.6 billion reduction in taxes, mostly on individual incomes, as well as reforms that would shift the tax burden to upper-income brackets. The move set the stage for unprecedented economic growth.

THE CIVIL RIGHTS CRISIS

Despite campaign promises to the black community, Kennedy dragged his feet on civil rights. Recognizing the power of southern Democrats, the White House appeased regional demands for patronage by awarding federal construction projects to southern states, raising price supports on cotton, and declining to introduce civil rights legislation. Instead, the president took moderate executive actions such as creating the Commission on Equal Employment Opportunity (CEEO) in 1961. Headed by Vice President Johnson, the CEEO sought to end employment discrimination in work done under government contract. However, the commission preferred voluntary compliance and seldom punished violators.

Although Kennedy claimed during the 1960 campaign that Eisenhower could eliminate federal support of segregated housing "with the stroke of a pen," the president became remarkably silent when that power passed into his own hands. Civil rights leaders began sending pens to the White House. Hoping to win congressional approval for a Department of Urban Affairs, Kennedy refused to challenge segregated housing. Only after Congress defeated his efforts in 1962 did the president act to end segregation in federally funded housing. More than previous presidents, however, Kennedy appointed African Americans to government positions and allowed them to work in areas other than race relations.

Kennedy showed a similar lack of interest in women's rights. Although the president personally accepted the sexual revolution, he never connected changing sexual values with issues of power. The "new woman," according to Helen Gurley Brown's 1962 best-seller, *Sex and the Single Girl*, "took the pill and lived in an apartment with a double bed. She spent money on herself and men spent attention on her. She was the old feminist ideal of the independent woman with a new twist—she was sexy." Rising female employment and the sexual revolution bolstered a growing sense of female autonomy. By 1960 nearly 40 percent of women more than sixteen years old held jobs outside the home. Yet women workers earned only three-fifths of what men received and seldom held political power.

Although the radical National Woman's Party continued to press for an equal rights amendment to the Constitution that would guarantee legal equality to both sexes, Kennedy, like his predecessors, listened primarily to the liberals in the government's Woman's Bureau who advocated economic gains without threatening the existing laws that provided specific protections for women workers. In 1962 he created the President's Commission on the Status of Women, charged with making policy recommendations. "Equality of rights . . . for all persons, male or female, is . . . basic to democracy," the commission reported in 1963. That year Congress passed the Equal Pay Act, which provided equal wages for "equal work." However, the law excluded numerous jobs and lacked enforcement provisions, and the traditional segregation of occupations by gender further eroded the concept of "equal work." Still, at a time when the proportion of women in the workforce continued to increase, the federal government had begun to address widespread economic inequalities.

Kennedy's limited support of equal rights reflected the values of liberal reformism. Believing that changes in social relations could not be forced on the nation, the White House intended to follow rather than lead public opinion. The president appointed few women to significant offices. So while issues of gender equality were largely ignored, problems of race moved to the forefront of the national agenda. Kennedy had hoped to limit government action on race issues to enforcement of the voting rights provisions of the Civil Rights Acts of 1957 and 1960. Yet his fear of white southern political power led him to appoint segregationist judges to federal courts in the South. One appointee openly referred to blacks as "niggers" and "chimpanzees."

African American activists resolved to move ahead of the White House to challenge legal segregation and force the federal government to protect equal rights. Following the nonviolent, direct action strategy of Martin Luther King and the sit-in demonstrators of 1960, the Congress of Racial Equality (CORE) embarked on interracial "freedom rides" in 1961 to desegregate interstate bus travel and commerce. As expected, violent mobs throughout the South viciously attacked the travelers, and local and state law enforcement authorities failed to provide minimal protection. The raw violence, coming on the eve of a summit meeting between Kennedy and Khrushchev, embarrassed the White House and compelled the federal government to intervene in areas of law enforcement that traditionally had been handled by the states. The president ordered federal marshals into the South and obtained court injunctions against interference with interstate travel. At the same time, however, the president's brother, Attorney General Robert Kennedy, asked the freedom riders for a "cooling-off period." "If we got any cooler," protested James Farmer, organizer of the freedom rides, "we'd be in a deep freeze." Meanwhile, the attorney general petitioned the Interstate Commerce Commission (ICC) to end segregation in interstate travel. Administration pressure led to the desired ICC ruling in 1961.

Thus, despite Kennedy's effort to remain aloof from the civil rights controversy, black activism and white intransigence demanded presidential intervention. In 1962 James Meredith, an African American air force veteran, won a federal court order to enter the all-white University of Mississippi. Governor Ross Barnett spoke for the southern leadership when he announced his refusal to comply with the ruling. Following Eisenhower's precedent of 1957, Kennedy federalized the National Guard and sent federal marshals and soldiers into the university town of Oxford. After a night of violence and bloodshed, Meredith gained entry into the university. However, Kennedy tried to avoid further antagonism of southern leaders by limiting federal interference to minimal legal protection and by refusing responsibility for local law enforcement.

While the White House sought to avoid racial confrontations, the Student Nonviolent Coordinating Committee (SNCC) proceeded with a voter registration campaign among disenfranchised blacks. This Voter Education Project, funded by northern liberal foundations but implemented primarily by courageous white and black students, soon provoked a violent reign of terror—beatings, bombings, and murders—to prevent the expansion of the African American electorate.

As in the case of the freedom rides, civil rights workers discovered that the federal government failed to provide adequate protection on the grounds that it lacked a statutory right to intervene. As liberals and activists protested White House inertia, the president introduced a civil rights bill in February 1963 that called for prosecution of voting rights violations, federal funds to encourage school desegregation, and extension of the Civil Rights Commission. "We are committed to achieving true equality of opportunity," said Kennedy, "because it is right."

African American leaders, however, wanted more fundamental changes and rejected Kennedy's modest proposal. In the spring of 1963 King's Southern Christian Leadership Conference (SCLC) carried the civil rights crusade to Birmingham, Alabama, purportedly "the most thoroughly segregated big city" in the nation. The movement's nonviolent strategy aimed at producing so much "creative tension" that segregationist leaders would feel compelled to negotiate a peaceful settlement. As noisy but peaceful marchers paraded downtown, local police chief "Bull" Connor ordered violent arrests that filled the jails. After weeks of futile demonstrations, civil rights leaders feared the crusade would fail for want of volunteers who could afford to be arrested and rearrested. African American leaders decided to find recruits among the city's youth, some as young as six years old. Birmingham police proceeded to attack the children with clubs, fire hoses, and vicious dogs. The brutality not only steeled the nerves of black protesters, but because of wide television coverage, it sent waves of outrage throughout the land.

Southern resistance flared again a few weeks later when Governor George Wallace stood in a doorway at the University of Alabama and tried to block the court-ordered admission of two black students. Federal marshals accompanying the students obliged the governor to step aside, but the ritualistic gesture of defiance encouraged President Kennedy to reaffirm his commitment to federal authority and civil rights. "We face . . . a moral crisis as a country and as a people," he told a television audience. "It cannot be met by repressive police action. It cannot be left to increased demonstrations in the streets." Kennedy's speech signaled the administration's determination to enact civil rights laws. But that night Mississippi's NAACP leader Medgar Evers was shot to death outside his home. Kennedy now introduced a broad new civil rights bill to prohibit racial discrimination in public accommodations, to authorize the Justice Department to initiate suits to desegregate public schools, to improve black employment opportunities, and to protect voting rights. Although African American leaders questioned loopholes in the proposal, few doubted the clarity of Kennedy's moral position.

As Congress began to consider the civil rights bill, black leaders staged a show of strength by organizing a March on Washington. The president initially discouraged the demonstration, but civil rights activists refused to retreat. On August 28, 1963, 250,000 marchers converged in the nation's capital and heard Martin Luther King Jr. proclaim, "I have a dream . . . that the sons of former slaves and the sons of former slave owners will be able to sit together at the table of brotherhood." King's passionate language electrified the crowd. However, other voices in Washington indicated differences within the African American community. John Lewis of SNCC attacked the administration for its "immoral compromises" with conservative politicians. "If any radical social, political, and economic changes are to take place in our society," he said, "the people, the masses must bring them about. . . . We must seek more than mere civil rights; we must work for the community of love, peace, and true brotherhood."

While liberals like Senator Hubert Humphrey lined up votes for the civil rights bill, southern representatives vowed to kill the measure by parliamentary procedures. But southern extremists spoke louder by detonating a bomb in a Birmingham church, killing four black girls. No local officials apologized for the violence. Such intransigence fed a counter-response from black nationalist Malcolm X, who had ridiculed the March on Washington. Recognizing the importance of achieving political power as a precondition for racial progress, Malcolm rejected the limited horizons of racial integration. "A revolutionary," he asserted in 1963, "is a black nationalist."

THE COLD WAR ON NEW FRONTIERS

In continuing the Cold War, Kennedy kept his eye on Moscow and Beijing, but the president also believed that the nations of Asia, Africa, and Latin America held the key to victory. To energize the nation's youth for that struggle, Kennedy created the Peace Corps in 1961, encouraging volunteers to serve "on a mission of freedom" around the world. Kennedy also launched a Food for Peace program to send surplus food to poor countries. By 1963 the plan was feeding 93 million people each day. Nor did Kennedy, unlike Eisenhower, insist that neutral nations take sides in the Cold War. In the former Belgian colony of the Congo, for example, the United States supported a United Nations peace mission to back a neutral government, although the White House allowed the CIA to provide secret payments and military aid to friendly Congolese politicians.

Kennedy also proposed "a new alliance for progress" in Latin America. Promising technical expertise and capital investment, the president envisioned major agrarian reform and public welfare within democratic institutions. In 1961 the administration pledged $20 billion to alleviate poverty and bring social reform. These funds boosted U.S. prestige, but Kennedy had no intention of altering Latin American politics. Instead, Washington continued to cooperate with conservative landed elites and their military allies.

American corporations also hesitated to invest in unstable countries. In 1962 Congress approved the Hickenlooper Amendment, which stopped foreign aid to countries that nationalized or excessively taxed corporate property. The next year the Foreign Assistance Act established an investment guaranty program that required recipients of U.S. aid to insure investors against losses due to nationalization. Most aid to Latin America went in the form of loans, rather than grants, and had to be repaid with interest and service charges (usually amounting to half the face value of the loan). And even these limited funds had to be spent within the United States at prevailing prices.

John F. Kennedy Library

The Executive Committee of the National Security Council deliberating during the Kennedy administration.

The Alliance for Progress aimed to blunt the appeal of Fidel Castro's revolutionary Cuba. During his last days in office, Eisenhower had broken diplomatic relations with Cuba and ordered the CIA to plan a military coup. As a presidential candidate, Kennedy endorsed the overthrow of Castro. Believing that Castro did not represent the Cuban people and could be toppled with sufficient pressure, Kennedy urged business leaders to boycott Cuba and banned the importation of Cuban sugar.

Anti-Castro activities culminated in a military invasion of Cuba at the Bay of Pigs in April 1961 by 1,400 Cuban exiles trained and organized by the CIA. But the CIA planned badly, choosing an indefensible landing position and mismanaging air attacks. Recognizing an imminent disaster, the White House refused to provide additional air support, which doomed the mission. Most seriously, the president had underestimated the strength of Castro's political base.

Although U.S. media had received unofficial leaks about the Bay of Pigs operation, the administration persuaded publications such as *The New York Times* to suppress the story. "There will not be, under any conditions, an intervention in Cuba," the president told a press conference five days before the mission. Secretary of State Dean Rusk lied blatantly: "The American people are entitled to know whether we are intervening in Cuba or intend to do so in the future," he said on the morning of the invasion. "The answer to that question is no. What happens in Cuba is for the Cuban people to decide." In justifying the invasion, Kennedy saw Castro as a pawn in the Cold War. "We are opposed around the world by a monolithic and ruthless conspiracy," he told the nation's leading news editors, "that relies primarily on covert means for expanding its sphere of influence." The president urged the news media to limit reporting of world events. "Every democracy," he claimed, "recognizes the necessary restraints of national security."

In the aftermath of the Bay of Pigs fiasco, Kennedy permitted the CIA to conduct illegal military activities against Castro, provided they were "plausibly deniable." The CIA proceeded to disrupt Cuban trade with the Soviet Union, in one case contaminating a shipload of sugar with bad-tasting chemicals. Secret CIA operations included support of anti-Castro exiles and underworld gangsters who attempted to assassinate the Cuban leader. Kennedy also exerted economic pressure by prohibiting trade with the island. Such destabilization efforts drew Castro closer to the Soviet Union.

Having failed in Cuba, however, Kennedy resolved to prove his strength on the issue of Germany. Although the Soviet Union wanted to formalize the existence of two German states— one linked to the communist bloc, the other to the West—and thereby force the Western Allies to leave Berlin, Washington demanded the unification of Germany through free elections (in which the larger population of West Germany would predominate). Soon after taking office, Kennedy asked Congress for increased military appropriations to build a preponderance of power that would force the Kremlin to accept U.S. terms. In this spirit he agreed to meet Khrushchev in Vienna in June 1961.

Kennedy underestimated Soviet resolve. In a blistering encounter, Khrushchev reminded the president that World War II had ended sixteen years earlier and demanded that the Western powers sign a final peace treaty that recognized the two German states and terminated the military occupation of Berlin. Kennedy refused to abandon Berlin. Instead of easing international tensions, the summit conference intensified the Cold War.

The president now asked Congress for another $3 billion military appropriation, which doubled the total military spending package in his first six months in office. Kennedy also called up military reserves and extended the draft. Finally, in a gesture that spread horror throughout the land, the president requested increased appropriations for civil defense and bomb shelters. Khrushchev then ordered the erection of a military barrier between East and West Berlin in August 1961, which ended the flood of refugees from East Germany and showed his determination to preserve two German states. Despite an extreme atmosphere of crisis, Kennedy resolved to test Soviet strategy by ordering 1,500 battle-ready troops to drive from West Germany into West Berlin, where they would be met by Vice President Johnson. Khrushchev decided not to worsen the situation. After U.S. troops entered West

Berlin, Khrushchev scrapped his deadline for settling the Berlin question, and the crisis passed.

The Cold War intensified that same month when the Soviet leader announced the resumption of nuclear bomb testing. Within a week, Kennedy declared that the United States would also resume underground testing. Two days later *Life* magazine published an article, endorsed by Kennedy, asserting (erroneously) that a national program of fallout shelters would ensure a 97 percent survival rate in the event of nuclear war. The news precipitated the first major protests against nuclear testing by peace organizations such as the National Committee for a Sane Nuclear Policy (SANE) and the Student Peace Union. As Soviet tests escalated to the 50-megaton level, the White House heightened tensions by revealing to Khrushchev that U.S. intelligence knew the extent of Soviet military weakness. The president proposed disarmament talks that would preserve the U.S. advantage. When the Soviets objected to international inspection, Kennedy ordered a resumption of atmospheric tests.

THE CUBAN MISSILE CRISIS

In admitting the nonexistence of a "missile gap," Kennedy increased Soviet concerns about the imbalance of power. The White House accentuated the problem by announcing a shift in nuclear strategy in 1962. Hereafter, U.S. missiles would be aimed not at Soviet cities but at nuclear missile sites. Such targets meant that a U.S. first strike could destroy Soviet power to retaliate. This disadvantage may have influenced Khrushchev's decision to place less expensive short-range missiles in Cuba. In the aftermath of sputnik, the United States had pursued a similar policy by establishing missile bases in Turkey and Italy. Khrushchev also wanted to discourage U.S. military action in Cuba.

During the summer of 1962, Soviet troops in Cuba began building sites to base missiles with a striking range of 2,000 miles, sufficient to reach East Coast cities or the Panama Canal. The Soviets had also placed nearly 100 nuclear warheads on the island—most attached to tactical rockets with a 15–20 mile range. The United States did not learn about the presence of the warheads until the 1990s, but when U-2 spy planes confirmed intelligence reports of the missiles, Kennedy summoned a top-level executive committee in October 1962 to consider U.S. responses. The choices ranged from immediate military attack (a "Pearl Harbor in reverse," objected Robert Kennedy) to a diplomatic retreat by closing U.S. missile bases in Turkey if the Soviets removed theirs from Cuba. A consensus eventually emerged that considered armed intervention only as a last resort. Kennedy also overruled his more militant advisers—the Joint Chiefs of Staff, National Security Adviser McGeorge Bundy, Secretary Rusk—and agreed to trade the removal of U.S. missiles in Turkey and Italy for Soviet missiles in Cuba. He did not reveal this concession to many in

EXHIBIT **4-2**   CUBAN MISSILE CRISIS

his administration nor to the public, lest he face criticism for "appeasement" of communism.

In a dramatic televised speech, Kennedy described Soviet intervention as "deliberately provocative" and demanded the removal of all missiles. "We will not prematurely or unnecessarily risk the cost of worldwide nuclear war in which the fruits of victory would be ashes in our mouth," he promised, "but neither will we shrink from that risk at any time it must be faced." As the world approached a nuclear holocaust, Kennedy announced the establishment of a "quarantine"—a naval blockade—to keep offensive weapons from Cuba.

Khrushchev had not anticipated Kennedy's outraged reaction. In a private letter to the president, the Soviet leader protested the demand for unconditional surrender. Yet Khrushchev did not want to start a war that "would not be in our power to stop." In a second, emotional letter, the Soviet leader emphasized that Soviet ships in the mid-Atlantic carried nonmilitary goods and that the missiles had already arrived in Cuba. He offered to remove the weapons provided that the United States end the blockade and agree to respect Cuban independence. "Only a madman," Khrushchev wrote, "can believe that armaments are the principal means in the life of a society."

The next day the president received still another message from Khrushchev that stiffened the terms for removal of the missiles. The Soviet leader now demanded the withdrawal of missiles from Turkey in exchange for withdrawal of those in Cuba. Months earlier, Kennedy had questioned the value of those outmoded weapons, but during the crisis, the White House publicly refused to discuss the question, fearing to suggest a wavering of national policy.

Kennedy decided to ignore Khrushchev's last letter and answer only the more conciliatory message that preceded it. The formal reply therefore made no mention of U.S. missiles in Europe (although Kennedy privately agreed to remove them from Turkey and Italy). Khrushchev then accepted the arrangement, and the crisis passed. Two months later, Kennedy admitted that the Cuban missiles would not have changed the military balance of power. "But it would have politically changed the balance of power," he explained. "It would have appeared to, and appearances contribute to reality." Although Khrushchev's retreat enhanced the president's reputation, the diplomatic victory obscured Washington's failure to change the government of Cuba. While Castro remained in power, the frustrated administration continued a secret program to assassinate the Cuban leader and overthrow the communist regime.

TOWARD DÉTENTE

The brush with nuclear war convinced both Kennedy and Khrushchev to seek an end to nuclear testing. At the same time, the international balance of power shifted dramatically when Soviet and Chinese leaders split over the issue of the future of world communism. The breakup of the Sino-Soviet alliance, although still incomplete, persuaded Moscow to seek accommodation with the West. One remaining stumbling block was Khrushchev's refusal to allow on-site inspections to verify compliance with a test ban treaty.

As the two superpowers resumed negotiations, Kennedy placed his faith in U.S. technology—satellite photographs and distant seismography. In a dramatic speech at American University in June 1963 the president introduced a major reevaluation of the Cold War. Explaining that the United States did not seek "a Pax Americana enforced . . . by American weapons of war," he assured the nation that "we can help make the world safe for diversity." Kennedy announced

Dr. Strangelove or: How I Learned to Stop Worrying and Love

Hollywood's version of the Cold War rested on two pillars of government authority: the Federal Bureau of Investigation for domestic spy films and the United States Air Force for war stories. The 1955 movie Strategic Air Command, *for instance, showed how SAC's vigilant pilots executed the nation's atomic–air defense strategy and served as the main deterrent to Soviet conquest. As the two nuclear powers expanded their arsenals and tested weapons that could annihilate human life, however, critics questioned whether atomic warfare could defend democratic principles or merely doom the entire world. Such fears prompted Stanley Kramer's* On the Beach *(1959), a wrenching movie that depicted the genocidal effects of nuclear confrontation.*

The Cuban missile crisis of October 1962 underscored the danger of starting a nuclear war. Indeed, President Kennedy's military advisors had considered such a strike against Cuba, and Premier Khrushchev had warned that only an "insane" person would allow such a calamity to occur. By then, filmmaker Stanley Kubrick had discovered Red Alert, *a 1958 novel by Peter George that described an air force general who orders a B-52 attack on the Soviet Union to eradicate the communist menace. Kubrick began to develop a movie that would depict a nuclear war "started by accident or madness."*

Since the Pentagon insisted that such a possibility was impossible, the military leadership refused to cooperate with the project. But as Kubrick proceeded to prepare a script that included an air force commander named General Jack D. Ripper who believes that the flouridation of drinking water was part of a "commie plot" to debilitate red-blooded soldiers, the madness of nuclear warfare assumed a crazy logic of its own. To preserve "the purity and essence of our natural fluids," Ripper orders a B-52 mission against Moscow. President Merkin Muffley promptly uses the newly installed hot line telephone to warn Premier Kissof of the impending tragedy and together the two make plans to shoot down the U.S. bombers. Assisting their efforts is Dr. Strangelove, a rehabilitated Nazi scientist who addresses the president as "mein Fuhrer."

Kubrick's satire thus targeted both the policy of nuclear deterrence and the military establishment that defended democratic principles, much as Joseph Heller's contemporary popular novel Catch 22 *(1961) had pilloried military bureaucracy. Audiences giggled hysterically when a battle scene occurs beneath an air force billboard that reads: "Peace Is Our Profession"; or when to*

the Bomb (1964)

Columbia Pictures/Archive Photos

save the world Group Captain Mandrake prepares to shoot a Coke machine to get change to make a telephone call only to be told by an officer "That's private property." Finally, the best technology cannot prevent a single plane from delivering its bomb, leading to a cascade of mushroom clouds and a nostalgic sound track promising "I'll be seeing you in all the old familiar places."

Strangelove appeared just months after the Senate ratified the atmospheric Test Ban Treaty, the first limit on nuclear proliferation. Social critic Lewis Mumford hailed the picture as "the first break" in the country's "cold war trance." Phyllis Schlafly, a Goldwater conservative who testified against ratification of the Test Ban Treaty, protested that such movies promoted "unilateral disarmament that leads to surrender to Communism." Others objected that the film was so funny it obscured Kubrick's warning about nuclear holocaust. In the end, U.S. policy remained committed to Mutual Assured Destruction (MAD), allowed arsenals to expand, and merely moved the testing underground.

he was sending a mission to Moscow to negotiate a test ban treaty, and in an act of "good faith" he ordered a halt on nuclear testing.

As questions of inspection and underground testing were set aside, negotiators quickly reached agreement. Yet the treaty required the approval of the Senate, the Pentagon, and public opinion. In seeking this support, the administration emphasized that the test ban constituted a victory because the United States held a clear lead in nuclear technology. Kennedy also assured the Pentagon that underground tests would continue, promises that were fulfilled after the Senate ratified the treaty in September 1963.

Although Kennedy expressed interest in improving relations with the Soviet Union and approved the sale of surplus U.S. wheat to Russia, he worried about a weakening of the Western Alliance. During the summer of 1963 the president journeyed to Europe and reaffirmed the impossibility of compromising with communism. "Today, in the world of freedom," he told a cheering throng in West Berlin, "the proudest boast is 'Ich bin ein Berliner.'" ("I am a Berliner.") Kennedy never wavered from his Cold War stance. In his last, undelivered speech, the president defined his sense of his historic mission: "We in this country, in this generation, are, by destiny rather than choice, the watchmen on the walls of world freedom."

COMMITMENTS IN VIETNAM

In seeking greater flexibility in the Cold War, Kennedy argued in 1961 that "the great battlefield for the defense and expansion of freedom today is the whole southern half of the globe—Asia, Latin America, Africa, and the Middle East—the lands of the rising peoples." Here the president saw communism "nibbling away" at the forces of freedom. Having been humiliated at the Bay of Pigs and having agreed in Vienna to a neutral Laos, Kennedy resolved to act decisively in Vietnam. Kennedy thus followed Eisenhower's policies, continued to reject the 1954 Geneva Accords, and refused to consider a neutral Vietnam state.

By 1961 the U.S.–backed regime of Ngo Dinh Diem was rapidly losing support to the newly established communist National Liberation Front (known as the Vietcong) as well as to noncommunist dissidents such as Buddhist priests. Kennedy responded to this pressure by increasing the number of military advisors and dispatching Green Berets and intelligence agents to engage in covert warfare in 1961. Although presidential advisors recommended additional military assistance, Kennedy hesitated to commit conventional forces and risk a repetition of the Korean War. The White House also urged Diem to offer political reforms to broaden support among Buddhists and the peasantry, but without success.

With increased U.S. military aid, the level of violence increased. In 1962 the Vietcong indicated a willingness to negotiate the neutralization of South

Vietnam, but the White House remained optimistic about military victory and rebuffed the approach. Meanwhile, U.S. advisors persuaded Diem to experiment with counterinsurgency based on "strategic hamlets." Assuming that guerrilla armies required a popular base of support, advisors proposed the encampment of the peasant population behind barbed wire. Depriving the Vietcong of their support base would cause them to disappear. However, the hamlets could not be defended, and the peasants resented being forcibly uprooted.

"Every quantitative measurement we have," declared McNamara with his faith in numbers, "shows we're winning this war." The State Department confirmed this optimism, announcing that 30,000 Vietcong were killed in 1962. Yet that figure was twice as large as the estimated size of the entire Vietcong organization at the beginning of the year. Exaggerated administration claims stemmed not only from poor calculations but also from a deliberate effort to deceive Congress and the nation about the nature of the U.S. commitment. When *The New York Times's* Saigon reporter David Halberstam reported failures of U.S. policy, Kennedy personally asked the newspaper to reassign him elsewhere.

By 1963 the Vietcong was stepping up terrorist attacks against the Diem regime. Yet Diem refused to institute political reforms. Tensions exploded in 1963 when South Vietnamese troops fired on a crowd of demonstrators and Buddhist priests set themselves on fire to protest political abuses. These events embarrassed the administration, but Kennedy took refuge in the domino theory. "For us to withdraw from that effort," he said, "would mean a collapse not only of South Vietnam, but Southeast Asia. So we are going to stay there." But the administration began to plan a military coup to remove Diem from power. On November 2, 1963, South Vietnamese army officers, encouraged by the U.S. embassy, killed their president.

The murder shocked Kennedy but did not alter his Vietnam policy. By November 1963 the administration had stationed 16,000 troops in South Vietnam. The previous month Kennedy had announced the withdrawal of 1,000 men by the end of the year and said that the U.S. commitment would end in 1965. His words probably reflected the same misplaced optimism that characterized U.S. policy toward Vietnam throughout the decade. Recently declassified audiotapes suggest that Kennedy still believed a military victory was possible. Perhaps, with Diem dead, the president would have considered a political solution to the war, just as he proposed a political response to the Cuban missile crisis. The remaining evidence provides no perfect answer.

ASSASSINATION AND THE YOUTH MOVEMENT

Kennedy did not live to fulfill his programs. On a political junket to Texas designed to strengthen the Democrats in the 1964 elections, the president was shot and killed by sniper fire in Dallas on November 22, 1963. The alleged assailant, Lee Harvey Oswald, denied his guilt but was killed in police custody by mobster Jack Ruby before he could testify. The mystery surrounding Kennedy's death contributed to the political turmoil of the decade. Although a special presidential commission headed by Chief Justice Earl Warren reported in 1964 that Oswald was a "loner" and had acted alone, the public widely believed the murder was part of a conspiracy. A 1966 Gallup poll found that a majority doubted the validity of the Warren report although a majority also opposed reopening the case.

The assassination shocked the nation—not only because of the sudden death of the president but also because of the disruption of the normal continuity of public life. To most citizens the events surrounding the assassination emerged as a shared emotional experience. Surveys found that 92 percent of the public learned of the assassination within two hours and that more than half of the entire population watched the same television coverage of the story. (For three days, the networks canceled all advertising!) Millions watched Jack Ruby shoot Oswald. The mass public mourning greatly magnified the slain president's stature. Local governments named and renamed public buildings in his honor; Kennedy's grave at Arlington National Cemetery became a national shrine; Kennedy memorabilia (picture books, coins, paintings, and jewelry) proliferated. Ironically, Kennedy created in death what had eluded him in life—a broad affirmation of consensus that transcended the differences of traditional politics.

The emotional intensity of the Kennedy assassination coincided with the coming of age of the first baby boomers (the cohort born just after World War II). Twice as numerous as their parents, teenagers formed a distinctive, self-conscious culture whose sheer numbers exerted tremendous economic and political power. Having grown up in the prosperous 1950s, the rising generation accepted affluence and consumption as expressions of its uniqueness. As children, baby boomers created an enormous market for diaper services, toys, and toddlers' shoes; as teenagers, the same generation consumed vast quantities of records, costume jewelry, and apparel. Purchasing power set the stage for the youth rebellion of the 1960s.

Nothing better expressed the teenagers' quest for personal independence than rock and roll. Just months after the Kennedy assassination in 1964, the British Beatles launched their first U.S. tour and instantly became icons of antiestablishment feelings. During the 1960s teenagers and college students crowded dance floors that reverberated to the rhythms of the "Motown sound," a hard-driving "soul" music named for the black Detroit record company that produced it. Black performers such as Ray Charles, James Brown, Otis Redding, Aretha Franklin, the Supremes, and the Temptations offered the new generation an alternative to sexually repressed music. Meanwhile, the arrival of British fashions such as long hair, miniskirts, and working-class blue jeans encouraged liberation of the body and a new confidence in defying social decorum.

The idea of choosing one's "lifestyle" reflected a changing morality associated with the "sexual revolution." Even before the introduction of the birth control pill in 1960, couples were engaging more frequently in nonmarital intercourse. The trend accelerated and received more attention during the 1960s. Surveys showed that the age of first sexual experience continued to decline and that the frequency of sexual intercourse within all social classes increased. Easier attitudes toward sexuality also led to a rise in unwanted pregnancies and an average of half a million illegal abortions each year.

The sexual revolution also undermined traditional definitions of obscenity and pornography. In a series of landmark cases in the late 1950s, the Supreme Court outlawed censorship of such literary classics as *Fanny Hill*, D. H. Lawrence's *Lady Chatterly's Lover*, and Henry Miller's *Tropic of Cancer*. By the mid-1960s Hollywood had replaced its 1930s production code with a rating system that permitted nudity and obscene language as well as "mature" themes. Traditional morality and censorship persisted on television, but commercial advertising increasingly introduced sexual themes and suggestive comments. Images of women, for example, shifted from dutiful housewives to sexually seductive singles.

The sheer number of baby boomers precipitated a large assault on adult institutions. As a result of economic prosperity and the service industry's demands for extended education, college enrollment doubled to 10 million in the 1960s. Increasingly independent college youth no longer accepted control of their private lives by student deans, who customarily had used curfews, sexual segregation, and threats of expulsion to dictate social behavior. During the 1960s most campuses abolished the doctrine of *in loco parentis* ("in place of parents"), which treated students as children rather than young adults. Students won the right to live in coeducational dormitories, to have opposite-sex visitors, and to stay out at night. This freedom of personal expression extended to campus political rights, including the publication of uncensored newspapers and magazines, the recruitment of political support, and public demonstrations.

Drugs became one of the most controversial routes to youth independence. Although earlier generations had consumed alcohol to defy adult morality, teenagers and college students increasingly used marijuana as a rite of initiation into youth culture. Harvard University psychologists Timothy Leary and Richard Alpert experimented with the government-provided hallucinogen LSD ("acid") and discovered states of "expanded" consciousness that approached religious ecstasy. When the university fired them for unprofessional conduct in 1963, Leary assumed the role of LSD "guru," advising a generation of students to "turn on, tune in, and drop out."

The cultural rebellion of middle-class youth paralleled an emerging political movement among a smaller segment of college students known as the

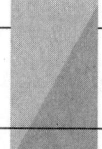

Bob Dylan (1941–   )

Bob Dylan's intense musical style and provocative songs made him a major catalyst and symbol of the cultural crisis of the 1960s. Dylan first captured national attention by merging blues and country music with the left-wing political content of the urban folk music scene. Then in

1965 he abruptly adopted the raucous sounds and electrified motifs of rock and roll, which he combined with surreal images and poetic phrasing to attack prevailing middle-class values and institutions.

Born Robert Zimmerman and raised in a small town on Minnesota's Iron Range in the 1950s, the young musician identified with the alienation expressed by actor James Dean and, like the Beat writers, concocted fantasies of escape. In 1960 he changed his name to Dylan and took off for New York in search of his hero, folksinger Woody Guthrie, troubadour for radical causes since the 1930s.

Dylan began singing in folk clubs in Greenwich Village, responding to the events and themes of the sixties. His 1962 song, "Blowin' in the Wind," denounced the complacence of middle-class society and quickly became an anthem of liberal dissent. He wrote many songs in support of the civil rights movement ("Oxford Town," "Who Killed Davey Moore?") and performed at the March on Washington in 1963. The Cuban missile

"New Left." Student-led civil rights activity in the South had ignited radical dissent across the country. After the sit-ins of 1960, veteran activist Ella Baker helped young African Americans organize the Student Nonviolent Coordinating Committee (SNCC), which combined a Christian social ethic with a commitment to participatory democracy. The courageous attacks on segregation by SNCC leaders such as John Lewis, Diana Nash, and Robert Moses inspired many liberal white students to engage in political struggle. Equally important was the young generation's despair at the continuing Cold War. Campus radicals organized Students for a Democratic Society (SDS) in 1962, issuing a manifesto called the Port Huron Statement, drafted by University of Michigan activist Tom Hayden. "We may be the last generation in the experiment with

crisis inspired "A Hard Rain's Gonna Fall." "Every line of it is actually the start of a whole song," he said, "but when I wrote it, I thought I wouldn't have enough time alive to write all those songs so I put all I could into this one."

Dylan's political faith eroded further after the Kennedy assassination. When given the Tom Paine Award in December 1963 by the Emergency Civil Liberties Committee at a swank New York hotel, he saw only the "mink and jewels." "It took me a long time to get young," he told the liberal audience, ". . . and I'm proud of it." For Dylan, the immense success of the Beatles's U.S. tour in 1964 suggested a way to reach the mass audience he had always sought. He began to perform with rock musicians and electrified his guitar to add a pulsating beat to his lyrical style. The result was 1965's "Like a Rolling Stone," Dylan's first major hit. With this success, he liberated political music from the enclaves of folk and brought lyrical protest into the cultural mainstream.

During the 1960s Dylan's gravelly voice resonated with the discontent of the youth movement. His lyrics became more metaphoric and symbolic; their juxtaposition of familiar Americana and surreal imagery suggested the absurdity and harsh hypocrisy of contemporary life. At the peak of his success in 1966 Dylan nearly died in a motorcycle crash, and he retreated from public view. When he returned two years later, he began to experiment with country music and gospel. Yet he would always be associated with the modern folk and rock music that he helped pioneer.

living," SDS announced. Attacking a complacent acceptance of poverty, racism, and militarism, the student New Left called for participatory democracy to overcome the alienation caused by bureaucratic decision making.

The first massive student protest erupted at the University of California at Berkeley in 1964 when administrators banned political recruiting on campus. Borrowing tactics from the civil rights struggle, the ensuing Free Speech Movement (FSM) organized a sit-in at which 800 students submitted to arrest. "There's a time when the operation of the machine becomes so odious," declared FSM leader Mario Savio, "that you can't take part . . . and you've got to put your bodies upon the gears . . . and you've got to make it stop." Otherwise, FSM warned, education merely prepared students to take their places

EXHIBIT **4-3   GROSS NATIONAL PRODUCT, 1960–1964**
(IN ROUNDED BILLIONS OF DOLLARS)

1960	515
1962	575
1964	650

Source: *Economic Report of the President* (1988).

in an oppressive corporate order. "You can't trust anybody over thirty," FSM activist Jack Weinberg taunted. A generation once courted by President Kennedy had now set its own agenda.

BUILDING THE GREAT SOCIETY

Five days after Kennedy was killed, President Lyndon Johnson stood before a joint session of Congress and pleaded earnestly, "Let us continue." Determined to preserve the liberal agenda, the new president now called for a "Great Society" to end poverty and racial injustice. Taking advantage of the public grief, he pushed legislation that Kennedy had initiated but failed to pass through Congress. By early 1964 Johnson had signed major laws involving economic development, social welfare, and civil rights. Ironically, this success diminished Johnson's appeal. Whereas Kennedy had appeared quick, witty, and inspired, Johnson emerged as a consummate politician, immensely experienced and skilled in political affairs but never quite reliable or sincere. The tall Texan was notorious for bullying subordinates and ignoring political criticism. Failing to charm the public, Johnson eventually personified the duplicity of government and widened the "credibility gap" between the presidency and the people.

In his first legislative triumph, Johnson persuaded Congress to pass Kennedy's tax reform program. The Revenue Act of 1964 affirmed the principle of deficit spending and stimulated a 7 percent boost in the gross national product (GNP) during its first year. To all appearances, government management had created unique economic expansion. The new tax laws encouraged productivity while reducing unemployment and inflation and brought prosperity for U.S. corporations. Profits jumped 57 percent between 1960 and 1964 as innovative technology, including pneumatic conveyors, copying machines, piggyback freight, and containerized shipping, increased efficiency and profits. Military and space contracts, particularly in the "Sunbelt" states of the South and Southwest, stimulated prosperity and corporate consolidation. By the end of the decade, 71 percent of manufacturing profits went to the nation's 400 largest firms.

In the reformist climate of the 1960s, however, the scope of corporate enterprise became an issue of public policy. In 1962 biologist Rachel Carson's best-selling book, *Silent Spring*, depicted the poisonous effects of environmental pollution and urged regulation of hazardous chemicals. Other critics charged that the interaction between private business and government threatened public interests and that personnel shifted too easily between corporate management and federal regulatory boards that set industry standards. Few government officials attempted to remedy the situation or protect consumer interests. But a private lawyer named Ralph Nader emerged as a consumer advocate. After his book *Unsafe at Any Speed* (1965) exposed the hazards of General Motors' Corvair, Senate hearings revealed that the world's largest corporation had investigated Nader's personal life in an effort to discredit his findings. Nader used a resulting jury award to start research centers to monitor the quality of consumer products as well as to investigate tax inequities, mine safety, radiation hazards, and pollution.

Prosperity both reflected and encouraged U.S. enterprise abroad. During the 1960s investment in western Europe doubled, and the total value of U.S.–owned overseas plants and equipment surpassed $100 billion. While U.S. firms exported $35 billion in goods each year, foreign subsidiaries of multinational businesses sold another $45 billion in goods. By the end of the decade the United States controlled nearly three-quarters of the world's oil and produced most of its machinery, electronics, and chemicals.

Amid prosperity, however, income distribution remained lopsided. The wealthiest fifth of U.S. families received more than 45 percent of the nation's personal income, whereas the poorest fifth earned 3.7 percent. Tax loopholes accentuated the problem. Tax-exempt bonds, a refuge for wealthy investors, amounted to nearly $86 billion in 1963. More than 150 persons with incomes exceeding $200,000 paid no taxes. Corporations benefited from similar loopholes. The percent of federal revenues derived from corporate income taxes decreased from 20 percent in 1955 to 12 percent in 1970. Yet nearly one-quarter of all U.S. citizens still lived in poverty.

Concerned about such inequities, Johnson vowed to wage an "unconditional war on poverty." Raised in the tradition of southern populism and having been a congressional New Dealer, Johnson believed that medical care, education, job training, and racial equality could complete the New Deal. Indeed, the ensuing legislative accomplishment dazzled the country, and the media compared Johnson's mastery of Congress to the achievement of the first hundred days of Roosevelt's New Deal of 1933.

The Economic Opportunity Act of 1964 created the Office of Economic Opportunity (OEO), launched training programs for the young, and offered loans and grants for self-help projects initiated by local communities. The bill's Community Action Program bypassed traditional leadership and called for a "participatory democracy" of the poor in shaping government-funded projects. The law mandated a Job Corps for youth and Volunteers in Service to America (VISTA), which assigned volunteers to assist needy communities. The OEO also introduced the Head Start program to provide preschool aid to children of the poor.

By the end of 1964 Congress had enacted most of Johnson's social welfare program, including $1 billion in housing legislation, federal grants for mass transportation, loans for college students, and aid for college construction. The president also expanded a food stamp program for the working poor. The Great Society thus promised to alleviate economic misery and social injustice for previously ignored citizens. The Kennedy administration had initiated some of these programs, but Johnson had greatly enlarged the agenda and his legislative skill translated liberal intentions into public policy.

EXPANDING CIVIL RIGHTS

Johnson's political genius also ensured passage of new civil rights laws. Although Kennedy had lined up support for his proposal in 1963, southern senators expected to weaken its provisions. Kennedy's death abruptly changed the political climate. "No memorial or eulogy," Johnson told a stunned joint session of Congress five days after Kennedy's death, "could more eloquently honor Kennedy's memory than the earliest possible passage of the Civil Rights Bill for which he fought so long." Linking the new measure to the martyred president, Johnson refused to compromise on its major provisions. With the support of northern Republicans, two-thirds of the Senate voted to end a southern filibuster—the first time the Senate halted such obstruction of a civil rights measure.

The Civil Rights Act of 1964 gave the federal government the power to sue to desegregate public accommodations and schools. The law also prohibited denial of equal job opportunities in all but the smallest businesses and unions and created the Equal Employment Opportunity Commission (EEOC) to sue for compliance. To be illegal, however, racial imbalances in employment had to be the result of deliberate intent, and the law prohibited the use of quotas or preferential treatment to accomplish racial balance. African Americans and liberals nonetheless celebrated this landmark step toward equal opportunity. But conservatives such as Arizona Senator Barry Goldwater attacked the law's extension of federal power. Die-hard southern segregationists such as Alabama's George Wallace detected a communist conspiracy at work.

Passage of the Civil Rights Act also opened an unexpected area for social change. During the debate in Congress, the National Woman's Party protested that prohibition of discrimination because of "race, color, religion, or national origin" had omitted the word "sex." Virginia Democrat Howard Smith, an opponent of the entire bill, then introduced an amendment adding the missing category. Although some suggested he was merely making a mockery of the measure, Smith probably sought to extend to white women the same rights now offered to blacks. Whatever his motives, nearly all the women in Congress endorsed the change, which carried both houses.

Subsequent failure of the EEOC to push for compliance with the anti-sex-discrimination law frustrated women reformers. Encouraged by the popularity of her book, *The Feminine Mystique* (1963), Betty Friedan joined other activists in forming the National Organization for Women (NOW) in 1966 to exert pressure on the government. Pledged to "take the actions needed to bring women into the mainstream of American society," NOW pushed for legal abortions, maternity leave, tax-deductible child care, and an equal rights amendment to end sex discrimination. Simultaneously, a younger generation of women working within the civil rights movement developed a commitment to equality for all groups and demanded equal treatment for themselves. The two strands of feminist reform later converged in the women's liberation movement.

THE ELECTION OF 1964

"I think we just delivered the South to the Republican Party," Johnson told an aide as he signed the Civil Rights Act of 1964. Angered at government interference in the private sector, Republican conservatives rallied behind Senator Goldwater, author of the best-selling book, *The Conscience of a Conservative* (1960). "Extremism in the defense of liberty is no vice," declared Goldwater in his acceptance speech to the stormy Republican National Convention, "moderation in the pursuit of justice is no virtue." The Republican nominee lamented crime in the streets, political corruption, aimlessness among youth, anxiety among the elderly, and the loss of spiritual meaning. His was the first candidacy to embrace the "social issue," the discomfort experienced by many voters over personally frightening aspects of social change in the 1960s. "I will give you back your freedom," said Goldwater. Meanwhile, his militant foreign policy speeches made Johnson look like a dove.

Alabama Governor George Wallace echoed Goldwater's agenda and captured national attention by winning one-third of the Democratic primary vote in Wisconsin, Indiana, and Maryland. Political commentators described Wallace's victories as a backlash against civil rights agitation and integration, but the conservative Democrat aimed his criticism at liberal paternalism and big government. "The American people," he said, "are fed up with the continuing trend toward a socialist state which subjects the individual to the dictates of an all-powerful central government." Wallace's surprising success revealed deep dissatisfactions among lower-middle-class whites about liberal support of African Americans instead of solutions to their own economic and social

Betty Friedan (1924–   )

At a time when psychologists insisted that a normal woman would achieve maximum fulfillment as wife, mother, housewife, and homemaker, author Betty Friedan challenged the cult of domesticity in her best-selling 1963 book, *The Feminine Mystique.* According to Friedan, middle-class

women responded to traditional expectations of domestic bliss with a bewildered "Is that all?" Her book sold 3 million copies, reached an estimated readership five times as large, and provoked a fundamental reexamination of women's place in U.S. society. Scarcely a single family was unaffected by its message.

The daughter of immigrant Jewish parents from Peoria, Illinois, Friedan had studied psychology and social science at Smith College and the University of California at Berkeley. "I didn't want to be like my mother" she later recalled. She worked as a journalist during World War II but lost her job to a returning war veteran. Despite a union contract forbidding such actions, she was fired from another job because of pregnancy. In 1949, she explained, no term existed to describe "sex discrimination."

During the 1950s Friedan lived in the suburbs of New York, where she raised three children and continued to pursue a journalism career as a freelance magazine writer. For a piece about her Smith College classmates fifteen years after graduation, she conducted a survey of their attitudes and feelings. Her research revealed a profound unhappiness among college-educated, middle-class women, but the article contra-

problems. Recognizing that Wallace threatened his support in the South, Goldwater persuaded the Alabaman to withdraw.

Johnson, himself a southerner, worried more about black activism and tried to silence further civil rights reform. African Americans defied his wishes. In 1964 the Student Nonviolent Coordinating Committee (SNCC) invited hundreds of white volunteers to participate in a voter registration campaign in Mississippi during the summer vacation. The integrated Missis-

dicted the assumptions of the day, and the editors of women's magazines refused to publish her findings.

Friedan decided to write a book. "Something is very wrong with the way American women are trying to live their lives today," she began. "It is no longer possible to . . . dismiss the desperation of so many American women." Friedan proceeded to demolish the "happy housewife" image of postwar society, arguing that middle-class women required a source of personal fulfillment, a career, to achieve satisfaction.

Having identified a major social problem, Friedan joined other feminists in seeking a solution. Her philosophy was quintessentially liberal. She demanded that women be given opportunities equal to those of men to achieve economic and political citizenship. In 1966 she helped found the National Organization for Women (NOW) "to bring women into full participation in the mainstream of American society now" and served as its first president until 1970. Besides demanding employment opportunities and legal rights, NOW advocated child care centers and "the right of women to control their reproductive rights." Working within the liberal consensus, Friedan also helped establish the National Women's Political Caucus in 1971 to pressure the major political parties to accept greater female participation.

Friedan's liberal agenda clashed not only with sexist values but also with a more radical feminism that emerged in the late 1960s. Viewing politics in traditional terms, she rejected the idea that "the personal is political" and dismissed the activism of lesbians within the women's movement as internally divisive. Nevertheless, Friedan continued to enjoy considerable stature as a foremother of contemporary feminism.

sippi Summer project encountered violent repression from vigilantes and local officials, which resulted in mass arrests, bombings, arson, beatings, and the murder of civil rights workers. Although only 1,200 blacks dared to register to vote during the summer's bloody events, a contingent of SNCC workers and new black voters went to the Democratic National Convention in Atlantic City to demand political representation.

Calling themselves the Mississippi Freedom Democratic Party, they argued

Frank Watte/Lyndon B. Johnson Library

Lyndon Johnson used the politics of consensus to win a 61 percent plurality in the 1964 election. Having signed civil rights legislation that year, he captured more than 90 percent of the black vote.

that the all-white Mississippi delegation should be unseated because African Americans could not participate in their selection. Johnson feared such reforms would cost white support and offered the delegates two at-large seats. In the end, no compromise was acceptable. The regular Mississippi Democrats, most of whom backed Goldwater, left the convention, and the unseated blacks remained embittered by liberal hypocrisy. As a gesture of reconciliation, Johnson chose the liberal Hubert Humphrey as his running mate, but many African Americans lost confidence in and respect for their white Democratic allies.

Johnson and Humphrey sought a politics of consensus in 1964 by defending civil rights legislation and promising moderation in Vietnam. "We seek no wider war," said the president, denouncing those who would "supply American boys to do the job that Asian boys should do." In the election, the Johnson-Humphrey liberal agenda received a record 61 percent plurality and amassed 43 million votes. The Democrats won more than 90 percent of the black vote but lost five states in the Deep South. The landslide gave the president greater than two-to-one majorities in both houses of Congress. Even without the white South, the president could now attempt to fulfill the promises of the liberal agenda.

THE TRIUMPH OF LIBERALISM

Johnson treated his election as a mandate and proceeded to expand his Great Society agenda, persuading Congress to enact a variety of programs for social reform. In 1965 he signed an education bill that based federal aid on the number of low-income families in each school district. The law enabled the federal government to influence local political decisions. For example, the Commissioner of Education ruled that school districts had to show a "good faith substantial start" toward desegregation or lose federal funds. In 1966 the Office of Education issued tighter guidelines and declared an end to "paper compliance with desegregation orders." Conservatives objected that federal aid was threatening local control over schools.

Johnson also pushed for health care for the elderly, leading to the pioneering Medicare program in 1965. The core of the legislative package provided for hospital and nursing home care for elderly citizens through payroll taxes administered by Social Security. The law also provided Medicaid grants to states that enacted health programs for poor people of all ages. By 1970 the cost of state health care nearly equaled that of Medicare. To accommodate conservative concerns about free enterprise, however, the law did not allow the government to control service fees.

The Great Society program peaked in 1965. Johnson signed a $1 billion Appalachia Assistance program, most of which went for road building in the economically depressed region. A portion of the $7.8 billion housing bill included rent supplements for low-income families. Johnson made the Department of Housing and Urban Development a cabinet-level office and followed that with approval of the Demonstration Cities and Metropolitan Development Act, which appropriated nearly $1 billion to attack urban blight. Congress also abolished the national-origins quota system for immigration, underscoring the rejection of race in federal policy. The Immigration Act of 1965 limited admission to 300,000 people a year but favored relatives of U.S. citizens and those with special skills rather than particular nationalities and encouraged a considerable increase in immigration from Asia and Latin America.

GUNS AND BUTTER

Despite the popularity of Johnson's initiatives, conservatives criticized the growth of government power and bureaucracy and resented the tax burdens to finance social reform. Southern leaders also objected to civil rights measures that demanded desegregation of public accommodations. Yet Johnson defended his program passionately, not only because it brought him political support but also because it satisfied a personal desire to be remembered as a

caring president. He would later compare his commitment to domestic reform to a love affair with a beautiful woman.

Johnson understood nevertheless that his ambitious program depended
on preserving a political consensus that would support deficit spending for
social legislation. He was constantly afraid that political opponents would undermine his support, and he feared that any weakness in Cold War foreign
policy would open him to criticism. In this context, he faced critical decisions
about the continuing war in Vietnam. "I knew from the start that I was bound
to be crucified either way I moved," he told biographer Doris Kearns after he
completed his term in office. "If I left the woman I really loved—the Great
Society—in order to get involved with that bitch of a war on the other side of
the world, then I would lose everything at home. All my programs. All my
hopes to feed the hungry and shelter the homeless. All my dreams to provide
education and health care to the browns and the blacks and the lame and the
poor." Yet Johnson believed, initially at least, that the country would support
both "guns and butter"— the war in Asia and the War on Poverty.

Like Kennedy, Johnson recognized the importance of undeveloped countries in the Cold War and opposed political or economic changes that might
destabilize U.S. interests. In 1965 he ordered U.S. troops into the Dominican
Republic when he suspected that communists controlled a constitutional
movement to seize power from the army. Johnson also followed Kennedy's
precedents in authorizing the CIA to promote friendly governments abroad.

In any case, U.S. military power appeared awesome and continued to grow.
By the late 1960s, the armed forces operated more than 3,000 military bases in
30 countries and had 1 million military personnel overseas. The nation's arsenal included 1,000 nuclear-armed intercontinental missiles and 70 nuclear-
armed and -powered submarines. The nuclear storehouse amounted to the
equivalent of 15 tons of dynamite for every person in the world. Total navy
tonnage exceeded that of all other nations combined. The cost of the military
establishment exceeded $216 million a day. Between 1945 and 1970 U.S. tax-
payers spent $1 trillion for military purposes. Yet the late 1960s brought the
United States the worst military and political disaster in its history.

Just hours after the assassination of President Kennedy, Johnson conferred
with the U.S. ambassador to South Vietnam, Henry Cabot Lodge, to assess the
status of the war. When Lodge reported that the Vietcong had escalated military activity, Johnson replied that he was "not going to be the President who
saw Southeast Asia go the way China went." Instead, he cancelled Kennedy's
order to withdraw troops from South Vietnam. Since South Vietnam had failed
to compete effectively against the Vietcong politically or militarily, Johnson
believed that U.S. military might would ensure victory in the Vietnamese civil
war. By early 1964, the White House approved plans to expand the war across
the border separating South and North Vietnam.

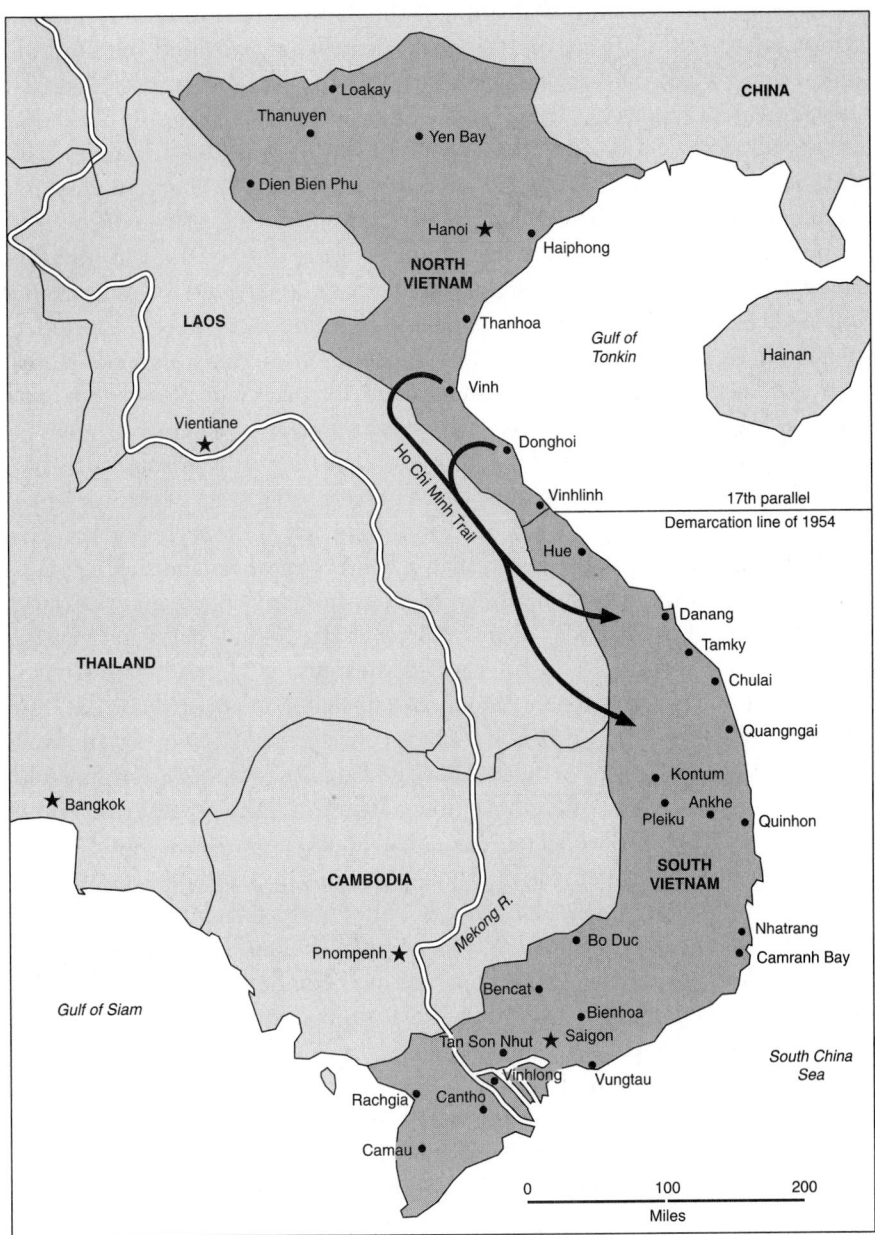

EXHIBIT **4-4** **VIETNAM**

To be sure, Johnson was determined to keep Vietnam from becoming an
issue in the presidential election. His 1964 State of the Union address made
no mention of foreign policy, the first such silence since the end of World

War II. Yet behind the scenes, top administration officials monitored the war closely and made decisions that brought the nation closer to military intervention. During the spring of 1964, U.S. destroyers patrolled the Gulf of Tonkin, and PT boats occasionally attacked North Vietnamese coastal installations. As military clashes increased, the State Department secretly drafted a congressional resolution for a declaration of war in May 1964. Two months later, South Vietnamese ships, accompanied by U.S. intelligence vessels, began bombarding North Vietnamese territory in the Gulf of Tonkin. When North Vietnamese patrol boats fired on one of the destroyers, U.S. fighter planes strafed the attackers. Secretary McNamara openly lied to Congress in denying U.S. involvement in these attacks. On August 4 the navy reported a second attack on U.S. ships, although subsequent analysis blamed "freak weather effects, and an overeager sonar man" for that claim. Newly opened records show that the second attack never occurred.

Johnson nevertheless used the allegation to order air reprisals on North Vietnamese bases. Insisting that the United States sought "no wider war," the president presented Congress with a reworded version of the secretly prepared May declaration of war, which stated that "Congress approves and supports the determination of the President as commander-in-chief to take all necessary measures to repel any attack against the forces of the United States and to prevent further aggression." The Tonkin Gulf Resolution passed in the House unanimously and in the Senate with only two dissenters, Wayne Morse of Oregon and Ernest Gruening of Alaska. A Harris poll showed 85 percent approval of air strikes against North Vietnam. Although Congress stopped short of a full declaration of war, which might have drawn China and the Soviet Union into the conflict, Johnson had won a free hand to conduct the war as he chose.

During the election campaign, Johnson stood as the candidate least likely to embroil the nation in a Vietnam war. But after his victory, he moved swiftly to approve measures to escalate U.S. military involvement. In December 1964 the president approved plans to begin a sustained bombing campaign of North Vietnam and accepted the deployment of U.S. ground forces to support the air war and engage the enemy in combat. These plans were made unilaterally, often in defiance of the opinion of such U.S. allies as France, Britain, even South Vietnam. Indeed, when South Vietnamese leaders suggested the possibility of opening negotiations with the National Liberation Front, U.S. officials refused to consider the possibility of a peaceful neutralization of the region. Moreover, Johnson feared that publicizing his military decision would increase international pressure to negotiate and would undermine congressional support for the Great Society. The decision to escalate the war thus remained secret.

The White House merely waited for an opportunity to begin the bombing campaign of North Vietnam. The excuse came after the Vietcong attacked a U.S. base at Pleiku in February 1965. Vowing not to be scared out of Vietnam, Johnson ordered air strikes, known as Operation Rolling Thunder, against North Vietnam. Claiming the bombings were merely retaliatory, the White House concealed the deepening commitment of air power from the public. The air war also required more ground troops to protect U.S. bases, and Johnson ordered 100,000 additional soldiers to Vietnam. In this way he hoped to maintain enough force to prevent the communists from winning but not enough to precipitate Chinese intervention.

The war against North Vietnam thus began as a policy change soon after Johnson came to office. Although a few administration officials, such as presidential advisor George Ball, opposed escalation of the war, Rusk, McNamara, Bundy, and the Joint Chiefs of Staff advocated a military solution to the political struggles in Indochina. Kennedy had resisted their pleas; Johnson, less confident about foreign policy and fearing the wrath of conservatives should he be responsible for "losing" Vietnam, determined to uphold an independent South Vietnam with ties to the Western alliance. In 1965 a Gallup poll found that 61 percent of the public approved increased troop deployments, indicating that Johnson was not running ahead of public opinion. But as the cost of the war became apparent, support for Johnson's war steadily weakened. And, tragically for Johnson, so did support for "the woman [he] really loved—the Great Society."

INFOTRAC COLLEGE EDITION

Using Keywords, enter the following search terms:

John F. Kennedy
Cuban Missile Crisis
New Left
Great Society
Lyndon Johnson
Student Nonviolent Coordinating Committee

RECOMMENDED READING

Taylor Branch, *Pillar of Fire: America in the King Years, 1963–1965* (1998). A thorough analysis of the civil rights movement, this volume emphasizes the role of individual participants.

Rebecca E. Klatch, *A Generation Divided: The New Left, the New Right, and the 1960s* (1999). A sociological study of political activism, this work examines the choices of activists on both sides of the spectrum.

Fredrik Logevall, *Choosing War: The Lost Chance for Peace and the Escalation of War in Vietnam* (1999). This study of U.S. policymaking between 1963 and 1965 describes the decisions that led to war in Vietnam.

Michael R. Beschloss, ed., *Taking Charge: The Johnson White House Tapes, 1963–1964* (1997). Based on transcriptions of White House telephone conversations, this volume vividly depicts the transition of power from Kennedy to Johnson.

Additional Reading

Although numerous authors have addressed the sixties, most confuse protest movements with the larger historical context. Good overviews include David Steigerwald, *The Sixties and the End of Modern America* (1995); David Farber, *The Age of Great Dreams: America in the 1960s* (1994); and Maurice Isserman and Michael Kazin, *America Divided: The Civil War of the 1960s* (2000). More speculative is Edward P. Morgan's *The Sixties Experience: Hard Lessons about Modern America* (1991). One political history critical of the liberal consensus is Allen J. Matusow, *The Unraveling of America: A History of Liberalism in the 1960s* (1984).

A balanced discussion of the Kennedy administration appears in James N. Giglio's *The Presidency of John F. Kennedy* (1991), which may be supplemented with the second volume of Herbert S. Parmet's biography, *JFK: The Presidency of John F. Kennedy* (1983). More critical is Bruce Miroff's *Pragmatic Illusions: The Presidential Politics of John F. Kennedy* (1976). A briefer book is David Burner's *John F. Kennedy and a New Generation* (1988). For an insightful study of the impact of personality, see Garry Wills, *The Kennedy Imprisonment* (1982). A fine study of U.S. leadership can be found in David Halberstam, *The Best and the Brightest* (1972). Historians' views of Kennedy are studied in Thomas Brown, *JFK: History of an Image* (1988).

Kennedy's problems with Congress are explored in Tom Wicker, *JFK and LBJ: The Influence of Personality upon Politics* (1968). The space program is well treated in Walter A. McDougall, *The Heavens and the Earth: A Political History of the Space Age* (1985); in Clayton R. Koppes, *JPL and the American Space Program: A History of the Jet Propulsion Lab* (1982); and in Tom Wolfe's journalistic *The Right Stuff* (1979). Problems of economic policy are described in Jim F. Heath's, *John F. Kennedy and the Business Community* (1969). For the Peace Corps, see Gerard T. Rice, *The Bold Experiment: John F. Kennedy's Peace Corps* (1985). Women's politics are covered in Cynthia Harrison, *On Account of Sex: The Politics of Women's Issues, 1945–1968* (1988). The career of a leading feminist is described in Daniel Horowitz, *Betty Friedan and the Making of the Feminine Mystique: The American Left, the Cold War, and Modern Feminism* (1998). For the experience of younger women, see Sara Evans, *Personal Politics: The Root of Women's Liberation in the Civil Rights Movement and the New Left* (1979).

A good survey of the civil rights movement can be found in Robert Weisbrot, *Freedom Bound: A History of America's Civil Rights Movement* (1990).

Kennedy's relationship to civil rights is analyzed critically in Victor S. Navasky, *Kennedy Justice* (1971), and more favorably in Carl M. Brauer, *John F. Kennedy and the Second Reconstruction* (1977). For Martin Luther King Jr., see Stephen B. Oates, *Let the Trumpet Sound: The Life of Martin Luther King, Jr.* (1982), and David J. Garrow, *Bearing the Cross: Martin Luther King, Jr., and the Southern Christian Leadership Conference* (1986). King's organization is studied in Adam Fairclough, *To Redeem the Soul of America: The Southern Christian Leadership Conference and Martin Luther King, Jr.* (1987). The legal framework is explained in Michael R. Belknap, *Federal Law and Southern Order: Racial Violence and Constitutional Conflict in the Post-Brown South* (1987). See also Hugh Davis Graham, *The Civil Rights Era: Origins and Development of National Policy* (1990). Another facet of government policy emerges in David J. Garrow, *The FBI and Martin Luther King, Jr.* (1981). The role of student activists is presented in Clayborne Carson, *In Struggle: SNCC and the Black Awakening of the 1960s* (1981). A fine oral history is Howell Raines's *My Soul Is Rested: The Story of the Civil Rights Movement in the Deep South* (1983).

For a thorough discussion of Kennedy's handling of the Cold War, see Michael R. Beschloss, *The Crisis Years: Kennedy and Khrushchev, 1960–1963* (1991). For the Bay of Pigs, see Trumbull Higgins, *The Perfect Failure: Kennedy, Eisenhower, and the CIA at the Bay of Pigs* (1988). The Cuban missile crisis is discussed in David Detzer, *The Brink* (1979). A detailed study of the German conflict can be found in Curtis Cate, *The Ides of August: The Berlin Wall Crisis, 1961* (1978). Another aspect of Kennedy policy emerges in Richard D. Mahoney, *JFK: Ordeal in Africa* (1983).

The Kennedy assassination has created a vast literature. A good starting point is Gerald L. Posner's *Case Closed: Lee Harvey Oswald and the Assassination of JFK* (1993).

For Lyndon Johnson, a good starting point is Irving Bernstein, *Guns or Butter: The Presidency of Lyndon B. Johnson* (1996), and Robert Dallek, *Flawed Giant: Lyndon Johnson and His Times, 1961–1973* (1998). Also insightful is Doris Kearns, *Lyndon Johnson and the American Dream* (1976). The internal workings of the administration are covered in Emmette S. Redford and Richard T. McCulley, *White House Operations: The Johnson Presidency* (1986). See also Carl Solberg's biography of the vice president, *Hubert Humphrey* (1984).

The Republican opposition is described in Mary C. Brennan's *Turning Right in the Sixties: The Conservative Capture of the GOP* (1995), and Robert Alan Goldberg, *Barry Goldwater* (1995). See also Stephan Lesher, *George Wallace: American Populist* (1994), and Jody Carlson, *George C. Wallace and the Politics of Powerlessness: The Wallace Campaigns for the Presidency* (1981).

The decision to intervene in Vietnam is best treated in David Kaiser, *American Tragedy: Kennedy, Johnson, and the Vietnam War* (2000). Other overviews of the Vietnam War include Marilyn B. Young, *The Vietnam Wars,*

1945–1990 (1991), and George L. Herring, *America's Longest War: The United States and Vietnam, 1950–1975* (1986). Another excellent introduction is Neil Sheehan, *A Bright and Shining Lie: John Paul Vann and America in Vietnam* (1988). Also useful are Stanley Karnow, *Vietnam: A History* (1983), and William S. Turley, *The Second Indochina War: A Short Political and Military History* (1986).

The best study of the Tonkin Gulf incident is Edwin E. Moise, *Tonkin Gulf and the Escalation of the Vietnam War* (1996). The limits of leadership are covered in Lloyd C. Gardner, *Pay Any Price: Lyndon Johnson and the Wars for Vietnam* (1995), and in Larry Berman, *Lyndon Johnson's War: The Road to Stalemate in Vietnam* (1989). A fine study of one leading official is Paul Hendrickson's *The Living and the Dead: Robert McNamara and Five Lives of a Lost War* (1996).

POLARIZED AMERICA: RACIAL TURMOIL AND VIETNAM, 1965–1968

President Lyndon Johnson dreamed of enlisting Americans behind a Great Society program of racial harmony and social reform. Yet Johnson could not contain the widening agenda of the civil rights movement, whose focus moved from nonviolent campaigns in the South to nationwide demands for African American political power and community control. Nor was the president able to forge a consensus for the fight for an anticommunist government in South Vietnam. As Johnson unleashed a bombing campaign against North Vietnam and sent the first U.S. combat troops to the South, he vowed that "come hell or high water, we're gonna stay there." Yet escalation of the U.S. role in Vietnam unleashed a torrent of dissent, led by a small but vocal antiwar movement, some of it infused with countercultural values.

Despite general prosperity, divisions over race relations, the Vietnam War, and social morality polarized public life. By articulating a conservative critique of "pseudo-intellectual government," Governor George Wallace mobilized a third-party race for the presidency. Wallace asserted that the "average man in the street" supported "a change on the domestic scene in this country." Meanwhile, Richard Nixon sought the White House by focusing on middle-class concerns about "social issues" such as crime, violence, and student protest. By 1968, the nation confronted the worst crisis since the Civil War.

THE VOTING RIGHTS CRUSADE

Many African Americans benefited from the widespread prosperity and made significant economic strides during Lyndon Johnson's tenure. As the ratio between black and white family income narrowed, black median family income increased by more than one-third between 1964 and 1969. Over the decade, the proportion of African American families living in poverty decreased from nearly 50 percent to less than 30 percent. Seeking to extend the benefits of inclusion to those left out of New Deal reforms, Johnson appointed African Americans to high-profile offices. Robert Weaver was named to head the Department of Housing and Urban Development, which the president upgraded to cabinet status, and became the first black in U.S. history to serve in such a high position. The president also selected Thurgood Marshall, former counsel for the National Association for the Advancement of Colored People (NAACP), to be the first black justice to serve on the Supreme Court. Meanwhile, Massachusetts voters elected Edward Brooke to the Senate in 1966, the first African American to sit in that body since Reconstruction.

Civil rights activists built on widespread liberal sympathy to win long-denied voting rights for African Americans. The Twenty-fourth Amendment to the Constitution, ratified in 1964, outlawed the poll tax, a historic barrier to black political participation in the South. But many southern states still used "literacy tests" to disqualify potential voters on the basis of race. When the Student Nonviolent Coordinating Committee (SNCC) initiated a voter registration drive in Selma, Alabama, local officials refused to cooperate, leading organizers to ask for help from Martin Luther King Jr. After King's nonviolent street demonstrations resulted in police harassment, 600 civil rights activists mounted a march to the state capital in Montgomery. On "Bloody Sunday"—March 7, 1965—state troopers used clubs and tear gas in a vicious attack on the peaceful protest. Broadcast on national television, the atrocity forced the White House to intervene. Johnson now summoned a joint session of Congress to request federal protection for black voter registrants. Borrowing the language of the civil rights movement, the first southern president since Woodrow Wilson declared, "All of us . . . must overcome the crippling legacy of bigotry and injustice—and we *shall* overcome."

As hundreds of clergy and civil rights supporters answered King's call to come to Selma, a federal judge nationalized the Alabama National Guard, permitting the Montgomery march to take place with official protection. Even so, Viola Liuzzo, a white volunteer from Detroit, was killed by racist vigilantes—the third casualty of the Alabama campaign. Violence against the protests helped to rally public opinion in support of the Voting Rights Act of 1965, a landmark piece of legislation that produced a revolution in southern politics. The new law abolished literacy tests and empowered the attorney general to assign federal examiners to register voters in states practicing racial discrimination. In one year, federal officials registered more than 400,000 African American voters. By 1968, 1 million southern blacks had qualified to vote. Although the voting rights measure remained a central pillar of the civil rights revolution, it led to a new form of racial separation in the South's political structure as blacks enlisted on the Democratic rolls and whites increasingly voted Republican.

RACIAL TURMOIL AND IDENTITY POLITICS

The Voting Rights Act marked the culmination of the effort to achieve racial integration in the South. After its passage, national attention shifted to the majority of African Americans who resided outside the region. Northern blacks lived primarily in decaying ghettos in the older industrial cities, where the exodus of manufacturing plants to the suburbs and Sunbelt states decimated urban tax bases and increased joblessness. In 1968 the Department of Labor reported that the black unemployment rate was three times as high as the white rate. Despite rising expenditures, welfare programs, such as Aid to Families with Dependent Children (AFDC), failed to meet the needs of impoverished families. Federally funded urban renewal projects added to the problem by destroying low-income housing without replacing it. As the black population of the central cities increased by 6 million between 1960 and 1977, 4 million whites moved out. Washington's heralded War on Poverty could not erase the fact that ghetto life remained depressingly bleak.

Moderate black leaders could not contain the mixture of impatience, rage, and militant consciousness that accompanied heightened aspirations and unchanging realities for most African Americans. Between 1964 and 1967, more than 100 urban riots and rebellions occurred as angry blacks attacked retail property in their communities in response to economic abuses and police harassment. Chanting "burn, baby, burn," young blacks in the Los Angeles community of Watts damaged nearly $750 million of property while dozens were killed and thousands injured in one explosive outbreak in the summer of 1965. The next year, black violence erupted in Chicago when angry whites attacked Martin Luther King's "open city" housing campaign. In 1967 central Detroit went up in smoke as African Americans and some whites went on a week-long rampage that brought out the National Guard and federal troops. A six-day riot in Newark, New Jersey, left twenty-seven dead, resulting in a special report to the governor that blamed law enforcement officials for "excessive and unjustified force." SNCC leader H. "Rap" Brown expressed the bitter mood of 1967, urging demonstrators in Cambridge, Maryland, to "burn this town down if this town don't turn around and grant the demand of Negroes."

Johnson reacted to the violence by appointing a National Advisory Commission on Civil Disorders chaired by Illinois Governor Otto Kerner. In a widely read report, the Kerner Commission concluded in 1968 that the nation was "moving toward two societies, one black, one white, separate and unequal." Blaming the riots on white racism and white institutional power, the commission urged a massive commitment to housing, education, jobs, and welfare as well as better law enforcement techniques. However, by then the White House was preoccupied with foreign policy and remained silent on the findings.

Stokely Carmichael (1941–   )

No single figure embodied the radicalization of 1960s protest among African Americans as much as Stokely Carmichael. Born in Trinidad, Carmichael went to public high school in the Bronx, New York, and graduated from predominantly black Howard University with a degree in phi-

losophy. Initiating his activism in the Deep South in 1961, he served several months in prison when he was arrested as a Freedom Rider, the first of thirty-five incarcerations he would experience.

After participating in the Mississippi Freedom Summer Project of 1964, Carmichael assumed the directorship of SNCC's voter registration campaign in Lowndes County, Alabama. There he proposed to arm field organizers and adopted the image of a snarling black panther as the insignia for a separate black political party. After succeeding John Lewis as SNCC chair in 1966, Carmichael warned of a "long hot summer" among discontented African American youth in the nation's ghettoes.

A few days after Carmichael's election to the SNCC post, he virtually assumed leadership of James Meredith's March Against Fear in Mississippi by chanting the slogan "Black Power, Black Power" to sharecrop-

The explosion of black anger after 1965 effectively killed the biracial, nonviolent civil rights coalition. Limited gains from liberal reform, the persistence of black poverty, and a vocal white backlash encouraged African Americans to see all whites as part of a rigid "establishment." When James Meredith, the first black to enroll at the University of Mississippi, launched a solitary march against fear through Mississippi in 1966, only to be shot by a sniper, civil rights leaders rushed forward to continue the demonstration. Now SNCC's Stokely Carmichael brushed aside talk of nonviolence and proclaimed "Black Power!" The words electrified the media and terrified whites. Martin Luther King urged Carmichael to adopt a more moderate slogan, but black pride and cultural identity could no longer be contained by nonviolent rhetoric. Refashioning itself as the Student National Coordinating Commit-

pers along the highway. "We are determined to win political power . . . by any means necessary," he stated. Carmichael coauthored a book entitled *Black Power: The Politics of Liberation in America* (1967) that urged the black community to abandon its "dependent colonial status" and "win its freedom while preserving its cultural integrity."

"Before a group can enter the open society, it must first close ranks," wrote the authors of *Black Power.* Carmichael implemented this philosophy by purging whites from SNCC. "If we are to proceed toward true liberation," he explained, "we must set ourselves off from white people." In seeking to shift the movement's focus from integration to black liberation, he dropped the word nonviolent from SNCC's name. One year later, Carmichael expressed sympathy for communism on a trip to Cuba and warned that black anti-imperialists in the United States were "preparing groups of urban guerrillas for our defense in the cities . . . a fight to the death."

Carmichael resigned from SNCC in 1967 and became prime minister of the Black Panther Party the following year. Yet his association with the Panthers was shortlived. Converted to Pan Africanism, he soon proclaimed that socialism was "not an ideology suited for black people . . . It's not a question of right or left. It's a question of black." He left the United States in 1969 and settled permanently in the African nation of Guinea.

---

tee, SNCC removed the word nonviolent from its name. As the organization purged nonblacks from leadership positions, Carmichael dismissed integration as "a subterfuge for the maintenance of white supremacy."

The magnetism of Black Power revealed widespread frustration within African American communities. "To be a Negro in this country," explained novelist James Baldwin, "is to be in a rage all the time." Eldridge Cleaver, an emerging leader of the Black Panther Party, expressed similar fury in his best-selling *Soul on Ice* (1968). For many young blacks, failure to gain equal rights, economic advancement, and cultural respect produced a powerful identity crisis, forcing a conversion from "Negro" values of assimilation and integration to "black" affirmations of ethnicity. Many blacks followed the lead of Malcolm X and changed their "slave" names to African or Muslim names. In Los

Angeles, Maulana Ron Karenga formed the US Organization to promote "back to black" cultural traditions and popularized Kwanza as an African American alternative holiday to Christmas.

Through his posthumously published autobiography, Malcolm X emerged as an important cultural force. Born Malcolm Little, he had converted to the black Nation of Islam (Black Muslims) religion while in prison and changed his name to symbolize independence from white domination. A persuasive, charismatic speaker, he initially opposed interracial cooperation and warned that any association with "evil whites" would thwart social justice. However, after breaking with the Black Muslims in 1964, Malcolm argued that capitalism functioned as an oppressive force and that people of all colors must cooperate to achieve a socialist alternative. Assassinated in Harlem in 1965, allegedly by associates of the Nation of Islam, Malcolm remained a prophet for black and white radicals seeking interracial cooperation.

The cultural aspects of Black Power—Afro hairstyles, soul food, ethnic identity—paralleled efforts to organize a black political movement. In 1967, Bobby Seale and Huey Newton founded the Black Panther Party in Oakland, California, to address the overwhelming problems of ghetto life. The Panthers considered urban riots as self-destructive and instead formed a community defense league to monitor local police. To dramatize the right to bear arms against the "occupation" of their communities by white authorities, Panthers marched into the California legislature with loaded rifles. By 1968, the Black Panther Party had devised a ten-point program embracing Marxist concepts of self-determination and opposition to "welfare colonialism." The Panthers also distributed a national weekly newspaper, established local health clinics, and provided free breakfasts and schools for black children. In 1968 Panther leaders won white radical support for the Peace and Freedom Party, which ran one of their members, Eldridge Cleaver, for president, but the movement exerted minimal influence on the election.

While the Black Panthers, SNCC, and Martin Luther King jockeyed for African American leadership, the cry of Black Power emboldened other ethnic groups. By the late 1960s, Mexican Americans in the Southwest and California proclaimed their "Chicano" pride. Chicano consciousness, however, could not hide the bleak facts of Mexican American economic existence, particularly for agricultural field-workers. To improve such conditions, California's Cesar Chavez and the United Farm Workers union used Christian nonviolence and product boycotts to win collective bargaining rights for the small but militant union.

Native Americans also moved from liberal reformism to militant assertions of cultural identity. When the state of Washington attempted to abridge native treaty rights to salmon fishing in the interests of conservation in 1964, local tribes invited the National Indian Youth Council to stage "fish-in" demonstrations. Four years later, the U.S. Supreme Court upheld the Indian position. Meanwhile, the Taos Pueblo in New Mexico rejected a federal offer of compensation for seizing sacred waters and initiated protests that led to a reversal of government policies. In 1966 Indian leaders adopted the phrase "self-determination" to oppose federal termination programs. Two years later, President Johnson embraced that language to demand "equality and dignity" for native peoples, and Congress passed the Indian Civil Rights Act, requiring tribal consent to state jurisdiction over civil or criminal matters. That year young activists formed the American Indian Movement (AIM), raised the cry "Red Power," and vowed to continue the struggle for cultural and political autonomy.

JOHNSON'S WAR

When Johnson authorized the Rolling Thunder air strikes against North Vietnam in 1965, he merely implemented an earlier decision to preserve the South Vietnamese government at all costs. Yet poor target accuracy and enemy anti-aircraft fire produced a high loss of planes and led to indiscriminate bombing of civilian targets, increasing the need for ground troops. By the summer of 1965, U.S. forces had begun large-scale combat operations in the South, engaging in "search-and-destroy" missions against the Vietcong (the National Liberation Front) while B-52s flew from Guam to bomb suspected enemy targets. By the end of the year, 180,000 U.S. ground troops were "in country" and the air force was attacking industrial areas in the North. "It used to be a war of the South Vietnamese assisted by the Americans," noted newspaper columnist Walter Lippmann. "It is now becoming an American war very inefficiently assisted by the South Vietnamese."

Johnson consistently had ruled out negotiations with the communists. During Christmas of 1965, however, the president ordered a bombing moratorium and sent diplomats across the globe to explore possibilities for peace. Yet the White House refused to recognize the National Liberation Front as a political force independent of North Vietnam. Contending that Hanoi had invaded South Vietnam in an instance of territorial aggression, Johnson denied that the United States had become involved in a civil war.

As troop commitments approached 400,000 in 1966, some members of Congress began to express reservations about the war. J. William Fulbright, chair of the Senate Foreign Relations Committee, held open hearings criticizing White House policy. And even though intelligence reports noted that air power was militarily ineffective, Johnson ordered the bombing of Hanoi. "We must continue to raise the price of aggression," he explained. The goal of the bombing had changed from breaking the enemy's will to cutting supply lines. The president promised to end the attacks if North Vietnam pledged to send no more troops south, but Hanoi responded that peace depended on withdrawal of U.S. forces. Because Johnson insisted that South Vietnam's independence must be preserved, he rejected Hanoi's demands.

Despite tremendous firepower, the president's limited war could not defeat the enemy. Military advisors repeatedly made the error of assuming that a reduction of Vietcong operations indicated diminished military capability rather than changes in strategy. In late 1966 Defense Secretary McNamara commissioned a study, later known as the Pentagon Papers, to evaluate the entire war policy, but the bombing continued, and reliable journalists in Vietnam denounced administration claims about the minimal number of civilian casualties.

By 1968 Johnson had ordered 500,000 soldiers to South Vietnam. As ground forces now confronted North Vietnamese regulars as well as Vietcong guerrillas, casualty figures soared. Meanwhile, the Vietcong controlled the timing and terms of 80 percent of all military confrontations. To destroy enemy bases, U.S. planes dropped napalm, jungle defoliants, and lethal herbicides throughout the country in a war in which it was difficult to distinguish between combatants and civilians. American fragmentation bombs left victims riddled with millions of tiny particles that could not be detected by x-rays. The Central Intelligence Agency (CIA) also launched Operation Phoenix, an assassination program against alleged Vietcong civilian leaders that claimed at least 20,000 victims.

THE ANTIWAR MOVEMENT

Less than a month after Johnson ordered the full-scale bombing of North Vietnam in 1965, 20,000 protesters participated in a Washington, D.C., demonstration sponsored by Students for a Democratic Society (SDS). College students, vulnerable to the draft and increasingly concerned about issues of social justice and personal freedom, denounced the war. "Teach-in" protests spread to major universities. At the University of California, Berkeley, 12,000 students and faculty participated in Vietnam Day in 1965. Draft calls reached 40,000 a month the following year, and rallies, marches, and draft-card burnings multiplied. Young men refused induction orders, thousands deserted the armed forces, and even more fled to Canada and Europe to avoid conscription. Protesters occupied military induction centers and harassed on-campus job recruiters for the military and the CIA.

The antiwar movement saw the use of technological violence against an economically impoverished people as equivalent to genocide. Defense contractors such as Dow Chemical, which manufactured napalm used to kill civilians in Vietnam, and Honeywell, which made antipersonnel fragmentation bombs, faced militant protests by activists. Carl Oglesby of SDS considered the conflict a laboratory for developing imperial techniques to halt social revolution in the third world. Yet most demonstrators identified with the spirit of Joseph Heller's cult novel, *Catch-22* (1960), an absurdist view of World War II that suggested that escape was the only sane response to war. Bolstered by celebrity activists such as folk singers Joan Baez and Phil Ochs, antiwar assemblies became instant communities in which outrage merged with political action.

African American organizers such as Stokely Carmichael played a key role in the antiwar crusade. Identifying with the colonized peoples of the third world and aware that blacks suffered disproportionate casualties in Vietnam, Carmichael made SNCC the first civil rights group to oppose the war in 1966. Coining the slogan "Hell No, We Won't Go!" the organization urged blacks to resist the draft. The next year African American heavyweight champion Muhammad Ali refused military induction on the basis of his status as a Muslim minister and remained defiant when boxing authorities stripped him of his crown. "No Viet Cong ever called me nigger," Ali explained.

Martin Luther King also responded to rising antiwar sentiment in the black community and issued a "declaration of independence" from the Vietnam War in 1967. The United States was the world's leading purveyor of violence, King asserted from the pulpit. As antiwar protest evolved into massive resistance, however, the movement struggled to maintain peaceful methods. A "stop-the-draft" week at the Oakland, California, Induction Center resulted in street battles between police and 20,000 activists. Late in 1967, 300,000 antiwar protesters rallied in New York City. The same day, the National Mobilization Against the War (MOBE) gathered more than 100,000 marchers to surround the Pentagon. When several hundred stormed the citadel, many protesters were arrested by military police, an event recorded in Norman Mailer's prize-winning *Armies of the Night* (1968).

Clergy from all three major denominations figured strongly in the antiwar crusade. In 1967, Catholic activists, including Father Philip Berrigan, poured blood on draft files in Baltimore. As efforts to destroy selective service records spread across the country, conscientious objectors in the military refused assignment to Vietnam. By 1968, the antiwar SDS boasted nearly 300 chapters and a national membership of 100,000. For many of the nation's increasingly politicized students and peace activists, the Vietnam War had become a symbol of all that was wrong with America.

THE COUNTERCULTURE

"There's battle lines being drawn / Nobody's right if everybody's wrong," suggested a popular rock song of the period. Alienation from the Vietnam War was enhanced by the spread of countercultural values and youth-oriented lifestyles—components of a changing morality associated with the questioning of social authority and the spread of the "sexual revolution." Flaunting the breakdown of old barriers, rock songs such as the Rolling Stones's "Let's Spend the Night Together" directly described sexual longing. "Life was free and so was sex," novelist Sara Davidson later wrote in *Loose Change* of Berkeley in the sixties.

Public fascination with new sexual standards and casual intimacy surfaced in books such as *The Harrad Experiment* (1967), a best-selling novel about a utopian sexual community of college students; in Ian Fleming's popular James Bond series; and in the pulp fiction of Jacqueline Susann, the most successful novelist of the period. Hollywood contributed to the shift in mores by replacing its 1930s production code with a rating system that permitted nudity and obscene language as well as "mature" themes. Television shows such as *The Smothers Brothers* and *Laugh-In* also broke precedent by joking about non-marital sex, divorce, and "up-tight" behavior. In country music, once the bastion of traditional morality, the widespread use of birth control pills and enhanced sexual frankness were reflected in the songs of superstars Tammy Wynette and Loretta Lynn.

As a psychedelic counterculture blossomed from Beat roots in San Francisco's Haight-Ashbury district, the mass media discovered the "hippie." "I never hold back, man. I'm always on the outer limits of possibility," declared Haight rock vocalist Janis Joplin. Young cultural dissidents wore their hair defiantly long and dressed in a free-form fashion that included bells, feathers, bandanas, beads, and earrings. Many survived in crash pads or in shared housing by panhandling, making crafts, selling "underground" newspapers, and dealing drugs. Some, like the communal Diggers, started free kitchens and health clinics. The most important facet of hippie culture involved its attempt to reject the mainstream's competitive individualism, materialism, and middle-class pretensions. Instead, the alternative culture prided itself on honest affection, physical pleasure, sharing, experimentation, and absolute inner freedom.

Few college students actually traveled to San Francisco during 1967's "Summer of Love" or identified themselves as hippies. Yet many sensed the counterculture's possibilities for social change and refashioned their private lives to emulate it. Many middle-class rebels believed their cultural lifestyles should reflect their political sensibilities and left the cities to form thousands of rural communes. Others published underground comics and newspapers, produced "guerrilla" theater and alternative film documentaries, created color-crazed "pop art" posters, or sought expression in traditional disciplines such as musical composition, dance, poetry, or prose. Many more adopted antiestablishment attitudes, spoke in "hip" language, wore blue jeans, and experimented with sexual freedom, marijuana, and rock music.

"Psychedelic" or "acid" rock bands such as the Jefferson Airplane, the Grateful Dead, and Joplin's Big Brother and the Holding Company integrated electric guitars with elaborate light shows, developing the piercing "San Francisco" sound. As introspective lyrics and "spaced-out" musical styles spread to the Beatles and Rolling Stones as well as to Bob Dylan, the Byrds, Jimi Hendrix, and The Doors, performers sought to fuse high art with popular culture. The underground culture was highly irreverent, a mood captured in essayist Tom Wolfe's *The Electric Kool-Aid Acid Test* (1968), a description of the exploits of writer Ken Kesey, whose Merry Pranksters traveled around the country in a psychedelically painted bus while promoting liberation through drugs, sex, and rock music. Satirical novels by Kesey, Kurt Vonnegut, and Thomas Pynchon won huge followings with absurdist portraits of "straight" life and social conventions. Youth culture received even wider exposure in provocative Hollywood films such as *Bonnie and Clyde* (1967), *The Graduate* (1967), and *Easy Rider* (1969).

Counterculture authors offered validation for alternative values that cherished the spiritual life and transcended competitive ego. Herbert Marcuse's *Eros and Civilization* (1955, 1962) condemned the use of sexual repression to bolster elite rule; Carlos Castaneda's *The Teachings of Don Juan: A Yaqui Way of Knowledge* (1968) rejected the narrowness of materialist rationality; R. D. Laing's *The Politics of Experience* (1966) depicted society's neglect of the inner self as insane. A popularized version of the new perspective found its way into Charles A. Reich's *The Greening of America* (1970), which predicted that the revolutionary counterculture was moving the nation toward an epoch of shared love and community.

Although radical activists insisted on the counterculture's hostility to consumer capitalism, the two forces were undeniably intertwined. Advertisers sought to tap expanded consumer tastes in a period of unprecedented prosperity by tying brand identity to youthful images and countercultural fantasies of liberation and revolution. By associating automobiles, carbonated beverages, cosmetics, and other products with the "rebellion" of the "Now Generation," hip marketers encouraged the public to adopt changing styles and fashions as a way of satisfying psychological needs for authenticity and individuality. Pop artist Andy Warhol illustrated the compatibility of the two worlds by creating silk-screen representations of everyday commodities such as soup and soda cans. The purpose of art was to alter consciousness and explore new sensibilities, not to elevate formal culture above popular expressions, lectured essayist Susan Sontag in her influential *Against Interpretation* (1964).

Radical feminists, however, remained adamantly hostile to the temptations of consumer capitalism. Drawing inspiration from the civil rights slogan, "The Personal Is Political," movement activists such Casey Hayden and Mary King began to organize women against the male domination of SNCC, SDS, and other groups. Despite the radical community's espousal of egalitarian values, they asserted, New Left men mirrored establishment culture by relegating women to office duties and other minor tasks. Feminists also complained that the male-oriented sexual revolution furthered female debasement by treating women as mere playthings and objects of conquest.

While their male colleagues greeted their efforts with ridicule and outright hostility, New Left women initiated "rap" sessions to share their grievances and address gender identity issues. In 1968, 200 radical feminists went public by organizing the first women's liberation demonstration. Calling themselves the

Bonnie and Clyde (1967)

The "long hot summer" of 1967 saw unprecedented civil disorder as angry African Americans vandalized ghetto neighborhoods in Detroit and Newark, creating scenes of violence that appeared on TV screens along with daily news coverage of the war in Vietnam. In August, the release of Arthur Penn's startling film of the Depression-era youthful criminals, Bonnie Parker and Clyde Barrow, added a cultural dimension to the national debate about the sources of social violence and demands for "law and order." For the nation's youth, who comprised the largest movie audience of the 1960s and turned the film into an instant box-office success, the saga of alienation, bank robbery, and sexual desire mirrored the tensions of contemporary society.

The movie opens with black-and-white photographs, reminiscent of Dorothea Lange's portraits of the 1930s, which produced a documentary

Photri Inc.

mood that evoked feelings of desperation. Bonnie (played by Faye Dunaway) is a bored, dreamy teenager, trapped as a small-town waitress, when she encounters the recently paroled Clyde (Warren Beatty) trying to steal her mother's car. When he shows off his revolver, she touches the barrel erotically and when he calls her "the best damn girl in Texas," Bonnie joins him in an adventurous romp through back country roads and Depression-worn towns, set against a background of frenetic banjo accompaniment.

"You ain't gonna have a minute's peace," warns Clyde. "You promise?" wisecracks Bonnie. Their fun, tempered somewhat by Clyde's sexual impotence, turns sober when their thievery leads to killing. But their criminality has a Robin Hood quality as they playfully expose middle-class hypocrisy and relate honestly to plain folks who look like they have emerged from John Steinbeck's novel, The Grapes of Wrath.

The characters' 1930s costumes as well as those in other successful movies such as They Shoot Horses, Don't They, *also set in the Depression, sparked a fashion fad. But the tone of the film belonged to the 1960s. Although Bonnie remains loyal to her man and allows Clyde to make the decisions, she has no illusions about forming a traditional household. Pointing to Clyde's conventional, often hysterical sister-in-law, a "preacher's daughter," Bonnie cries: "She's what's the matter with me." In contrast to Clyde's dysfunction, moreover, Bonnie appears sexually alive, embodying the sexual revolution that preceded a feminist consciousness.*

"If Bonnie and Clyde were here today, they would be hip," said the film's screenwriters, David Newman and Robert Benton. "Their values have been assimilated in much of our culture—not robbing banks and killing people, of course, but their style, their sexuality, their bravado, their delicacy, their cultivated arrogance, their narcissistic insecurity, their curious ambition have relevance to the way we live." As the outlaws created a "gang" of family and friends, creating a community on the run, they appealed to 1960s fantasies of a mobile youth culture, escaping from adult institutions and living more "naturally."

The movie's romanticism of crime infuriated traditional critics, such as The New York Times' *Bosley Crowther, who denounced "the excess of violence." Director Penn acknowledged that the bloody finale was influenced by images of the Kennedy assassination. Others praised the film's tragic elements that linked the frustration of the past to the current political repression that provoked violent reactions.*

Women's International Terrorist Conspiracy from Hell (WITCH), activists protested against "sexism" and capitalism's "objectification" of women's bodies by picketing the Miss America Pageant and throwing "instruments of torture" such as brassieres and high-heeled shoes into a "freedom trash can." Feminists focused on women's control of their own bodies by embracing an agenda that included the right to legal abortions, dissemination of birth control literature, and passage of tougher laws against rape and spousal abuse.

THE WAR AT HOME

As dissent against the Vietnam War increased, the White House fought to curtail public criticism. Since the early 1960s, FBI Director J. Edgar Hoover had directed counterintelligence (COINTEL) efforts against both the Ku Klux Klan and the civil rights movement. The FBI program was soon expanded to include the wiretapping and bugging of Martin Luther King, whom the director feared as a potential "black messiah." Black Panther militancy toward local police aroused Hoover's anger in 1967, and he ordered counterintelligence activities to "expose, disrupt, misdirect, discredit, or otherwise neutralize the activities of black nationalists." After King joined SNCC leaders in opposing the Vietnam War, the FBI broadened its covert capabilities to disrupting the New Left. The COINTEL program also targeted women's liberation groups.

Other government agencies initiated similar operations against the antiwar movement. Since many campuses encouraged antigovernment activity, Johnson ordered Army Intelligence to join the FBI in putting thousands of students and faculty under surveillance. By 1968 the army had compiled 100,000 dossiers on antiwar dissidents. The president also authorized the CIA's Operation Chaos to conduct domestic surveillance— in violation of the agency's charter—against activists, demonstrators, and even "suspicious" members of Congress. When the CIA notified Johnson that domestic dissent appeared to be independent of foreign funding, he rejected the finding. The courts were also used to impede the antiwar movement, as when the Justice Department indicted pediatrician Dr. Benjamin Spock and Yale chaplain William Sloane Coffin for promoting draft evasion.

EXHIBIT **5-1**   **ARRESTS OF PERSONS UNDER AGE 18, 1966–1969**
(IN ROUNDED FIGURES)

1966	1,149,000
1969	1,500,000

Source: *Historical Statistics of the United States, Colonial Times to 1970* (1975).

EXHIBIT **5-2   U.S. NATIONAL DEFENSE
AND VETERANS OUTLAYS, 1966–1968**
(IN BILLIONS OF DOLLARS)

1966	64.0
1968	88.8

Source: *Statistical Abstract of the United States* (1987).

Johnson thought he could fight poverty and communism simultaneously, that he could finance the Vietnam War without cutting Great Society funding. Yet as military costs rose to $2 billion a month in 1966, the president admitted the impossibility of spending large sums for both "guns and butter." Civil rights demonstrations, urban rioting, and campus protests added to a weakened liberal position. In Chicago, Martin Luther King's open-housing marches into white ethnic neighborhoods provoked violent retaliation. When the White House submitted a federal equal housing bill, two attempts to end a Senate filibuster failed, and the administration settled for a modest rat-control appropriation. In a year of record federal expenditures, Congress abolished the school milk program and cut appropriations for education. The War on Poverty also faced reductions when big-city mayors complained that the community action program had been taken over by minority professionals and other patronage entrepreneurs.

Congressional uneasiness with domestic programs also reflected the soaring inflation caused by war spending. Johnson persuaded Capitol Hill to suspend Kennedy's investment tax credit and accelerated depreciation allowances in 1966, but these minor tax increases provided insufficient funds to finance the war. The president suffered a severe legislative setback when Congress refused to accept a war tax surcharge and preferred spending cuts or tax reform. Although the White House won a small tax surcharge in 1968, the delay in increasing taxation encouraged a crippling inflation that would retard economic growth for the next twenty-five years and bring into question the use of government spending as national policy. Rising prices and war outlays produced a phenomenal rise in the federal deficit, which more than doubled between 1966 and 1967 and nearly tripled during 1968 to more than $25 billion.

EXHIBIT **5-3   CONSUMER PRICE INDEX, 1966–1968**
(IN ROUNDED PERCENTS)
(1967 = 100)

1966	97
1967	100
1968	104

Source: *Historical Statistics of the United States, Colonial Times to 1970* (1975).

Democrats warned that education, jobs, housing reforms, and an end to discrimination were necessary to end domestic strife. Yet voters responded to escalating welfare costs, rising inflation, higher crime rates, black militancy, and antiwar demonstrations by participating in a conservative backlash in the 1966 congressional elections. By stressing increasing crime and the need for law and order, Republican candidates made large gains in both houses of Congress. In California, former movie actor Ronald Reagan, an ex-Democrat, captured the governorship by blaming a cultural elite of liberal politicians, intellectuals, and bureaucrats for the expanding welfare state.

The conservative backlash enabled Alabama's George Wallace to attract a national following. "A bearded professor . . . thinks he knows how to settle the Vietnam War," Wallace told one audience, but he "hasn't got enough sense to park his bicycle straight." Wallace articulated deeply held resentments against liberal government programs, ghetto rioting, and student rebellions and appealed to working people concerned about the rising crime rate and fearful of the loss of traditional values. In 1968 he launched a presidential campaign through the American Independent Party, calling for repeal of civil rights laws and for a military victory in Vietnam. "When I become your president," he declared, "I'm going to ask my attorney general to seek an indictment against any college professor who calls for a communist victory. . . . That's treason."

Despite Wallace's popularity among workers, blue-collar support of the war barely outpaced that of the rest of the nation in a period marked by increasing skepticism over Johnson's credibility. Yet a majority of voters saw peace demonstrations as "acts of disloyalty against the boys fighting in Vietnam." To "hawk" and "dove" alike, the war had become a volatile political issue. Organized labor, led by AFL-CIO President George Meany, remained loyal to the Democratic Party and backed the Vietnam crusade. In 1967 a New York City march "supporting our men in Vietnam" attracted 70,000 people. Nevertheless, Johnson's Democratic consensus seemed to be unraveling.

THE CHAOS OF 1968

Disaffected from the Vietnam War he had helped to orchestrate, Defense Secretary Robert McNamara resigned in late 1967 to head the World Bank. On the eve of Tet (the Vietnamese New Year) early the next year, disaster struck. As Johnson deployed immense firepower to repel the siege of a desolated marine outpost at Khe Sanh, the Vietcong launched a coordinated attack on every major population center in South Vietnam. In Saigon, commandos penetrated the U.S. embassy grounds. In Hue, communist forces executed police officials and political enemies while the South Vietnamese army retaliated against Buddhists, students, and teachers who appeared to be "VC collaborators." By the

EXHIBIT **5-4**   **THE TET OFFENSIVE**

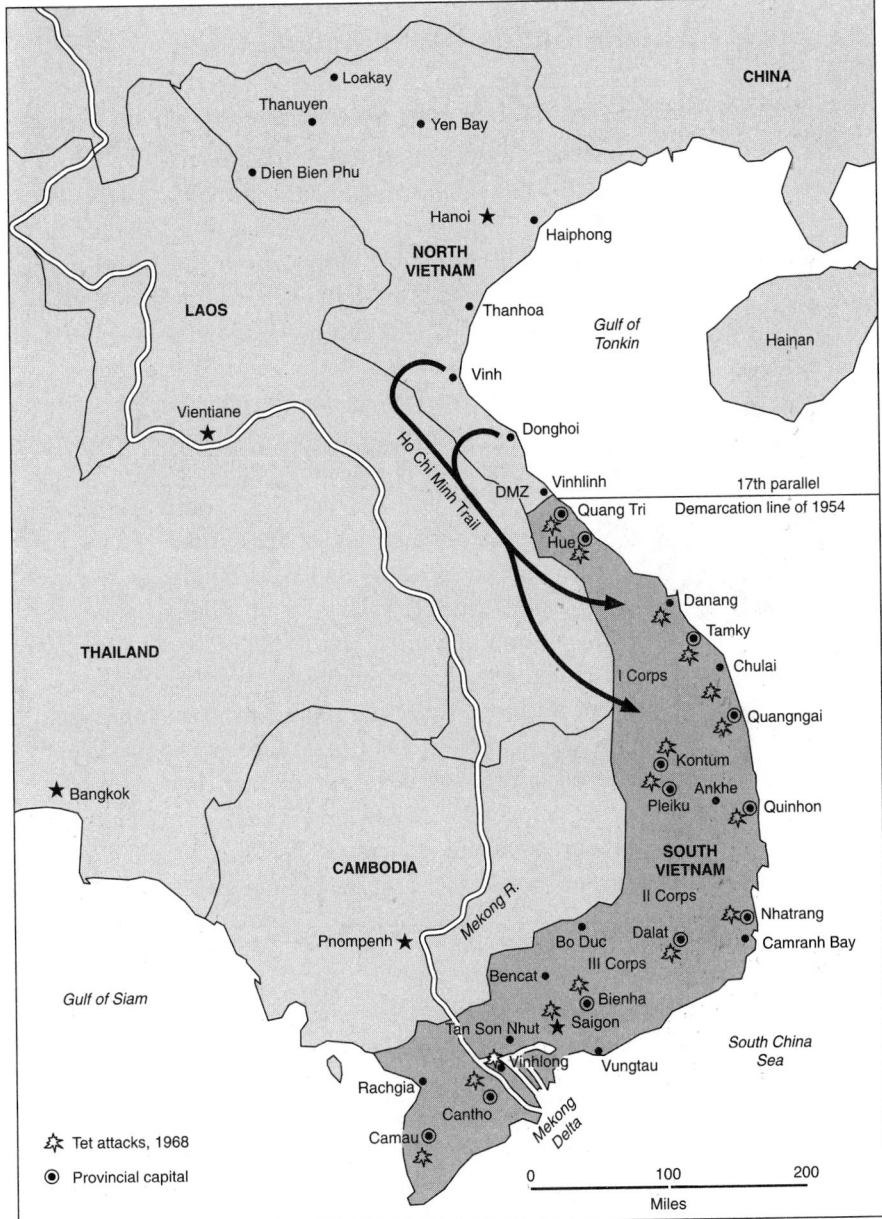

time the cities were once again under Saigon's control, the United States had lost 4,000 soldiers and suffered nearly 20,000 injuries.

The Tet Offensive had cost the lives of 32,000 communist insurgents and greatly depleted Vietcong strength, forcing Hanoi to rely on regular troops to

William Childs Westmoreland (1914–   )

General William Childs Westmoreland, the commander of U.S. military forces in Vietnam from 1964 to 1968, embodied the strengths and weaknesses of the U.S. presence in Southeast Asia. A picture-book soldier, he was ramrod straight, 6 feet tall, jut-jawed, brave, meticulous, and self-

disciplined. In Vietnam he was determined to prove that superior technology and organization skills could defeat a guerrilla army but, like civilian leaders, he underestimated the passion and power of the enemy, and he failed to appreciate the political dimensions of the war.

Born in Spartanburg, South Carolina, Westmoreland devoted his entire life to the military. He attended West Point, saw service in World War II, and commanded a parachute troop in Korea. He then went to the Pentagon's manpower office and enrolled in an advanced management program at the Harvard School of Business. Indistinguishable from the other corporate executives in the seminars, the young general became a proficient administrator and later used his association with former classmates who had become defense contractors to increase worker performance and productivity in military procurement and manpower allocation. In 1960 President Dwight Eisenhower appointed him superintendent of West Point.

pursue its military objectives. Yet the campaign showed the futility of the U.S. strategy. In one telling instance, a general ordered the army to destroy a "friendly" village to "save" it from the communists, highlighting the difficulty of assessing civilian loyalty in a civil war. As documentation of military atrocities surfaced in coming months, the public would learn the moral consequences of waging war in Vietnam. Yet the immediate lesson of Tet was that the enemy merely had to survive to prevent the United States from "winning." The offensive also exposed the inability of South Vietnamese troops to defend positions without U.S. assistance or air strikes.

By drastically undermining support for Johnson's war policy at home, Tet provoked one of the most tumultuous years in U.S. political history. Although General William Westmoreland insisted that the tide in Vietnam had turned,

Chosen to lead U.S. troops in Vietnam in 1964, Westmoreland drew upon his vast administrative skill. Even to the general's critics, his logistic achievements seemed astounding. Under his command, the military constructed deep-water ports, jet airfields, tactical airstrips, hundreds of helicopter pads, storage facilities, and miles of telephone cable and radio grids, as well as bridges, roads, canals, and seaways. Westmoreland's demand for troops also appeared voracious and increased from 16,000 in 1964 to 520,000 in 1968.

Such power inflicted immense damage but could not defeat the elusive enemy. Nor could the seemingly unending war justify the tremendous drain on U.S. resources. When political leaders recognized that victory could not be achieved, President Johnson appointed Westmoreland Chief of Staff of the Army in 1968 and ordered him back to Washington. "We have curtailed the tide of Communist aggression," Westmoreland stated in his final report on the war; " . . . the enemy has not won a single major victory."

The general never accepted responsibility for the defeat in Vietnam. "However desirable the American system of civilian control of the military," he argued in his memoirs, "it was a mistake to permit appointive civilian officials lacking military experience and knowledge . . . to wield undue influence in the decision-making process."

he now requested another 200,000 troops and mobilization of the reserves—proposals that would have added $12 billion to war costs already reaching $30 billion a year. As opposition to the conflict intensified, newly appointed Defense Secretary Clark Clifford found extensive "dove" sentiment within the Pentagon. In March 1968 antiwar Senator Eugene McCarthy of Minnesota astounded the nation by taking 42 percent of the vote in the New Hampshire Democratic presidential primary, a serious political defeat for the White House. Days later, New York Senator Robert Kennedy announced his candidacy. Within a week, Johnson relieved Westmoreland of the Vietnam command and summoned a meeting of senior advisors to reassess the war effort.

The White House conference included twelve of the most prestigious members of the nation's foreign policy, business, and legal establishment.

President Johnson listened somberly to the advice of the administration's "wise men" at a meeting in the Oval Office on March 26, 1968. Five days later, Johnson withdrew from the presidential contest.

Nearly all had supported the escalation of bombing in 1967. But now they concluded that the present policy could not achieve its objectives without full citizen support and major budgetary sacrifices, and they warned that the war threatened the position of the U.S. dollar abroad. The bombing of North Vietnam had damaged the administration in Washington more than the regime in Hanoi, scolded former Secretary of State Dean Acheson. Johnson agonized about his response. Then, on the evening of March 31, 1968, he gave a dramatic televised speech announcing the suspension of the bombing of North Vietnam and a willingness to negotiate with the communist enemy. In a surprising postscript, he also announced his withdrawal from the presidential race.

Four days later, on the day North Vietnam agreed to peace talks, a self-proclaimed racist named James Earl Ray assassinated Martin Luther King in Memphis, Tennessee. King had come to the city to support a strike of predominantly African American sanitation workers. The murder provoked a spasm of racial violence and riots in more than 100 cities and sent smoke from black neighborhoods circling above the Capitol Dome in Washington, D.C. King had hoped to draw attention to the need for jobs and housing with a Poor People's March on Washington that spring, but without his presence the demonstration lost focus. Goaded by his assassination, Congress at last passed the long-delayed open-housing bill, which banned discrimination in the sale and rental of about four-fifths of the nation's housing and provided more than $5 billion in mortgage and rent subsidies.

Johnson's withdrawal from presidential politics emboldened sentiment for a negotiated end to the war and sparked heated campaigns by peace candidates Senators McCarthy and Kennedy. The White House choice, Vice President Hubert Humphrey, remained on the sidelines, but in June Kennedy won the California primary, only to be killed minutes after his victory by Sirhan Sirhan, a Palestinian opposed to the senator's support for Israel. Bitterly divided over the Vietnam War and related social issues, the Democratic Party drifted for want of leadership.

The assassinations of King and Kennedy underscored the national political and cultural crisis. At New York's Columbia University, cooperation between African American activists and SDS briefly surfaced in the spring of 1968 when the two groups separately occupied university buildings to protest campus ties to the war as well as planned expansion into a Harlem community park. Yet blacks called off their action just before New York City police viciously smashed the SDS occupation. The confrontation, which brought nearly 700 arrests, set the tone for clashes at every major university—more than 3,000 campus protests occurred during 1968. Public opinion polls found that most respondents blamed the demonstrators, not the police, for the violence.

As the Democratic Party prepared to nominate Vice President Humphrey, several thousand peace activists and young radicals descended on Chicago to hold a "festival of life" and demonstrate at the national convention. Their protest was coordinated by a coalition of antiestablishment groups, including the Youth International Party (Yippies), a group of cultural dissidents organized by antiwar leaders Jerry Rubin and Abbie Hoffman. Mayor Richard Daley refused to allow demonstrators to protest in the streets or camp in city parks and ordered mass arrests and the use of indiscriminate force, permitting what a presidential commission later called a "police riot." While street crowds chanted "the whole world is watching!" police attacked protesters, passers-by, and the media with clubs and mace. Inside the convention, party leaders defeated a dovish platform and proceeded to nominate Hubert Humphrey.

THE "NEW" NIXON

With his party split, Humphrey's chances seemed slim against Republican nominee Richard Nixon. After losing a bitter race for the California governorship in 1962, Nixon had joined a prestigious New York law firm and refurbished his image as an elder statesman with extensive world travel that provided him with the opportunity to consult foreign leaders. Vowing to "bring the American people together," the candidate declared that 1968 was the

Robert Francis Kennedy (1925–1968)

Robert Kennedy's assassination signaled the end of hope in a turbulent era desperately in need of conciliation. Kennedy had served as the New Frontier's principal power broker. He was his brother's presidential campaign manager in 1960, attorney general during the stormy civil rights movement, and personal advisor on foreign policy during John F. Kennedy's presidency.

As a tough Irish American, Kennedy helped to shape counterinsurgency in Vietnam, personally supervised the CIA's covert campaigns in Cuba, and had a reputation as a cool-handed operator with a ruthless streak. Dallas changed all that. The heir-apparent to the presidency, Bobby Kennedy began a new career in 1964 as the junior senator from New York. Deeply affected by his loss, he used his prestige to push for greater commitments to those without privilege or power. He visited Cesar Chavez's striking farmworkers in California, heard testimony on malnutrition in Mississippi, and held hearings on the squalor of reservation life in New Mexico. Kennedy warned in 1967 that "we cannot measure national spirit by the Dow-Jones Average, nor national achievement by the gross national product."

The senator was not among the first to question the Vietnam War. However, early in 1966 he issued a cautious call for a coalition government in Saigon. A year later he took the floor to condemn the Johnson administration's bombing: "We are all participants . . . We must also feel as men the anguish of what it is we are doing." In 1967 Kennedy delivered a spontaneous tirade on national television against U.S. slaughter of the Vietnamese

"time for a complete housecleaning" in Washington. Regarding Vietnam, Nixon promised to "end the war and win the peace in the Pacific," although he provided no specifics other than to hint at a Great Power settlement. "We're going to build this country up so that no one will dare use the U.S. flag for a doormat again," he stated.

Nixon's most emphatic message addressed voter fears concerning domestic instability and safety on the streets. "The first civil right of every American," he

people. Commentators began to speculate on his availability as a presidential candidate, but Kennedy was too much of a professional to risk splitting the Democratic Party in a personal vendetta against an incumbent president. Johnson's political fall in 1968 moved the senator to action.

The eighty-five-day presidential campaign of Robert Kennedy stirred an emotional groundswell seldom seen in election politics. Kennedy's proposals for a draft lottery, corporate development of the ghettoes, and Vietnam negotiations were modest, but he symbolized the lost idealism of the New Frontier, the flickering hope that all classes and races could share in the American Dream. He campaigned on the streets with his jacket off, tie loose, and sleeves rolled up. Excited crowds swarmed the primary trail just to touch his hand.

When Martin Luther King was assassinated, Kennedy went directly to a ghetto street gathering in Indianapolis and shared his own feelings of loss by quoting the Greek poet Aeschylus. A nearby graffito explained his remarkable following among African Americans: "Kennedy white but alright / The one before, he opened the door." Yet the secret to the Kennedy campaign was the compassion he expressed toward all the nation's working people and dispossessed. Despite his stance against the war, the strict Catholic and father of ten scored large primary pluralities in white districts that had previously supported George Wallace.

Kennedy was the only leader of his era who might have united white working people, antiwar students, and racial minorities in a coalition for change. His assassination by a Palestinian Arab incensed at the candidate's support for Israel was a harsh blow to the nation. At the Democratic Convention in Chicago delegates wept and sang the "Battle Hymn of the Republic" in his memory.

declared, was to be free of violence. In the face of student protests and ghetto riots, the nominee called for recognition of "the Silent Americans"—working people "forgotten" by high-minded liberals and unruly radicals. Nixon's vice presidential running mate, Governor Spiro Agnew of Maryland, a Greek American, had achieved national prominence by attacking violent black power and antiwar demonstrators and by espousing the traditional social values and law-and-order requirements of white ethnics and George Wallace supporters.

The conservative Nixon campaign enhanced its prospects by advancing the political use of television advertising. Professional marketers merged the candidate's calm voice with a series of still black-and-white images, associating the nominee with serene competence, respect for tradition, and faith in the American people. Campaign operatives also staged ten regional live broadcasts enabling Nixon to answer questions from specially selected panels of "ordinary" citizens. Nixon used these opportunities to court the traditional Democratic constituency of white southerners, northern Catholics, lower-middle-class Jews, and blue-collar workers—the so-called middle Americans who resented liberal preoccupation with racial minorities and who despised the influence of counterculture values. "Our objective in the next four years should not be to get more people on welfare rolls—we want to get more people on payrolls," Nixon declared. His TV commercials carried this warning: "VOTE AS IF YOUR WHOLE WORLD DEPENDED ON IT."

As the seriousness of the Republican challenge intensified, President Johnson moved toward a settlement of the Vietnam War. In September, Johnson had rejected private North Vietnamese overtures. But in the following month the president announced a complete halt of the bombing and began active campaigning for Humphrey. However, Republican operatives, fearing Nixon's defeat, used intermediaries to urge the South Vietnamese government to refuse participation in the peace talks and wait for a better deal once the Democrats lost. The Saigon regime then opposed the seating of the National Liberation Front at the Paris negotiations. Although FBI wiretaps of the South Vietnamese Embassy and other sources confirmed the arrangement, the Johnson administration had no evidence of Nixon's personal involvement and feared a constitutional crisis should the deal be exposed.

Despite Humphrey's dramatic narrowing of Nixon's lead in the last week of the campaign, he never overcame the burden of White House incumbency or the Democratic Party's association with lawlessness and the disorder of the Chicago convention. In the North, Humphrey managed to preserve the historic New Deal coalition of labor, blacks, Jews, and Catholics. Yet the Democrats took only 35 percent of the overall white vote and failed to retain the loyalty of sufficient numbers of middle-class citizens. By positioning himself as a moderate capable of healing the nation's bitter social divisions, Nixon won the 1968 election by less than 1 percentage point in one of the closest races in U.S. history. Wallace's American Independent Party, which had hoped to force the contest into the House of Representatives, amassed nearly 14 percent of the vote and claimed 45 electoral votes in the Deep South. Together, Nixon and Wallace carried 57 percent of the national electorate, although Democrats maintained control of both houses of Congress by substantial margins.

The turbulence of 1968 shook public faith in the political system. As the credibility gap and violent dissent brought widespread alienation from the

EXHIBIT **5-5**   **THE ELECTION OF 1968**

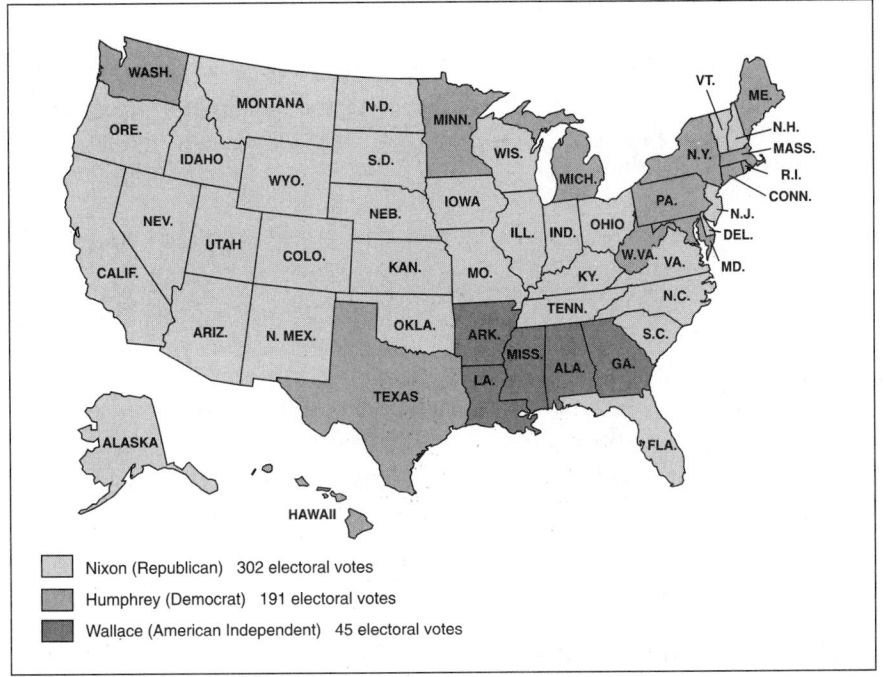

Nixon (Republican)   302 electoral votes

Humphrey (Democrat)   191 electoral votes

Wallace (American Independent)   45 electoral votes

White House and conventional politics, the U.S. death toll in Vietnam passed 30,000. At year's end more than 500,000 soldiers remained in that distant outpost of national aspirations. Fatigued by bitter divisions of war, race, and culture, a weary nation looked to Richard Nixon to restore tranquility at home, achieve a dignified peace abroad, and stabilize the domestic economy.

INFOTRAC COLLEGE EDITION

Using Keywords, enter the following search terms:

    Tet Offensive
    Malcolm X
    Richard Nixon
    Thurgood Marshall
    Cesar Chavez
    George Wallace
    Black Panther Party

RECOMMENDED READING

Robert D. Schulzinger, *A Time for War: The United States and Vietnam, 1941–1975* (1997). This overview of the Vietnam War places Johnson's escalation in full context.

Douglas C. Rossinow, *The Politics of Authenticity: Liberalism, Christianity, and the New Left in America* (1998). The author breaks new ground by tying antiwar activism and participatory democracy to Protestant moralism in Texas and the South.

Dan T. Carter, *The Politics of Rage: George Wallace, the Origins of the New Conservatism, and the Transformation of American Politics* (1995). A key source for understanding the rise of populist conservatism in the 1960s.

Thomas Frank, *The Conquest of Cool: Business Culture, Counterculture, and the Rise of Hip Consumerism* (1997). This innovative work establishes connections between countercultural values and the 1960s innovations of Madison Avenue.

Additional Reading

For overviews of the 1965–1968 period, descriptions of the Johnson administration, and accounts of civil rights and ethnic identity movements, see the sources listed in Chapter 4. Additional overviews of the 1960s include David Burner, *Making Peace with the Sixties* (1996); Douglas T. Miller, *On Our Own: Americans in the 1960s* (1996); and Irwin Unger and Debi Unger, *America in the 1960s* (1988). Accounts of reform and its limitations include Irwin Unger, *The Best of Intentions: The Triumph of the Great Society Under Kennedy, Johnson, and Nixon* (1996), and Jill Quadagno, *The Color of Welfare: How Racism Undermined the War on Poverty* (1994).

For further discussion of African American radicalism, see Philip S. Foner, ed., *The Black Panther Party: A Brief History with Documents* (1996). The definitive history of feminism can be found in Ruth Rosen's *The World Split Open: How the Modern Women's Movement Changed America* (2000). The origins of radical feminism are traced in Sara Evans, *Personal Politics: The Root of Women's Liberation in the Civil Rights Movement and the New Left* (1979).

Surveys of the Vietnam War are listed in the readings for Chapter 4. For criticism of the notion that a liberal media helped to lose the war, see Clarence R. Wyatt, *Paper Soldiers: The American Press and the Vietnam War* (1993).

For the antiwar movement, student activism, and the counterculture, see the listings in Chapter 4. Additional sources include Terry Anderson, *The Movement and the Sixties: Protest in America From Greensboro to Wounded Knee* (1995). See also the perceptive Peter Levy, *The New Left and Labor in the 1960s* (1994). Media treatment of dissidents is described in Melvin Small,

Covering Dissent: The Media and the Anti-Vietnam War Movement (1994), and Todd Gitlin, *The Whole World Is Watching: Mass Media and the Making and Unmaking of the New Left* (1980).

Changes in sexual conventions are outlined in David Allyn, *Make Love, Not War: The Sexual Revolution, An Unfettered History* (2000). Drugs and the counterculture are discussed in Jay Stevens, *Storming Heaven: LSD and the American Dream* (1987), and Martin A. Lee and Bruce Shlain, *Acid Dreams: The CIA, LSD, and the Sixties Rebellion* (1985). For the intellectual roots of the counterculture, see Theodore Roszak, *The Making of the Counter Culture* (1969). A good study of cultural dissent can be found in Jonah Raskin, *For the Hell of It: The Life and Times of Abbie Hoffman* (1997). For popular culture, see David Pichaske, *A Generation in Motion: Popular Music and Culture in the Sixties* (1989), and Jon Weiner, *Come Together: John Lennon in His Time* (1991). Youth-oriented Hollywood films are analyzed in portions of Michael Ryan and Douglas Kellner, *Camera Politica: The Politics and Ideology of Contemporary Hollywood Film* (1990).

For FBI activities, see David J. Garrow, *The FBI and Martin Luther King, Jr.* (1981); Richard Gid Powers, *Secrecy and Power: The Life of J. Edgar Hoover* (1987); and Athan G. Theoharis and John Stuart Cox, *The Boss: J. Edgar Hoover and the Great American Inquisition* (1988). Conservative political activism is described in Stephan Lesher, *George Wallace: American Populist* (1994); in Kent Schuparra, *Triumph of the Right. The Rise of the Califomia Conservative Movement, 1945–1966* (1998); and in segments of Jerome L. Himmelstein, *To the Right: The Transformation of American Conservatism* (1990).

For the politics of 1968, see William H. Chafe, *Never Stop Running: Allard Lowenstein and the Struggle to Save American Liberalism* (1993); David Halberstam, *The Unfinished Odyssey of Robert Kennedy* (1968); and David Farber, *Chicago '68* (1988). The Nixon campaign is described in the relevant segment of Roger Morris, *Richard Milhous Nixon: The Rise of an American Politician* (1990); in Stephen E. Ambrose, *Nixon: The Triumph of a Politician, 1962–1972* (1989); and in William C. Berman, *America's Right Turn: From Nixon to Bush* (1994).

THE EMBATTLED
PRESIDENCY, 1968–1976

Richard Nixon's election revealed widespread impatience with liberal social values and positioned the Republican Party as an advocate of George Wallace's populist conservatism. Nevertheless, the Nixon administration embodied enormous contradictions. While defending individual responsibility and demanding reduced federal power, the president expanded the welfare state and broadened the scope of regulatory reform, making strong commitments to environmental policy. Overseas, the White House worked with National Security Assistant Henry Kissinger to sustain respect for U.S. power and military strength. Yet the Nixon administration ended the nation's painful commitment to Vietnam and pulled off the most dramatic diplomatic triumph of the entire Cold War era by forging a détente with historic communist rivals.

Nixon also brought his personal demons to the White House. Having forged his reputation in Congress and the vice presidency as a bitter anticommunist, he resented the social superiority of affluent reformers like the Kennedys. Nixon hoped to use the presidency to get back at a "soft" liberal establishment he believed to have been "poisoned by the elite universities and the media." Despite its accomplishments, Nixon's presidency unraveled because his animosity toward adversaries led to the political abuses associated with the Watergate scandal. As Gerald Ford served out his predecessor's second term, disillusionment over Vietnam and Watergate threatened to erode national confidence and public trust in government.

THE INDOCHINA BIND AND
THE NEW FEDERALISM AT HOME

Aware that massive commitments of military force in Vietnam had destroyed Lyndon Johnson's presidency, Nixon sought to prevail in Southeast Asia by combining Cold War diplomacy with the selective use of force. He believed that the Soviet Union might be willing to pressure North Vietnam into a negotiated settlement in exchange for superpower negotiations about arms control and Berlin. Yet within one month of taking office, the administration faced a North Vietnamese military offensive. Responding assertively but hoping to limit public criticism from neutralist Cambodia, the president dispatched B-52 bombers in a secret campaign against communist sanctuaries located within Vietnam's southwest neighbor. Meanwhile, the White House sent Henry Kissinger to engage the North Vietnamese in secret talks in Paris.

Although negotiations floundered over Hanoi's insistence that North Vietnamese troops remain in the South and that the Saigon government be replaced with a coalition, the new president announced what appeared to be a policy change in the spring of 1969. In what was called the Nixon Doctrine, Nixon promised that "Vietnamization" of the war would permit gradual withdrawal of U.S. ground troops while expanding the air campaign against the North. Meanwhile, Saigon would receive sufficient military assistance to complete the struggle against the communists. Yet Hanoi continued to ignore U.S. threats, leading Kissinger to fume that "a little fourth-rate power like North Vietnam" had to "have a breaking point." As polls during the fall of 1969 revealed that 57 percent of Americans favored a specific deadline for total disengagement in Vietnam, domestic public opinion became a serious obstacle to the White House's Indochina strategy.

The administration's major challenge at home was the maintenance of economic prosperity. Since the end of World War II, the Bretton Woods system of international exchange rates and the open market arrangements of the General Agreement on Tariffs and Trade (GATT) had provided enormous advantages for U.S. business. During the 1960s, U.S. multinational corporations took part in an unprecedented wave of mergers. Reduced tariffs and lower investment barriers enhanced their global position. Between 1960 and 1974, the foreign assets of U.S. banks leaped from $3 billion to $155 billion. Integration into the world economy was of great interest to financial figures such as David Rockefeller, who in 1973 created the Trilateral Commission, a "think tank" of business leaders, social planners, and politicians from western Europe, Japan, and the United States devoted to such issues as long-term development and global stability.

As U.S. military spending, foreign aid, and overseas investment diverted capital from the economy at home, however, the "golden age" of postwar prosperity appeared to be increasingly fragile. These trends accelerated in 1971 when the Organization of Petroleum Exporting Countries (OPEC) raised oil prices, tripling the U.S. balance of trade deficit. The "dollar drain" reduced U.S. gold reserves and lowered currency values. As inflation set in, corporate debt and government budget deficits intensified the competition for credit, leading

EXHIBIT **6-1**   **U.S. NATIONAL DEFENSE AND VETERANS OUTLAYS,
1968–1976**
(IN BILLIONS OF DOLLARS)

1968	88.8
1970	90.4
1972	89.9
1974	92.7
1976	108.0

Source: *Statistical Abstract of the United States* (1987).

to a rise in interest rates. As a result of both trends—inflation and higher interest rates—consumers suffered a substantial reduction in spending power and a threat to savings. The deterioration of "real" wages also encouraged labor unrest, leading to a wildcat strike by the Teamsters Union, an extended walkout by automakers, and a brief disruption of mail delivery by postal workers during the first strike by federal employees in U.S. history.

Nixon acted to reduce inflation by cutting government spending and by encouraging higher interest rates, but these measures merely brought "stagflation"—a combination of rising prices and high unemployment. Desperate to reverse negative economic trends, the president suspended gold payments for dollars in 1971, thereby taking the nation off the gold standard and ending participation in the Bretton Woods system. Nixon established the first peacetime economic controls since 1947 and ordered a ninety-day freeze on wages, prices, and rents and also placed a surtax on imports. Such unprecedented administrative measures ironically came from a Republican chief executive who claimed to support smaller government. Even though Nixon created a Cost of Living Council to monitor rising costs, continuing stagflation compelled him to end the import surtax after devaluing the dollar.

Because of the continuing structural weaknesses of the economy, Nixon ignored his own warnings and stepped up the federal government's social welfare activity. Under the leadership of White House advisors John Ehrlichman and Harvard sociologist Daniel Patrick Moynihan, the administration created

EXHIBIT **6-2**   **CONSUMER PRICE INDEX, 1968–1976**
(1967 = 100)

1968	104.2
1970	116.3
1972	125.3
1974	147.4
1976	170.5

Source: *Economic Report of the President* (1988).

a new set of executive agencies—including the Office of Management and Budget (OMB), the Domestic Council, and the Urban Affairs Council— which worked with the Democratic Congress to expand Great Society reform. By indexing Social Security payments to the cost of living, the government enabled millions of older Americans to raise their incomes above the poverty level. Nixon nearly tripled the caseload of Aid to Families with Dependent Children (AFDC), the nation's largest welfare program. Congress also quadrupled food stamp coverage when midwestern agricultural interests lobbied to extend the program to the able-bodied and to the nonelderly poor. In 1969 the White House introduced a $6 billion Family Assistance Plan that offered a guaranteed annual income to needy families and proposed to triple the number of welfare recipients. Nixon also called for a comprehensive health care plan based on employer mandates. And even without the additional welfare benefits, federal income maintenance costs surpassed defense outlays for the first time in history.

Nixon also responded to public concern about environmental deterioration and safety issues and substantially broadened federal regulatory power. In 1970 the president approved creation of the Occupational Safety and Health Administration (OSHA), an agency empowered to set mandatory standards to protect employees from workplace hazards. Nixon made environmental protection a matter of national priority. After signing the Endangered Species Act in 1969, the president endorsed the National Environmental Policy Act, which required the government to issue ecological impact statements about pending legislation or programs. The Clean Air Act of 1970 set emission standards for new cars and reorganized antipollution agencies into the Environmental Protection Agency (EPA). The new bureau outlawed the use of the pesticide DDT and implemented a congressional ban on the production and stockpiling of biological and chemical weapons. Environmental rules contributed to a sixfold increase in the length of the *Federal Register*'s guide to regulations during the Nixon presidency.

Although the Republican administration expanded government power, Nixon courted public opinion by packaging his reforms as a limitation on Washington's influence. For example, the president described his Family Assistance Plan as "workfare" because it contained employment requirements for some recipients. When Democrats complained of inadequate support levels for the proposal, however, they joined antiwelfare conservatives in defeating the measure in Congress. Angered by the lack of cooperation from liberals, Nixon made major cuts in Head Start, the Job Corps, and the War on Poverty. He also introduced a "revenue sharing" plan to reduce government spending, which had reached nearly one-third the gross national product, and sought to give the states primary responsibility for welfare programs. Despite Nixon's much-heralded "new federalism," however, federal budget deficits continued to mount.

ᴇxʜɪʙɪᴛ **6-3   U.S. GOVERNMENT SPENDING AS A PERCENTAGE**
OF GROSS NATIONAL PRODUCT, 1969–1976

1969	30.5
1976	33.9

Source: *Historical Statistics of the United States, Colonial Times to 1970* (1975).
Economic Report of the President (1977).

AFFIRMATIVE ACTION AND THE BURGER COURT

The Nixon White House assumed a wildly contradictory approach to race relations, an area of government activism often criticized by social conservatives. In the South, radio crusaders such as Reverends Carl McIntyre and
Billy James Hargis had contributed to a conservative social climate in the
1960s by combining evangelical enthusiasm with harsh assaults on liberal social programs as communist inspired. As Sunbelt cities exploded in the next
two decades (the Southwest would claim five of the nation's ten largest cities
by 1980), evangelical churches expanded their traditional influence. Between
1965 and 1974, the Southern Baptist Convention gained almost 2 million followers, and its total membership reached 12.5 million. Meanwhile, mainstream liberal Protestant denominations lost members to charismatic sects
whose leaders professed divinely inspired powers of healing and prophecy.

Resentment of Washington's civil rights agenda also resonated among
George Wallace's supporters in northern and midwestern industrial cities.
Blue-collar and middle-class white ethnic decendants of immigrants often invoked traditional virtues such as patriotism, religion, the work ethic, and family loyalty. Hostile to the counterculture and the national media, millions of
Italian, Greek, and Slavic Americans centered their families and social lives
around communal practices from the past, a phenomenon reflected in such
Hollywood films as *The Godfather, Parts I and II* (1971, 1974), *Rocky* (1976),
and *Saturday Night Fever* (1977).

Many working-class whites blamed "permissive" schools, "liberal" media,
misguided judges, and amoral officials for rising welfare costs, higher taxes, increased drug use, and criminal activity (crime rates doubled between 1960 and
1980). In cities such as Philadelphia, voters elected tough law and order mayors
like Police Commissioner Frank Rizzo. Neighborhood anticrime groups such
as the Guardian Angels and New York's Jewish Defense League (JDL) established foot patrols to protect city residents, leading to increased racial tensions
in some cases. The most controversial expression of white ethnic power centered on the campaign against court-ordered busing. Busing, which was designed to achieve racial integration in northern public schools, raised fears that
inner-city youth would bring crime, drug use, and poverty into stable, white

neighborhoods. Grassroots antibusing activists such as Boston's Louise Day Hicks led demonstrations and boycotts in the 1970s to protest the imposition of school integration by liberal government officials.

As federal courts integrated public schools in the South and reduced the region's proportion of African Americans in segregated educational facilities to 8 percent, Nixon professed to endorse racial equality and due process. Yet in northern suburbs, the White House tailored civil rights enforcement to meet the preferences of white Wallace supporters and Republican conservatives. When the Supreme Court unanimously sanctioned busing to promote school integration in 1973, Nixon rejected use of "arbitrary" guidelines and proposed a congressional moratorium on the forced transfer of pupils. Federal judges responded by slowing racial integration in the North, and the Supreme Court confined busing to districts that intentionally segregated. By 1974 half of African American students in northern and western states remained in schools whose racial composition was at least 95 percent black.

Insisting that "black capitalism" offered the surest road to equal opportunity, Nixon followed White House advisor Moynihan's call for a civil rights policy of "benign neglect." The president denounced racial quotas as "a dangerous detour away from the traditional value of measuring a person on the basis of ability." Yet the Nixon administration quietly extended the implementation of affirmative action (the principle of compensatory racial justice) to include employment and union membership practices. Affirmative action drove a wedge between Democratic constituencies in organized labor and in the civil rights movement. Lyndon Johnson's Department of Labor had responded to historic patterns of racial prejudice by requiring government construction contractors to end job discrimination. In 1969 Nixon's Secretary of Labor George P. Shultz introduced the "Philadelphia Plan," a program that applied a proportional system of minority hiring in federally funded construction and required contractors to file affirmative action policies with the Labor Department.

In 1971 the Supreme Court upheld preferential hiring in *Griggs v. Duke Power Co.* (1971) by ruling that job applicants could not be subjected to aptitude tests or arbitrary job qualifications if such policies sustained discriminatory patterns. The decision paved the way for antibias suits against fire and police departments and against building contractors. Congress advanced affirmative action by expanding the enforcement powers of the Equal Employment Opportunity Commission (EEOC). By 1974 the Washington bureaucracy provided more than $240 million a year in "set-asides" for minority contractors. By then, racial and ethnic minorities constituted one-fifth of the federal government's civilian labor force, and affirmative action affected one-third of the nation's work force.

The Labor Department had not originally targeted women workers, but in 1970 Nixon approved an agency directive that ordered equal treatment of

Saturday Night Fever (1977)

In June 1976, New York Magazine *published a story about current youth culture titled "Tribal Rites of the New Saturday Night." "They know nothing of flower power or meditation, pansexuality, or mind expansion. No waterbeds or Moroccan cushions, no hand-thrown pottery, for them. No hep jargon either, and no Pepsi revolutions. In many cases, they genuinely can't remember who Bob Dylan was, let alone Ken Kesey or Timothy Leary. Haight-Ashbury, Woodstock, Altamont—all of them draw a blank."*

    Observing that the youth of the 1960s had lived in a time of prosperity and so could afford to "run free [and] indulge themselves in whatever treats they wished," author Nik Cohn noted that the economic shortages of the 1970s had reduced opportunities for self-indulgence. "So the new generation takes few risks," he wrote. "It goes through high school obedient; graduates, looks for a job, saves, and plans. Endures. And once a week, on Saturday night, its one great moment of release, it explodes."

Paramount Pictures/Archive Photos

Here was the inspiration for one of the decade's box-office hits, Saturday Night Fever, *which catapulted actor-dancer John Travolta to stardom and defined the mass culture of disco music, dance, and fashion. At a time when teenage gangs prowled urban streets, "tagged" public places with graffiti, and accounted for a surge in city crime, the movie softened the image of young toughs, treating them not as delinquents but as victims of social class and circumstances. "They got it all locked up," says one of the kids in the movie. "Ain't nobody gonna give you a chance."*

Set in Bay Ridge, Brooklyn, an Italian working-class neighborhood, the movie contrasted the ambitions of Tony Manero (Travolta) with the limits imposed by social class, family, church, and peer culture. It also reflected economic and social trends in the 1970s—Tony's father is an unemployed construction worker, his housewife-mother talks about getting a job, and his older brother decides to abandon the celibate priesthood for new age spirituality. As Tony's domestic world distingegrates, the local disco club Odyssey 2001 presents a fantasyland of mirrors and strobe lights as well as a dance contest that promises fame for couples who perform with flamboyance and precision.

Tony rises to the opportunity but is distracted by a new acquaintance, Stephanie McDonald (played by Karen.Lynn Gorney), who pretends to be sophisticated. "There's a world of difference between us," she says defiantly, explaining that her job in Manhattan gives her opportunities unimagined in the borough of Brooklyn. "You're nowhere," she tells Tony, "on your way to no place." Unlike Tony's other dance partners, who use sex to catch the guys, Stephanie demands respect.

In the end, Tony decides to follow her across the Brooklyn Bridge and take his chances in the metropolis. The movie thus suggested the possibility of leaving behind old neighborhoods, old values, old rules. But Tony's implied mobility requires not only talent, but determination. "I'm an able person," he announces hopefully.

The movie's success reflected that optimistic message. Instead of following violent gangs or finding a community through nihilistic "punk" culture, Travolta's character appealed to dreams of upward social mobility through hard work, self-discipline, and good character. This vision was punctuated by the pulsating rhythms of the soundtrack, which featured original disco music by the BeeGees (the album grossed four times as much as the movie). Yet the film's resolution was ambiguous. As both characters discard their working-class bravado to become mutually supportive friends, not lovers, it is far from clear whether Tony and Stephanie can "make it" in the upscale but calculating world across the river.

both sexes in recruitment, job opportunities, pay, and the granting of seniority rights. Congress supplemented such coverage in 1972 by prohibiting sex discrimination in all federally funded educational programs and thereby legislated equal support for men and women in collegiate athletics. Democratic pressure also led the administration to continue civil rights reform when Congress renewed the Voting Rights Act in 1970. The law retained federal registrars in southern states and suspended literacy tests for another five years. It also triggered the deployment of registrars anywhere in the country where more than half of the minority population of voting age had failed to register.

Nixon's support for minority voting rights played a key role in the president's "southern strategy." Anticipating that newly enfranchised African Americans would vote Democratic, the president hoped to attract white southerners to the Republican Party and end Democratic domination of the region. The White House courted white votes in the South by balancing its qualified support for civil rights with a series of controversial nominations to the Supreme Court. As a presidential candidate, Nixon had denounced the court for "permissiveness" for abolishing compulsory prayer in public schools and for requiring procedural protections for criminal suspects. When Chief Justice Earl Warren retired in 1969, the president chose Minnesota moderate Warren E. Burger to replace him. When a second vacancy occurred that year, the White House nominated South Carolina Judge Clement F. Haynsworth. After the Democratic Senate questioned the conservative Haynsworth about a judicial conflict of interest, however, he became the first Supreme Court nominee to be rejected in forty years.

The president responded to the Haynsworth defeat by nominating another southerner, G. Harold Carswell, but the Florida judge failed to win Senate confirmation after revelations concerning white supremacist statements made earlier in his career. Infuriated, the president denounced "regional discrimination" and claimed that the power of appointment had been abrogated by liberals hostile to a strict interpretation of the Constitution. Yet the White House eased tensions by selecting Harry A. Blackmun, a well-qualified moderate, whom the Senate easily confirmed. When two more vacancies occurred in 1971, the appointments of Lewis F. Powell Jr. and William Rehnquist provided Nixon with the conservative ideological consistency he desired.

Despite White House efforts to mold a conservative majority, however, the Burger Court had a mixed record. The high tribunal outlawed domestic national security wiretaps without judicial permission in 1972 and ruled the death penalty unconstitutional because of its cruelty and inconsistent application. In *Roe v. Wade* (1973), its most controversial decision, the Court struck down state abortion laws covering the initial three months of pregnancy as a violation of a woman's right to privacy and an intrusion into the physician-client relationship, although the justices said that states could prohibit abortions during the final term and regulate midterm pregnancies affecting a woman's health. The Court balanced these "liberal" decisions by limiting the immunity of witnesses from prosecution, permitting nonunanimous jury verdicts in state criminal cases, and compelling journalists to testify before grand juries. Moreover, in 1975 the Court reversed earlier rulings by providing a "local option" for obscenity and pornography censorship. The following year the Court approved death penalty statutes if they were carefully constructed and applied without discrimination.

RADICAL CULTURE AND IDENTITY POLITICS

President Nixon's continuation of the war in Vietnam and his conservative policies at home inspired the spread of a broad radical movement infused with counterculture values and identity politics. One expression of the dissident culture occurred during the summer of 1969 at Woodstock, an upstate New York rock music festival whose 400,000 participants gathered to celebrate love, community, and peace. As leading bands performed, many in the crowd shared marijuana, shed their clothes, and celebrated the rise of an idealistic "new generation" and spiritually advanced "Age of Aquarius." Woodstock marked the coming of age of a youth-oriented popular culture devoted to personal liberation, affinity with nature, and rejection of traditional authorities. Yet as rock music developed into a $1 billion industry, the youth market embraced capitalist commodities such as blue jeans, waterbeds, granola, "hip" cosmetics, specialized hair accessories, and Hollywood movie hits like the documentary *Woodstock* (1970).

Countercultural interest in spirituality stimulated new concern about ecological issues. The focus on planet Earth initially surfaced as a result of the U.S. space program. In 1969 the landing of astronauts Neil A. Armstrong and Colonel Edwin E. Aldrin Jr. on the Moon in the *Apollo 11* spacecraft was televised worldwide. "That's one small step for a man," said Armstrong, "one giant leap for mankind." Space photographs confirmed that Earth was a small and frail island of life in an immense universe. Environmentalists like Barry Commoner explained that humans lived within Earth's atmosphere and needed to limit air pollution from manufacturing and auto exhausts. In *The Closing Circle* (1971), Commoner declared that the industrial system interfered with nature's attempts to regulate Earth's air, water, and soil. An international study, *The Limits to Growth* (1972), concluded that economic growth threatened to exhaust the planet's resources by the end of the twentieth century.

By April 1970, when environmentalists organized university teach-ins to celebrate the first Earth Day, a national ecological movement had begun. Activists directed attention toward toxic residues from fossil fuels and petrochemical fertilizers, nonbiodegradable waste from plastics and detergents, industrial pollutants that turned rivers into fire hazards, and damage to the atmosphere's ozone layer from aerosol sprays and other chemicals. The environmental movement took its cues from such writers as E. F. Schumacher, author of *Small Is Beautiful* (1973), who criticized the materialism of western capitalism and insisted that human survival depended on a harmonious relationship with nature that required a livable technology of solar, geothermal, and wind power. Urban cooperative stores and rural communes sought to simplify consumer habits through use of organic foods and natural fibers.

Radical culture also embraced the feminist revolution, which used liberatory "rap groups" and "consciousness-raising" sessions to build collective self-esteem among growing numbers of middle-class women. Inspired by the politics of identity, Gloria Steinem launched *Ms.* magazine in 1971. Calls for the restructuring of patriarchy and capitalism appeared in such provocative books as Kate Millett's *Sexual Politics* (1969), Shulamith Firestone's *The Dialectic of Sex: The Case for Feminist Revolution* (1970), and Robin Morgan's *Sisterhood Is Powerful* (1970). These works not only inspired the spread of women's studies classes and programs but also contributed to bonds of solidarity among radical women whose empowerment derived from their criticism of the social and moral conventions of the status quo.

Opponents of economic discrimination against women constituted another segment of the feminist movement. Demanding that the market treat women equally as individuals, these activists worked with such groups as the National Organization for Women (NOW), the academic Women's Equity Action League (WEAL), and the Professional Women's Caucus (PWC). While reformers promoted "equal pay for equal work," groups like the National Women's Political Caucus helped to break down gender barriers to holding office. As congresswomen such as Shirley Chisholm and Bella Abzug assumed prominence in the early 1970s, radical and reformist feminists joined forces to endorse the equal rights amendment (ERA), which Congress approved and sent to the states for ratification in 1972. The following year, women's rights activists celibrated *Roe v. Wade*, the Supreme Court's landmark decision on abortion, as a victory for women's freedom to control their bodies. After 1973 abortion clinics and hospitals performed more than 1.5 million legal abortion procedures each year. Meanwhile, a growing feminist health movement explored alternative methods of birthing, healing, and treatment of women's diseases such as breast cancer.

The women's liberation movement inspired protests among homosexuals of both genders. The movement originated in 1969, when New York City police raided the Stonewall Inn, a gay men's bar in Greenwich Village, and angry patrons fought back against harassment for the first time. Gay men and lesbians soon announced a national gay power and civil rights movement that portrayed homosexuality as a chosen lifestyle instead of as a disease or criminal pastime. Their efforts at self-validation inspired the American Psychiatric Society to drop its classification of homosexuality as a mental disorder in 1975. The anniversary of the Stonewall riot continues to serve as an occasion for yearly marches to celebrate gay pride.

Native Americans, seeking to overcome a legacy of economic devastation, government abuse, and social demoralization, also turned to identity politics. In 1969 members of the American Indian Movement (AIM) began an eighteen-month occupation of San Francisco Bay's Alcatraz Island, the site of a former federal prison, to demand that the government permit them to establish a cultural center on its grounds. The protest was part of an effort by Indian leaders to revive historical traditions of worship, dance, poetry, and healing in community centers and university Native American studies programs. Activists also pursued economic and political goals. Passage of the Alaska Native Land Claims Act in 1971 returned nearly $1 billion and 40 million acres to that state's original inhabitants. Yet the overall plight of indigenous peoples remained abysmal. As the Native American population neared 1 million, average income remained less than that of African Americans.

In 1972 AIM protested government corruption and neglect of Native Americans by mounting a "Trail of Broken Treaties" march to Washington that resulted in a takeover of the Bureau of Indian Affairs. The following spring AIM focused attention on the Pine Ridge reservation in South Dakota, where Sioux dissidents were protesting federal collusion in tribal corruption. Hundreds of AIM activists occupied the village of Wounded Knee, took hostages, and confronted federal marshals in a series of armed clashes. The siege lasted seventy-one days, but U.S. officials refused to reopen disputed treaty talks.

Mexican Americans comprised another group that turned to radical politics to assert ethnic identity. During the 1970s population growth and endemic poverty in Mexico encouraged between 3.5 and 6 million residents to immigrate illegally to the United States. These "undocumented aliens" willingly accepted low-paying jobs, mainly in the Southwest, and eventually constituted 10 percent of California's labor pool. Although Chicanos continued to work as migrant field hands, a larger number found employment in the service sector or worked for nonunion subcontractors in the garment trades. Unionization of Mexican American women became a national issue in the early 1970s when the Amalgamated Clothing Workers organized a consumer boycott to support a strike against the manufacturer of Farah pants. After the workers gained a union contract, the company gradually moved its operations to Mexico. As a contingent labor force, Mexican Americans received only 70 percent of median white income. By 1980 one-fifth of the Chicano community lived in poverty, and median educational levels for Chicanos remained less than tenth grade.

Building on the success of Cesar Chavez's farm workers union, Mexican American activists such as Corky Gonzales and Jose Angel Gutierrez organized civil rights protests in Denver and south Texas in the late 1960s and early 1970s. In Los Angeles and Denver, young Chicanos asserted independence from Anglo authorities by wielding weapons as Brown Berets. The rural New Mexican activist Reies Lopez Tijerina also armed followers to protest the loss

Phyllis Schlafly (1924-   )

"Politics is too important to be left to politicians," declared conservative Republican Phyllis Schlafly in 1969. "More women should strive for the elected positions now held by men, and more women should support those who do." Women's leadership, she added, "can raise the moral tone of politics. They keep their ideals while playing the game." Although spoken in the language of feminism, Schlafly's appeal did not reflect a feminist agenda. In fact, it was just the opposite. During the 1970s she would emerge as the nation's most vocal opponent of the proposed equal rights amendment (ERA).

Long involved in Republican politics, Schlafly preferred to identify herself as an Alton, Illinois, "housewife" and mother of six. Born into a pious Roman Catholic family in Depression St. Louis, she had watched her mother enter the workforce when her father lost his job. After achieving academic success at Radcliffe and obtaining a government job in Washington, she married a wealthy corporate lawyer—"who rescued me from the life of a working girl," she later said—and moved to southern Illinois. While busy as a homemaker, Schlafly still found time to participate in community organizations and Republican politics. As a supporter of the conservative Robert Taft, she ran unsuccessfully as a "powder-puff" candidate for Congress in 1952.

Endorsing the anticommunist crusade of the 1950s, Schlafly cultivated expertise on national defense issues as a leader of the Daughters of the American Revolution. In 1963 Schlafly was the only woman to testify in the Senate in opposition to the ratification of the nuclear test ban treaty. She achieved celebrity status in Republican circles the next year when her campaign biography of Barry Goldwater, *A Choice, Not an*

of historic land claims. Mexican American students at southwestern universities adopted confrontational tactics to establish Chicano studies programs and assert ethnic pride. The cultural awakening produced scholarly journals such as *Aztlan,* the popular magazines *El Grito* and *La Raza,* and moving explorations of Chicano roots by novelists and poets such as Raymond Barrio, Rudolfo Anaya, Lorna Dee Cervantes, and Angela de Hoyos.

Echo, sold 3 million copies. Goldwater's loss failed to dampen her spirits. Pursuing her enthusiastic opposition to detente, she proceeded to coauthor a series of small books exposing Soviet perfidy and the failure of liberals to stand up to the communist menace. When her ardent conservatism cost her the leadership of the National Federation of Republican Women, she organized an independent network of her supporters and began publishing a newsletter called "The Phyllis Schlafly Report."

Since she worked outside the Republican establishment, Schlafly earned no rewards from Nixon's victory in 1968. When the president opened diplomatic relations with China and signed the SALT disarmament treaty, she broke with the administration. But congressional passage of the ERA in 1972 rejuvenated her career. "Their motive is totally radical," she said of the new feminists. "They hate men, marriage, and children. They are out to destroy morality and the family. They look upon husbands as exploiters, children as an evil to be avoided (by abortion if necessary), and the family as an institution which keeps women in 'second-class citizenship.'" She announced a new lobbying group called Stop-ERA and led her conservative army into battle.

Arguing that feminists were selfish and socially irresponsible, she wrote articles, gave lectures, organized public demonstrations, and sought private meetings with key legislators in the states. Her 1977 book, *The Power of the Positive Woman,* warned that the ERA would "mandate the gender-free, rigid, absolute equality of treatment of men and women" and would create "a constitutional mandate that the husband no longer has the primary duty to support his wife and child." She also protested that the ERA would permit women to serve equally with men in the armed forces. Schlafly's moment of greatest triumph occurred when the ERA failed to gain ratification by the necessary three-fourths of the states in 1982.

As Mexican Americans gained an economic foothold, middle-class and professional organizations substituted political lobbying for protest. By the 1970s the Congress of Mexican American Unity served as an umbrella for 200 civic groups, and Mexican Americans played a major role in the National Council of La Raza, a consortium of twenty-six Hispanic organizations. In the Los Angeles area and in San Antonio, Mexican Americans elected public officials, used political clout to fight discrimination, and campaigned for bilingual education. In 1974 the Supreme Court ruled in *Lau v. Nichols* that public schools were required to teach children in a language they understood.

Radical African Americans engaged in the most bitterly contested assertions of identity politics. Activists organized an extended student strike at San Francisco State and an armed march on a building at Cornell University to demand the creation of black studies programs and more hiring of minority faculty. Meanwhile, the Black Panthers continued to face the wrath of the FBI and local police, resulting in the death of some forty activists by December 1969. In one episode, Chicago police and state officers raided the apartment of Panther leaders Fred Hampton and Mark Clark and shot them to death while they slept. Even so, the Black Panthers continued organizing, even in the nation's prisons. In California, several bloody confrontations led to the shooting death in 1970 of Panther prisoner George Jackson. The following year, New York Governor Nelson Rockefeller ordered state troopers to storm Attica prison, where white, Puerto Rican, and black inmates had taken over the facility to protest degrading conditions. The confrontation resulted in the killing of thirty-three prisoners and ten guards held as hostages. By middecade, control of the Panthers had shifted to African American women, including Elaine Brown and Erika Huggins.

ANTIWAR PROTEST, KENT STATE, AND POLITICAL STALEMATE

Amid declining public support for the Vietnam War in the fall of 1969, peace activists organized a series of huge antiwar rallies. On October 15, Vietnam Moratorium Day, more than 200,000 protesters, many of them demonstrating for the first time, marched in Boston, New York, and Washington, D.C. One month later, 250,000 marched to the Washington Monument. When 10,000 demonstrators were tear-gassed after breaking away from the rally to storm the Justice Department, Attorney General John Mitchell remarked that "it looked like the Russian Revolution."

President Nixon responded to antiwar activism by assuring the nation in a televised speech that protest was not necessary since the administration was "Vietnamizing the search for peace." "Precipitate withdrawal" from Vietnam would be a "popular and easy course," he acknowledged, but defeat and humiliation would bring the "collapse of confidence in American leadership." Promising an all-volunteer army and an end to the draft, Nixon marginalized protesters as a "vocal minority" in contrast to the compliant "silent majority." Vice President Spiro Agnew dismissed demonstrators and news commentators as an "effete corps of impudent snobs who characterized themselves as intellectuals." Complaining that the media legitimized the antiwar message,

Nixon Presidential Materials Project

Vice President Spiro T. Agnew executed the Nixon administration's rhetorical campaign against anti–Vietnam War dissenters and other critics.

Agnew took particular aim at the "tiny enclosed fraternity of privileged men" in TV journalism that offered "instant analysis" of presidential speeches.

The White House's difficulty in managing wartime information surfaced when newspapers published the first photographs of the recently uncovered My Lai massacre. After the Tet Offensive of 1968, 347 unarmed South Vietnamese peasants, mostly women, children, and the elderly, had been massacred by U.S. troops under the command of Lieutenant William Calley. The case epitomized the bitter divisions caused by the Vietnam War. Whereas critics described the act as racially motivated genocide, defenders argued that villages like My Lai were often staging grounds for Vietcong attacks on U.S.

troops. Others contended that the beleaguered company had cracked under the strains of a war in which commanders were expected to produce high enemy body counts. Although Nixon expressed sympathy for Calley, a military court convicted the lieutenant of murder in 1971. After the president reduced Calley's sentence, the lieutenant was paroled and received an honorable discharge in 1974.

Nixon hoped to build support for a peace agreement that would leave the South Vietnamese government in place. By the spring of 1970 the president had withdrawn 110,000 U.S. troops from Southeast Asia as part of "Vietnamization." To impress the North Vietnamese with U.S. resolve, however, the White House decided to expand the war to Cambodia. On April 30, 1970, Nixon went on television to tell a stunned nation that 25,000 U.S. and South Vietnamese troops had entered Cambodia in an "incursion" designed to "shorten the war." He described the operation's purpose as "cleaning out major North Vietnamese and Vietcong occupied territories" and destroying the "main headquarters for the entire Communist military operation in South Vietnam." The president also hoped to bolster the anticommunist military regime that recently had taken control of the Cambodian capital. Proclaiming that the United States could not act "like a pitiful, helpless giant," Nixon protested that he would rather be a one-term president than allow the nation to become a "second-rate power."

The Cambodian invasion revitalized the antiwar movement. As student protests spread, Nixon dismissed activists as "bums," and Ohio Governor James Rhodes ordered the National Guard to police several dissident campuses. At Kent State, antiwar protesters trashed the town business district and burned the university's Reserve Officers' Training Corps (ROTC) building. The next day, May 4, 1970, a small number of campus demonstrators failed to respond to an order to disperse during a noon rally and threw rocks and bottles at guardsmen deploying tear gas. Several of the tense troopers wheeled around and fired into the crowd. The attack wounded nine and killed four, including two students leaving class. The Kent State deaths electrified a nation already shocked by news of the Cambodian invasion. University presidents had warned Nixon that peace could not be restored on campuses without ending the war, but Vice President Agnew attributed the violence to "elitist" permissiveness toward "psychotic and criminal elements . . . traitors and thieves and perverts . . . in our midst." Public opinion polls showed that majorities sympathized not with the students, but with the National Guard.

In the most extensive student unrest in U.S. history, post–Kent State strikes closed 350 universities and colleges and mobilized millions of demonstrators, many first-time protesters. At Mississippi's Jackson State, two more students were killed when state police responded to antiwar activism at the predominantly African American college by firing on a dormitory. Later that summer, the National Chicano Moratorium organized a peaceful march of 20,000 pro-

EXHIBIT **6-4**   **THE THRUST INTO CAMBODIA, 1970**

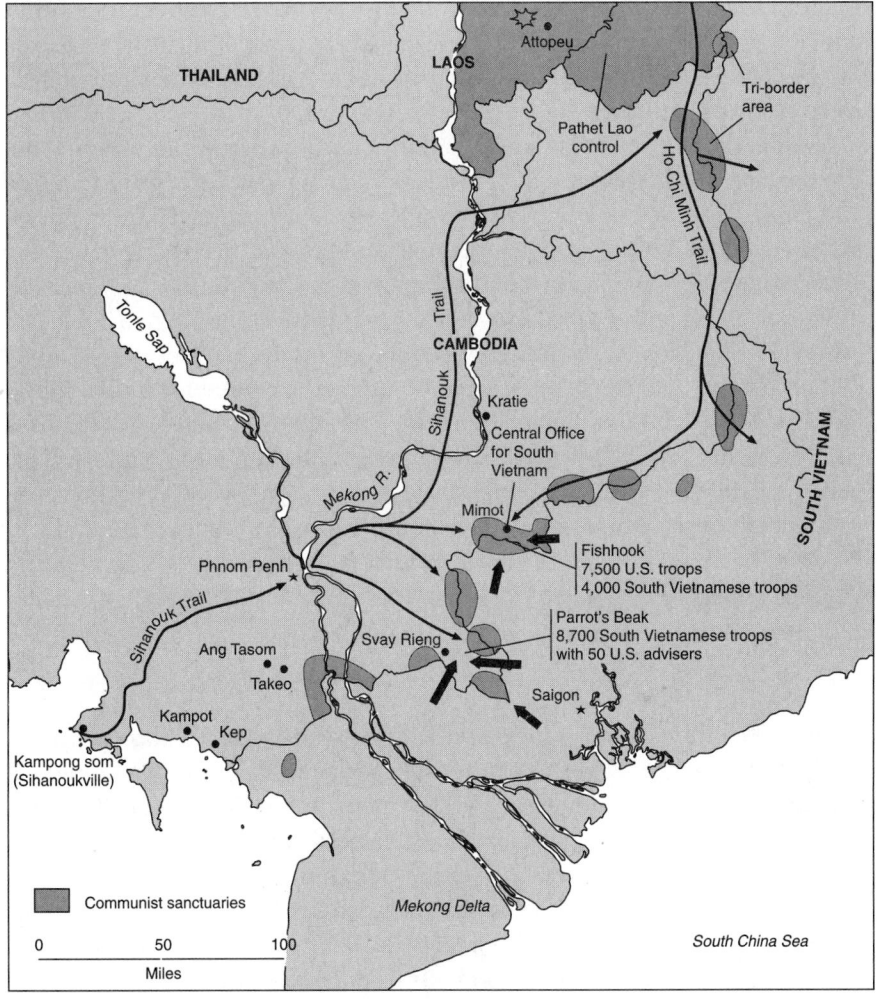

testers in Los Angeles to emphasize that Mexican Americans accounted for nearly one-fifth of the Vietnam War casualties from the Southwest. At an ensuing street festival, county deputies made mass arrests that resulted in the death of Chicano journalist Ruben Salazar.

Despite Nixon's showdown with the antiwar movement, the president withdrew U.S. troops from Cambodia two months later. Aware of the military's failure to uncover communist installations and sensitive to growing peace sentiment, Congress set a summer deadline on the Cambodian deployment, the first such limit imposed on the commander in chief during the Indochinese conflict. While the administration mounted "protective-reaction" air strikes to increase the pressure on North Vietnam in the fall of 1970, the Pentagon continued to withdraw ground forces. With the decline in draft quotas and U.S. casualties, the press curtailed coverage of the war. Yet Nixon purposely taunted antiwar demonstrators as he campaigned for Republican congressional candidates.

While the White House sought a position of strength from which to negotiate with North Vietnam, the president announced early in 1971 that U.S. and South Vietnamese troops had invaded Laos, where the CIA had organized covert bombing campaigns against communist insurgents since the 1960s. The new escalation inspired spring marches of hundreds of thousands of protesters, including 2,000 members of Vietnam Veterans Against the War (VVAW), who threw their military decorations on the Capitol steps. In one demonstration, 30,000 activists blocked Washington commuter traffic. Monitored by a unit jointly commanded by the CIA and local police, 12,000 dissidents were swept off the streets in the largest mass arrest in U.S. history. Such police activity involved widespread suspension of legal procedures, however, and federal courts later awarded the victims modest damages.

POPULIST CONSERVATISM AND THE WAR AGAINST DISSENT

Domestic conflict over the Vietnam War revealed profound class divisions. Many Americans viewed the blatant sexuality and drug use of the radical counterculture as self-indulgent and destructive. Indeed, an "underground" trade in drugs took its toll in substance-related deaths, including three rock superstars—Jimi Hendrix, Janis Joplin, and Jim Morrison. Drug use led Charles Manson's self-styled "family" of hippie revolutionaries to murder seven wealthy Hollywood Hills residents in 1969, a case that received extensive media attention and drew comments from President Nixon.

Movement extremists also generated criticism for revolutionary rhetoric and violence. Some members of Students for a Democratic Society (SDS) formed the "Weathermen" and went underground to escape police. Other young radicals aligned themselves with "third world" Marxists and attacked the United States as racist and imperialist. Intent on "bringing the war home," secret affinity groups bombed at least fourteen government and military installations between 1969 and 1974. Three members of the Weathermen lost their lives in a 1970 explosion in a Greenwich Village townhouse used to assemble bombs. That year a bomb planted at a mathematics research facility at the University of Wisconsin killed a graduate student. Activists and police engaged in repeated confrontations—from Santa Barbara, California, where street people reacted to police harassment by burning down a branch of the Bank of America; to the University of California at Berkeley, where thousands of residents protested police destruction of a "people's park" built on university property.

Until the inauguration of the Selective Service lottery system in 1969, predominantly middle-class activists were exempted from the draft as college students—only 20 percent of the 3 million who served in Vietnam came from middle- or upper-class families. In contrast, limited educational and job opportunities pushed poor and working-class men into military service, although the most effective draft evaders often were inner-city blacks who simply ignored Selective Service requirements. Polls of white northern workers revealed that nearly half supported the immediate withdrawal of troops by 1970. Yet fully half of those favoring disengagement were hostile to antiwar actions. Although the peace movement depicted ordinary soldiers as pawns of higher-ups, many citizens viewed attacks on the armed services and on the war as extensions of class privilege legitimizing escape from military duty.

Working-class criticism of antiwar protest and counterculture lifestyles often found expression in white country music, as in Merle Haggard's "Okie from Muskogee" (1969) or in "The Fightin' Side of Me" (1970), a song confronting those who were "runnin' down our country." Similar convictions about the immorality of protest surfaced in 1970 when New York City construction workers assaulted college students participating in a nonviolent antiwar demonstration on Wall Street. After receiving praise for their patriotism from President Nixon, the labor unions mobilized thousands of supporters in a "Victory in Vietnam" parade down New York City's Broadway.

Convinced that domestic disunity would undermine Kissinger's secret diplomacy, Nixon turned to coercive measures to create a wartime consensus. When the liberal *New York Times* reported the secret bombing of Cambodia, the White House ordered "national security" wiretaps on the telephone lines of four journalists and thirteen administration aides. To ascertain the source of future "leaks," Nixon officials hired private investigators to make additional wiretaps. Federal prosecutors also accused Father Philip Berrigan and other Catholic radicals of participating in an alleged plot to kidnap Henry Kissinger, although the defendants were acquitted. In another case, the administration indicted eight organizers of the demonstrations outside Chicago's 1968 Democratic Convention for conspiracy to violate antiriot laws. Led by Yippies Abbie Hoffman and Jerry Rubin, the defendants used the trial to showcase the revolutionary culture of the protest movement and mocked the court and government prosecutors. The judge reacted to continuing protests by defendant Bobby Seale by having the Black Panther leader gagged and chained. After five months of contentious testimony and repeated contempt citations, the jury rejected nearly all of the government's arguments.

Nixon officials used the increased militancy among dissidents to press for a more formal program of domestic intelligence. In 1970 presidential aide

Tom Huston proposed an interagency intelligence unit composed of the FBI, CIA, National Security Agency, and Pentagon intelligence groups that would conduct illegal burglaries, wiretappings, mail openings, solicitation of campus informants, and interceptions of international communications. After the Huston plan had been approved by the president and had been implemented for five days, however, J. Edgar Hoover squelched the plan because it threatened FBI control of domestic security. But government agencies continued to rely on secret and illegal methods to monitor and disrupt domestic dissenters. The Internal Revenue Service used tax audits to harass individuals and organizations with "extremist views and philosophies."

The Nixon administration faced another public relations challenge in 1971 when *The New York Times* began to publish the secret Pentagon Papers. The documents, a history of the Vietnam War commissioned by former Defense Secretary Robert McNamara, illustrated the continuity of government duplicity during the Kennedy and Johnson administrations. Fearing that future leaks might threaten Soviet and Chinese confidence in U.S. ability to conduct secret negotiations, the administration sought a court order to stop publication of the papers, but the Supreme Court ruled that the government had no grounds for preemptive censorship. Dissatisfied with the Court's finding, the White House ordered a Special Investigations Unit (the "plumbers") to investigate Daniel Ellsberg, a former Defense Department planner who had confessed to releasing the Pentagon Papers. After the Justice Department indicted Ellsberg for espionage and conspiracy, the plumbers burglarized the office of Ellsberg's psychiatrist to gain confidential information on the defendant.

DÉTENTE, CHILE, AND THE ELECTION OF 1972

Seeking to press the North Vietnamese to accept a workable settlement of the Indochinese war, Nixon turned for help to the People's Republic of China and the Soviet Union. Washington had refused to recognize China since the communist revolution of 1949. Cold warriors like Nixon had continually warned that recognition would lead to the abandonment of the Nationalist government on Taiwan (Formosa) and would legitimize communist subversion of established regimes. However, when the Chinese made diplomatic overtures in 1969, Nixon reasoned that he could win concessions from both Beijing and Moscow and could stabilize global tensions if he took advantage of the deepening rift between the two communist rivals.

Nixon and National Security Assistant Kissinger initiated the new balance of power by easing restrictions on U.S. travel to mainland China. In 1971 the United States announced the end of a twenty-one-year embargo on Chinese trade. Washington also accepted the People's Republic of China's admission to the United Nations, even though China claimed the seat of the Republic of China located on Nationalist Taiwan. In 1972 Nixon formalized détente when he visited China and signed a joint communiqué with Chinese Premier Zhou Enlai in which the two nations pledged "peaceful mutuality." The most important part of the negotiations involved a U.S. promise to withdraw military forces from Taiwan.

Nixon followed the agreement with China by traveling to Moscow for disarmament negotiations. The resulting Strategic Arms Limitation Treaty (SALT) of 1972 limited the construction of antiballistic missile sites and nuclear delivery systems. Although the accord did not rule out the development of new weapons, it represented the Cold War's first advance toward regulating existing arsenals and was the biggest step toward nuclear disarmament since the atmospheric test ban treaty of 1963. The Nixon-Brezhnev talks also produced consensus on the status quo in divided Berlin and a trade pact providing for the sale of nearly one-fourth of the U.S. grain crop to the Soviets. When Secretary Leonid I. Brezhnev visited Washington in 1973, the two leaders signed additional agreements covering nuclear arms, cultural exchange, and the peaceful use of atomic energy.

Recognizing the limits of U.S. strength, Nixon and Kissinger acknowledged the Soviet Union as a superpower with virtual nuclear parity. Despite this acceptance, détente reaffirmed the president's conviction that communist negotiating partners only respected military strength and that Washington should never appear weak. The White House saw U.S. hegemony in the Western Hemisphere as a symbol of national credibility and power. Thus, the administration reacted harshly to the election of Marxist Salvador Allende as president of Chile in 1970. Although Nixon shared Kennedy's and Johnson's distrust of the CIA's intelligence capability, he and Kissinger ordered the agency to destabilize the Allende regime. The CIA provided secret funds to opposing politicians, friendly media, and anticommunist unions, and the U.S. government and private lending agencies refused to provide credit to Chile, thereby creating severe economic shortages and political chaos. Allende was assassinated in a bloody 1973 coup by Chilean military leaders, who executed thousands of dissidents and abolished democracy.

As the administration prepared for the 1972 presidential election, the Democratic Party became the main political vehicle for antiwar criticism, demands for social justice by racial minorities, and women's rights. Under the "McGovern rules," instituted after 1968, Democratic convention delegates and nominees were chosen in open primaries, not by party bosses. The new procedures also required proportional representation of women and racial minorities—the percent of female delegates jumped from 10 percent to 40 percent between 1968 and 1972. Because upper-middle-class citizens more frequently participated in

Daniel Ellsberg (1931–   )

Converted from righteous advocate of the Cold War crusade to antiwar activist, Daniel Ellsberg played a central role in bringing down the Nixon presidency. Born in Chicago during the Depression, Ellsberg attended an exclusive preparatory school on a full scholarship before getting an

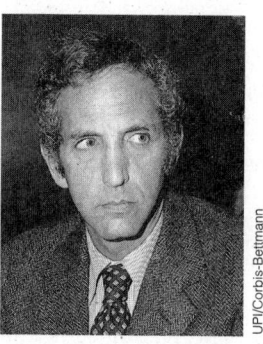

economics degree from Harvard. Yet he abandoned the academic life in 1954 by volunteering for the Marines and by becoming an infantry sharpshooter. Two years later, Ellsberg resumed his studies at Harvard and Cambridge. His Ph.D. thesis in economics focused on strategic military planning.

A tall, lean man with a sharp-featured, narrow face, Ellsberg embraced the Cold War as an advisor to Senator John Kennedy on foreign policy. In 1959 he signed on with the Rand Corporation, a California consultant to the Defense Department, as a strategic analyst whose speciality was nuclear warfare. By 1964, Ellsberg had become convinced that the future of democracy hinged on the war in Vietnam. He served as a special international security aide in the Pentagon. Then he volunteered to become State Department liaison with the counterinsurgency effort in the Vietnamese countryside. By 1967, he was special assistant to the deputy ambassador.

With a Boy Scout's enthusiasm for containing communist aggression, Ellsberg often donned military gear to accompany counterinsurgency teams on "clearing operations" in Vietnam. Yet by 1966 he began to note the failure of pacification campaigns, the rising number of civilian casualties, widespread corruption in the South Vietnamese government and

primaries than did working-class voters, the new system favored consideration of the cultural issues endorsed by the more affluent. As a result, delegates openly debated abortion rights, the legalization of marijuana, and gay liberation. More than 100 convention participants publicly acknowledged their homosexuality in 1972.

The Democratic Convention nominated South Dakota's George McGovern, a liberal senator who had criticized the Vietnam War. McGovern called

military, and repeated reports of the torture of Vietcong prisoners. Ellsberg informed Defense Secretary McNamara that, although the war was stalemated, its level of violence continued to increase and that official reporting was not telling decision makers what they needed to know. On leaving Saigon in 1967 he proposed a high-level study of U.S. policy in Vietnam. By the time McNamara ordered such an assessment, Ellsberg had returned to Rand and became one of thirty-six researchers to work on the project.

The Pentagon study convinced Ellsberg that the war stemmed from a sordid history of aggression perpetuated by several presidents. Seeing no justification for U.S. policy and feeling guilty about his complicity in pacification, Ellsberg made copies of the secret study report, soon to be known as the Pentagon Papers, and resigned from Rand in 1970. Once he became convinced that the Nixon administration was about to repeat the mistakes and deception of its predecessors, he released portions of the Pentagon Papers to *The New York Times.*

Although a court injunction temporarily halted publication of the Pentagon Papers, the Supreme Court overruled any prior restraint on publishing them. Nevertheless, the Nixon administration indicted Ellsberg for conspiracy, theft, and violation of espionage laws. To discredit the disaffected strategist, the White House assigned his case to a newly formed Special Investigations Unit. In September 1971 the "plumbers" broke into the Los Angeles office of Ellsberg's psychiatrist. This government misconduct resulted in dismissal of all charges against the man who had leaked the Pentagon Papers and the prosecution of leading White House aides for subverting the Fourth Amendment.

for a "politics of conscience" embracing tax reform and a shift from defense spending to social needs. Citing Nixon's ties to big business, he castigated the Republican administration as "the most corrupt in history." Yet the Democratic candidate's plan for a guaranteed national income lacked credibility, and he was forced to replace his vice presidential running mate when press reports announced that the nominee had repeatedly been hospitalized for depression. The McGovern campaign hoped to take advantage of the Twenty-sixth

EXHIBIT **6-5   U.S. NATIONAL DEFENSE AS A PERCENTAGE OF TOTAL FEDERAL OUTLAYS, 1968–1976**

1968	46.0
1970	41.8
1972	34.3
1974	29.5
1976	24.1

Source: *Statistical Abstract of the United States* (1987).

Amendment, which in 1971 gave the vote to eighteen-year-olds. Yet young voters tended to support Wallace. By crusading against busing and the "suffocating bureaucracy in Washington," Wallace won Democratic primary victories in Florida, Michigan, and Maryland before being paralyzed by an assassin's bullet in May 1972.

Nixon's campaign followed the strategies of Kevin Phillips's *The Emerging Republican Majority* (1969), which sought to refashion the New Deal electoral coalition by recruiting Wallace voters, white southerners, urban supporters in the Southwest, working-class Catholics, suburbanites, and rural Americans. These voters were philosophically opposed to the costly welfare programs established in the 1960s and clung to traditional moral and social values. Acknowledging such disaffection, Nixon instructed aides about the "gut" issues of the campaign—crime, busing, drugs, welfare, and inflation. The president called for a congressional moratorium on busing, denounced "arbitrary" government orders, and attacked racial quotas. "The way to end discrimination against some," he declared, was "not to begin discrimination against others." The White House also pointed to Kissinger's prediction that peace was "at hand" in the Vietnam negotiations.

Nixon won 61 percent of the popular vote and the entire electoral college except for Massachusetts and the District of Columbia and nearly equaled Lyndon Johnson's landslide of 1964. While McGovern received only 29 percent of the vote in the South, the president became the first twentieth-century Republican to win a majority of white Catholic and working-class voters. The Republicans also took nearly 80 percent of the Wallace vote and thereby signaled an end to the New Deal electoral coalition of the 1930s.

ENDING THE VIETNAM WAR

Empowered by a mandate at the polls, Nixon and Kissinger continued to press for an acceptable resolution of the Vietnam War. In the spring of 1971, Washington dropped its demand that a peace agreement provide for the

North's withdrawal of troops from the South. Yet the administration faced a new crisis a year later when North Vietnamese regulars invaded the central highlands, forcing further retreat by Saigon's army. Emboldened by South Vietnam's successes with pacification, however, the president refused to be intimidated by the communist advances. Denouncing Hanoi's leaders as "international outlaws," the commander in chief ordered the mining of the North's ports. He also authorized massive B-52 air strikes against enemy industrial sites, flood-control dikes, and railroad lines leading to the People's Republic of China. Within months, Hanoi dropped demands that a peace accord provide for the replacement of the Saigon government. In turn, the United States agreed to stop bombing the North. Kissinger and North Vietnamese negotiators secretly agreed to a military cease-fire in October 1972. Yet the White House allowed the South Vietnamese to veto the truce, and Kissinger abruptly announced the suspension of negotiations and the resumption of the air war.

After the 1972 presidential election, Kissinger won minor changes in the prospective agreement with the North Vietnamese. When communist negotiators consulted with their superiors in Hanoi, however, the president charged them with breaking off the talks. In the "Christmas Bombing" of 1972—the most intensive air attack in military history—B-52s targeted populated areas in North Vietnam. As the campaign resulted in the loss of 15 U.S. bombers and the 121 members of the crews, congressional critics charged that Nixon and Kissinger were conducting war "by temper tantrum." Yet the attack supported the administration's repeated contention that brute force would push Hanoi toward peace on U.S. terms. By the end of the year Nixon had caused nearly 4 million tons of bombs to be dropped on Indochina, twice the amount ordered by Johnson and 1.5 times the total tonnage deployed by all armies in World War II.

Having demonstrated U.S. military power, Nixon announced in January 1973 that Kissinger had brokered an agreement that would "end the war and bring peace with honor." The Paris Peace Accord provided for the withdrawal from the South of remaining U.S. troops in exchange for North Vietnam's repatriation of 587 U.S. prisoners of war. Under the terms of the treaty, Washington recognized the Vietnamese National Liberation Front (Vietcong) and resolved the nineteen-year controversy over the two Vietnams by declaring that the seventeenth parallel was a provisional boundary instead of a political or territorial line. American military involvement in Vietnam ended in March 1973 with the withdrawal of the last combat troops and a televised homecoming of U.S. prisoners of war. Although Kissinger and his Vietnamese counterpart shared the 1973 Nobel Peace Prize, the terms of the accord hardly varied from those of the preelection agreement and were virtually identical to the ones Nixon had opposed in 1968.

WATERGATE

Despite the fact that Nixon ended the divisive U.S. presence in Vietnam, his second term would be remembered by Watergate, a series of political scandals arising from the president's desire to forge a Vietnam consensus and win a re-election landslide. As early as 1969 White House officials had ordered "national security" investigators to conduct surveillance of Senator Edward M. Kennedy, a potential Democratic candidate for the presidency. Kennedy had delayed reporting a late-night accident in which he had driven his car off a coastal bridge, drowning Mary Jo Kopechne, a former campaign aide. Nixon officials organized the Committee to Re-Elect the President (CREEP) in 1971. The panel created 400 dummy corporations to channel secret contributions and collected $55 million from corporate donors seeking preferential treatment. The committee also used "dirty tricks" such as signing the names of Democratic candidates to misleading literature to discredit presidential contenders.

Seeking information on Democratic National Chairman Lawrence O'Brien, CREEP Director John Mitchell approved covert entry into Democratic headquarters at Washington's Watergate complex in June 1972. When an electronic listening device malfunctioned, five CREEP operatives returned for a second entry and were arrested. Although Nixon press secretary Ron Ziegler dismissed the crime as a "third-rate burglary," an address book notation linked the team to White House "plumbers" G. Gordon Liddy and E. Howard Hunt. Immediately, CREEP and White House aides began a cover-up, destroying campaign records, lying to the FBI and to the grand jury, removing incriminating evidence from a White House safe, and pressuring law enforcement agencies for "cooperation." Although the disclosure would not be made for two years, Nixon initiated the Watergate cover-up by personally ordering aides to request that the CIA stop the FBI from tracing the source of Watergate funds.

By the time the trial of the Watergate burglars opened in early 1973, two of the men had received promises of executive clemency in return for continued silence. In March White House counselor John Dean brought new demands to Nixon at an Oval Office meeting in which he warned of a "cancer on the presidency" and estimated that eventual hush money payments could reach $1 million. However, the next day Nixon ordered Mitchell to continue the cover-up. Despite these precautions, news reports soon linked top White House aides to the Watergate affair. Attempting to place responsibility on Dean, Nixon fired the White House counsel and asked for the resignation of his key assistants, John Ehrlichman and H. R. Haldeman. The president also acceded to the appointment of a special Watergate prosecutor.

As a Senate Select Committee chaired by Democrat Sam Ervin began dramatic televised hearings on the scandal in 1973, Dean testified about the president's knowledge of the cover-up. He also produced evidence of the plumbers unit, the illegal Huston plan, and an administration "enemies list" submitted to the Internal Revenue Service (IRS) for possible audits. Even more astounding, White House aide Alexander Butterfield revealed that Nixon had installed secret tape-recording devices in the Oval Office. Although the president's attorneys claimed that executive privilege and the separation of powers gave him the right to preserve the confidentiality of conversations with advisors, a federal court ordered him to turn over nine tapes to the courts.

When Special Prosecutor Archibald Cox refused White House demands to stop subpoenas and cited the president's "noncompliance" with court orders, Nixon stunned the nation by ordering Attorney General Elliot Richardson to fire Cox and to abolish the special prosecutor's office. Richardson refused and resigned in protest. When Deputy Attorney General William Ruckelshaus objected to the presidential order, Nixon fired him and secured the compliance of Solicitor General Robert F. Bork. The "Saturday Night Massacre" produced wide protests, and Nixon agreed to relinquish the tapes and appoint a new special prosecutor. Yet three of the subpoenaed tapes were missing, and evidence revealed that extensive blank spots on the others had been caused by manual erasures.

By the fall of 1973 both President Nixon and Vice President Agnew faced income tax problems. Agnew had been under investigation for participation in a kickback scheme with Maryland contractors. In October the vice president pleaded "no contest" to tax evasion and resigned. Adhering to the succession provisions of the Twenty-fifth Amendment, ratified in 1967, Nixon nominated House Republican leader Gerald R. Ford for the vice presidency, and Congress quickly confirmed his choice. When the IRS announced that it was reexamining Nixon's tax deductions for the donation of his vice presidential papers, he assured a televised meeting of newspaper editors that "I'm not a crook." The agency subsequently reported that the president owed $450,000 in back taxes and penalties.

NIXON'S FALL

Weakened by Watergate, Nixon found the implementation of his foreign policy constrained. As the military draft expired in 1973, the army adopted voluntary recruitment for the first time since 1948. Moreover, the president was forced to submit to a congressionally imposed deadline of August 1973 for funding combat activities in Indochina. The compromise finally ended the bombing of Cambodia—one of Nixon's most fiercely protected projects. Congress also overrode a presidential veto to pass the War Powers Act of 1973. The landmark legislation required the chief executive to inform Congress within forty-eight hours of the deployment of overseas military forces and established a sixty-day limit on the commitment of troops without congressional

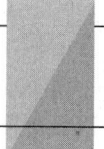

John Sirica (1904–1992)

Beneath the dark judicial robes of John Sirica sat the oldest son of a poor Italian immigrant barber. Although in 1973 he was chief judge of the federal district court in Washington, D.C., John Sirica never forgot his humble beginnings. "I came up rough-and-tough," he liked to say. "If it had not been for the Republican Party, I might never have done much better than my father." And now standing before him were four members of the Spanish-speaking Cuban exile community of Miami who were on trial for their participation in the Watergate break-in. They triggered an instinctive sympathy. If it had not been for the Republican Party, the judge suspected, they might not be in his courtroom either.

Sirica had barely worked his way through law school. Poorly educated and unsuccessful as a lawyer, he managed to get a job as an assistant government attorney in 1929. Returning to an unprofitable private practice, he served as chief counsel for a congressional committee investigating corruption in the Federal Communications Commission in 1944 but to his annoyance, Democratic politicians squashed the case. After World War II, Sirica strengthened his position in Republican circles by campaigning actively for Eisenhower. He was also a close friend of Senator Joseph McCarthy. In recognition of the attorney's loyalty, Eisenhower appointed him to the federal court in 1957. The judge soon gained a reputation for brusqueness and impatience with abstruse legal argument. The severity of his sentences earned him the nickname "Maximum John," but many of his decisions were overturned on appeal.

By 1973, Sirica's seniority made him chief judge of the Washington,

consent. Although no president has ever acknowledged the constitutionality of the statute, the War Powers Act provided the most important limitation on executive military initiative since the dawn of the Cold War.

Nixon's ability to assert U.S. power also was challenged by a new Middle East war. Just as Watergate revelations climaxed in the fall of 1973, Egyptian

D.C., district court. As a loyal Republican, he felt a special obligation to ensure a fair trial for the seven men accused of organizing the break-in at Democratic Party headquarters at the Watergate complex in June 1972. When to establish a conspiracy of silence, they all pleaded guilty, Sirica replied: "I don't think we should sit up here like nincompoops."

Exercising his authority as a federal judge, he interrupted the courtroom examinations to ask specific questions about payments and uncovered additional incriminating evidence. After a jury convicted the burglars, Sirica delayed sentencing to pressure the defendants to talk. To his delight, one of the men broke his silence under pressure, and Sirica eventually presided over the trials of many high-level coconspirators. Meanwhile, congressional investigators issued a subpoena for tape-recorded evidence to President Nixon, but the White House rejected the request on grounds of executive privilege. The constitutional dispute came to Sirica's docket. "One question kept nagging at me," he recalled. "If Nixon himself were not involved why would he stand on such an abstract principle . . . when by voluntarily turning over the tapes he could prove himself innocent and put the Watergate case behind him?" Sirica ordered the release of the subpoenaed material.

Nixon's compliance merely intensified the judge's outrage because, while listening to the presidential tapes, he discovered that the man he had supported in 1972 was vulgar, devious, and dishonest. On the day before his seventieth birthday, in his last act as chief judge, Sirica ordered the release of grand jury files to the House of Representatives, which was debating Nixon's impeachment. This material contained explosive and incriminating evidence that forced the president to resign. "I was often described as an 'obscure federal judge' and that was true," Sirica observed, "but I was not a damn fool."

and Syrian troops invaded territories claimed by Israel. When the Soviet Union airlifted supplies to Egypt, the United States responded by providing military equipment for the Israelis. In response, Arab oil producers ended the sale of petroleum products to nations friendly to Israel. After the United Nations brokered a cease-fire, the Soviets threatened to move troops to the

Middle East to supervise the truce. Nixon immediately placed U.S. forces on worldwide alert, forcing Moscow to agree to the creation of a U.N. peacekeeping force. Kissinger then resumed diplomatic relations that had been broken off with Egypt since 1967 and used "shuttle diplomacy" to arrange for U.N. buffer units to monitor the fragile cease-fire.

Despite Kissinger's triumphs, the Arab oil embargo dramatized U.S. dependence on foreign energy sources and intensified chronic inflation. Fearing recession, Nixon had relaxed wage and price guidelines in 1973. When the sale of 8.5 million tons of grain to the Soviet Union led to an increase in retail food prices, however, the president imposed a second freeze and again raised the dollar price of gold. After failing to lower inflation and reduce the trade deficit, Nixon conceded defeat in 1974 and allowed price controls to expire. However, the oil boycott quadrupled the price of petroleum and dramatically inflated the cost of gasoline, diesel fuel, heating oil, plastics, fertilizers, and synthetic fibers. Dwindling supplies produced endless lines at the gas pumps and generated public criticism of energy hoarding by industry. Meanwhile, inflation reached a twenty-five-year high of 12 percent.

Higher energy costs compelled federal officials to promote the use of domestic fuel sources. With only 6 percent of the world's population, the United States consumed 30 percent of global energy production. Nearly 40 percent of this amount came from overseas. Congress reacted to the oil embargo in late 1973 by authorizing construction of a controversial pipeline across Alaska. Rejecting plans to ration oil or tax oil company profits, Nixon created a Federal Energy Administration to develop nuclear reactors and coal-burning facilities. "We can't live in a Garden of Eden and still have a technological society," Atomic Energy Commissioner Dixie Lee Ray scolded in 1974. After launching what he termed "Project Independence," the president ordered government thermostats to be lowered to 68 degrees Fahrenheit, cut official air travel, requested the relaxation of environmental regulations affecting energy consumption, and reduced the speed limit on interstate freeways to 55 miles per hour.

Richard Nixon's presidency did not survive the energy crisis. In March 1974 a grand jury indicted former White House aides Haldeman, Ehrlichman, Mitchell, and four others for perjury and hush money payments and named the president himself as an unindicted coconspirator. Four months later, Ehrlichman and former aide Charles Colson were convicted of ordering the burglary of Ellsberg's medical records. This verdict was supported by a federal court ruling that a president has no constitutional right to authorize a break-in, even if he were targeting foreign intelligence operatives or threats to national security. The House of Representatives voted 406–4 to investigate whether sufficient grounds existed for Nixon's impeachment, and the Burger Court unanimously ruled that the president had to surrender all subpoenaed tapes. "When the claim of privilege is based only on a generalized interest in confidentiality," ruled the Court, "it cannot prevail over the fundamental demands

EXHIBIT **6-6**   **THE MIDDLE EAST**

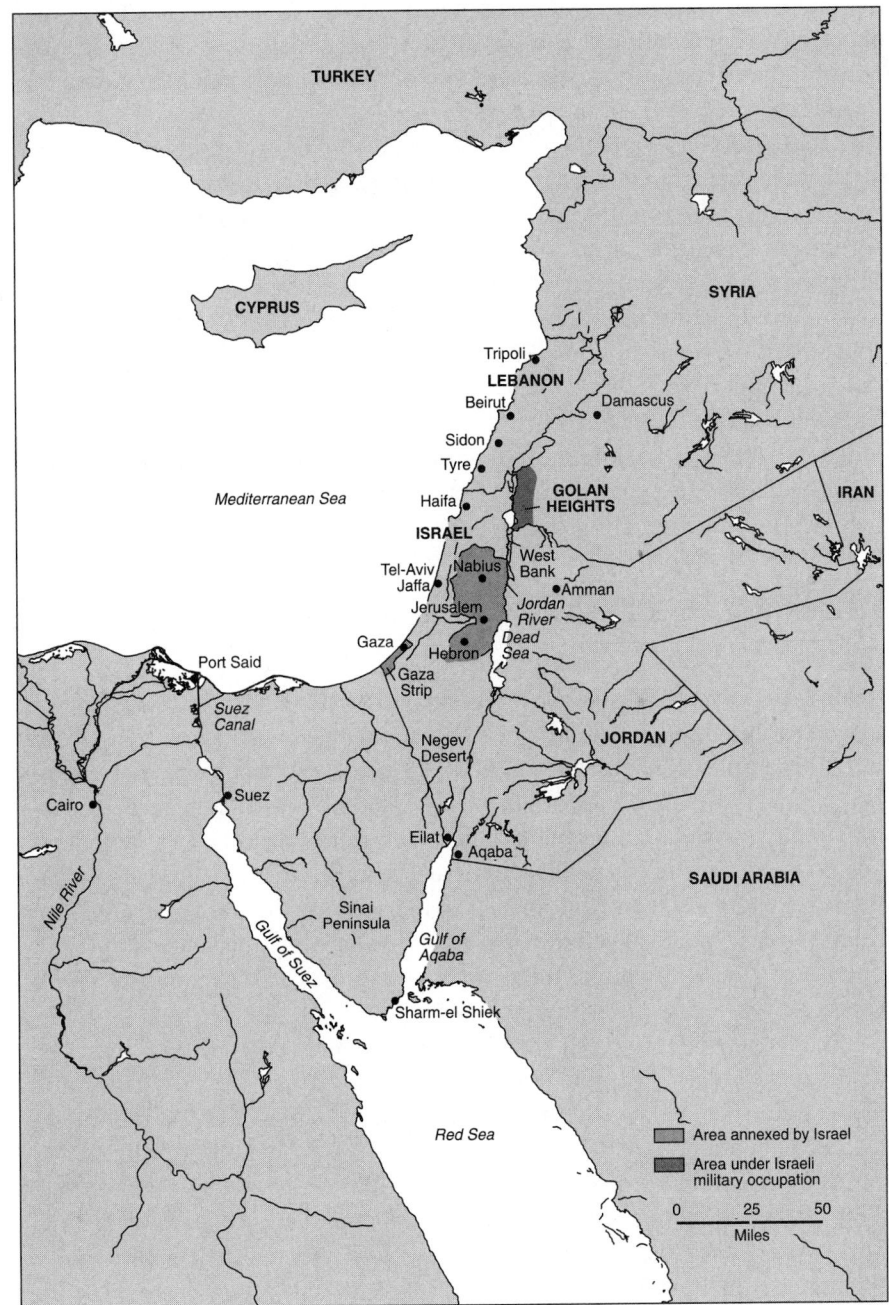

of due process." The House Judiciary Committee now voted three bills of impeachment against Nixon and charged him with obstruction of justice, abuse of power, and unconstitutional defiance of its subpoenas.

The "smoking gun" of Watergate emerged when subpoenaed tapes revealed that the president had played a key role in the early cover-up. As a result, on August 9, 1974, Richard Nixon became the first chief executive in U.S. history to resign from office. "Our long national nightmare is over," newly inaugurated President Ford told the nation. "Our Constitution works. Our great republic is a government of laws and not of men." As the first White House occupant not elected as either president or vice president, Ford faced a nation whose faith in leaders had been shaken by Vietnam and Watergate. Public opinion was stunned, therefore, by the announcement that the new president was pardoning Nixon "for all offenses against the United States." In personal testimony before Congress, Ford insisted there had been "no deal," that he had granted the pardon to remove the disruptive Watergate issue from the national spotlight. The president also offered clemency to Vietnam-era draft law violators and deserters, but only 6 percent of the 350,000 eligible applied.

THE FORD SUCCESSION

Ford chose former New York Governor Nelson D. Rockefeller as his vice president, although the Empire State billionaire faced hostile questions about his political finances. Sensitivity to political ethics also resulted in passage of the Campaign Finance Law of 1974. Although the Supreme Court later invalidated the act's spending limits, the law established check-offs on federal income tax returns to finance elections and created strict disclosure requirements for campaign contributions. Two years later, Congress restricted the proliferation of political action committees. Meanwhile, lawmakers updated the Freedom of Information Act of 1966 by setting deadlines for government response to citizen requests for documents.

In foreign policy, Ford relied on Nixon's Secretary of State Henry Kissinger to pursue the policy of détente. Late in 1974 the president went to Vladivostok to discuss arms limitations with the Soviet Union and agreed to an accord setting negotiating guidelines. At Helsinki in 1975 Ford and Soviet leader Brezhnev joined European leaders in signing a declaration that acknowledged the primacy of human rights and recognized the territorial boundaries that emerged after World War II. As Cold War tensions eased, Kissinger sought stability in the strategically important Middle East by pushing Israel and Egypt to accept an interim peace pact.

However, the Ford administration faced a Congress that sought to regain the initiative in formulating foreign policy. Criticizing the Helsinki Accords for implicitly recognizing communist annexations and satellite regimes in eastern

Europe, congressional leaders denied the Soviets most-favored-nation trade status until Moscow relaxed emigration restrictions on Jews and other dissenters. Congress also sought to control the CIA in 1974 by passing the Hughes-Ryan Amendment, which required the president to report covert actions to Congress "in a timely fashion." The administration soon faced a test case in East Africa's Angola, where it opposed a nationalist movement supported by the Soviets and Cubans. Ford authorized funding for a covert operation in the civil war, but Democrats voted to cut off this aid in 1976. Congressional distrust of the CIA intensified when a select committee led by Senator Frank Church exposed agency involvement in foreign assassination plots and other covert actions.

Congress also defeated administration pleas for increased South Vietnamese military aid. Without such support, the Saigon government could not stop communist advances. On April 30, 1975, one day after military helicopters evacuated 1,000 citizens from the U.S. embassy, North Vietnamese troops marched into Saigon and renamed it Ho Chi Minh City. A symbol of the limits of U.S. power, the war in Southeast Asia brought the deaths of 1.5 million Vietnamese and left 10 million homeless. More than 58,000 members of the U.S. armed forces died in Vietnam, more than 300,000 were wounded, and the conflict's financial cost surpassed $150 billion. Although the United States rescued 120,000 Vietnamese refugees as hostilities ended, the humiliating defeat was an incalculable blow to U.S. national cohesion and pride.

Two weeks before the fall of Saigon, Khmer Rouge rebels had taken control of the Cambodian capital while the U.S.–supported government fled. In May 1975 a patrol boat under orders from the revolutionary regime seized the U.S. merchant ship *Mayaguez*. Just as the vessel was being released, Ford ordered aerial bombing and a coastal island assault. Fifteen marines were killed in the ensuing combat, and twenty-three others died in a helicopter crash. Yet the Ford administration used the confrontation to suggest that the United States had resumed world leadership after the Vietnam War.

At home, inflation and unemployment continued to plague an economy suffering from international competition, sagging growth and profits, and rising social welfare costs. As the era of post–World War II prosperity drew to a close in 1974, Congress appropriated funds for housing, public schools, transportation, and educational benefits for Vietnam veterans. In response, Ford campaigned for Republican congressional candidates by introducing a Whip Inflation Now (WIN) program of reduced government spending. Yet Watergate, the Nixon pardon, and the ailing economy helped to assure the Democrats a two-thirds majority in the House and added strength in the Senate. After the election, Ford agreed to the Comprehensive Employment and Training Act (CETA), a program that provided temporary jobs in state and local governments for skilled workers. The empowered Democrats now raised Social Security stipends and extended unemployment benefits in states hit by the recession. While agreeing to some tax relief, Congress also ended oil depletion write-offs for large energy corporations and curbed investment-related tax shelters.

Seeking to bring the nation together amid the Vietnam War and continuing racial turmoil, Richard Nixon had adopted a two-track policy. Overseas, the president turned to the creative diplomacy of Henry Kissinger to establish détente with the communist Soviet Union and the People's Republic of China. Yet the easing of Cold War tensions failed to bring the anticipated peace with honor in Southeast Asia. On the domestic front, Nixon embraced environmental regulation, price control, increased social welfare spending, affirmative action, and racial integration of some public schools. Nevertheless, the president's obsession with a Vietnam consensus and his political competitiveness intensified polarization at home. Facing mounting antiwar protests and criticism from liberals, Nixon turned to repressive tactics, resulting in the Watergate scandal that destroyed his presidency. As Gerald Ford presided over the final chapter of the Vietnam saga and struggled to deal with a sagging economy, Americans looked for leaders to restore morale and address the nation's problems.

INFOTRAC COLLEGE EDITION

Using Keywords, enter the following search terms:

Henry Kissinger
Organization of Petroleum Exporting Countries
Busing
Roe v. Wade
Equal Rights Amendment
Kent State
Pentagon Papers
Watergate
Gerald Ford

RECOMMENDED READING

Jeffrey Kimball, *Nixon's Vietnam War* (1998). This provocative study attributes the president's military escalations to the "mad bomber theory"—the belief that Hanoi's fear of an unpredictable adversary would produce a favorable settlement.

Lewis Sorley, *The Better War: The Unexamined Victories and the Final Tragedy of America's Last Years in Vietnam* (1999). The author presents a fresh approach to the subject by highlighting the surprising success of pacification under Nixon.

Stanley I. Kutler, ed., *Abuse of Power: The New Nixon Tapes* (1997). The transcripts of uncensored Nixon Watergate conversations are presented in this well-edited collection, providing chilling insights into the president's personal foibles and obsessions.

Jill Quadagno, *The Color of Welfare: How Racism Undermined the War on Poverty* (1994). This analysis includes a critical view of the Nixon administration's politicized approach to the needs of racial minorities and the poor.

Additional Reading

The definitive work on the Nixon administration is Melvin Small's *The Presidency of Richard Nixon* (1999). For a critical perspective, see the relevant portions of Stephen E. Ambrose, *Nixon: The Triumph of a Politician, 1962–1972* (1989), and of *Nixon: Ruin and Recovery, 1973–1990* (1991). A more sympathetic view appears in Joan Hoff, *Nixon Reconsidered* (1994). See also the relevant segments of Roger Morris, *Richard Milhous Nixon: The Rise of an American Politician* (1990), and of John Robert Greene, *The Limits of Power: The Nixon and Ford Administrations* (1992). For Nixon's domestic policies, see Allen J. Matusow, *Nixon's Economy: Booms, Busts, Dollars, and Votes* (1998).

Nixon's social policies are treated in the relevant segments of Irwin Unger, *The Best of Intentions: The Triumph of the Great Society Under Kennedy, Johnson, and Nixon* (1996). For racial matters, see Hugh Davis Graham, *The Civil Rights Era: Origins and Development of National Policy* (1990), and the first segments of Dan T. Carter, *From George Wallace to Newt Gingrich: Race in the Conservative Counterrevolution, 1963–1994* (1996). Nixon's political activities are described in the early sections of William C. Berman, *America's Right Turn: From Nixon to Bush* (1994). See also Dan T. Carter, *The Politics of Rage. George Wallace, the Origins of the New Conservatism, and the Transformation of American Politics* (1995).

For global diplomacy in the Nixon years, see Robert S. Litwak, *Détente and the Nixon Doctrine: American Foreign Policy and the Pursuit of Stability* (1984), and Robert D. Schulzinger, *Henry Kissinger: Doctor of Diplomacy* (1989). The later stages of the Indochina War can be followed in many of the sources listed in Chapters 4 and 5. Other important works include Harry G. Summers Jr., *On Strategy: The Vietnam War in Context* (1981), and Michael P. Sullivan, *The Vietnam War: A Study in the Making of American Policy* (1985). For war-related controversies, see Stuart I. Rochester and Frederick Kiley, *Honor Bound: The History of American Prisoners of War in Southeast Asia, 1961–1973* (1998), and Jerry Lembcke, *The Spitting Image: Myth, Memory, and the Legacy of Vietnam* (1998).

Antiwar activism during Nixon's presidency is treated in the relevant portions of Tom Wells, *The War Within: America's Battle Over Vietnam* (1994), and in Kenneth J. Heineman, *Campus Wars: The Peace Movement at American State Universities in the Vietnam War Era* (1993). For working-class responses to student protest and the New Left, see Christian G. Appy, *Working-Class War: American Combat Soldiers and Vietnam* (1993), and the last segment of Peter B. Levy, *The New Left and Labor in the 1960s* (1994). The relationship between antiwar politics and the counterculture is discussed in Peter N. Carroll, *It Seemed Like Nothing Happened: America in the 1970s* (2000). For cultural history, see Michael X. Delli Carpini, *Stability and Change in American Politics: The Coming of Age of the Generation of the 1960s* (1986), and the relevant portions of John D'Emilio and Estelle Freedman, *Intimate Matters: A History of Sexuality in America* (1988).

Space technology and its implications are explored in the relevant segments of Walter A. McDougall, *The Heavens and the Earth: A Political History of the Space Age* (1985). The best overview of the environmental movement is Samuel Hays and Barbara D. Hays's *Beauty, Health, and Permanence: Environmental Politics in the United States, 1955–1985* (1987). For ecological controversies in the resource-rich western states, see Richard White, *It's Your Misfortune and None of My Own: A History of the American West* (1991).

Feminist agitation in the 1970s is the subject of the appropriate segments of Ruth Rosen, *The World Split Open: How the Modern Women's Movement Changed America* (2000), and of Alice Nichols, *Daring to Be Bad: Radical Feminism in America, 1967–1975* (1989). The ERA is described in Donald G. Mathews and Jane Sherron De Hart, *Sex, Gender, and the Politics of ERA* (1990), and in the provocative work by Mary Frances Berry, *Why ERA Failed: Politics, Women's Rights and the Amending Process of the Constitution* (1986). For the abortion rights controversy, see David Garrow, *Liberty and Sexuality: The Right to Privacy and the Making of Roe v. Wade* (1994), and Kristin Luker, *Abortion and the Politics of Womanhood* (1984). Struggles for homosexual rights are described in Barry D. Adam, *The Rise of a Gay and Lesbian Movement* (1987), and in the relevant sections of D'Emilio and Freedman, *Intimate Matters*.

Mexican American history of the 1970s can be found in Rodolfo Acuna, *Occupied America: A History of Chicanos* (1988), and in Juan Gomez Quinones, *Chicano Politics: Reality and Promise, 1940–1990* (1990). For Native Americans, see Philip Reno, *Mother Earth, Father Sky, and Economic Development* (1981), and the later segments of Francis Paul Prucha, *The Great Father: The United States Government and the American Indians, Volume II* (1984).

Assertions of black power in the early 1970s are treated in segments of William L. Van Deburg, *New Day in Babylon: The Black Power Movement and American Culture, 1965–1975* (1992), and in Harvard Sitkoff, *The Strug-*

gle for Black Equality, 1954–1980 (1981). For the Black Panthers, see Philip
S. Foner, ed.,*The Black Panthers Speak* (1995). For African American political activity, see Katherine Tate, *From Protest to Politics: The New Black Voters in American Elections* (1993).

White ethnicity and populist conservatism are the focus of Richard D.
Alba, *Italian Americans: The Twilight of Ethnicity* (1985), and of Richard
Krickus, *Pursuing the American Dream: White Ethnics and the New Pop-
ulism* (1976). Two excellent case studies are Ronald P. Formisano, *Boston
Against Busing: Race, Class, and Ethnicity in the 1960s and 1970s* (1991),
and Jonathan Rieder, *Canarsie: The Jews and Italians of Brooklyn Against
Liberalism* (1985). For conservatism, see Mark Gerson, *The Neoconservative
Vision: From the Cold War to the Culture Wars* (1995), and Jerome L. Him-
melstein, *To the Right: The Transformation of American Conservatism* (1990).

Reassessments of the radical political and cultural movements of the
Nixon era appear in the relevant portions of Todd Gitlin, *The Twilight of Common Dreams: Why America Is Wracked by Culture Wars* (1995); in E. J.
Dionne Jr., *Why Americans Hate Politics* (1991); and in Maurice Isserman
and Michael Kazin, *America Divided: The Civil War of the 1960s* (2000). Far
more critical is Peter Collier and David J. Horowitz, *Destructive Generation:
Second Thoughts About the '60s* (1989). The political consequences of radical
activism and liberal social policy are graphically portrayed in Thomas Byrne
Edsall with Mary D. Edsall, *Chain Reaction: The Impact of Race, Rights, and
Taxes on American Politics* (1991).

Watergate is summarized in Stanley I. Kutler, *The Wars of Watergate*
(1990). For a view of the scandal sympathetic to Nixon, see Len Colodny and
Robert Gettlin, *Silent Coup* (1992). See also Michael Schudson, *Watergate in
American Memory: How We Remember, Forget, and Reconstruct the Past*
(1992). For FBI abuses, see Richard Gid Powers, *Secrecy and Power: The Life
of J. Edgar Hoover* (1987), and Athan G. Theoharis and John Stuart Cox, *The
Boss: J. Edgar Hoover and the Great American Inquisition* (1988). For Ford's
presidency, see John Robert Greene, *The Limits of Power and the Presidency
of Gerald R. Ford* (1995). See also James L. Sundquist, *The Decline and Resurgence of Congress* (1981).

STRUGGLING GIANT: THE CARTER AND REAGAN YEARS, 1976–1988

"We want to have faith again. We want to be proud again," declared newly elected President Jimmy Carter. Promising to overcome the legacies of Vietnam and Watergate, Carter pledged to restore public trust in government. But energy shortages, severe economic dislocation, and global instability combined to sink esteem for the White House. As a wave of populist conservatism swept the nation in the late 1970s, Republican Ronald Reagan offered to rekindle the national sense of mission.

Reagan mobilized a new coalition of social conservatives, free-market advocates, and foreign policy hawks in response to economic stagnation at home and declining influence abroad. His ambitious program of government deregulation, welfare cuts, tax relief, and increased military spending led to the most dramatic change of government since the New Deal. Although "Reaganomics" was credited with the business boom that dominated the 1980s, trade imbalances and federal budget deficits threatened to eradicate prosperity. Meanwhile, the country was divided over identity politics, cultural allegiances, and conflicting social values.

JIMMY CARTER: THE ENERGY CRISIS AND ECONOMIC STAGNATION

Gerald Ford hoped to translate public goodwill into victory at the polls in 1976. The president was the object of sympathy when two female assailants botched separate assassination attempts, leaving him unharmed. Ford and running mate Senator Robert Dole of Kansas campaigned against excessive federal spending. Yet they faced a formidable Democratic opponent in former Georgia Governor James ("Jimmy") Earl Carter Jr., a virtual unknown. As chair of the Democratic Campaign Committee, Carter had helped the party dominate the

Promising to restore public trust in government after the Vietnam War and Watergate, newcomer Jimmy Carter refashioned the Democratic Party's electoral coalition in 1976.

congressional elections of 1974. Yet, except for his service in the navy, the Georgia politician had never worked for the federal government.

Carter played up his outsider status by attacking a "confused and overlapping and wasteful federal bureaucracy" and by calling for tax reform, a national health program, and a comprehensive energy policy. Supported by African American leaders such as Atlanta's Andrew Young, the candidate also sought to capture the votes of white southerners who had deserted the Democrats in the previous two presidential elections. Indeed, the Georgian's credentials as a "born-again" Christian helped to defeat George Wallace in the southern primaries. Yet Carter also took pride in his experience as a nuclear engineer and

EXHIBIT **7-1**   **U.S. GROSS NATIONAL PRODUCT, 1976–1980**
(IN CURRENT DOLLARS IN BILLIONS)

1976	1782.8
1978	2243.7
1980	2732.0

Source: *Economic Report of the President* (1988).

member of the business-oriented Trilateral Commission. Defeating a wide range of candidates in the early primaries, Carter easily won the Democratic nomination. To bring geographic and ideological unity to the ticket, the nominee chose Senator Walter F. Mondale, a Minnesota liberal, as his running mate.

Although Carter called for "a time of healing" after Vietnam and Watergate, he also expressed populist anger toward elites. "It's time for the people to run the government," the candidate stated softly, "and not the other way around." When Carter accused Ford of trying to "hide" in the White House Rose Garden, the president agreed to hold three televised debates, the first such exercise since 1960. The TV exposure quickly transformed the challenger into a viable candidate.

By receiving a majority of the white male vote, Ford swept the West and carried three key midwestern states. Yet Democrats rebuilt the New Deal coalition by winning overwhelmingly among northeastern union workers, African Americans, and middle-class liberals. Because of strong support from black and white evangelicals, Carter captured all southern states except Virginia—90 percent of the candidate's national plurality came from the South. Winning by a margin of 2 percent of the popular vote, Carter edged past Ford in a 297–240 victory in the electoral college, the closest finish since 1916. Despite the tightness of the race and the candidates' sole reliance on public campaign financing for the first time in U.S. history, voter participation remained less than 55 percent.

As Carter assumed the presidency, he faced a stagnating economy whose performance was worsened by inflation, federal budget deficits, and increased national debt. Delays in the modernization of manufacturing facilities had produced a sharp decline in worker productivity by the 1970s. Foreign com-

EXHIBIT **7-2**   **U.S. CONSUMER CREDIT OUTSTANDING, 1977–1980**
(IN ROUNDED BILLIONS OF DOLLARS)

1977	279
1980	369

Source: *Economic Report of the President* (1988).

EXHIBIT **7-3**   **U.S. FEDERAL SOCIAL WELFARE EXPENDITURES, 1976–1980**
(IN ROUNDED BILLIONS OF DOLLARS)

1976	197.0
1978	239.7
1980	302.6

Source: *Statistical Abstract of the United States* (1987).

petition particularly hurt the automobile industry, whose managers were slow to recognize consumer demand for smaller, energy-efficient cars in an era of rising gas prices. By the following decade, Japan would produce more autos and trucks than the United States for the first time in history and rank as the world's largest steel manufacturer. Plant and mill closings devastated midwestern "rust belt" cities such as Detroit, Gary, and Youngstown and contributed to declining property values and the failure of regional businesses. Western mining operations were also victimized by the recession.

Pressed by organized labor to respond to the recession, Congress passed an emergency public works program in 1977. The next year Carter signed the Humphrey-Hawkins Act, which set a ceiling on acceptable inflation rates and sought to reduce unemployment by making the federal government the employer of last resort. The president also approved a generous price-support system for farmers suffering from commodity surpluses. Yet Republicans embraced proposals advanced by Senator William Roth and Representative Jack Kemp that called for a 30 percent reduction in federal income taxes and government spending cuts. Carter encouraged the Federal Reserve Board to fight inflation by raising interest rates while the president established voluntary guidelines for wage and price increases. Responding to a tax rebellion initiated by California voters, the president also promised future tax relief.

Despite the administration's attempts to control spending, spiraling energy costs continued to spur inflation. In a major television address, Carter depicted the emergency as the "moral equivalent of war." Pleading for the conservation of electricity and fuel, he called for limits on oil imports and for subsidies to develop alternative energy. The White House also proposed a tax on excessive energy consumption and a contingency plan for gas rationing. In 1979 the crisis deepened when the Organization of Petroleum Exporting Countries (OPEC) hiked oil prices another 50 percent. After convening a domestic summit, Carter returned to television to depict the nation's inability to deal with its problems as a national "crisis of confidence." The president outlined a massive, ten-year energy program but faced congressional opposition from those who wanted to cut consumption by deregulating prices. The stalemate was resolved when Carter accepted gradual deregulation of domestic energy prices and limited rationing powers. Congress also agreed to impose a windfall profits tax on oil companies

Reverend Andrew Young (1932–   )

Andrew Young often recalled an old slavery proverb: "The Lord can make a way out of no way." The son of an African American dentist who raised his family in a racially integrated neighborhood of New Orleans, Young graduated from Howard University and received a degree from

Hartford Theological Seminary. He presided over small Congregational churches in Georgia and Alabama in the late 1950s and led early voter registration drives. Appointed assistant director of the National Council of Churches in 1959, he channeled funds into the burgeoning civil rights movement.

Young joined the Southern Christian Leadership Conference (SCLC) in Atlanta in the early 1960s, where he pursued voter registration, served as a trusted aide to Martin Luther King Jr., and rose through the organizational hierarchy. In 1972 he became the first African American from Georgia to be elected to the House of Representatives in more than a century. Four years later, Young supported Jimmy Carter for president because the former Georgia governor had compiled an excellent civil rights record and had a positive working relationship with black leaders.

Seeking to fashion a foreign policy that fused U.S. ideals and interests, Carter chose Young as his United Nations spokesperson. The new

and to fund a Department of Energy and synthetic fuels program. Per capita energy use declined 20 percent between 1978 and 1981.

The energy crisis placed new emphasis on the use of nuclear reactors as a source of electrical power. Vowing to reverse this trend, environmental activists turned to civil disobedience at sites such as Seabrook, New Hampshire, to call attention to the health, safety, and financial dangers associated with atomic plants. In 1979 a near "meltdown" of the reactor core at a nuclear facility at Three Mile Island, Pennsylvania, focused public attention on the credibility of energy company managers and government regulators. "The history of the nuclear power industry," consumer advocate Ralph Nader told more

ambassador enhanced Washington's global image by denouncing white minority rule in South Africa and Rhodesia. Yet the administration soon discovered the difficulty of applying evangelical principles to foreign policy.

As Carter brokered peace talks between Israel and Egypt at Camp David, Jewish leaders criticized the president for inadequate support of Israeli interests. Relations with the Jewish community deteriorated in 1979 when the president's brother hosted a Libyan business delegation and blamed criticism of the meeting on the "Jewish media." Carter was slow to distance himself from such remarks and courted further trouble by comparing the zeal of the guerrilla Palestine Liberation Organization (PLO) to that of the nonviolent U.S. civil rights movement. Two weeks later, in his role as temporary U.N. Security Council president, Young discussed the timing of a PLO resolution with the organization's U.N. representative, a Columbia University professor.

Young believed he had taken a "risk for peace" by encouraging the PLO to recognize the state of Israel. Yet he was forced to resign because he misled State Department officials about engaging in a meeting contrary to U.S. policy. Portrayed as a conservative by civil rights activists and as a moderate by Congress, he now attracted criticism as a radical. Despite the setback, Young would be elected mayor of Atlanta in the 1980s and would continue to emphasize the spiritual component to the quest for equal rights.

than 100,000 demonstrators gathered in Washington, "is replete with cover-ups, deceptions, outright lies, error, negligence, arrogance, greed."

While the economy stagnated, Carter sought to establish a consumer protection agency and a hospital cost-control plan. Although the administration met defeat for these proposals in Congress, it succeeded in getting legislation to create a Department of Education, to establish a chemical contamination cleanup fund, to control strip mining, and to restrict the development of federal lands in Alaska. Carter also signed measures that deregulated the airline, railroad, trucking, communications, and banking industries and that authorized a multibillion dollar loan to save automaker Chrysler from bankruptcy.

Pressed by Republican advocates of tax relief, Carter finally agreed to substantial cuts, although he postponed implementing them until 1981.

Unable to protect Democratic constituencies from rising oil prices and economic structural problems, the administration watched helplessly as "stagflation" worsened. Annual inflation reached 13.5 percent for 1980—the highest level since 1947—and the prime lending rate exceeded 22 percent. As loan rates surpassed the limits of potential home and car purchasers, economic stagnation pushed unemployment to more than 7 percent. When bloated budget deficits forced government borrowing, foreign investors sold off depreciated dollars, and the crisis worsened.

Carter's unfamiliarity with Washington compounded his political difficulties. Billing himself as an outsider, the Georgian chose advisors who lacked experience in congressional dealings and who could not win confidence on Capitol Hill. Carter attributed his legislative failures to narrow economic interests and single-issue lobbyists. Yet he often failed to follow his visionary televised appeals with detailed political negotiations among congressional leaders. As the president's approval ratings fell from a high of 75 percent upon taking office to less than 25 percent, the public viewed the nation's leader as hesitant, evasive, and removed from their problems.

SUPERPOWER LIMITS AND THE IRAN HOSTAGE CRISIS

Having promised to cut defense spending and to take a fresh approach to foreign policy, Carter canceled production of the B-1 bomber, which air force leaders wanted as a replacement for the aging B-52. The president proclaimed that the United States was at last free "of the inordinate fear of communism . . . the fear that led to the moral poverty of Vietnam." Carter also deferred development of the neutron bomb and proposed to withdraw ground troops from South Korea. Building on the foundations laid by Nixon and Ford, the president stabilized relations with the Soviet Union by signing a second Strategic Arms Limitation Treaty (SALT II) in 1979. The new accord set limits on the number of long-range missiles, bombers, and nuclear warheads that could be held by the superpowers. Such cooperation reflected an easing of Cold War tensions in Europe, where West Germany had opened diplomatic and trade relations with the Soviet bloc. Washington also exchanged ambassadors with China and agreed to sever diplomatic ties with Taiwan.

The search for political stability in the oil-rich Middle East and the chance to exert global leadership led the White House to promote peace between Egypt and Israel. After a dramatic visit to Jerusalem by Egypt's Anwar Sadat in 1977, Carter brought the Egyptian leader and Israeli Prime Minister Menachem Begin to Maryland's Camp David for a summit. When further negotiations stalled two years later, the president flew to the Middle East to continue low-key diplomacy. Egypt and Israel finally signed a historic peace treaty in Washington in 1979. Yet Palestinian Arabs living in Israeli-occupied territories were not part of the accord and remained the most important stumbling block to regional peace.

Carter had greater success in linking foreign policy to the aspirations of third-world people. Stressing the importance of human rights in his global strategy, he became the first president to visit black Africa. Andrew Young, the administration's African American ambassador to the United Nations, denounced apartheid in South Africa and defended the president's refusal to recognize the white minority government of Rhodesia (now Zimbabwe) until blacks were given political rights.

Carter also continued Nixon's and Ford's negotiations to return the Panama Canal to Panama by 2000. Despite strong opposition by Republican conservatives and a lengthy Senate debate, the president signed the Panama Canal treaty in 1978, although the United States reserved the right to intervene to preserve the Canal Zone's neutrality. By awarding Panama $1 billion and by negotiating the canal's sovereignty, the Carter administration removed the most obvious symbol of U.S. military aggression in the hemisphere. Congress also approved a small amount of emergency aid for Nicaragua when a 1979 revolution by Sandinista nationalists overthrew a brutal military dictatorship once supported by Washington.

Despite such achievements, Carter was devastated when the Soviet Union sought to contain Islamic nationalism on its southern flanks by invading neighboring Afghanistan in 1979. Placing the action in a Cold War context, the president raised alarms about "the most severe threat to world peace since the second World War." Carter promptly suspended grain sales to the Soviets and ordered a boycott of the 1980 Olympic Games in Moscow. The president also asked the Senate to shelve ratification of SALT II. Defense-minded senators from both parties had denounced the treaty for restricting development of cruise missiles while permitting the Soviets to improve "Backfire" bombers and other weapons. Yet the main objection to the accord centered on difficulties in verifying compliance, a persistent point of contention between the two superpowers. Another area of disagreement involved charges that the Soviets habitually violated the human rights of domestic dissidents.

Fearing that the Afghan operation signaled a Soviet move into Africa and the oil-rich Persian Gulf, the White House issued the Carter Doctrine of 1980. "An attempt by any outside force to gain control of the Gulf region," it proclaimed, would be regarded as an assault on U.S. "vital interests" and would be repelled "by any means necessary." To demonstrate national resolve, Carter prevailed upon Congress to resume registration for the draft. He also proposed a 25 percent growth in defense spending in the next five years. The administration already had responded to claims that the U.S. military had deteriorated after the Vietnam War by increasing annual outlays by

EXHIBIT **7-4**   **U.S. NATIONAL DEFENSE AND VETERANS OUTLAYS,
1976–1980**
(IN BILLIONS OF DOLLARS)

1976	108.0
1978	123.5
1980	155.2

Source: *Statistical Abstract of the United States* (1987).

nearly 50 percent. Carter provided additional support for the military by endorsing Pentagon plans for the deployment of Trident submarines armed with nuclear missiles.

Ironically, the Soviet Union did not present Carter with his most daunting foreign policy challenge. Instead, the administration floundered as a result of a crisis arising from the 1979 overthrow of Iran's pro-Western Shah Mohammed Reza Pahlavi. Led by Moslem cleric Ayatollah Ruhollah Khomeini, Shiite fundamentalists demanded a religious state that would end ties with the United States and that would purge Western secularism and materialism. Many Iranians remained embittered by the CIA coup that had restored the shah in 1953. Like Nixon and Kissinger, Carter recognized Iran's importance as an oil-rich nation that bordered the Soviet Union, purchased U.S. arms, and functioned as a reliable client state. The president first supported the shah but then watched helplessly as the dictator's regime crumbled. Forced into exile, the deposed leader sought medical treatment in the United States. When Kissinger and the Rockefeller family convinced Carter to grant the shah's request for U.S. entry on humanitarian grounds, outraged Iranian militants seized the U.S. embassy in Tehran, took embassy personnel hostage, and demanded repatriation of the shah and his fortune.

After the United States refused to negotiate with the militants in Tehran, the Iranian government assumed control of the hostages. Carter then froze Iran's assets in the United States, severed diplomatic relations, and ordered trade sanctions. By portraying the president as singularly committed to the release of U.S. citizens, the White House dramatized their plight. Months later, under pressure to break the deadlock, Carter ordered a military rescue, but two helicopters malfunctioned in a desert sandstorm, eight commandos were killed, and the mission failed. Protesting the decision to resolve the crisis through military means, Cyrus R. Vance became the first secretary of state to resign because of a disagreement about policy since William Jennings Bryan did so in 1915.

After engaging in complex negotiations with intermediaries regarding Iranian assets held in U.S. banks, Tehran agreed to release the fifty-two remaining hostages—but only after Jimmy Carter left office. Hours after the inauguration

EXHIBIT 7-5   LOCATION OF U.S. HOSTAGE RESCUE EFFORT IN IRAN

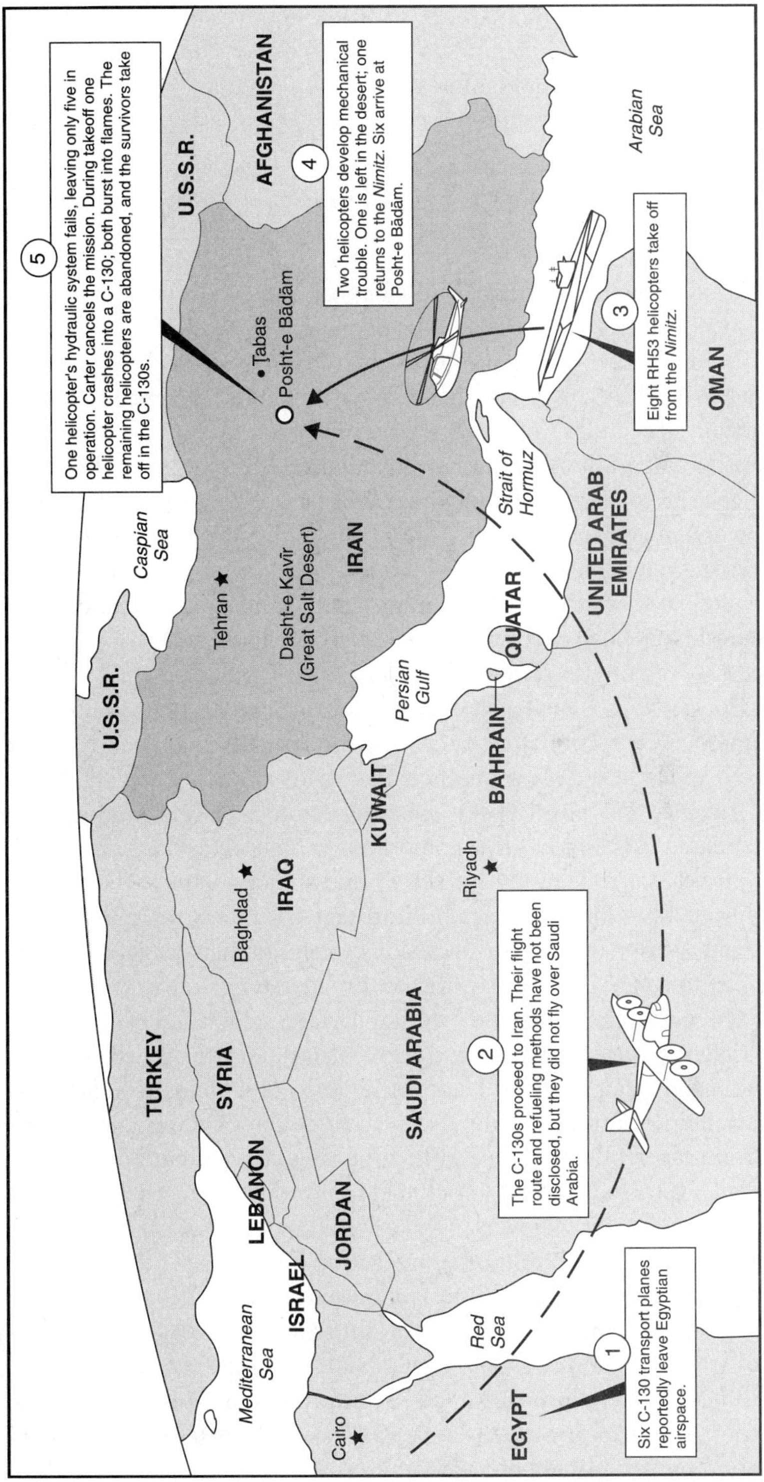

1 Six C-130 transport planes reportedly leave Egyptian airspace.

2 The C-130s proceed to Iran. Their flight route and refueling methods have not been disclosed, but they did not fly over Saudi Arabia.

3 Eight RH53 helicopters take off from the *Nimitz*.

4 Two helicopters develop mechanical trouble. One is left in the desert; one returns to the *Nimitz*. Six arrive at Posht-e Bādām.

5 One helicopter's hydraulic system fails, leaving only five in operation. Carter cancels the mission. During takeoff one helicopter crashes into a C-130; both burst into flames. The remaining helicopters are abandoned, and the survivors take off in the C-130s.

of a new president on January 20, 1981, the captives ended 444 days of incarceration. The Iranian standoff remained a bitter symbol of the diminished global power of the United States in the post–Vietnam War era and helped to produce a major power shift in Washington.

THE CHRISTIAN RIGHT AND SOCIAL CONSERVATISM

The evolving political climate in Washington reflected a major upsurge in conservative social views. As the number of one-parent families in the United States increased by 79 percent in the 1970s and the birth rate declined to record lows, evangelical Christians began to denounce increased tolerance of birth control, abortion, premarital sex, divorce, and pornography. In 1979 Reverend Jerry Falwell founded the Moral Majority and used his televised pulpit to mobilize evangelical Protestants who sought a Christian republic. By revitalizing political involvement and social activism among fundamentalists of the Southwest and the West, Falwell fused anticommunism with a condemnation of "modernist" teachings such as evolution. The movement complained that a liberal "Eastern Establishment" had destroyed reverence for religion and proper education by imposing "value-free" standards on churches and schools.

Condemning "secular humanism" as a misguided philosophy that placed man above God, fundamentalists preached against "sin" and "moral decadence" and attacked abortion, the equal rights amendment (ERA), gay rights, and "satanic" rock music. They also struggled to replace evolutionist teachings with creationist doctrines that conformed to biblical teaching. Using computer lists, direct mail, telephone marketing, and audiocassettes, the Christian Right organized 50 million born-again Protestants. The new religious conservatism fostered a variety of popular television evangelists such as Pat Robertson, who went on to create cable TV's Christian Broadcasting Network (CBN).

The most intense debate over family values centered on abortion. Insisting that the fetus was a sacred form of human life, the Roman Catholic Church and groups such as National Right to Life denounced legalized abortion as murder of the unborn. Conservatives like Phyllis Schlafly argued that abortion placed the individual needs of the potential mother above those of family and society. Abortion opponents viewed sex as a procreative ritual and childbearing as a God-given privilege, so they also objected to "family planning." A broad movement of conservative Catholics, Protestants, and Jews began to picket abortion clinics and mount massive demonstrations in the late 1970s. Although the Supreme Court refused to reverse *Roe v. Wade* or grant states the power to outlaw abortion outright, pro-lifers succeeded in limiting taxpayer support of the procedure. In 1976 Congress passed an amendment introduced by Illinois's Henry J. Hyde barring Medicaid funds for abortions for women on welfare.

The ERA became another focal point of the conservative cultural crusade. Stop-ERA organizer Schlafly lobbied furiously against the measure by claiming it would "neuterize" society and would relieve men of the obligation to support their families. Fearing that the ERA would force women into the male-dominated labor market and require placement of children in day care, opponents linked the amendment to an attack on the family. As the debate shifted from issues of equality to a conflict over traditional values, anti-ERA activists raised the specter of a military draft that would place women in combat. Feminists appeared to cut themselves off from less privileged cohorts by suggesting that women should discard the traditional protections offered by men. The ERA fell three states short of ratification in 1982 and six votes shy of reconsideration the following year. Nine states in the traditional South were among those that rejected the measure.

The ERA controversy illustrated the conflict between individual rights and traditional obligations. Similar polarization marked the confrontation over affirmative action. As the courts and regulatory agencies seemed to penalize nonminorities for the past policies of employers, the costs of civil rights reform became more broadly distributed, and whites complained of "reverse discrimination." The controversy was particularly bitter in higher education, where institutions set aside admissions slots for minority students even if their grades and test scores were lower than those of rejected white applicants. In the *Bakke* case of 1978 the Supreme Court ruled that affirmative action numeric quotas in medical school admissions violated civil rights law although race could be considered to secure a more diverse student body.

THE 1980 ELECTION AND REAGANOMICS

Having responded to inflation with reduced federal spending and tight monetary policies, President Carter faced an uprising of traditional Democratic constituencies in the labor and civil rights movements. When Senator Edward Kennedy challenged Carter for the 1980 presidential nomination, the White House used the powers of incumbency to prevail in the party primaries. Yet Carter faced a more effective opponent when Ronald Reagan defeated George Bush in the race for the Republican nomination. A minor star in 1940s movies, Reagan had forged anticommunist credentials as president of the Screen Actors Guild during the Hollywood Red Scare. As his movie career declined in the early 1950s, the actor became the national spokesperson for defense contractor General Electric. Moving into politics, Reagan espoused fiscal and social conservatism and Cold War interventionism. After winning the governorship of California in 1966, he attracted attention as a militant opponent of student activism, as a critic of government bureaucracy, and as a supporter of the Vietnam War.

Reverend Jerry Falwell (1933–   )

As leader of the Moral Majority, a political and social lobby for Protestant fundamentalists, Jerry Falwell was America's most influential conservative voice of the 1980s. His Sunday evening cable TV program reached into 34 million homes. His enterprises and holdings included television's National Christian Network, Liberty Baptist College, and an 18,000-member Baptist Church in Lynchburg, Virginia. Falwell traveled 200,000 air miles each year by private jet to raise the annual $100 million needed to sustain these interests. Once described as the "sleeping giant" of U.S. politics, the Virginia preacher was credited with controlling the votes of an estimated 21 million evangelicals.

Falwell came from a successful but disreputable Lynchburg family that included bootlegging and a dance hall among its enterprises. A bright student and an accomplished athlete with a flair for rowdiness, he studied mechanical engineering at a local college. One night Falwell attended a Baptist service, fell in love with (and subsequently married) the church pianist, and instantly became a born-again Christian. Two months later he decided to enter the ministry and transferred to a Baptist Bible college in Missouri. Upon graduation in 1956, Falwell returned to Lynchburg to found an independent fundamentalist church in an abandoned bottling facility.

Falwell immediately arranged to broadcast services by radio. Six months later, his *Old Time Gospel Hour*, which merely recorded the service as it occurred, made it to television. A 6-footer with a large waistline and a deep, booming voice, the minister wore dark suits and always carried a Bible. His upbeat theology conveyed images of success and messages of hope and redemption. At the same time, Falwell never strayed

By 1980 Reagan had become the leading voice of the nation's conservatives by questioning detente with the Soviets, by demanding a strong defense, and by attacking government social spending as inflationary. The Republican candidate promised to "take the government off the backs of the people" by

from the fundamentalist belief in the accuracy of the Bible or from resistance to anything that conflicted with spiritual command.

In 1977 the Lynchburg preacher reversed long-standing fundamentalist isolation from social action and politics by affirming a religious leader's right to disseminate views on abortion, pornography, and homosexuality. During that year, Falwell helped singer Anita Bryant lead a political campaign to repeal a Florida county ordinance granting equal rights to homosexuals, whom the minister accused of "perversion and immorality." In 1978 and 1979 he fashioned "Clean Up America" campaigns to counteract "a tide of permissiveness and moral decay." These efforts climaxed in the founding of the Moral Majority in 1979.

Falwell described the independent Moral Majority as a united front for God and country. He professed to speak for the vast majority of citizens who subscribed to traditional values in opposition to the "godless minority" that ruled the country. In *Listen America!* (1980), Falwell explained that this "coalition of God-fearing moral Americans" would "reverse the politicalization of immorality." The enemy was "secular humanism" in government—the attempt to solve problems apart from God. "I believe in the separation of church and state but not in the separation of God and government," Falwell remarked.

After signing up more than 2 million members, the Moral Majority registered twice that number as new voters for the 1980 elections and urged another 10 million to vote. Falwell had created a massive political action movement. Yet he rejected party affiliations and simply chose to identify himself as "a noisy Baptist" who had a "divine mandate" to fight for laws to save America. Politicizing the struggle between "good and evil," Falwell's mobilization of evangelical social conservatives dramatically realigned national politics and helped set the stage for the election of Ronald Reagan.

cutting government "waste, extravagance, abuse, and outright fraud." He also identified with the social values advanced by the Christian Right and Reverend Falwell. By promoting family cohesion, religious worship, and traditional education, the nominee expressed the desire of Protestant evangelicals

EXHIBIT **7-6**   **THE ELECTION OF 1980**

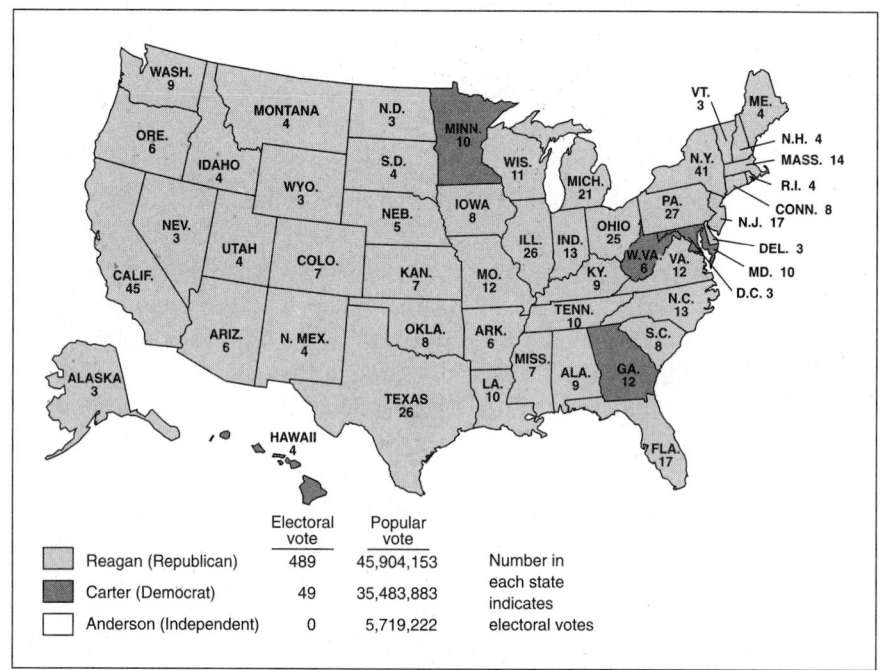

	Electoral vote	Popular vote	
Reagan (Republican)	489	45,904,153	Number in each state indicates electoral votes
Carter (Democrat)	49	35,483,883	
Anderson (Independent)	0	5,719,222	

and conservative Catholics to redeem the nation from moral permissiveness and collectivist values.

Asking voters if they were "better off" than they had been four years earlier, Reagan assured a frustrated electorate that it did "not have to go on sharing scarcity." Instead, the candidate proclaimed "an era of national renewal" and promised to restore U.S. global power. Democratic allusions to Reagan as a right-wing threat to peace backfired when the challenger appeared relaxed and amiable in a nationally televised debate. Although Reagan won support from corporate leaders seeking to reduce social costs and to regain a competitive edge in the world economy, his rejection of Carter's notion of "limits" attracted a broad coalition of upscale professionals, young entrepreneurs, and blue-collar workers anxious about economic opportunity. As the White House waited in vain for settlement of the Iranian hostage crisis, Reagan and vice presidential candidate George Bush captured 51 percent of the popular vote, compared with 41 percent for Carter and Mondale. Running as an independent, Representative John B. Anderson, a moderate Illinois Republican, received nearly 7 percent of presidential ballots.

The one-sided nature of the 1980 contest surfaced in the electoral college vote, where the Republicans prevailed by an overwhelming 489–49. His support of a constitutional amendment to ban abortion allowed Reagan to attract more than three-fifths of born-again white Protestants, who helped him capture seven southern states that Carter had carried in the previous contest. Meanwhile, Republicans won control of the Senate for the first time since 1952.

George Bush had accused Reagan of espousing "voodoo economics" during the Republican primaries. Yet the former governor insisted that he could reduce government spending while increasing outlays for defense, could lower taxes while balancing the federal budget, and could simultaneously restore economic prosperity. Such reasoning originated with "supply-side" economists such as Arthur Laffer of the University of Southern California and consultants associated with conservative think tanks such as the Heritage Foundation and the American Enterprise Institute. These advisors insisted that government regulations and high taxes held back production and inflated prices. Supply-side policy called for generous tax cuts and government deregulation. Reagan argued that investors would anticipate improvements from his economic program and would spur market recovery. As supply-side economics gained ground in Congress, the president called for the largest tax cut in U.S. history.

While many Democrats lashed out against "Reaganomics," Office of Management and Budget Director David Stockman appeared before Congress to demonstrate that tax relief would not interfere with a balanced budget, even if accompanied by added military spending. Although Stockman acknowledged that tax cuts served the interests of the administration's wealthy supporters, he insisted that the budget plan could sustain economic growth without inflation. Accordingly, Democrats cooperated in passing the Economic Recovery Act of 1981, which enacted a three-year individual income tax reduction of 25 percent. The law offered incentives for individual retirement accounts (IRAs), reduced capital gains taxes and maximum tax rates, increased amounts exempted from estate and gift taxes, and indexed returns to inflation. Congress also lowered corporate tax rates, accelerated depreciation allowances, and reduced the windfall profits tax on oil. Although House Democrats subsequently tightened loopholes and restored some cuts, Reagan's tax relief pumped billions of dollars into the economy.

REAGAN DEREGULATION

Reagan sought to implement a conservative agenda by altering the direction of the Supreme Court. In 1981 he appointed Arizona judge and free-market advocate Sandra Day O'Connor as the first female justice to sit on the Court, despite her moderate support for abortion rights. When Chief Justice Warren Burger retired in 1986, the White House chose Antonin Scalia, a conservative academic, to fill the vacancy and elevated William Rehnquist, the panel's most conservative member, to the presiding chair. Reagan anticipated further judicial influence when he selected constitutional scholar Robert H. Bork to fill a third vacancy in 1987. However, Democrats and Republican moderates rejected Bork's strict interpretation of constitutional rights protections as "extremist." Forced to abandon the nominee after a campaign by feminists and civil rights activists, the president settled on the less abrasive Anthony M. Kennedy, a California judge.

The Reagan administration also pursued conservative policies by abandoning suits in favor of affirmative action and school desegregation, by opposing busing, by reducing legal services budgets for the poor, and by stacking civil rights agencies with obstructive appointees. Most important, the president sought to lessen Washington's commitment to the welfare system. Viewing discretionary social spending as counterproductive and inflationary, the White House hoped to restore post–World War II prosperity by returning to a budget in which safety net functions were confined to Social Security. Accordingly, Reagan and Congress cut $35 billion from domestic programs in 1981 through a drastic reduction of welfare. Confining the provision of benefits to the "truly needy," the government removed 400,000 families from Aid to Families with Dependent Children (AFDC) and took nearly 1 million people off the food stamp rolls. Discretionary social expenditure as a share of gross national product declined by more than a third during Reagan's tenure.

Committed to free-market reform, Reagan's administration accelerated Carter's steps toward deregulation. A 1982 court order divested American Telephone and Telegraph (AT&T) of local telephone service business and permitted its subsidiaries to enter computer processing and information fields. The Banking Act of 1982 enabled lenders to increase new services such as interest-bearing checking and money market accounts. Meanwhile, continued federal airline deregulation introduced lower fares and more flexible schedules. However, the policy soon led to conflicts with organized labor. When Reagan reduced the authority of the Occupational Safety and Health Administration (OSHA) in 1981, union leaders complained that the government had abandoned workers to suffer from excessive noise levels and lethal chemical exposures. After airline controls were lifted, air traffic controllers protested that the Federal Aviation Administration (FAA) had not allocated sufficient resources to deal with increased domestic flights. When 12,000 controllers went on strike, the president dissolved their union and ordered the FAA to replace them with military personnel. This antiunion strategy signaled the government's support for reduced labor costs amid global competition.

The administration also provoked the ire of environmentalists when it cut Carter's energy windfall profits tax and eliminated federal funding for alternative fuels. Further conflict emerged when Secretary of the Interior James G. Watt leased off-shore drilling rights to oil and gas interests and proposed the harvesting of timber from national parks. After activists won Watt's resignation in 1983, the head of the Environmental Protection Agency (EPA) was forced to resign and another official was convicted of perjury in a scandal involving EPA

collusion with industrial polluters. Congress responded with legislation imposing stricter handling of hazardous wastes, agreed to a new Superfund to clean
toxic dumps, and overrode a presidential veto to appropriate billions of dollars
to combat water pollution. Experts estimated that the cleanup costs for three
U.S. government nuclear waste disposal sites alone would surpass $100 billion.

Responding to the White House's lack of interest in environmental regulation, ecologists warned that pollution crossed national boundaries. For example, depletion of Amazon rain forests by developers and fast-food cattle
interests was dangerously lowering global atmospheric oxygen levels. Sulfuric
emissions from the burning of cheap coal by U.S. factories and power plants resulted in acid rain that was defoliating trees and contaminating lakes in Canada
and the northern Midwest. As the federal government moderated regulations
to accommodate industrial interests, figures revealed that Earth's atmosphere
had lost 2.3 percent of its ozone layer—an essential shield of ultraviolet rays
that cause skin cancer and excessive heating by the sun.

Despite Reagan's conservative agenda, however, the White House often
compromised with congressional Democrats. As unemployment approached
11 percent in 1982, the president approved a gas tax that funded a four-year
outlay for highway and other transportation projects. After Reagan created a
bipartisan commission on the impending bankruptcy of the Social Security
system, he signed the commission's recommendations for increased payroll
taxes into law. Yet Congress refused to implement the White House's "new
federalism," a proposal to shift welfare programs to the poorly funded states.
Congress also ignored the president's plan to provide tuition tax credits for private school education because the plan was perceived as a threat to public
schooling and racial integration. Nor did Congress approve requests to abolish
the Departments of Education and Energy. Constitutional amendments concerning balanced budgets, abortion, and public school prayer also met defeat.

REELECTION AND THE REAGAN DOCTRINE

Reagan's tax cuts coincided with a sharp drop in global oil prices and a return of
prosperity. "We Brought America Back," the White House announced in 1984.
Seeking to strengthen voter faith in the Republican Party as the promoter of
opportunity, campaign videos proclaimed that it was "Morning in America."
Democrats disagreed on how to regain the electorate's confidence. African
American minister and civil rights advocate Jesse Jackson represented a "rainbow coalition" of racial minorities, feminists, peace activists, and the poor. Senator Gary Hart of Colorado cultivated urban professionals involved in the "high-
tech" service economy. Yet former Vice President Mondale emerged as the
1984 Democratic presidential nominee by deferring to party power bases in
labor, education, and the big cities. At the urging of feminists, Mondale chose

Representative Geraldine A. Ferraro of New York as his running mate—the first woman nominated for national executive office by a major party.

Democrats tried to preserve the alliance of unions, beneficiaries of big government, and urban developers that had financed their party's presidential races since World War II. Yet global competition reduced tolerance of government regulation and social spending among those business interests once friendly to the Democratic Party. Meanwhile, the diminished role of manufacturing eroded union membership and bargaining power. Both parties now competed for financial backing by relying on election specialists, media advisors, and legal consultants. Democrats increasingly leaned on their upper-middle-class base by combining calls for fiscal integrity with a focus on education, the environment, and civil rights.

Although Mondale won the AFL-CIO's first-ever presidential endorsement in 1984, he lost the confidence of many voters when he acknowledged that he would raise taxes to ease the budget deficit without shifting the burden to the affluent. The Democrats emerged from the election with 90 percent of African American ballots, nearly two-thirds of the Hispanic vote, and a hefty majority among the working poor. Yet Reagan's communications skills fused with sophisticated polling and advertising techniques to produce a stunning Republican victory.

The president won 59 percent of the popular vote and captured majorities in every state but Mondale's Minnesota and the District of Columbia. Republicans did particularly well among evangelical Christians, southern whites, white males, and the affluent. More surprising was Reagan's comfortable majority among eighteen to twenty-nine year-olds, a group who preferred Republican promises of economic growth to the "status quo" politics of the losers. The election dramatized the conversion of "Reagan Democrats"—Republican voters from working-class families once loyal to the New Deal— who were more comfortable with the president's promarket policies than with the Democrats' social liberalism.

Reagan contrasted the "evil empire" of the Soviet Union with the moral superiority of the United States—the "blessed land" of a "chosen people." President Carter had translated this moral imperative into a demand that allies such as Chile and El Salvador adhere to high standards in guaranteeing human

EXHIBIT **7-7   VOTER PARTICIPATION, 1980–1984**
(AS A PERCENTAGE OF ALL ELIGIBLE VOTERS)

1980	52.8
1984	53.3

Source: *Statistical Abstract of the United States* (1996).

rights. In contrast, Reagan's U.N. Ambassador Jeane J. Kirkpatrick rejected this policy as naive and insisted that right-wing "authoritarian" dictatorships were capable of democratic change, whereas left-wing "totalitarian" regimes were not. Blaming "world terrorism" and most global conflict on Soviet adventurism in developing nations, national security planners fashioned an unofficial "Reagan Doctrine" to rebuild the Central Intelligence Agency's (CIA) capabilities. The president persuaded Congress to lift the Carter-era restrictions in Angola and personally designated the anticommunist UNITA to be the recipient of military aid. The United States also supplied anticommunist rebels in Afghanistan, Cambodia, Ethiopia, and Nicaragua.

Although the administration insisted that communism contributed to the worst human rights abuses, the White House faced intense congressional pressure when the white minority government of South Africa violently suppressed black demonstrations. As U.S. civil rights leaders led daily antiapartheid protests at Washington's South African embassy, conservative Republicans embraced the campaign to demonstrate opposition to racism. Reagan responded with a policy of "constructive engagement" that called for peaceful persuasion of an anticommunist ally. Not satisfied, Congress then handed the president his most dramatic foreign policy reversal by overriding his veto of South African trade sanctions in 1986. After the defeat, Reagan recognized the government of reformer Corazon Aquino when Philippine dictator Ferdinand E. Marcos was ousted by a democratic movement. American officials also escorted dictator Jean-Claude Duvalier out of Haiti. As relations cooled with military governments in Chile and Paraguay, Reagan announced that the United States encouraged democratic movements among right-wing allies.

THE MIDDLE EAST QUAGMIRE

The United States faced its most daunting challenges in the Middle East, where it sought to protect regional oil fields and shipping lanes and to support Israel and "moderate" Arab leaders. When Reagan sent a contingent of marines to act as peacekeepers during a civil war in Lebanon in 1982, the troops clashed with Syrian forces and with Moslem militias allied with Iran. Islamic revolutionaries deployed massive truck bombs to destroy the U.S. embassy and marine headquarters, killing 241 U.S. servicemen. For the first time in history, Congress invoked the War Powers Act. Although Reagan did not recognize the statute's constitutionality, he agreed to withdraw all troops within eighteen months. Like its predecessors, the Reagan administration underestimated the region's pervasive currents of nationalism and fundamentalism and failed to address the ongoing dispute between Israel and the Palestinians.

Perceived as a supporter of Israeli expansion and as an imperial power in

Jeane J. Kirkpatrick (1926–   )

Like her boss Ronald Reagan, Jeane Kirkpatrick became a prominent Republican after years of loyalty to the Democratic Party. While a staunch Democrat, Kirkpatrick went to Barnard College and Columbia University but delayed her career to meet family responsibilities. She returned to academic life in the early 1960s, joined the faculty of Georgetown University, and completed her Ph.D. in political science at Columbia in 1968. Quickly establishing herself as a prolific and respected scholar, Kirkpatrick did important work on U.S. politics and foreign policy.

Kirkpatrick grew steadily estranged from liberal politics after 1968. She particularly objected to the influx of Democratic dissidents she described as "antiwar, antigrowth, antibusiness, antilabor." As a result of the Vietnam War, moreover, she found that Democrats expressed a reluctance to wield military power to defend U.S. interests against Soviet and other threats. Kirkpatrick preferred an older version of liberalism best articulated in the 1970s by Senators Henry Jackson of Washington and Hubert Humphrey of Minnesota. Characterizing herself as a "welfare conservative," she defended the "noble tradition of caring in domestic affairs, of . . . providing minimum standards of well-being" while simultaneously contrasting the success of American society to "the failure and tyranny of communist societies."

The issue of foreign policy finally prompted her break with the Demo-

the Middle East, the United States continued to be the target of violent attacks, kidnappings, and hijackings. After declaring a trade embargo against radical Libya, which the White House accused of supporting terror campaigns, the president unleashed an air and naval attack in 1986. Once Washington linked the Libyans to the bombing of a West German discotheque frequented by U.S. soldiers, the administration orchestrated a second military attack against Libya that destroyed the family quarters of Libyan leader Muammar al-Qaddafi.

The administration also sought to contain revolutionary Iran. Reagan em-

cratic Party during the Carter administration, whose approach to world affairs she saw as guilt-ridden and irresolute. Kirkpatrick voiced these concerns in a biting article for the conservative journal *Commentary*. Titled "Dictatorships and Double Standards," her polemic attacked the failure of Carter's foreign policy as "clear to everyone except its architects." Kirkpatrick particularly scored the administration for opposing pro–U.S., right-wing authoritarians while tolerating leftist or revolutionary regimes unfriendly to the United States. She argued that for all their faults, right-wing authoritarians more easily accepted democratic reforms than did left-wing totalitarians. "Liberal idealism," she concluded, "need not be identical with masochism, and need not be incompatible with the defense of freedom and the national interest."

Impressed by the article, Reagan appointed Kirkpatrick ambassador to the United Nations shortly after his election in 1980. During her five years at the U.N., she acquired a reputation as a combative advocate of U.S. policy, but her role as U.N. ambassador increasingly frustrated her. Kirkpatrick called the body a "dismal show" where conflicts never were resolved. When Reagan did not appoint her to a high-level policy-making position, she resigned in 1985 and returned to Georgetown. Almost simultaneously, she joined the Republican Party.

One of the few prominent women to serve in the Reagan administration, Kirkpatrick often received press consideration as a possible candidate for elective office or for a future political appointment. Adored by conservatives and vilified by liberals, Jeane Kirkpatrick remained an outspoken beacon of plain talk and provocative viewpoints.

---

bargoed military shipments to Tehran and pledged never to negotiate with terrorists. Nevertheless, in 1985 the president permitted National Security Council officials to arrange a secret exchange of U.S. weapons to Iran for the release of U.S. hostages in Lebanon. When a Beirut newspaper leaked details of the arms-for-hostage accord in 1986, the administration abruptly ended the relationship. Reagan subsequently sent naval forces to the Persian Gulf to protect the passage of Middle East oil tankers. Yet the covert arrangement with Tehran would haunt the president for the remainder of his term.

EXHIBIT **7-8**   **LEBANON, 1983**

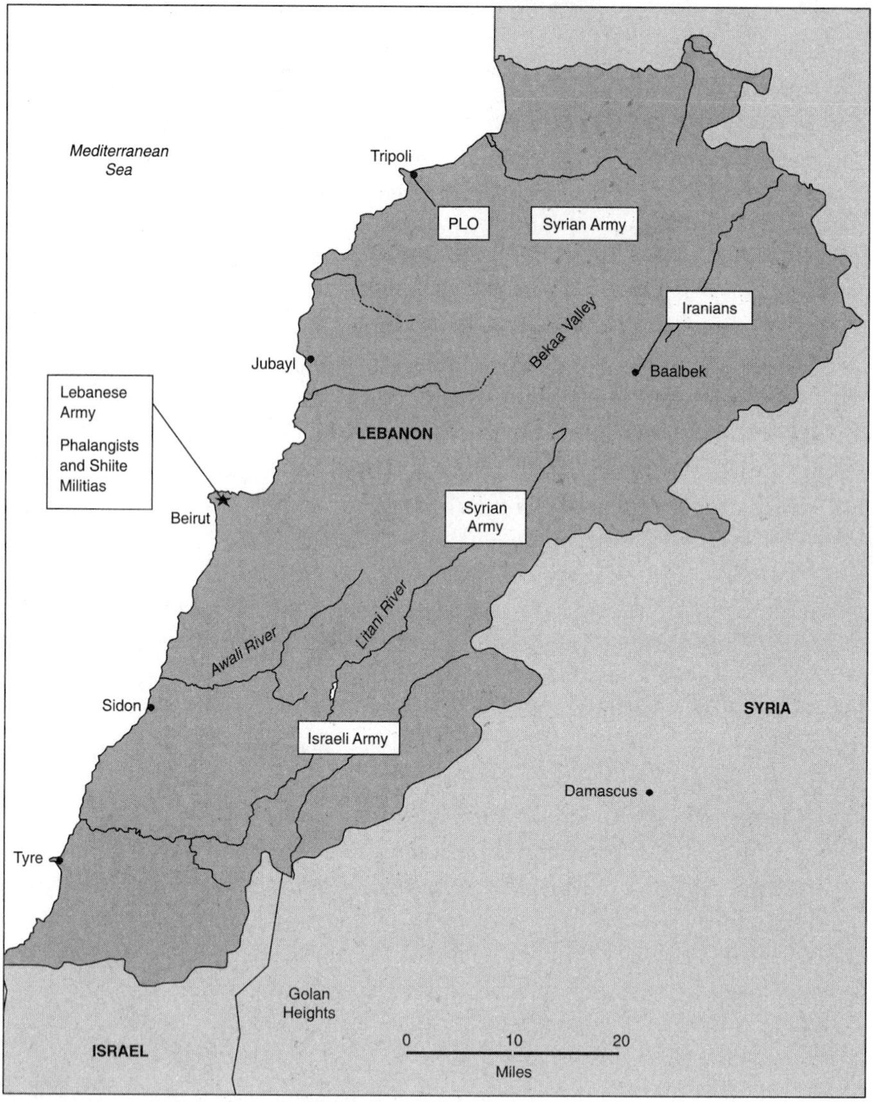

Mediterranean
Sea

Tripoli

PLO   Syrian Army

Iranians

Jubayl   Bekaa Valley   Baalbek

Lebanese
Army

Phalangists
and Shiite
Militias

LEBANON

Beirut

Syrian
Army

Awali River   Litani River

Sidon   **SYRIA**

Israeli Army

Damascus

Tyre

Golan
Heights

ISRAEL   0   10   20

Miles

THE CRUSADE IN CENTRAL AMERICA

Pushing for supremacy in the Cold War, Reagan officials pursued a vigilant anticommunist policy in the Caribbean and Central America. Cuba's Fidel Castro had permitted 125,000 exiles to flee to Florida in 1980, but the United States charged that many were criminals, mental patients, or social undesirables. As relations between Havana and Washington worsened, Castro consolidated ties with the Marxist government of the tiny Caribbean island of Grenada. When

EXHIBIT **7-9**　**PERSIAN GULF SHIPPING LANES**

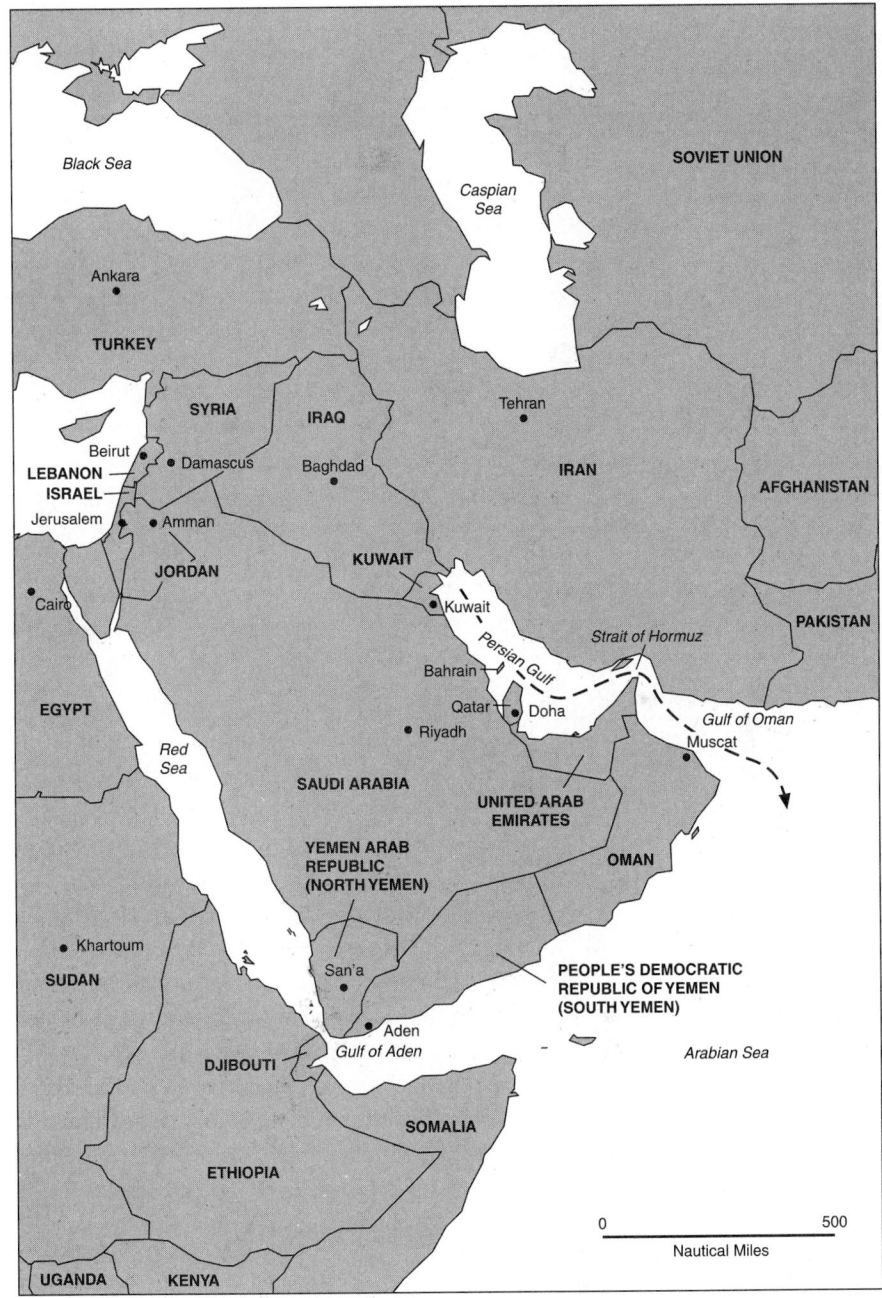

dissident communists murdered Grenada's prime minister and other leaders in
1983, Reagan used the pretext of civil strife to mount an invasion against Cuba's
ally. Labeling the operation a "rescue mission" to protect 1,000 U.S. medical

EXHIBIT **7-10**   **CENTRAL AMERICA AND THE CARIBBEAN**

students, the president dispatched a small force of marines, rangers, and paratroopers to take control of the island. Polls revealed public endorsement of the nation's first military "victory" in the post–Vietnam War era.

In Central America's impoverished El Salvador, the Reagan administration pursued a more controversial policy by arming a right-wing military government whose security forces and "death squads" killed 30,000 civilians in a bloody civil war in the early 1980s. When a centrist leader won internationally supervised elections in 1984, Congress approved additional funding to defeat left-wing guerrillas. Yet efforts to incorporate the rebels into the political structure were threatened in 1988 when right-wingers regained control of El Salvador's legislature. In neighboring Nicaragua, Reagan authorized the CIA to support a rebel army of "contras" to overthrow the Sandinista government, which the White House saw as a front for communist expansion. Administration policy in Central America was strongly opposed by many religious leaders, particularly in the Catholic community. After learning of CIA assassination manuals and the secret mining of Nicaraguan ports, Congress passed the Boland Amendments of 1982 and 1984, which prohibited the use of military or intelligence funds for covert action against Nicaragua's government.

Frustrated by congressional interference with so-called freedom fighters, Reagan officials violated Boland Amendment restrictions by secretly raising more than $36 million from private donors and conservative allies such as Saudi Arabia and Taiwan. Meanwhile, CIA Director William Casey, National

Security Advisor Rear Admiral John M. Poindexter, and National Security Council aide Lieutenant Colonel Oliver North coordinated an illegal scheme to help the contras by diverting unlawful profits from the illegal Iranian arms sales. The top-secret campaign depended on illegal CIA operations and pressure on the governments of Honduras and Costa Rica to permit Nicaraguan contra rebels to operate from their territory.

Disclosure of the Iran-Contra fund diversion in 1986 created the greatest crisis of Reagan's tenure. Having weathered an assassin's bullet in his first months in office, the president had forged a reputation as a "Teflon" leader who survived both misfortune and criticism with ease. However, after denying the arms sale to Iran had ever occurred and after insisting that missiles were not traded for hostages, Reagan faced questions about his involvement in the violations of the Boland Amendments. A commission led by former Senator John Tower concluded in 1987 that the commander in chief had mismanaged his staff but had no knowledge of the contra funding. Reagan fired North, accepted Poindexter's resignation, and agreed to the appointment of a special prosecutor. After televised hearings in which North gave a passionate defense of his actions, a joint panel of the House and Senate cited the administration for violating congressional restrictions on covert activity and for "pervasive dishonesty and inordinate secrecy." When the Nicaraguan government agreed to peace talks with its domestic rivals in 1988, Congress ended military aid to the contras.

Despite embarrassment, the Reagan administration managed to survive the scandal. After Special Prosecutor Lawrence Walsh won convictions of North and Poindexter for obstructing Congress, an appeals court reversed the verdicts because the Iran-Contra committee had granted the defendants limited immunity. After the perjury indictment of Defense Secretary Caspar W. Weinberger, public consideration of the matter was closed when Weinberger and five other officials received presidential pardons from Reagan's successor in 1992. Although the president had been compelled to testify as a witness in court proceedings, he never accepted legal or moral responsibility for the actions committed in his name, nor acknowledged how Iran-Contra had diminished his political effectiveness.

COLD WAR CATHARSIS

Having won the White House with promises to revitalize national defense, Reagan initiated the largest peacetime military buildup in U.S. history. Congress approved an $18 billion increase in defense spending in a 1981 budget that embraced construction of neutron bombs, production of the B-1 bomber canceled by Carter, and creation of a rapid deployment force. Insisting that the United States could win the Cold War by forcing the Soviets to spend beyond their means, Reagan prevailed on Congress to raise annual military expenditures by nearly 50 percent between 1981 and 1986. The most controversial feature of the president's plan was the Strategic Defense Initiative (SDI), introduced in a 1983 television address. Dubbed "Star Wars," the massive research and development project sought to explore the use of space satellites and laser weapons to fend off nuclear missiles. Although Congress appropriated a fraction of the proposed funding, many scientists joined the Soviets in expressing concerns about the potential militarization of space.

Since Reagan viewed arms control as an inadequate response to an aggressive Soviet military machine, he acknowledged the possibility of a "limited" nuclear war in which damage might be confined to Europe. By 1982, however, grassroots activists on both sides of the Atlantic had mounted a "nuclear freeze" movement that demanded that the superpowers declare a verifiable moratorium on testing, deployment, and production of atomic weapons. Public concern about the dangers of nuclear war mounted under Reagan. Three chilling cult movie classics—*Mad Max* (1980), *Road Warrior* (1981), and *Blade Runner* (1982) —portrayed the bleak human and physical landscapes resulting from nuclear apocalypse. In 1983 astronomer Carl Sagan gave credence to such fears by warning that radioactive dust clouds from atomic war might block the sun's rays and produce a "nuclear winter" that would condemn the human species to imminent death. That year's television special, "The Day After," graphically illustrated the potential effects of a nuclear explosion on a typical midwestern town.

Strategic thinkers such as Daniel Ellsberg and Robert McNamara led campaigns for nuclear disarmament, and 600,000 protesters rallied in New York City's Central Park in the largest demonstration to that point in U.S. history. When the nuclear freeze resolution came before the House, the White House argued that passage would weaken the U.S. bargaining position in the SALT negotiations, and the proposal met a narrow 204–202 defeat. Nevertheless, the president declared that nuclear war should be deterred at all costs and committed the nation to SALT II. Congress moderated the arms race in 1985 by eliminating funding for half the MX missiles the administration requested.

EXHIBIT **7-11**   **NATIONAL DEFENSE SPENDING, 1980–1988**
(IN ROUNDED BILLIONS OF DOLLARS)

1980	134.0
1982	185.3
1984	227.4
1986	273.4
1988	290.4

Source: *Statistical Abstract of the United States* (1996).

Soviet Secretary Gorbachev and President Reagan at the Geneva summit of 1985, the first of four such meetings between the two superpower leaders.

Despite militant anticommunism, Reagan embraced some accommodation with the Soviet Union. In 1981 he responded to the agricultural lobby by ending the Carter embargo on grain sales to Moscow. Two years later Reagan negotiated a five-year wheat sales pact. As the Soviets initiated democratic political reforms, European allies and Congress pushed the White House toward negotiations with Soviet Communist Party leader Mikhail Gorbachev. At the Geneva conference of 1985, the first summit in six years, Gorbachev expressed a desire for *glasnost* ("openness") at home and abroad. Seeking to modernize his economy through Western investment and lower defense costs, the Soviet leader persuaded Reagan to work toward a 50 percent cut in nuclear weapons.

When Reagan and Gorbachev met again in Iceland in 1986, they nearly reached consensus on major arms reduction, but the Soviets insisted that the United States first confine development of Star Wars to laboratory research. Nevertheless, the summit resulted in an intermediate nuclear force (INF) treaty the following year that allowed Reagan to keep Star Wars but provided for the dismantling of thousands of medium- and short-range missiles in Europe. The pact included the most extensive system of weapons surveillance ever negotiated by the two superpowers. Following Moscow's announcement in 1988 that it intended to withdraw troops from Afghanistan, the U.S. Senate took a major step toward ending the Cold War by ratifying the INF treaty.

THE NEW ECONOMY

As Cold War tensions eased, the U.S. economy thrived with innovations in information services and expanded international trade. By 1980 more than two-fifths of the workforce was employed in the "knowledge" sector, accounting for more than one-third of the gross national product. As electronics firms introduced desktop computers with silicon chips to digitally process, store, and display information, innovations such as electronic mail and the Internet communications "web" accelerated the pace of data transmission. Other applications of electronic technology included mobile telephones, facsimile (fax) machines, telephone answering devices, videocassette recorders, and compact disc players.

Telecommunications increasingly shaped the way Americans did business and filled leisure time. The National Aeronautics and Space Administration (NASA) had established a global communications system in the 1960s by deploying satellite relay stations in space. When the development of fiber-optic cables and photonic amplifiers stimulated the growth of cable television in the 1980s, space satellites began transmitting TV signals worldwide. By the early 1990s, cable and satellite networks offered twenty-four-hour news, sports, music, movie, and shopping channels to more than 60 percent of U.S. households.

High-tech products also reached consumers through new retail facilities and manufacturers' outlets in suburban shopping malls. In 1989 the largest shopping complex in the nation—Mall of America—opened in Bloomington, Minnesota. Urban strip malls, discount stores, mail-order sales, TV shopping channels, amusement "theme" parks, and credit card services helped to push consumer debt to more than $744 billion by 1991. Fast-food outlets provided another key to economic growth. Begun in 1954 by Ray Kroc, McDonald's grew into a hamburger franchising operation with nearly 10,000 worldwide

EXHIBIT **7-12**   **U.S. GROSS NATIONAL PRODUCT, 1981–1987**
(IN CURRENT DOLLARS IN BILLIONS)

1981	3,052.6
1983	3,405.7
1985	4,010.3
1987	4,486.2

Source: *Economics Report of the President* (1988).

EXHIBIT **7-13**   U.S. CONSUMER CREDIT OUTSTANDING, 1980–1987
(IN ROUNDED BILLIONS OF DOLLARS AS OF DECEMBER OF EACH YEAR)

1980	369
1981	390
1983	468
1985	657
1987	756

Source: *Economics Report of the President* (1988).

outlets. The diversified fast-food industry proliferated around the world with formula-produced soft drinks, pizza, fried chicken, and ice cream products.

The high-tech, global service economy created new clusters of corporate power and influence. As U.S. trade with Asia surpassed that with Europe in the 1980s, San Francisco became a major center of international business and global investment planning. The growth in the service sector, which accounted for nearly three-quarters of all employment by the 1990s, attracted professional and white-collar workers to the capital cities of the Midwest and to computer software centers like California's Silicon Valley. Meanwhile, tourism and the retirement industry served as development magnets in the Sunbelt states of Arizona, California, Florida, and Texas, where half the nation's population growth occurred in the 1980s.

Spurred by investment from Japan and the Middle East, U.S. financial managers prospered in the 1980s. Yet profits were sustained partially through questionable techniques such as the sale of high-risk "junk" bonds, an innovation of Wall Street broker Michael R. Milken that permitted small companies to borrow huge sums to absorb larger firms. Stocks benefited from leveraged buyouts, with which executives staged hostile corporate takeovers by purchasing the equity of other shareholders. Mergers and acquisitions consolidated the airlines, communications, and banking industries. Yet the resulting volatility contributed to the greatest one-day loss in stock market history in 1987 when the Dow Jones average lost nearly one-fourth of its value. The market only regained its footing when the Federal Reserve poured capital into the banking system. Federal authorities then sought to discourage further abuse by prosecuting junk bond dealer Milken for securities fraud and charging several Wall Street brokers with insider trading and stock fraud.

The banking boom also generated economic instability. Beginning in 1980, federal deregulation phased out interest rate ceilings on savings accounts and increased federal deposit insurance to $100,000. Commercial banks could now extend high-interest loans to developing nations and engage in risky real estate development at home. Congress also permitted savings and loans (S&Ls) to invest in the money market and to pump funds into commercial real estate. Subsequent mismanagement and fraud led to the bankruptcy of hundreds of financial institutions by the decade's end.

Congress responded to the S&L crisis in 1989 with a bailout to cover depositor losses and a massive fund for buying and selling off failed institutions. This expensive intervention was paid for by taxpayers, eroding confidence in the government's ability to monitor financial greed. Five U.S. senators were reprimanded by colleagues for exerting improper influence on behalf of one banker.

YOUNG URBAN PROFESSIONALS AND THE NEW AGE

The global economy and information age provided expanded opportunities for the skilled college graduates of the baby boom era. Clustered around high-tech service centers, young, urban professionals, or "yuppies," specialized in law, marketing, computer trades, the media, health services, and government. Their intensity and informality revitalized U.S. business with team play, networking skills, and a strong entrepreneurial spirit. Urban professionals such as Apple Computer cofounder Stephen Jobs saw the workplace as an arena for translating personal growth goals into practical life strategies. Attorneys in "public interest" law organized class action lawsuits against corporate polluters, cigarette companies, and employers charged with discriminatory labor policies.

By emphasizing countercultural values such as self-fulfillment and openness to change, the new professionals helped to reshape consumption patterns. "Postmodern" condominiums, theaters, and specialty shops contributed to the gentrification of urban neighborhoods. Although the high rents that accompanied renovation of historical districts often displaced less affluent tenants and shopkeepers, the new middle class played an active role in neighborhood associations and campaigns to make cities safer and more livable. Improvement also took on a personal character. Instructional work-out videos and manuals produced by actress Jane Fonda led millions in daily exercise routines. Jogging, bicycling, body building, indoor sports, and hot tubs provided convenient outlets for professionals with limited recreational time and disposable income. Such activities would be supplanted in the 1990s by more "extreme" pursuits that included roller blading, snowboarding, hang gliding, windsurfing, and bungee jumping.

Eating habits also changed. Urban professionals opted for tasty, lower-calorie, nutritional meals that did not require extensive preparation. Carry-home specialties (often reheated in microwave ovens) replaced home-cooked meals. The new diet featured natural and organic foods, frozen yogurt desserts, fresh-ground coffees, domestic wines, "light" beers, and mineral waters. A proliferation of gourmet restaurants included specialists in "California cuisine"—an aesthetically presented cookery that replaced salty and fatty foods with fresh fish, poultry, and vegetables. Espresso bars and microbreweries served as additional gathering places for young urbanites.

Trends in popular music reflected the diversity of cultures made possible by enhanced communications. Although country and western, gospel, soul, and rock music continued to attract loyal fans, the disco rhythms of big-city gay and black dance clubs found their way to the airwaves and recording studios in the mid-1970s. In turn, disco and mainstream rock soon were supplanted by the more confrontive sounds of heavy metal and punk. After the launching in 1981 of MTV (Music Television), a twenty-four-hour cable outlet originally devoted to rock videos, young consumers could sample musical styles ranging from techno-pop, reggae, rap, and hip-hop to grunge, alternative rock, and new folk.

Facing competition from specialized cable programming, network television struggled to attract new audiences. Widely viewed 1980s TV series—*Hill Street Blues, Miami Vice, St. Elsewhere,* and *L.A. Law*—explored the work life of urban professionals. In the film industry, new computer technologies produced sophisticated animations such as *Who Framed Roger Rabbit?* (1988), Disney's *The Little Mermaid* (1989), and Steven Spielberg's dinosaur saga, *Jurassic Park* (1993).

Countercultural lifestyles also influenced the spiritual practices of many urban professionals. As second marriages, stepparenting, and two-income families became more common, some religious denominations offered greater roles for women and increased involvement in such social issues as homelessness. Alternative religions also prospered—by 1987, 20 percent of Americans between eighteen and twenty-four years of age (31 percent on the West Coast) claimed a religious belief outside the mainstream faiths. Young cultural dissidents of the 1960s and 1970s had experimented with Asian spiritual traditions such as Zen Buddhism, Tibetan Buddhism, yoga, the *I Ching*, and martial arts. These interests led some to join such sects as the Church of Scientology, the Hari Krishnas, and the Unification Church of Korea's Reverend Sun Myung Moon. Others experimented with "New Age" fusions of science and spirituality that embraced holistic practices associated with natural medicine, acupuncture, biofeedback, and meditation.

MULTICULTURAL POPULATIONS

The global economy, together with overseas political repression, stimulated the mobility of labor, leading 20 million people to immigrate legally to the United States between 1950 and 1990. More than 8.3 million newcomers arrived in the 1980s, the most numerous of whom were Hispanics, two-thirds of whom came from Mexico. Although Chicanos faced a struggle for survival, they established significant power bases in southwestern cities like Los Angeles and San Antonio, producing national leaders such as future cabinet official Henry G. Cisneros. Film director Louis Valdez captured the authentic textures of

Madonna Louise Veronica Ciccone (1958–   )

"I was born and raised in Detroit," an unknown Madonna Ciccone scribbled in an audition statement for a New York movie producer, "where I began my career in petulance and preciousness. By the time I was in fifth grade, I knew I either wanted to be a nun or a movie star. During high school I became slightly schizophrenic as I couldn't choose between class virgin or the other kind."

Known simply as Madonna, Ciccone emerged as a major cultural icon of the 1980s, the most financially successful female entertainer in history. One of eight children in a middle-class Catholic family, she was devastated when she was six years old by the death of her mother. In 1978 she dropped out of the University of Michigan and flew to New York with $37 in her pocket. After enrolling for classes with the third-string troupe of the prestigious American Dance Center, she rented a fourth-floor "walk-up" in Manhattan's East Village, worked at Dunkin' Donuts, posed in the nude for art classes, and sifted through garbage for food.

After a one-year stint as a back-up vocalist and dancer for a Parisian disco act, Madonna returned to the United States and began singing with "alternative" music bands and lip-synching on the Lower Manhattan disco and hip-hop club circuit. Adopting a trampy, punk look that featured rags, safety pins, and the use of underwear as outer garments, the aspiring performer set her mind on a pop music career. Building on personal contacts with club musicians and disk jockeys, Madonna garnered a Warner Bros. recording commitment in 1983. Her first album, the disco-oriented *Madonna*, attracted little attention until the vocalist took it upon

Mexican American life in films such as *Boulevard Nights* (1979), *Zoot Suit* (1981), and *La Bamba* (1987).

Impoverished migrants from Central America and the Caribbean contributed to the stream of newcomers. Cuban Americans ranked as one of the most successful of the recent immigrants. An annual average of 20,000 Cubans had migrated to the United States through the 1960s, most skilled profession-

herself to promote club exposure and airplay. The collection eventually sold 9 million copies, and three of its cuts rose to the Top Ten.

Madonna benefited from the immense popularity of MTV, whose twenty-four-hour cable television programming placed her videos on "heavy" rotation. An appearance as a charming street-waif in the film *Desperately Seeking Susan* (1984) contributed to the performer's mystique. Abandoning bracelets and crucifixes for a white silk wedding dress and for a belt buckle reading "Boy Toy," Madonna cut a new song titled "Like a Virgin" (1984). The album of the same name sold 11 million copies and featured "Material Girl," a simultaneous tribute to and parody of Marilyn Monroe. Another collection, *True Blue* (1988), reached sales of 17 million and included the controversial "Papa Don't Preach," a portrait of a pregnant single woman who chooses to keep her baby.

Aware of Madonna's loyal following among young women, including many African American and Hispanic fans, the Pepsi corporation agreed to sponsor a 1989 concert tour and to pay the performer $5 million for three commercials. When the video for "Like a Prayer," the title song of Madonna's new album, included footage of the singer kissing a black saint and dancing provocatively before burning crosses, the company pulled the commercial and severed its relationship with the star. "Express Yourself," the album's second hit, told listeners never to settle for "second best"—for anything less than truth and self-respect.

During the 1990s Madonna leveraged her fame and financial success into careers as a movie performer, book publisher, record company owner, and producer. The star's mixture of toughness and vulnerability continued to speak to many women. Sampling a diversity of postures and styles, she brilliantly embodied the era's postmodern synthesis of high and mass culture.

als or white-collar workers. In the following decades, working-class Cubans joined the exodus, particularly when Fidel Castro allowed thousands to leave the island in 1980. As the Cuban American population reached 1 million, its leaders made Miami the financial and cultural center of Latin America. Yet the poverty of the city's underclass and its geographic location attracted the international narcotics trade in the 1980s. The multibillion-dollar industry

EXHIBIT 7-14   NUMBER OF IMMIGRANTS TO THE UNITED STATES,
1980–1990
(IN ROUNDED FIGURES)

1980	531,000
1985	570,000
1990	1,500,000

Source: *Statistical Abstract of the United States* (1996).

brought rising cocaine addiction, rampant police corruption, soaring crime and homicide rates, and schemes for laundering proceeds from drug sales.

As Los Angeles replaced New York as the leading port of entry in the 1970s, Asian immigrants accounted for more than 40 percent of newcomers to the United States. A half-million Filipinos emigrated to America during the 1980s. Taking advantage of the liberal provisions of the Immigration Act of 1965, more than 6 million newcomers from China, Taiwan, Hong Kong, and Korea arrived between 1970 and 1995. Many of these immigrants established small businesses, particularly retail food stores and restaurants. Asian Americans also worked in low-wage service and garment trades, sometimes as "sweatshop" seamstresses who received minimal pay and no benefits from unregulated clothing subcontractors. Yet the children of Asian immigrants frequently sought college training. The richness of Chinese ethnic culture and family life was conveyed in Amy Tan's popular novel, *The Joy Luck Club* (1989). Nearly 840,000 refugees from the Indochina War, some aided by government relocation funds, also came to the United States.

Public reaction to immigration depended upon perceived labor needs. When officeholders in the Southwest and West complained that poor migrants created excessive social welfare burdens, several states passed laws to make English their official language. Under the Immigration Act of 1986, employers could be fined for knowingly hiring illegal aliens or undocumented laborers, although the law provided amnesty to some illegal immigrants. Ironically, professionally trained foreigners were actively pursued by U.S. corporations, research facilities, and medical institutions. Seeking to exploit the "brain drain" from eastern Europe and Asia, Congress passed the Immigration Act of 1990, which increased the legal immigration quota and made allowances for skilled newcomers, particularly engineers, scientists, and professionals. To encourage aliens to become citizens, naturalization procedures were moved from the courts to the Justice Department. By the mid-1990s legal immigration to the United States had risen to an annual 900,000.

Native Americans also sought opportunities for economic development and control of natural resources. Beginning in 1977 more than a dozen U.S. tribes filed federal lawsuits based on historic land claims. Three years later the Supreme Court upheld an award that compensated the South Dakota Sioux for U.S. seizure of the Black Hills a century earlier. After three tribes in northern Maine won another settlement, the U.S. Civil Rights Commission asked the federal government to negotiate several eastern Indian land disputes. Native American tribes also obtained the right to federal funding on the same basis as states and received recognition of claims to fishing and other resources. These assertions of economic sovereignty were sustained by the Supreme Court and by the Indian Gaming Reservation Act of 1988, which enabled tribes to build reservation gambling casinos.

Economic vitality accompanied renewed interest in Native traditions of spirituality, dance, drumming, and storytelling. Powwows, cleansing sweats, and vision quests counteracted historical legacies of racism by enhancing Native American self-esteem and ethnic pride. Indian leaders also compelled archeologists and anthropologists to turn over ancestral remains for respectful treatment and reburial. The cultural renaissance found expression in the literary works of Leslie Marmon Silko, Gerald Vizenor, and Louise Erdrich. Five hundred years after Columbus first explored the New World, the U.S. Native American population surpassed 2 million. Yet poverty, unemployment, alcoholism, and suicide continued to plague young people whose reservations and urban communities were untouched by capital investment or tourist development.

Like Native Americans, African Americans won added recognition of their cultural contributions during the 1980s but also saw economic opportunities decline among poorer members of the community. As black studies programs and the perspectives of people of color began to find their way into university curricula, Alex Haley's *Roots* (1976), a personal story of black genealogy, popularized African American history for a mass audience. More than 130 million viewers, or at least half the nation, watched at least one segment of the televised version of the book. African American artists considered their work an assertion of cultural independence. Race-conscious poetry emerged from literary figures such as Nikki Giovanni and Maya Angelou. Critically acclaimed black novelists included Nobel Prize winner Toni Morrison, whose *Beloved* (1987) explored psychological themes within a historical context. Alice Walker's *The Color Purple* (1982) portrayed a direct connection to the African legacy. Other significant African American novelists included Ishmael Reed, Al Young, Terry McMillan, and John Edgar Wideman.

Black creative energies had an enormous impact on the performing arts. Pulitzer Prize–winning playwright August Wilson used African techniques of storytelling and ensemble performance in *Ma Rainey's Black Bottom* (1984) and *Fences* (1987). Filmmaker Spike Lee brought black themes to mainstream audiences with provocative features such as *Do the Right Thing* (1989) and *Malcolm X* (1992). New directors like John Singleton incorporated inner-city gang life into movies such as *Boyz in the Hood* (1991). Rap music and hip-hop, products of black street subculture, spawned a new generation of

African American recording artists and pop cultural icons. As black spending power reached nearly $500 billion a year, mainstream African American entertainment and sports figures such as Bill Cosby, Eddie Murphy, Michael Jackson, Whitney Houston, Michael Jordan, and Oprah Winfrey became mainstays of international television, movies, and the celebrity press.

African American consumer power was buttressed by an increasingly prosperous black middle class. Government statistics revealed that 70 percent of the African American population lived above the poverty level (compared with 90 percent for whites). The annual income of black men leaped by half in the 1980s, while wage rates for African American women rose to equal those of white women. More than a million blacks were attending college by the 1980s, and African Americans constituted an increasing percentage of the nation's social service professionals. Economic well-being translated into political power. Between 1964 and 1980 the number of elected black officials jumped from 103 to more than 4,000. In the 1980s major cities such as Chicago, Philadelphia, Los Angeles, and New York chose African American mayors, and Virginia's L. Douglas Wilder became the first black governor. By 1993, thirty-eight African Americans sat in the House of Representatives.

Despite achievements, African Americans were particularly disadvantaged by conservative tax and investment policies that drained capital from inner cities, factories, and public schools, and by the stagnant minimum wage rates of the 1980s. More than 30 percent of African Americans continued to live in poverty. By 1985, jobless rates among adult black men averaged 60 percent. Although economic opportunities for affluent African Americans broadened in the 1980s, black poverty increased. By 1990, an African American citizen was nearly three times as likely to be without a job as was a white citizen. The inability of black men to support families contributed to large numbers of African American women having babies without getting married. By the mid-1980s, 60 percent of black infants were born out of wedlock, and more than half of all African American children less than six years of age lived in poverty. Although blacks constituted less than 13 percent of the U.S. population, African American families constituted more than half of Aid to Families with Dependent Children recipients.

As the inner city became the warehouse for society's unwanted, poverty and hopelessness produced an urban underclass—a population of unemployed and untrained people who relied on hustling and crime to survive. By the early 1990s violent street gangs contracted with powerful drug syndicates to sell "crack," an inexpensive but highly addictive cocaine derivative. As gang members sought territorial sovereignty, communities across the nation were terrorized and helpless to protect themselves. Government crime statistics for the 1980s showed that 30 percent of violent assaults and 60 percent of robberies were committed by blacks.

CULTURE WAR

Women activists focused identity politics on economic barriers in the 1980s, attacking the last legal bastions of sex segregation. Following the settlement of several class-action bias suits, the Supreme Court outlawed sex discrimination in private clubs and organizations. By 1980, women constituted the majority of university students and received ten times as many professional degrees as they had a decade earlier. Education improved women's occupational prospects. By the 1990s, 58 percent of women over sixteen years of age participated in the labor force, and women held nearly half of all jobs. Although women rarely reached top executive positions, they constituted nearly half of all managerial and professional employees and began to build lucrative careers as entrepreneurs. As wages for skilled female labor caught up to prevailing rates for men, however, the larger number of women in clerical, office, retail sales, and other low-status jobs continued to earn only three-quarters the rates of their male counterparts. Detecting a "feminization" of poverty, social critics noted that households headed by women were five times more likely to be destitute than those with male breadwinners.

Homosexuals also stepped up efforts to win inclusion in public life. Forming groups such as the National Gay Task Force, activists fought for local civil rights ordinances, mounted court cases against discrimination, and organized for acceptance of gays into the military and other institutions. Despite growing solidarity, however, the gay male population was decimated by the acquired immunodeficiency syndrome (AIDS) epidemic, first detected in 1981. Gays ultimately organized campaigns to close bathhouses (the scene of unprotected promiscuous sex), to limit sexual partners, and to promote the use of condoms, but activists accused the federal government of delaying AIDS research and condemned the media for failing to issue explicit warnings against dangerous sexual practices. By 1997, more than 400,000 AIDS patients had died in the United States.

Feminist, gay, and multicultural assertions of identity politics generated heated responses from social conservatives, particularly evangelical Christians who supported the televised ministries of preachers such as Jim Bakker, Jimmy Swaggart, Robert Schuler, and Oral Roberts. Even though Swaggart was defrocked for sexual misconduct and Bakker received a long prison sentence for financial irregularities, televangelists and Christian popular media remained influential forces. Pat Robertson used his national television audience to campaign for the Republican presidential nomination in 1988, although he finished poorly. Nevertheless, through Robertson's Christian Coalition, an issue-oriented political lobby, evangelical conservatives assumed a major role in the Republican Party.

Fatal Attraction (1987)

Released in the fall of 1987, British director Adrian Lyne's Fatal Attraction *turned out to be one of the surprise movie hits of the Reagan decade. In an age of AIDS, increasing family insecurity, and escalating tensions between men and women, the film offered a disturbing tale of contemporary sexual mores. Feminists considered the movie part of a backlash against women's liberation.*

Conceived eight years earlier by British screenwriter James Dearden, Fatal Attraction *told the story of a willful female book editor (played by Glenn Close) who seduces a married lawyer whose family is out of town (Michael Douglas). Close's liberated, single, career woman dresses in black leather, lives in a sparsely decorated New York apartment, and approaches the one-night affair in a casual and off-handed manner.*

Much to the surprise of family man Douglas, his bedmate turns insanely possessive the next morning, slitting her wrists to command his attention. Close skillfully conveys the precarious ego lurking behind her character's ex-

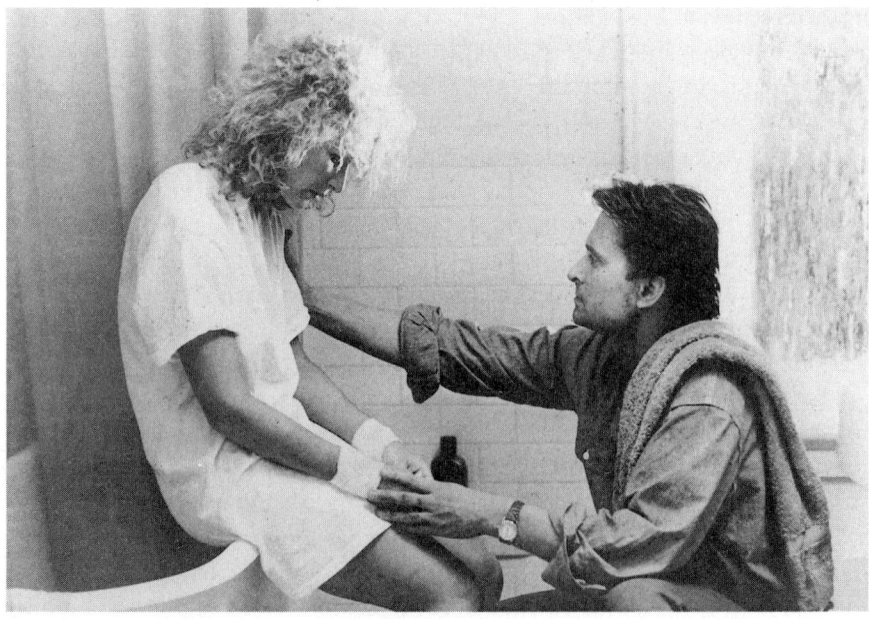

Movie Star News/Photri Inc.

terior. Initially sympathetic to feminist consciousness, the film suggests that single women are unfairly victimized by the diminished attractiveness of age and by unequal power relationships with male partners. As the obsessed Close hounds the attorney at his office and home, she echoes themes of feminist empowerment by insisting that she will not be used and discarded by men who refuse to take the consequences of their caprices. The point is subsequently reinforced by the disclosure that she is pregnant with his child.

From here on, Fatal Attraction *abandons a complex rendering of Close's character and turns her into a pathological creature, a terrifying figment of male paranoia who refuses to hold to rules to which she has agreed. First pouring acid on Douglas's car hood, then kidnapping his daughter from school, and finally invading the sanctity of his dream family, Close gradually works her way into an all-out assault on society's central institution. Under the delusion that Douglas's wife is an intruder into her own marital life with the attorney, Close comes at the sympathetically drawn homemaker with a knife. In a memorable bathroom scene reminiscent of teenage "slasher" movies, the courageous wife and mother finishes the job that Douglas is unable to complete by killing the monster.*

Feminist critics complained that Hollywood once again had characterized passionate and single women as antisocial beings who aroused the deepest fears of men. Indeed, Dearden's original script had the Close character commit suicide to the strains of the opera Madame Butterfly. *But the filmmakers found that trial audiences wanted a more forceful resolution to the story. Reviewers reported that male viewers openly cheered on Close's demise, leading director Lyne to suggest that the movie was "almost like a living thing that feeds off the public and takes on new shape." Yet critics also noted that many women appreciated the film's depiction of male irresponsibility.*

One of the most discussed movies of the 1980s, Fatal Attraction *reflected profound cultural ambivalence about the lifestyles of young urban professionals, the parameters of the sexual revolution, and the tensions associated with emancipated roles for women. As the AIDS epidemic heightened the dangers of sexual intimacy and the traditional family seemed under threat by mass media and popular culture, the movie appeared as a dark parable in an age of uncertain relationships.*

As birth rates slowly rose during the 1980s, cultural traditionalists re-asserted the importance of "family values" and moral authority. Insisting that social commitments were more important than individual rights, critics such as the scholar Allan Bloom attacked the dominance of secular values among professionals and academicians. Reagan's Secretary of Education, William J. Bennett, a Catholic intellectual, called for more emphasis on intellectual standards and ethical training. Defenders of family discipline also assailed the mass media for subjecting children to sex, violence, and antisocial messages. Concerned about the loss of parental control, Mary "Tipper" Gore, the wife of Tennessee Senator Al Gore, led a successful campaign in the late 1980s to convince popular music recording companies to place warning labels on products containing sexually explicit lyrics. Another parents' group, Mothers Against Drunk Driving (MADD), sponsored national advertising, pressed for tougher sentences for drinking offenders, and helped to pass legislation denying federal highway funds to states that did not raise the drinking age to twenty-one. Sensitivity to victims' rights led the Supreme Court to restrict repeated death penalty appeals in 1991 and to allow juries to consider testimony about murder victims from victims' families before sentencing.

Drug use stimulated another battle to sustain traditional values. As cocaine addiction spread to the middle class and victimized top entertainment and sports figures, some corporations began mandatory testing of job applicants and employees. After the Supreme Court upheld the right of public school officials to search students without warrants, the federal government ordered drug tests for many civilian employees. Under the Omnibus Drug Act of 1986, Congress authorized a "war on drugs" that included enforcement, education, and treatment. The United States even sent troops to Bolivia to wipe out cocaine-processing laboratories. Yet when Colombian drug cartels began to smuggle less-refined cocaine across U.S. borders, domestic dealers began producing "crack" and inner-city gang warfare intensified.

Family values advocates stepped up the campaign against abortion during the 1980s with massive demonstrations at clinics. In 1989 the Supreme Court concluded that unborn children had protectable rights and prohibited the use of tax-supported facilities for abortions not essential to save the mother's life. Two years later the tribunal upheld a congressional ban on federal funding for abortion counseling. In 1992 the Court permitted states to erect abortion restrictions that did not interfere with the privileges granted in *Roe v. Wade*. Social conservatives also protested that homosexuality was undeserving of government support. In *Bowers v. Hardwick* (1986), the Supreme Court upheld a Georgia law that made sodomy a criminal offense and thereby refused to extend constitutional rights of privacy to consensual relations between homosexuals. The issue of government endorsement of homosexuality surfaced the next year when the National Endowment for the Arts (NEA) funded a Cincinnati arts show featuring homoerotic photography by Robert Mapplethorp. Although Congress reauthorized NEA financing in 1990, it limited grants to work "sensitive to the general standard of decency."

Traditionalists also denounced sperm donation for artificial insemination and in vitro fertilization (in which an egg is fertilized before placement in the womb). When a New Jersey woman agreed to act as a paid "surrogate" mother but sued to keep the baby in 1987, a state court ruled that she had contractual obligations to surrender custody to the natural father and his infertile wife. The resulting furor inspired several state laws that prohibited compensation of surrogate mothers. Advances in artificial life support contributed to medical controversy. After the parents of a comatose patient, Karen Ann Quinlan, sued to disconnect an artificial respirator in 1975, eighteen states followed with laws declaring that legal death was defined by the cessation of brain activity, not of heartbeat. In 1990 the Supreme Court acknowledged an individual's right to refuse medical treatment but upheld legislation requiring "clear and convincing evidence" of a patient's wishes. The next year, Congress ordered health care groups to inform clients about the right to complete "living wills" to anticipate such requests. Calling for "right-to-die" protection for terminally ill people in pain, Michigan's Dr. Jack Kevorkian began a campaign to legalize physician-assisted suicide.

THE REAGAN LEGACY

In the wake of Vietnam and Watergate, Americans yearned for a resurgence of national pride. Media events such as the 1976 Bicentennial, the 1982 dedication of the Vietnam Memorial, the 1984 Olympics, and the gala 1986 Statue of Liberty celebration sought to unite a fragmented society around patriotic values. Yet wounds like those produced by the Vietnam War continued to fester. In Hollywood movies such as *Rambo* (1982), the Vietnam War veteran emerged as a symbol of the latent anger generated by the conflict. Frank portraits of the war also appeared in such films as *Platoon* (1986), *Full Metal Jacket* (1987), and *Hamburger Hill* (1987), as well as in popular novels by veteran Timothy O'Brien.

The space program offered another chance to forge national identity. After a series of manned spaceflights resulted in linkage with a Soviet satellite in 1975, NASA used its *Skylab* space station to launch vehicles to explore the solar system and photograph the distant Milky Way. The agency also inaugurated a series of manned space flights. In 1986, however, an explosion killed seven *Challenger* space shuttle astronauts, including the project's first civilian, a New England schoolteacher. Despite the tragedy, shuttles continued to perform space missions such as synthesizing chemicals in a vacuum. Meanwhile, space technology fascinated moviegoers and video-game players. Films such as *Star Wars* (1977) and its sequels, the *Star Trek* film series (of which the first was released in 1978), and *E.T., The Extra-Terrestrial* (1982) thrilled audiences with computer-generated morality tales involving exotic creatures, cyborgs, and rapid galactic travel.

Despite the renewal of national optimism, the Reagan administration never overcame bloated foreign trade and federal budget deficits. Because Treasury shortfalls prompted government borrowing on international exchanges, foreign consumers had fewer dollars with which to buy U.S. exports. Overseas manufacturing by U.S. multinationals also cost thousands of jobs at home. Congress sought to relieve domestic producers by curbing some imports in 1985, but Reagan vetoed the measure as protectionist. Yet as the trade deficit with Japan mounted in 1987 and Tokyo "dumped" below-cost computer chips on the U.S. market, the president overcame free-market sentiments to approve tariffs on Japanese electronic exports. He also signed a measure permitting retaliation against unfair trade practices and providing aid to industries and workers facing overseas competition. When Congress passed another bill requiring manufacturers to provide sixty days' notice of plant closings and major layoffs, Reagan let it become law without his signature.

The administration's reluctance to raise taxes combined with increased military and domestic spending thwarted efforts to control federal budget deficits. Facing a large budget shortfall in 1985, Congress passed the Gramm-Rudman-Hollings Act. The legislation established deficit-reduction targets and required the president to make across-the-board cuts if the targets were not met. Yet the House failed to agree on spending limits, and in 1986 the Supreme Court ruled the automatic cuts unconstitutional. Concerned with containing the deficit, Congress eliminated many business deductions and raised capital gains taxes, adding some $120 billion in revenues over the next five years. Nevertheless, the federal budget deficit multiplied 2.6 times between 1985 and 1987. With the national debt soaring into the trillions by the end of Reagan's term, the United States became the world's largest borrower.

Ronald Reagan insisted that a U.S. military buildup and lower taxes would counteract the foreign policy reverses and economic stagnation of the Carter

EXHIBIT **7-15**   **U.S. FEDERAL SPENDING AND BUDGET DEFICITS, 1980–1988**
(IN ROUNDED BILLIONS OF DOLLARS)

Year	Outlays	Deficit
1980	590.9	73.8
1982	745.7	127.9
1984	851.8	185.3
1986	990.3	221.2
1988	1,064.1	155.2

Source: *Statistical Abstract of the United States* (1996).

years. Yet Reagan's policies resulted in bloated trade and budget deficits as well as mixed results overseas. Seeking to extend their party's White House reign, Republican strategists searched for ways to sustain electoral goodwill amid an unevenly distributed and tenuous economic boom, continuing cultural conflicts at home, and a persistently unstable world environment.

INFOTRAC COLLEGE EDITION

Using Keywords, enter the following search terms:

Jimmy Carter
Three Mile Island
Jerry Falwell
Ronald Reagan
Jesse Jackson
Iran-Contra

RECOMMENDED READING

David Skidmore, *Reversing Course: Carter's Foreign Policy, Domestic Politics, and the Failure of Reform* (1996). This thoughtful work explains the tragic consequences of Jimmy Carter's high-minded approaches to domestic reform and international relations.

John W. Sloan, *The Reagan Effect: Economics and Presidential Leadership* (1999). A primer in Reaganomics that explores the impact of tax cuts and reduced government.

Beth A. Fischer, *The Reagan Reversal: Foreign Policy and the End of the Cold War* (1997). The author evaluates the extent to which Reagan's military buildup led to victory in the global struggle against communism.

David M. Reimers, *Unwelcome Strangers: American Identity and the Turn Against Immigration* (1998). A valuable source for tracing anti-immigrant sentiment in the late twentieth century.

Additional Reading

Carter's rise to the Oval Office is portrayed in Patrick Anderson, *Electing Jimmy Carter: The Campaign of 1976* (1994). The Carter White House is the focus of Erwin C. Hargrove's *Jimmy Carter as President: Leadership and the Politics of the Public Good* (1988), and of Charles O. Jones's *The Trusteeship Presidency: Jimmy Carter and the United States Congress* (1988). See also Kenneth Earl Morris, *Jimmy Carter, American Moralist* (1996). Assessments of Carter's presidency appear in Burton I. Kaufman, *The Presidency of James Earl Carter* (1993), and in John Dumbrell, *The Carter Presidency: A Re-Evaluation* (1993).

For Carter's domestic policy, see Anthony S. Campagna, *Economic Policy in the Carter Administration* (1995); Laurence E. Lynn, *The Presidency as Policymaker: Jimmy Carter and Welfare Reform* (1981); and Laurence H. Shoup, *The Carter Presidency and Beyond: Power and Politics in the 1980s* (1980). A useful collection can be found in Gary M. Fink and Hugh Davis Graham, eds., *The Carter Presidency: Policy Choices in the Post–New Deal Era* (1998). Pressure group politics are discussed in William F. Grover, *The President as Prisoner: A Structural Critique of the Carter and Reagan Years* (1989).

For foreign policy, see Robert A. Strong, *Working in the World: Jimmy Carter and the Making of American Foreign Policy* (2000); Gaddis Smith, *Morality, Reason, and Power: American Diplomacy in the Carter Years* (1986); and Timothy P. Maga, *The World of Jimmy Carter: U.S. Foreign Policy, 1977–1981* (1994). Oil diplomacy figures in portions of Daniel Yergin, *The Prize: The Epic Quest for Oil, Money, and Power* (1992), and in Michael A. Palmer, *Guardians of the Gulf: A History of America's Expanding Role in the Persian Gulf, 1933–1992* (1992).

The revitalization of evangelical Christianity is placed in historical context in George M. Marsden, *Religion and American Culture* (1990), and in Robert Wuthnow, *The Restructuring of American Religion: Society and Faith Since World War II* (1988). The social and cultural influence of religious conservatives is addressed in Steve Bruce, *The Rise and Fall of the Christian Right: Conservative Protestant Politics in America, 1978–1988* (1988); in Michael Lienesch, *Redeeming America: Piety and Politics in the New Christian Right* (1993); and in Sara Diamond, *Spiritual Warfare: The Politics of the Christian Right* (1989). For Jerry Falwell, see Dinesh D'Souza, *Falwell Before the Millennium: A Critical Biography* (1986). See also Duane M. Oldfield, *The Right and the Righteous: The Christian Right Confronts the Republican Party* (1996). Catholic conservatives are the focus of Patrick Allitt, *Catholic Intellectuals and Conservative Politics in America: 1950–1985* (1993). The abortion rights controversy is discussed in David Garrow, *Liberty and Sexuality: The Right to Privacy and the Making of* Roe v. Wade (1994), and Kristin Luker, *Abortion and the Politics of Womanhood* (1984).

The evolution of post-1945 conservative political and social thought is summarized in Mark Gerson, *The Neoconservative Vision: From the Cold War to the Culture Wars* (1995); in Melvin J. Thorne, *American Conservative Thought Since World War II: The Core Ideas* (1990); and in Jerome L. Himmelstein, *To the Right: The Transformation of American Conservatism* (1990). For the influence of secular conservatives, see J. David Hoeveler Jr., *Watch on the Right: Conservative Intellectuals in the Reagan Era* (1991); James Allen Smith, *The Idea Brokers: Think Tanks and the Rise of the New Policy Elite* (1991); and Sidney Blumenthal, *The Rise of the Counter-Establishment: From Conservative Ideology to Political Power* (1986).

The definitive introduction to the Reagan administration is William E. Pemberton, *Exit with Honor: The Life and Presidency of Ronald Reagan* (1997). See also Michael Shaller, *Reckoning with Reagan: America and Its President in the 1980s* (1992). For a controversial biography that uses a fictional narrator, see Edmund Morris, *Dutch: A Memoir of Ronald Reagan* (1999). Critical assessments of the president include Robert Dallek, *Ronald Reagan: The Politics of Symbolism* (1984), and Paul D. Erickson, *Reagan Speaks: The Making of an American Myth* (1985). For a psychological analysis, see Garry Wills, *Reagan's America: Innocents at Home* (1987).

Reagan's mastery of political discourse is explored in William K. Muir, *The Bully Pulpit: The Presidential Leadership of Ronald Reagan* (1992), and in the final chapter of David Green, *Shaping Political Consciousness: The Language of Politics in America from McKinley to Reagan* (1987). See also Jeffrey Bell, *Populism and Elitism: Politics in the Age of Equality* (1992), and portions of William C. Berman, *America's Right Turn: From Nixon to Bush* (1994). Reagan's administrative style and conservative approach to economic growth is the subject of John W. Sloan's *The Reagan Effect: Economics and Presidential Leadership* (1999). See also Amos Kiewe and David W. Houck, *A Shining City on a Hill: Ronald Reagan's Economic Rhetoric, 1951–1989* (1991). A portrait of the president's most innovative appointment appears in Nancy Maveety, *Justice Sandra Day O'Connor: Strategist on the Supreme Court* (1996).

Reagan's cuts in domestic spending are analyzed in the final segments of Michael B. Katz, *The Undeserving Poor: From the War on Poverty to the War on Welfare* (1989). See also George Lipsitz, *The Possessive Investment in Whiteness: How White People Profit from Identity Politics* (1998). The administration's approach to race is surveyed in Robert Detlefsen, *Civil Rights Under Reagan* (1990). See also the relevant portions of Dan T. Carter, *From George Wallace to Newt Gingrich: Race in the Conservative Counterrevolution, 1963–1994* (1996).

Relationships between politics, economics, and the plight of working families are explored in Thomas Byrne Edsall, *The New Politics of Equality: How Political Power Shapes Economic Policy* (1984), and Greg J. Duncan, *Years of Poverty, Years of Plenty: The Changing Economic Fortunes of American Workers and Families* (1984). For Reagan's labor policy, see the relevant segments of James A. Gross, *Broken Promise: The Subversion of U.S. Labor Relations Policy, 1947–1994* (1995).

Environmental policy under Reagan is assessed in the last portions of Richard H. K. Vietor, *Energy Policy in America Since 1945: A Study in Business–Government Relations* (1984). For balanced evaluations of the domestic impact of the Reagan presidency, see Sidney Blumenthal and Thomas Byrne Edsall, eds., *The Reagan Legacy* (1988).

For Reagan's involvement in foreign policy, see the relevant portions of John Prados, *Keeper of the Keys: A History of the National Security Council from Truman to Bush* (1991), and of Francis P. Wormuth and Edwin P. Firmage, *To Chain the Dog of War: The Powers of Congress in History and Law* (1986). A useful analysis appears in Coral Bell, *The Reagan Paradox: American Foreign Policy in the 1980s* (1989).

Reagan's Persian Gulf policies are discussed in sections of Michael A. Palmer, *Guardians of the Gulf: A History of America's Expanding Role in the Persian Gulf, 1933–1992* (1992). For Iran-Contra, see Robert Busby, *Reagan and the Iran-Contra Affair: The Politics of Presidential Recovery* (1999), and Roxanne Y. Sutherland, *Defusing a Rhetorical Situation Through Apologia: Ronald Reagan and the Iran-Contra Affair* (1992). Central American policy is assessed in the appropriate portions of Robert Kagan, *A Twilight Struggle: American Power and Nicaragua, 1977–1990* (1995); of Raymond Bonner, *Weakness and Deceit: United States Policy and El Salvador* (1984); and of William M. LeoGrande, *Our Own Backyard: The United States in Central America, 1977–1992* (1998). See also Mark P. Lagon, *The Reagan Doctrine: Sources of American Conduct in the Cold War's Last Chapter* (1994).

Cold War policy in the Reagan years is explored in Beth A. Fischer, *The Reagan Reversal: Foreign Policy and the End of the Cold War* (1997), and in Strobe Talbott, *Deadly Gambits: The Reagan Administration and the Stalemate in Nuclear Arms Control* (1984). See also Keith L. Shimko, *Images and Arms Control: Perceptions of the Soviet Union in the Reagan Administration* (1991). Star Wars is the focus of Rebecca S. Bjork, *The Strategic Defense Initiative: Symbolic Containment of the Nuclear Threat* (1992). For Cold War overviews, see the later sections of John Lewis Gaddis, *The Long Peace: Inquiries into the History of the Cold War* (1987), and of Thomas J. McCormick, *America's Half-Century: United States Foreign Policy in the Cold War* (1989).

A brief introduction to the world market can be found in Henry C. Dethloff, *The United States and the Global Economy Since 1945* (1997). See also Robert Schaeffer, *Understanding Globalization: The Social Consequences of Political and Economic Change* (1997). For the computer revolution, see Katie Hafner and Matthew Lyon, *Where Wizards Stay Up Late: The Origins of the Internet* (1996), and portions of George Basalla, *The Evolution of Technology* (1988).

The rise of upwardly mobile professionals is treated in Michael X. Carpini, *Stability and Change in American Politics: The Coming of Age of the Generation of the 1960s* (1986). See also Landon Y. Jones, *Great Expectations: America and the Baby Boom Generation* (1980). Ties between yuppie lifestyles and the earlier protest culture are addressed in Lauren Kessler, *After All These Years: Sixties Ideals in a Different World* (1991), and in Annie Gottlieb, *Do You Believe in Magic? The Second Coming of the Sixties Generation* (1987). See also Jack Whalen and Richard Flacks, *Beyond the Barricades: The Sixties Gen-*

eration Grows Up (1989). For perspectives on 1980s consumerism, see Debora Silverman, *Selling Culture: Bloomingdale's Diana Vreeland and the New Aristocracy of Taste in Reagan's America* (1986), and Warren J. Belasco, *Appetite for Change: How the Counterculture Took on the Food Industry, 1966–1988* (1990). The social ethics of professionals are the subject of Robert N. Bellah et al., *Habits of the Heart: Individualism and Commitment in American Life* (1985). A more critical account can be found in portions of Christopher Lasch's *The True and Only Heaven: Progress and Its Critics* (1991). For the New Age, see John P. Briggs and F. David Peat, *Looking Glass Universe: The Emerging Science of Wholeness* (1984), and Wade Clark Roof, *A Generation of Seekers* (1993).

The roots of 1970s feminism are vividly portrayed in Alice Echols, *Daring to Be Bad: Radical Feminism in America, 1967–1975* (1989). See also Rochelle Gatlin, *American Women Since 1945* (1987). The ERA is the focus of Donald G. Mathews and Jane Sherron De Hart, *Sex, Gender, and the Politics of ERA* (1990), and of the provocative Mary Frances Berry, *Why ERA Failed: Politics, Women's Rights and the Amending Process of the Constitution* (1986). Struggles for homosexual rights are described in Barry D. Adam, *The Rise of a Gay and Lesbian Movement* (1987).

The "postmodern" roots of multiculturalism can be traced in Andreas Huyssen, *After the Great Divide: Modernism, Mass Culture, Postmodernism* (1986). For the politicization of cultural studies see Benjamin Barber, *An Aristocracy of Everyone: The Politics of Education and the Future of America* (1992). Harsh critiques of multiculturalism and "political correctness" include Allan Bloom's *The Closing of the American Mind* (1987), and Roger Kimball's *Tenured Radicals: How Politics Has Corrupted Our Higher Education* (1990). For a reassertion of ideas about pluralist democracy, see Arthur M. Schlesinger Jr., *The Disuniting of America: Reflections on a Multicultural Society* (1993). Identity politics is criticized by radical activist Todd Gitlin in *The Twilight of Common Dreams: Why America Is Wracked by Culture Wars* (1995). Historian David A. Hollinger seeks to resolve the conflict in *Postethnic America: Beyond Multiculturalism* (1995).

Treatments of the new wave of immigration include Gil Loescher and John A. Scanlan, *Calculated Kindness: Refugees and America's Half Open Door, 1945 to the Present* (1986), and David Reimers, *Still the Golden Door: The Third World Comes to America* (1985). See also the later segments of John Bodnar, *The Transplanted: A History of Immigrants in Urban America* (1985), and of Roger Daniels, *Coming to America: A History of Immigration and Ethnicity in American Life* (1991).

Asian ethnicity is the focus of Roger Daniels, *Asian America: Chinese and Japanese in the United States Since 1850* (1988); Ronald Takaki, *Strangers from a Different Shore: A History of Asian Americans* (1989); and Stephen S. Fugita and David J. O'Brien, *Japanese American Ethnicity: The Persistence of*

Community (1991). For Hispanics, see Alejandro Portes and Robert L. Bach, *Latin Journey: Cuban and Mexican Immigrants in the United States* (1985). Mexican Americans are the subject of Rodolfo Acuna, *Occupied America: A History of Chicanos* (1988), and of Juan Gomez Quinones, *Chicano Politics: Reality and Promise, 1940–1990* (1990).

For native peoples, see the later segments of Francis Paul Prucha, *The Great Father: The United States Government and the American Indians, Vol. II* (1984). An overview of recent African American history is presented in Manning Marable, *Black American Politics: From the Washington Marches to Jesse Jackson* (1988). See also the useful Katherine Tate, *From Protest to Politics: The New Black Voters in American Elections* (1993). One of the most important African American leaders is portrayed in Adolph L. Reed Jr., *The Jesse Jackson Phenomenon* (1986), and in the relevant segments of Allen D. Hertzke, *Echoes of Discontent: Jesse Jackson, Pat Robertson, and the Resurgence of Populism* (1993).

A growing literature on the postindustrial workplace includes Jon C. Teaford, *Cities of the Heartland: The Rise and Fall of the Industrial Midwest* (1993), and Kathryn Marie Dudley, *The End of the Line: Lost Jobs, New Lives in Post-Industrial America* (1994). See also Eileen Boris, *Home to Work: Motherhood and the Politics of Industrial Homework* (1994). For nonelite social perspectives, see David Halle, *America's Working Man: Work, Home, and Politics Among Blue-Collar Property Owners* (1984); Craig Reeinarman, *American States of Mind: Political Beliefs and Behavior Among Private and Public Workers* (1987); and Clarence Y. H. Lo, *Small Property Versus Big Government: Social Origins of the Property Tax Revolt* (1990).

The cultural confrontations of the post-Vietnam era are the focus of James Davison Hunter, *Culture Wars: The Struggle to Define America* (1991); of John Kenneth White, *The New Politics of Old Values* (1988); and of Ira Shor, *Culture Wars: School and Society in the Conservative Restoration, 1969–1984* (1986). See also Jeffrey Goldfarb, *The Cynical Society: The Culture of Politics and the Politics of Culture in American Life* (1991). Racial conflict is analyzed in Lawrence H. Fuchs, *The American Kaleidoscope: Race, Ethnicity, and the Civic Culture* (1990), and in Edward G. Carmines and James A. Stimson, *Issue Evolution: Race and the Transformation of American Politics* (1989).

Critical approaches to Reagan-era conservatism include Thomas Ferguson and Joel Rogers, *Right Turn: The Decline of the Democrats and the Future of American Politics* (1986); Herbert I. Schiller, *Culture, Inc.: The Corporate Takeover of Public Expression* (1989); and Michael Parenti, *Democracy for the Few* (1995). See also Donald L. Bartlett and James B. Steele, *America: What Went Wrong?* (1992).

THE TURN TO CENTRISM: BUSH AND CLINTON, 1988–2000

Ronald Reagan won the highest public opinion rating any previous chief executive had received upon leaving office. Shortly thereafter, the bipolar Cold War ended with the dissolution of the Soviet Union. Despite the apparent victory, Reagan's successors faced a complex and dangerous global environment—a "new world order" in which nationalist and religious extremists continued to resort to destabilizing violence and terror. At home, Presidents George Bush and Bill Clinton sought to sustain prosperity and social cohesion in a period of reduced ideological fervor but declining trust in government. Although Clinton favored a more "hands-on" personal and political style than Bush, both leaders emphasized enactment of moderate programs embracing environmental protection, volunteer services, welfare reform, and budget reduction. While the global market and information revolution contributed to a booming U.S. economy by century's end, the two major parties sharpened their partisan attacks while simultaneously appealing to the centrist sentiments of the huge middle class.

GEORGE BUSH AND THE END OF THE COLD WAR

Democrats prepared for the 1988 presidential election by exploiting the weaknesses of Reaganomics. During the 1980s workers and middle-class citizens had experienced no notable increase in income. In contrast, Reagan's tax cuts helped to boost the earnings of the richest 1 percent of families by 87 percent—the greatest upward redistribution of income in U.S. history. Tax breaks and reduced federal regulation had encouraged financial speculation and corporate mergers and led cost-conscious companies to downsize and phase out skilled manufacturing positions. Democrat Jesse Jackson responded to these trends by refashioning a second presidential campaign around populist issues. Appealing to white workers and farmers as well as racial minorities, Jackson campaigned

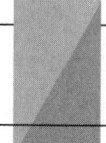

Jesse L. Jackson (1941–   )

"God hasn't finished with me yet," Baptist minister Jesse L. Jackson told the 1984 Democratic National Convention after finishing third in the party's presidential sweepstakes. Four years later, Jackson swept across the country in a fiery presidential campaign that brought him nearly a third of all Democratic primary votes. By the

1990s, Jackson's biracial reform agenda had earned him a reputation as the conscience of the Democratic Party and as a spokesperson for the nation's people of color.

Jackson was the illegitimate son of a teen-age domestic from the cotton mill town of Greenville, South Carolina. He won an ath-letic scholarship to the University of Illinois but transferred to predominately black North Carolina Agricultural and Technical College in Greensboro after Illinois placed him on academic probation. Arriving in Greensboro months after students initiated the 1960 lunch-counter sit-ins, he became the star quarterback, student body president, and leader of the demonstrations. Chosen for a Rockefeller Foundation grant, Jackson attended the Chicago Theological Seminary but left short of graduation to work with Martin Luther King Jr.

King made the young activist head of the Southern Christian Lead-ership Conference's Operation Breadbasket—a campaign that used boy-cotts and mass picketing to win jobs and contracts for black workers and businesses. Citing Jackson's lack of organizational loyalty and discipline, however, the SCLC suspended the young minister. Jackson seized the opportunity to create his own group, Operation PUSH (People United to Save Humanity).

With PUSH, Jackson sought to build a national campaign to restore African American pride. "I may be poor, but I am somebody," Jackson chanted with the black youngsters he addressed in the public schools, where he conducted self-help motivational programs that cautioned against drug abuse, teenage pregnancy, truancy, and high drop-out rates. Between 1971 and 1983, PUSH attracted $17 million in government grants and private donations, although critics pointed to the organization's chaotic financial administration and poor management. "I'm a tree-shaker, not a jelly-maker," Jackson later explained.

Jackson was an influential supporter of Jimmy Carter in 1976 and 1980 and organized voter registration drives in 1983. After the election of Chicago African American reform mayor Harold Washington, he announced his candidacy for the presidency, criticizing Democratic leaders for being "too silent" and "too passive" about Ronald Reagan's policies. Jackson promised to represent "the poor and dispossessed of this nation" and to forge a "rainbow coalition" for those who were "rejected and . . . despised." Yet his campaign faltered when a black reporter revealed that the candidate had privately referred to Jews as "hymies." Jackson apologized but never managed to repair the break with the Jewish community. Relations worsened when he was slow to disavow the support of Louis Farrakan, a Nation of Islam leader given to anti-Semitic pronouncements.

Addressing a broad constituency of peace activists, organized labor, environmentalists, farmers, and racial minorities, Jackson launched the National Rainbow Coalition and announced his second presidential candidacy in 1987. He condemned "economic violence" against those "locked out of the system." He proposed to tax corporate mergers, to enact protections against plant closings and farm foreclosures, and to invest public employee pension funds in social programs. "If I can win, you can win. We the people can win!" Jackson told voters in the 1988 Democratic presidential primaries. Astounding political professionals, the candidate finished a strong second.

Jackson continued to raise racial issues as a media commentator in the 1990s. He played a key role in popularizing the term "African American" and in convincing Congress to make Reverend King's birthday a national holiday. He campaigned against South African apartheid, supported a U.S. role in restoring democracy in Haiti, and pushed for statehood for the District of Columbia. Recognized as a prime authority on racial discrimination, he participated in negotiations to end bias in corporations, the media, and professional athletics. Ever the caretaker of souls, Jackson denounced drugs and gang violence with customary fervor. Yet he also spoke out against police brutality against people of color, "hate" crimes, and investor neglect of the inner city.

for higher taxes on corporations and the regulation of plant closings and relocations overseas.

Although Jackson received nearly a third of the Democratic primary vote,
Massachusetts Governor Michael Dukakis, a political centrist, emerged as
the party nominee when front-runner Gary Hart was forced out of the race
by accusations of marital infidelity. A Greek American with extensive public
administration experience, Dukakis heralded the use of tax incentives, an educated labor force, and a balanced budget in fashioning an economic "miracle" in his home state. Combining proposals for national health insurance and
investment in education with fiscal moderation, the governor chose Senator
Lloyd Bentsen, a Texas conservative with expertise in finance, as his vice presidential partner.

Aware of the uneven distribution of Reagan-era prosperity, Republican
campaign strategist Lee Atwater prepared the party for the 1988 election by
concentrating on social issues. Seeking a coalition of nonaffluent white southerners and middle-class voters in northern suburbs, Atwater positioned the
Republicans as supporters of family values, defenders of patriotism, and opponents of crime. After defeating Senate Minority Leader Robert ("Bob") Dole
in early primaries, Vice President George Bush won the party nomination. A
Yale graduate, a World War II pilot, and the son of a former Republican senator from Connecticut, Bush had a successful early career in the Texas oil business. After two terms in the House, he served the Nixon White House as U.N.
ambassador, chair of the Republican National Committee, and liaison to
China. Bush spent the final year of the Ford presidency as the director of the
Central Intelligence Agency (CIA). A social moderate and an internationalist,
he chose Dan Quayle, a conservative Indiana senator, as his running mate.

Bush attacked Dukakis as an "ice man," a Harvard elitist whose membership in the rights-oriented American Civil Liberties Union (ACLU) betrayed
liberal social values. Republicans focused on the Democratic governor's opposition to the death penalty and his vetoes of legislation requiring public school
students to recite the Pledge of Allegiance and of a bill banning prison fur-
loughs for first-degree murderers. Television ads dramatized the case of Willie
Horton, a black convict serving a life sentence for murder who had raped a
white woman while on furlough from a Massachusetts prison. The Republican
candidates also celebrated Reagan's restoration of national dignity and the tam-
ing of the Soviet Union. Promising to sustain Reagan's legacy of domestic prosperity and deregulation, Bush issued an emphatic promise: "Read my lips—no
new taxes!" To soften his image, the vice president spoke of a "kinder" and "gen-
tler" nation whose volunteer charities formed "a thousand points of light."

Failing to respond to the Republican assault on his moral integrity and
having no broad-based appeal, Dukakis suffered a humiliating defeat. In November the Bush-Quayle ticket captured 54 percent of the popular vote and
swept the Republican Party to its fifth victory in the last six presidential elec-

EXHIBIT **8-1**   **THE ELECTION OF 1988**

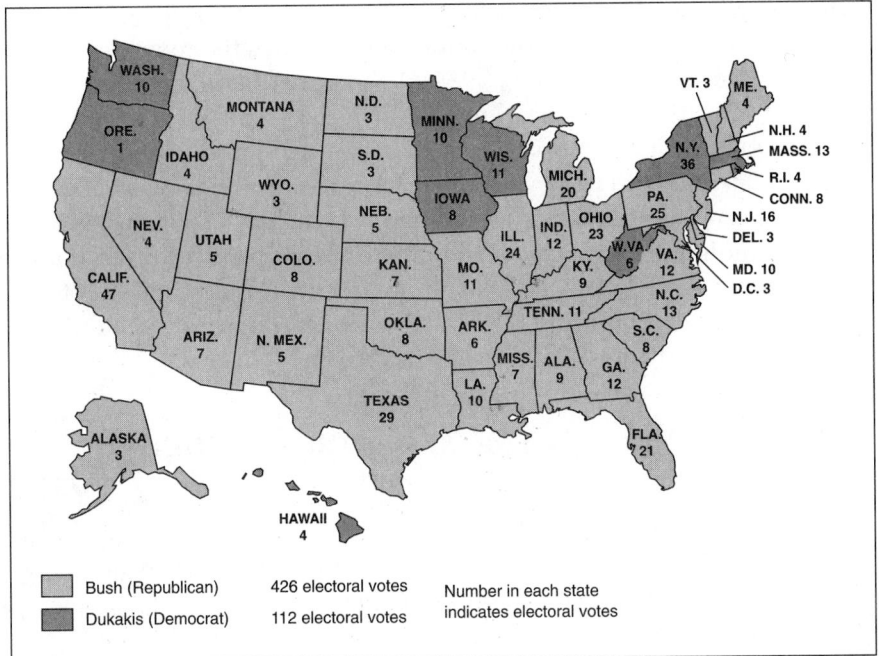

Bush (Republican)   426 electoral votes   Number in each state
Dukakis (Democrat)   112 electoral votes   indicates electoral votes

tions. By taking nearly two-thirds of the white male vote as well as most of that of southerners and suburbanites, Republicans tightened their grip on the key "Reagan Democrats." Once again, political apathy and cynicism lowered participation rates to barely more than half of eligible voters.

As Bush took office in 1989, East Germany dismantled the Berlin Wall, and democratic movements began to replace eastern Europe's communist governments. Once the Soviet Union withdrew its troops from Afghanistan and held its first free elections at home, the president met with Soviet leader Mikhail Gorbachev in 1990, and the two leaders accepted a framework for mutual nuclear disarmament and agreed to stop producing chemical weapons. The Cold War effectively ended in that year when the Conference on Security and Cooperation in Europe (comprising thirty European nations plus the United States and Canada) sponsored a treaty drastically limiting U.S. and Soviet military presence on the continent. After signing the Strategic Arms Reduction Treaty (START) in 1991, both nuclear superpowers eliminated most short-range nuclear weapons. When Gorbachev resigned as president the same year, the Soviet Union dissolved, breaking up into its constituent republics, the most powerful of which was Russia.

Although Bush waited for signs of reform before providing aid to the former Soviet republics, he welcomed Boris Yeltsin, the Russian president, as a negotiating partner. Meeting in Moscow in early 1993, the two leaders signed

START II, which reduced world tensions by providing for the gradual elimination of all land-based nuclear missiles. Yet instead of bringing peace, the
end of the Cold War destabilized world politics. When the communist federation in Yugoslavia dissolved in 1992, Croatian and Serbian military forces
mounted armed attacks on the Muslim-dominated breakaway state of Bosnia-
Herzegovina. Although the Croats soon recognized Bosnian independence,
the Serbian army and nationalist militias initiated a genocidal campaign of
"ethnic cleansing" to rid Bosnia of Muslims. Instead of taking unilateral action, the Bush administration joined European allies in imposing sanctions on
Serbia. When the Bosnian Serbs cut off supply lines to the capital city of Sarajevo, Congress authorized the U.S. military to participate in a multilateral
force charged with delivering food and medical supplies.

THE GULF WAR AND THE NEW WORLD ORDER

Although Bush hesitated to deploy military force in southeastern Europe, the
administration showed greater interest in the Persian Gulf, where oil reserves
provided resources for western Europe and Japan—Washington's partners in
the global economy. In the summer of 1990, Iraq's President Saddam Hussein
invaded his oil-rich neighbor Kuwait, annexed it, and placed troops on the Saudi
Arabian border. The U.N. Security Council unanimously condemned Iraq as an
aggressor and demanded unconditional withdrawal. The council then ordered
an economic embargo against Iraq and authorized U.N. members to use all
necessary means to liberate Kuwait. Taking the leadership in forging a military
coalition with the Russians and twenty-six other countries, including Saudi Arabia, Egypt, and Syria, Bush organized Operation Desert Storm. Under the leadership of General Colin Powell, whom the president had appointed as the first
African American Chair of the Joint Chiefs of Staff, and of General H. Norman
Schwarzkopf, 540,000 U.S. and 160,000 Allied troops participated in the largest
military mobilization since World War II.

After a heated debate and a close 52–47 vote in the Senate early in 1991,
Congress authorized the Bush administration to use force to back the U.N.
mandate. The Gulf War began with a massive six-week air and missile campaign. Once Iraq's air force, communications, and weapons facilities had been
destroyed, Bush set a deadline for Hussein's withdrawal from Kuwait. The
United States then orchestrated a broad attack on Iraqi ground forces. Hussein's troops quickly retreated or were left isolated while his infantry fled
Kuwait. Fearing the rise of nationalistic sentiment in Iraq, however, Bush
sought to avoid the extensive casualties and controversy of a prolonged war. Accordingly, the White House deferred to Arab allies by terminating the one-
sided rout within hours, thereby leaving Hussein in power. Nevertheless, Bush
declared that the "Vietnam Syndrome" no longer paralyzed U.S. foreign policy.

EXHIBIT **8-2**   THE PERSIAN GULF WAR

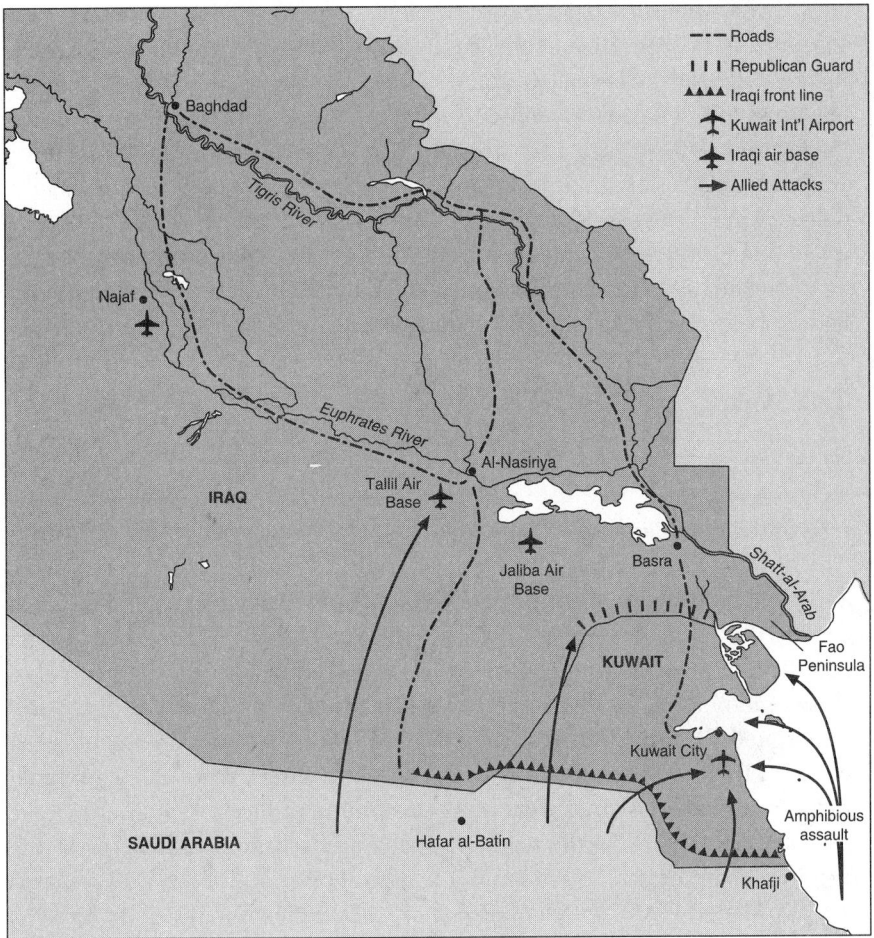

The most decisive U.S. military victory since World War II, the Gulf War was heralded as the fruit of a post–Cold War "new world order." Envisioning a historic opportunity to stabilize the volatile Middle East, Bush arranged peace talks among Israel, neighboring Arab states, and Palestinians. Under U.S. and Russian auspices, the Madrid Conference of 1991 broke new ground by focusing on a "comprehensive" settlement based on exchanging "territory for peace." The following year the administration signaled its commitment to international humanitarianism by sending troops to Somalia after famine and factional warfare prompted the U.N. Security Council to request military protection for food relief efforts.

In the absence of Cold War hostilities, Bush sought to promote democracy in Central America. Panamanian leader General Manuel Noriega Morena had been indicted by the Reagan administration for drug trafficking and money laundering. When Noriega halted free elections and incited violence against U.S. citizens in 1989, Bush mobilized 24,000 troops to invade Panama. After inflicting hundreds of casualties and detaining thousands, the army forced Noriega to surrender and took him to the United States to stand trial. Once U.S. military authorities installed the country's duly elected leader as president, the Bush administration granted Panama's new government nearly a half-billion dollars in aid. Congress awarded a smaller sum to Nicaragua, where a conservative defeated the leftist Sandinista government in internationally supervised elections in 1990. Tensions also eased in El Salvador when Washington brokered a peace treaty in 1992 that ended a twelve-year civil war.

THE STRUGGLING ECONOMY

At home, the Bush White House pursued an activist record on environmental reform to bolster its moderate credentials. The president agreed to the Montreal Protocol of 1989, by which eighty nations banned dangerous chemicals and pledged to halve the production of ozone-depleting substances. He approved the Clean Air Act of 1990, which called for the reduced emission of industrial pollutants that cause acid rain, placed new pollution controls on autos, and phased out the use of chemicals threatening the ozone layer. Bush also signed a treaty limiting carbon dioxide emissions, cited by scientists as a cause of the greenhouse effect and global warming. After an Exxon tanker ran aground in Alaskan waters in 1989, spilling millions of gallons of crude petroleum and causing the worst environmental disaster in U.S. history, the president supported the creation of a federal cleanup fund for oil pollution. He also signed the Energy Policy Act of 1992, which encouraged natural gas development and alternative fuel use.

Other Bush reforms included federal support for volunteer service programs, child care, and transportation projects. Yet the president faced increasing controversy over his domestic agenda. When an overextended real estate market decimated the savings and loan industry, the White House was forced to ask Congress for a massive infusion of funds to reimburse investors and rehabilitate delinquent banks. Subsequent anxiety over federal budget deficits led to the greatest controversy of George Bush's tenure. In return for reduced federal spending and a promise to cut the deficit within five years, House Democrats compelled the administration to accept a tax hike in 1990. Although the agreement stipulated that one-fourth of government savings were to come from entitlement cuts, the remainder was to be implemented through defense reductions and increased tax rates on top incomes. Complaining that federal taxation already amounted to nearly one-fifth of the gross

EXHIBIT **8-3**   **U.S. FEDERAL BUDGET DEFICITS, 1988–1992**
(IN ROUNDED BILLIONS OF DOLLARS)

1988	155
1990	221
1992	290

Source: *Statistical Abstract of the United States* (1996).

domestic product, Republicans condemned the president for betraying his campaign promise of "no new taxes."

Bush's problems deepened as an economic recession took hold in 1991. Concerned about maintaining his credibility with conservatives, the president recommitted his administration to Reaganite policies. The White House endorsed a constitutional amendment to protect the flag, although Congress merely passed a law prohibiting flag desecration that the Supreme Court overturned on First Amendment grounds. Bush encountered further controversy when he sought to replace retiring African American Justice Thurgood Marshall with federal appeals court judge Clarence Thomas. A black conservative, Thomas had administered cuts as Reagan's chair of the Equal Employment Opportunity Commission (EEOC). The nomination became more contentious when African American law professor Anita Hill, a former EEOC employee, charged Thomas with sexual harassment, a highly sensitive issue among professional women. Anxious to address concerns over the abuse of women in the workplace, the Senate held special televised hearings on Hill's allegations. Nevertheless, Thomas won confirmation in a close 52–48 vote.

As Bush prepared to face voters in 1992, unemployment hovered at 7.5 percent. Since the 1970s, automation, plant consolidations, bankruptcies, transfer of factories overseas, and reduced union membership had contributed to a loss of skilled manufacturing jobs, stagnating wage scales, and decimated pension protection. As a result, the least affluent two-fifths of families had experienced an absolute decline in earnings while income for the rich soared. Critics pointed to the fact that chief executive officers at large corporations made nearly 150 times the pay of the average factory employee. As the recession deepened, Bush's disinterest in domestic affairs and his opposition to government activism

EXHIBIT **8-4**   **PERCENTAGE DISTRIBUTION OF U.S. HOUSEHOLD AGGREGATE INCOME, 1993**

Top 1 percent of household income receivers	20.3
Top 5 percent of household income receivers	47.0

Source: *Statistical Abstract of the United States* (1996).

EXHIBIT **8-5**   **U.S. FEDERAL SOCIAL WELFARE SPENDING, 1980–1990**
(IN ROUNDED BILLIONS AND AS A
PERCENTAGE OF GROSS NATIONAL PRODUCT)

Year	Amount	Percentage
1980	303	11.4
1985	451	11.3
1990	617	11.1

Source: *Statistical Abstract of the United States* (1996).

reinforced accusations that he was a disengaged leader out of touch with pressing needs. Enacting a ninety-day moratorium on all new government regulations in 1992, the president opposed legislation for gun control, voter registration at state motor vehicle bureaus, and additional aid to the cities. Bush also vetoed bills to permit workers to leave jobs for family emergencies, to expand civil rights protections in the workplace, and to cap campaign spending in congressional races.

BILL CLINTON AND THE 1992 ELECTION

During the height of the Gulf War, Bush's approval ratings had surpassed 90 percent. Yet the president's success in defeating Saddam Hussein removed foreign policy as a leading source of consideration and opened the door for Democratic criticism of the White House's economic policy. As the 1992 presidential campaign approached, an assortment of Democrats called for tax reform, targeted spending cuts, balanced budgets, and attention to education and the environment. The nominee turned out to be the virtually unknown governor of Arkansas—William ("Bill") Jefferson Clinton.

Raised by a widowed mother, Clinton had aspired to political life since boyhood. During the height of the Vietnam controversy in the mid-1960s, he attended Georgetown University and worked for antiwar Senator J. William Fulbright of Arkansas. Clinton was also opposed to the U.S. presence in Vietnam and accepted a prestigious Rhodes scholarship to attend Oxford University and managed to avoid the draft. A graduate of Yale Law School, he won election as the nation's youngest governor in 1978. After cofounding the centrist Democratic Leadership Council, Clinton pushed the party to adopt moderate positions on the budget and on social issues such as abortion, crime, and welfare. With Tennessee Senator Albert ("Al") Gore Jr. as his running mate, the nominee opposed "tax and spend" liberalism and promised to "reinvent government" and to reform welfare. However, the "New Democrat" also criticized the "trickle-down economics" of the Republicans. Rallying to the cry, "it's the econ-

EXHIBIT **8-6**   THE ELECTION OF 1992

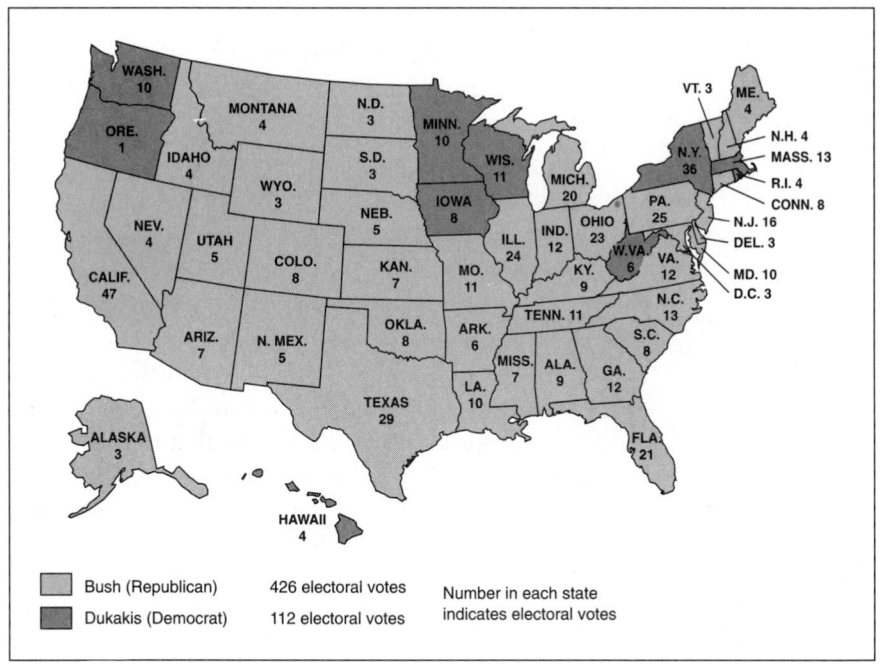

| | Bush (Republican) | 426 electoral votes | Number in each state |
| | Dukakis (Democrat) | 112 electoral votes | indicates electoral votes |

omy, stupid," Clinton aides promoted their candidate as an agent of change who would rescue the middle class by "Putting People First."

Bush survived a spirited primary challenge from former Nixon speech-writer Patrick ("Pat") Buchanan, who fused conservative social values and economic nationalism. Yet Buchanan's strident references to "culture wars" alienated party moderates and independents, particularly the half of the electorate now living in suburbs. Bush was also hurt by the third-party candidacy of H. Ross Perot, a self-made billionaire who promised to break the Washington gridlock by taking government away from the "politicians." Launching his campaign on a cable TV talk show, Perot called for federal spending cuts and a balanced budget, tighter trade regulations, and a national industrial policy.

Although Perot performed well in three televised debates, Clinton outdid his rivals as a master of modern media. Through televised "town meetings"

EXHIBIT **8-7**   U.S. VOTER PARTICIPATION, 1988–1992
(AS A PERCENTAGE OF ELIGIBLE VOTERS)

1988	50.3
1992	55.1

Source: *Statistical Abstract of the United States* (1996).

Patrick ("Pat") Buchanan (1938–   )

"I'm entitled to be a heretic," Pat Buchanan once declared. Combining radical conservatism and populist social values, the scrappy media commentator and Republican campaigner embodied some of the most jarring contradictions of 1990s political life.

The third of nine children, Buchanan grew up in the suburbs of Washington, D.C. A product of Catholic schooling from the primary grades to Georgetown University, Buchanan absorbed the Cold War notion that communism was the ideological enemy of Christianity.

After graduating from the Columbia University School of Journalism on a scholarship, the ambitious writer found work as a reporter and editorialist for the conservative Republican *St. Louis Globe-Democrat*. An avid reader of William F. Buckley's *National Review*, Buchanan supported Barry Goldwater in 1964. Viewing Richard Nixon as the conservative hope for the next presidential race, he joined the former vice president's staff, brought Maryland Governor Spiro Agnew to his boss's attention, and served as press secretary and speech writer in the 1968 campaign.

Once Nixon won, Buchanan became a special assistant who briefed the president on media coverage. The first in the administration to grasp the significance of George Wallace's populism, Buchanan drew up press releases that contrasted the traditional values of Nixon's "new majority" of "middle Americans" with the "liberal elitism" of the media and intelligentsia. After returning to journalism to produce a widely syndicated newspaper column, Buchanan cofounded *Crossfire*, a television commentary series on the Cable News Network (CNN). During Ronald Reagan's second term, he resurfaced in public life as director of communications and supplied the media with White House rhetoric on the Nicaragua "freedom fighters."

(including an effective pitch for the youth vote on MTV), the Arkansas governor established personal rapport with voters. By positioning himself as a centrist, Clinton overcame questions concerning his personal life and captured a plurality

Dissenting from Bush's globalism, Buchanan campaigned furiously against U.S. involvement in the Gulf War. "There are only two groups that are beating the drums for war in the Middle East," he declared on television, "the Israeli Defense Ministry and its amen corner in the United States." If the United States went to war, he warned, fighting would be done by "kids with names like McAllister, Murphy, Gonzales, and Leroy Brown." Buchanan expanded upon such populism when he challenged Bush for the Republican presidential nomination in 1992. Portraying the incumbent as rich, indifferent, and out of touch, Buchanan tapped voter frustration about economic stagnation by taking 40 percent of the New Hampshire primary vote. At the Republican Convention, he expanded his perspective to warn of an emerging "cultural war . . . for the soul of America."

Mobilizing against Republican front-runner Bob Dole in 1996, Buchanan forged a coalition of Reagan Democrats, protectionists, social conservatives, and supporters of the far right. A bitter opponent of the North American Free Trade Agreement (NAFTA), he agreed with labor leaders and progressive activists such as Ralph Nader in condemning corporate plant closings and overseas relocations. Buchanan shocked Republican officials by denouncing "blood-sucking multinational banks" and "the money lenders of the Fortune 500." Yet he also blamed unemployment on illegal immigration, a problem he sought to rectify with a security fence across the entire border with Mexico.

After a narrow victory over Dole in New Hampshire, Buchanan sought to rally the Christian right by stressing opposition to abortion, but consensus-oriented politicians minimized the candidate's exposure at the 1996 convention. A dissident among Republican supporters of the global economy, Pat Buchanan had become a politician with no institutional base. Four years later, he won the presidential nomination of a badly split Reform Party but managed to win less than 0.5 percent of the popular vote.

of independent votes, equaling Bush's total among whites and making strong inroads among Republican suburbanites. Taking seven of the ten largest states and several southern states, Clinton scored 43 percent in contrast to 37 percent for Bush and to 19 percent for Perot—certainly not a mandate. In winning only their second presidential contest since 1964, however, the Democrats benefited from a voter turnout of 55 percent of eligible voters, the highest rate in twenty years.

CLINTON'S POST–COLD WAR DIPLOMACY

Clinton's inaugural address focused on economic revitalization and citizen assumption of personal responsibility. However, amid the instabilities of the post–Cold War period, global politics assumed a more important role than the leader of the world's sole superpower anticipated. The president responded to this challenge by engaging in personal diplomacy and leading the United States into multilateral commitments overseas. Yet without the focus of the anticommunist crusade, U.S. foreign policy appeared to lack cohesion and direction.

Weeks after taking office, Clinton met with Russian President Yeltsin. As the two nations extended a mutual moratorium on nuclear testing, the White House promised emergency aid to the struggling Russians. When Yelstin sent the army to the province of Chechnya in 1994 to subdue a separatist revolt, poorly equipped troops suffered major losses and inflicted huge civilian casualties. Yet after continued support from Clinton, the Russian leader prevailed in his country's first democratic elections and temporarily withdrew the military from Chechnya.

Anxious to preserve stability in the Middle East, the Clinton administration continued Bush's enforcement of economic sanctions against Iraq until international inspectors certified the dismantling of Baghdad's chemical, biological, and nuclear weapons. After receiving information that Hussein had sponsored a plan to assassinate former President Bush, Clinton unleashed cruise missile attacks on Baghdad intelligence headquarters in 1993. The White House orchestrated a second series of strikes after Hussein attacked Kurdish enclaves in northern Iraq. When Baghdad mobilized a large military force at Kuwait's border in 1994, the president redeployed troops to the region before the Iraqis withdrew. Hardened by these provocations, the United States insisted on enforcing sanctions despite their huge toll on Iraq's civilians and children. By 1996, Iraq agreed to permit the United Nations to administer its foreign oil sales and to channel oil revenues to food and medical relief, although reports of suffering persisted. Meanwhile, U.S. aircraft and missile power enforced the "no fly" zone with periodic raids on Iraqi installations.

The complexities of post–Cold War policy emerged in Somalia, where the U.S. military turned the food relief effort begun by Bush over to the United Nations in 1993. Finding themselves in the middle of factional strife, commanders initiated a campaign to capture General Mohammed Farah

Aidid, a powerful warlord who refused to engage in peace talks. When fighting erupted, Aidid's followers killed eighteen U.S. soldiers and paraded their bodies before jubilant crowds. Under intense congressional pressure, Clinton ordered more troops to Somalia, but only to assure an orderly withdrawal. Condemned for allowing the Somalia operation to drift from humanitarian aid to involvement in a civil war under multilateral auspices, the White House promised to seek purely political solutions to the conflict.

Although peacemaking failed in Somalia, the Clinton administration continued to seek an important role as an international power broker. After a military coup overthrew Haiti's freely elected Jean-Bertrand Aristide in 1991, President Bush had supported a U.N. oil and arms embargo against the regime but returned thousands of refugees who had entered the United States after fleeing the Caribbean island. Clinton upheld the refugee policy but supervised an agreement to restore democracy. When Haitian ships blocked a U.S. attempt to implement the accord, the president backed reimposition of the U.N. embargo and threatened an invasion. In a final attempt to win a peaceful transition of leadership, Clinton sent personal emissaries to negotiate a settlement. Once the Haitian military accepted Washington's offers of relocation and financial assistance in 1994, the president dispatched troops to the island to maintain order while Aristide completed his term of office. Although opposed by many in Congress, the deployment restored democracy.

Anxious to please the large population of Cuban Americans in southern Florida, Clinton mixed conciliatory and hard-line stances toward the communist government of Cuba's Fidel Castro. Once Cuba's subsidies from the Soviet Union disappeared, the Bush administration had sought to expedite the overthrow of Cuban communism by tightening trade sanctions. Clinton followed a different course by relaxing travel restrictions and by permitting humanitarian relief and cultural exchanges with the island. Yet in 1996 the president signed the Helms-Burton bill, permitting citizens to sue some foreign companies that did business with the Cuban government, although Clinton postponed enactment of the controversial law.

Although the Cold War was over, communist North Korea aroused U.S. anxiety when it appeared to be assembling materials to develop nuclear weapons. Clinton dispatched Jimmy Carter to forge an agreement by which Japan and South Korea financed construction of atomic reactors incapable of producing weapons-grade materials. In another effort at alleviating tensions with a communist power, the administration prevailed on Vietnam to assist efforts to locate the remains of more than 2,000 U.S. servicemen missing in action from the Vietnam War. While extending formal diplomatic recognition to the former adversary in 1995, Clinton celebrated "the opportunity to bind up our wounds." In yet another effort at personal diplomacy, the White House appointed former Senator George Mitchell to coordinate peace talks on British-held Northern Ireland. After the nationalist Irish Republican Army (IRA) agreed to a cease-fire and supervision of its arsenal in 2000, Britain turned power over to a self-ruling assembly of all factions.

The struggle to realize a peaceful and stable "new world order" received its greatest challenge in Bosnia. As Serbian militias continued "ethnic cleansing" and shelled the capital city of Sarajevo, Clinton called for North Atlantic Treaty Organization (NATO) air strikes against Serbian positions. In 1995 the president convened a peace conference near Dayton, Ohio, which established a cease-fire between the warring parties and organized internationally supervised elections. The agreement also called for the deployment of U.S. troops to the region as part of a NATO peacekeeping force, a multilateral provision that Congress acceded to but did not endorse.

Clinton exerted his strongest efforts at personal diplomacy in the Middle East. After the Israelis conducted secret talks in Norway with Yasir Arafat's Palestine Liberation Organization, the president invited Arafat and Israeli Prime Minister Yitzhak Rabin to Washington in 1993 to sign a Declaration of Principles. Marked by a historic handshake between the former adversaries, the pact provided for mutual recognition and a renunciation of armed conflict. It also established an interim period of Palestinian self-rule in territories occupied by Israel, to be followed by negotiations for a permanent settlement. One year later, Israel and Jordan signed another treaty. Although the Israelis and Palestinians remained far apart in views, the administration sought to preserve the peace process without success.

CLINTON AND THE DOMESTIC AGENDA

As Americans reassessed the importance of government in the post–Cold War era, the Clinton administration struggled to redefine Washington's role at home. Relying for support on Democratic interest groups, the new president initially stumbled. Clinton was forced to withdraw the nominations of several women to the Justice Department when his staff conducted inadequate background checks. White House sponsorship of diversity also suffered when the president prepared an executive order ending discrimination against homosexuals in the armed forces. Having made campaign promises to gay activists, and viewing bias as an obstacle to the optimal use of human resources, Clinton did not anticipate the firestorm of opposition that erupted from the military and Congress. Under intense criticism for undermining the morale of the armed forces, he amended the order to permit homosexuals to serve only if they did not publicly acknowledge their sexual orientation or engage in homosexual acts ("don't ask, don't tell"). Satisfying neither gays nor conservatives, the policy remained a source of controversy and branded Clinton with a reputation for "waffling" on his principles.

EXHIBIT **8-8**   **BOSNIA, 1995**

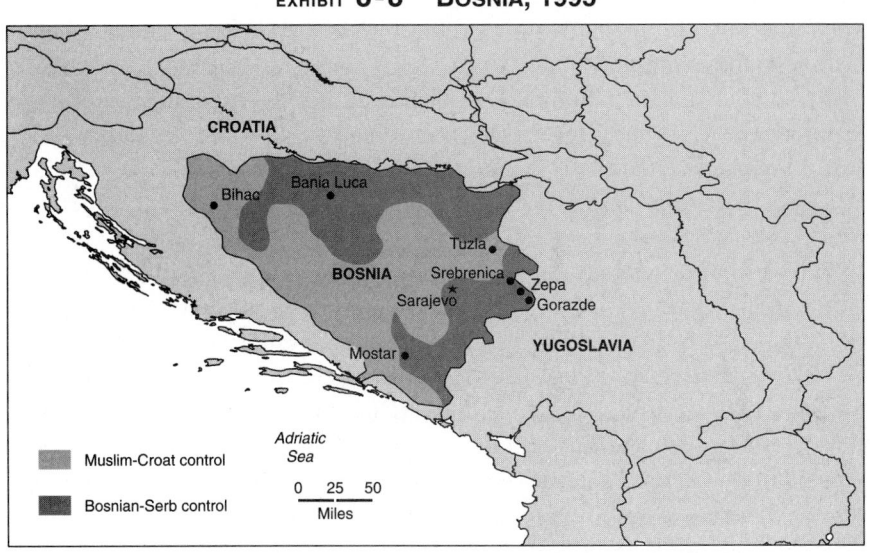

Accepting the advice of Democratic congressional leaders, the president proposed to enact an energy tax to fund a massive jobs programs. Yet as the economy showed signs of recovery, the measure came under strong attack from critics of government spending. Reversing direction, Clinton moved toward fiscal conservatism by accepting the idea that prosperity would not be restored until reduced federal budget deficits lowered interest rates and ensured investors against inflation. The White House now produced a five-year budget that cut defense outlays, payments to Medicare providers, and discretionary spending, while increasing taxes on gasoline, wealthy income receivers, and affluent Social Security recipients. In the House, where not one Republican supported the budget, the measure passed by a single vote; in the Senate, Vice President Gore was forced to break a tie in favor of passage.

Democrats heralded the fiscal discipline of the 1993 budget as the cornerstone of the decade's prosperity. Acknowledging public discomfort with big government, Clinton assigned Gore to chair a committee to trim government bureaucracy. Meanwhile, the administration contrasted itself from its Republican predecessor by addressing reforms that appealed to the middle class. The president signed three measures opposed or vetoed by George Bush—motor voter registration legislation, the family leave act, and the Brady bill establishing a five-day waiting period for handgun purchases. Clinton also won approval for a National Service Plan, which provided college students with earnings from community service to help pay for tuition. Another statute extended the terms of tuition loans without using private lenders. The president moved further to the political center by appointing moderates Ruth Bader Ginsburg and Stephen G. Breyer to the Supreme Court.

Viewing U.S. participation in the global economy as essential to national prosperity, the Clinton administration emphasized the need to ratify the North American Free Trade Agreement (NAFTA), which Bush had signed in 1992. The treaty eliminated taxes or rules impeding the flow of commerce between the United States, Mexico, and Canada. Seeking to overcome the objections of union activists and environmentalists, Clinton had completed supplemental agreements establishing labor and pollution standards. Nevertheless, the AFL-CIO joined nationalists such as Ross Perot in arguing that lower trade barriers would encourage multinational corporations to desert the United States for cheaper labor in Mexico. Ironically, Republican free-trade supporters such as House Minority Leader Newt Gingrich provided the administration with the necessary votes to overcome the resistance of Democratic protectionists and human rights reformers. After the enactment of NAFTA, ten nations at the Pacific Summit joined the United States in calling for extended trade liberalization.

Despite the accomplishments of its first term, the Clinton administration suffered a devastating defeat when Congress refused to act on a national health insurance plan advanced by a panel led by the president's wife, Hillary Rodham Clinton. As advances in medical technology prolonged life but increased costs, health care spending accounted for nearly 12 percent of the gross national product. Seeking to contain costs through comprehensive coverage and to establish medical care as a civil right, the administration proposal divided responsibility between government and private business. The White House task force proposed to enroll consumers in health care alliances that would contract for medical coverage with private insurers. Government regulation of premiums, costs, and quality would assure "managed competition" in a system in which employers absorbed most costs. Once the complex regulations of the proposal were made known, however, public anxieties about government bureaucracy merged with opposition by medical industry interests to kill the measure.

Immobilized by the failure of its central reform, the administration returned to more modest proposals in 1994. Congress passed Clinton's Goals 2000 legislation, a program to establish the first national educational standards. The president also received funding to encourage defense contractors to diversify production for civilian markets. Yet polls showed that crime remained the most important and troubling issue for Americans. Overall crime rates had remained static or declined since the early 1980s. Yet violent offenses by juveniles had increased 50 percent since 1988—young offenders accounted for one-fifth of violent crime arrests in 1994. Disturbed by the random violence emanating from an urban youth culture of weapons, drugs, and gangs, voters demanded that the federal government provide greater support for local law enforcement.

The Clinton administration responded with the Omnibus Crime Act. A patchwork of differing philosophies, the law appealed to conservatives by providing grants to the states to hire more police and build prisons. It also expanded the federal death penalty and mandated life imprisonment for three-time violent federal offenders ("three strikes, you're out"). Yet the legislation addressed liberal concerns by funding crime prevention programs, banning many assault weapons, appropriating money to fight violence against women, and setting up special courts to rehabilitate nonviolent drug abusers. Despite such concessions, civil rights activists were furious that the law's penalties for possession of crack cocaine, a mainstay of inner-city street life, were far more stringent than the punishment for more expensive powder cocaine, consumed by affluent whites.

Disregarding the centrist nature of the Clinton program, Republican politicians insisted that the Democrat-led Congress was politically vulnerable. Following exposure of a series of financial scandals involving House leaders in 1992, the states had ratified a constitutional amendment that outlawed pay raises for sitting members of Congress. By 1994, less than one-fifth of Americans believed that government would "always" do what was right. Charging the Democratic leadership with a forty-year record of cronyism and greed, House Minority Leader Gingrich prepared to take control of the House by drafting a campaign manifesto called the "Contract with America." Signed by 350 Republican House incumbents and candidates, the document promised action on mandatory term limits, a balanced budget amendment, welfare reform, tougher law enforcement, government deregulation, "profamily" legislation, and a strong national defense.

REINVENTING REFORM

The Contract with America helped Republicans regain majorities in both houses of Congress. Although Democrats retained a majority of the women's vote in 1994, they carried less than 40 percent of white males. Ideologically opposed to big government, first-year Republicans influenced the most independent Congress since 1947. The House opened the new session by eliminating many of its own committees and reducing the size of its staff. Under Gingrich's leadership, Congress curbed unfunded federal government mandates and enacted a presidential line-item veto on spending measures. A constitutional amendment requiring a balanced budget passed the House but twice fell short of the required two-thirds Senate majority. Another amendment to limit congressional terms to twelve years failed to receive sufficient support.

Stunned by his party's loss of Congress, Clinton declared that the era of big government was over. Yet Republicans overplayed their hand. Promising a 1995 budget that would eliminate the federal deficit in seven years, Gingrich and Senate Majority Leader Dole combined substantial tax cuts with reductions in the growth of Medicare and Medicaid and decreased aid to education and the environment. Following a Democratic television campaign, Clinton vetoed the Republican budget and the government shut down twice. To the dismay of voters, Washington "beltway" politicians appeared to be engaged in a destructive game of "gridlock," the result of capture of the White House by one political party and control of Congress by its opponents. Yet public opinion placed more of the blame on Gingrich and Dole than on the president.

With public support, Clinton eventually embraced moderate reductions in domestic spending that spared popular social programs. As the 1996 election approached, chagrined Republicans accepted a minimum wage increase they formerly had opposed. In turn, Democrats agreed to a telecommunications bill that promised lower consumer costs and required manufacturers to equip large-screen televisions with "V-chips" allowing parents to block offensive programming. (Studies showed that young people watched five hours of television daily and that cartoons and other children's programming contained more violence than prime-time shows.) Continuing to seek centrist credentials, Clinton signed the Kennedy-Kassenbaum bill, which enabled workers to carry health insurance from job to job and increased medical insurance tax deductions.

The high point of bipartisan cooperation emerged with the Welfare Reform Act of 1996, the most far-reaching change to federal public assistance since its inception in the 1930s. Half of African American and Hispanic families headed by women lived in poverty. Critics had long pointed to the need to break the cycle of "dependence" among "welfare mothers" who were recipients of Aid to Families with Dependent Children (AFDC). Declaring that government assistance provided a second chance, not a way of life, Clinton promoted welfare reform as a means of bringing the poor into the economic mainstream. The new law returned aid programs to the states through federal block grants, compelled nearly a half-million adult recipients to find work in two years, and placed a five-year limit on help to the needy. When liberals accused the president of abandoning women and the poor, he promised to seek tax incentives for businesses that hired former welfare recipients and to provide extra funds for job training.

As the presidential election approached, Clinton readdressed the needs of middle-class families. Responding to continuing concerns about excessive sex and violence on television, he asked the networks to adopt a ratings system to protect young viewers. Attacking cigarette smoking as "the most significant public health hazard facing our people," the president authorized the Food and Drug Administration (FDA) to limit the marketing of tobacco to minors. Appropriating the middle ground of social controversy, Clinton signed the Sanctity of Marriage Act, a Republican measure prohibiting federal recognition of same-sex unions.

THE ELECTION OF 1996 AND THE CENTRIST AGENDA

Hoping to benefit by Clinton's midterm slip in the polls, Republican presidential candidates included former education secretary Lamar Alexander, publishing magnate Steve Forbes, and free-trade opponent Pat Buchanan. Nevertheless, Dole emerged as the Republican nominee by winning key southern primaries. Dole and running mate Jack Kemp called for economic growth through a tax cut, reduced government regulation, and delegation of welfare and anticrime programs to the states. Yet Dole's campaign focused primarily on Whitewater, a scandal involving financial abuses during Clinton's governorship in Arkansas, and on allegations of improper fundraising by the Democrats. Once again, Perot's Reform Party entered the fray by focusing on campaign finance reform.

Running for reelection, Clinton and Gore targeted the votes of babyboomer parents and suburban women ("soccer moms") by promoting education, job training, and computer literacy as a "bridge to the twenty-first century" information age. Democratic "attack ads" also lambasted Republicans

EXHIBIT **8-9**   **THE ELECTION OF 1996**

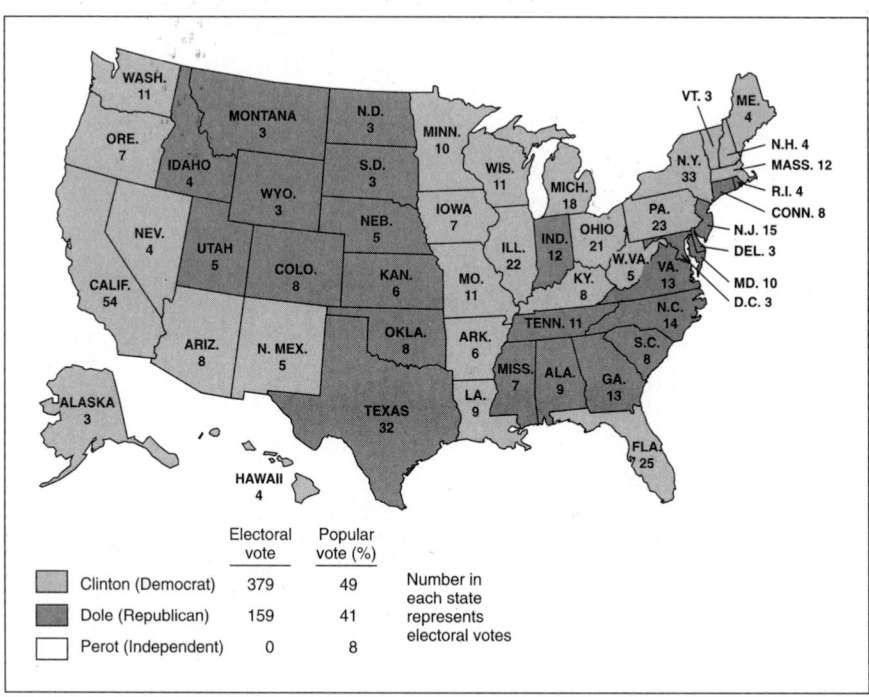

	Electoral vote	Popular vote (%)	
Clinton (Democrat)	379	49	Number in each state represents electoral votes
Dole (Republican)	159	41	
Perot (Independent)	0	8	

for trying to cut Medicare. Benefiting by a booming economy, Clinton breezed to victory by accumulating 49 percent of the popular vote compared to 41 percent for Dole and 8 percent for Perot. Although Dole and Kemp carried most of the mountain West and the Southeast, Democrats took seven of the eight largest states, equaled the Republican total among men, outpaced their opponents among independents, and consolidated their hold among suburbanites and women. Yet voters once again ensured divided government by allowing Republicans to maintain control of Congress.

Clinton used his second term to pursue the centrist agenda favored by the middle class. On the environmental front, the White House protected millions of acres of federal wilderness and created national parks and monuments in western states such as California and Utah. In the Pacific Northwest the administration sought to preserve old-growth forests and salmon runs by limiting the timber harvest in national forests. Yet the Senate blocked U.S. implementation of a treaty on the prevention of global warning.

Finely tuned to consumer needs, Clinton approved a bailout that saved the Amtrak railroad system from bankruptcy, signed a massive transportation appropriation, and agreed to legislation allowing competition among banks, security firms, and insurance companies. The administration addressed the needs of working families by creating a medical insurance program for poor children, raising minimum wages, and expanding the earned income tax credit. To respond to charges of excessive spending and to keep interest rates at historic lows, the president endorsed a Republican plan to balance the budget. By consenting to reduce capital gains and corporate taxes, Clinton authorized the largest tax cut since Ronald Reagan. He also pleased Republicans by agreeing to a congressional moratorium on state taxation of Internet commerce. Spending cuts and continued prosperity produced results: in 1998 the United States experienced the first federal budget surplus in decades, and the Treasury predicted even larger surpluses in the new century.

Convinced that U.S. prosperity rested on ties to the global economy, Clinton promoted participation in the World Trade Organization (WTO), which had replaced the General Agreement on Tariffs and Trade (GATT) in 1995. Although Congress failed to grant the White House "fast-track" negotiating authority for trade pacts, it extended permanent trading partner status to the People's Republic of China despite Beijing's poor human rights and labor record. The president also fostered economic ties with communist regimes in Cuba, North Korea, and Vietnam.

Seeking a stable Europe, Clinton asked that peacekeepers remain in Bosnia and received congressional support for the admission of Poland, Hungary, and the Czech Republic into NATO. Yet the absence of a single enemy increased the partisan nature of foreign policy. After 224 people were killed in the bombing of U.S. embassies in Kenya and Tanzania in 1998, the White House ordered raids on suspected terrorist installations in Sudan and Afghanistan, only to come under criticism for the poor reliability of its intelligence. The next year the president led a brief but violent NATO air campaign against Serbia when a civil war resulted in the brutal suppression of that country's Albanian Muslims. Skeptical that U.S. interests were at stake, the Republican House failed to support a resolution authorizing the Kosovo bombing. When the administration pleaded for ratification of the comprehensive nuclear test ban treaty it had carefully negotiated, the Senate fell three votes shy of agreement.

A DIVIDED SOCIETY

Blessed with declining unemployment and negligible inflation, the Clinton era witnessed the most sustained economic boom in U.S. history. Detroit played a large role in the recovery by producing minivans, light trucks, and sports utility vehicles that tapped the huge family market at home and abroad. Yet the most dramatic growth occurred in the information and telecommunications industries, where computer technology and software applications stimulated an economic revolution. By 2000, about half of all households contained at least one personal computer and over two-fifths of adults used the World Wide Web (the Internet), first organized in 1991. Although more than three-quarters of electronic commerce involved business-to-business transactions, an increasing number of consumers went on-line to make retail purchases, engage in financial transactions, arrange for travel and entertainment, download music and graphics, access information, pursue schoolwork, or socialize in "chat rooms" related to special interests or preferences. Millions of others communicated by electronic mail, creating a virtual subculture of global computer users.

Commercial web sites and Internet services produced a crop of "dot.com" millionaires whose "start-up" companies helped to fuel the strongest stock market in history. By 2000, well over half of U.S. families held Wall Street investments. Nevertheless, as financial conglomerates organized mergers in banking, utilities, retailing, publishing, entertainment, and telecommunications, critics such as Noam Chomsky raised fears concerning corporate control of information and news. The segmented nature of the workforce also belied promises of economic democracy. In a job market dependent upon high-tech skills and training, only 25 percent of working age people possessed college degrees. Unskilled and semiskilled employees, usually African Americans, Hispanics, or women, often filled menial and service positions bereft of health care plans, pensions, or other benefits.

At the close of the century, national poverty rates remained at 13 percent—the same percent prevailing at the height of Lyndon Johnson's Great Society. Anticorporate activists such as Ralph Nader contended that the highly touted global market contributed to the polarization of social classes by exporting high-wage jobs and rewarding reduced employee costs. When

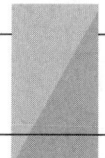

William ("Bill") Henry Gates III (1955–   )

"I wrote my first software program when I was thirteen," recalled Bill Gates, the richest person in the world. "It was for playing tic-tac-toe." Gates became enamored with computers when a system was installed at the Seattle private school he attended. He and childhood friend Paul

Allen took entry-level software programming jobs to pay for computer play time. While at Harvard in 1977, Gates read about a personal computer (PC) kit that featured a powerful microprocessor (a transistor chip that performed basic calculations). Gates and Allen realized that computers needed software programs to instruct them to perform complex tasks such as word processing and data retrieval. After dropping out of college, Gates joined Allen in forming Microsoft—the company that would personalize the computer revolution and become the information age's most successful enterprise.

Microsoft's task was facilitated by corporate giant International Business Machines (IBM), which licensed Microsoft's software for its personal computers instead of purchasing it outright. This arrangement allowed Gates and Allen to offer software to other manufacturers, who marketed their PCs as "IBM-compatible." Yet as Microsoft sought to capture the consumer market in the 1980s, it had difficulty replacing words with pictures to signal programming commands. The company did not develop a user-friendly format until 1990, when Windows 3.0 adopted the graphic commands of Apple Computer's Macintosh, and did not achieve the full potential of Apple's "point and click" system until five years later.

Microsoft established a distinctive, informal work climate for its 17,000 employees, who were hired on the basis of intellectual curiosity and teamwork skills instead of previous expertise. A similar disdain for traditional methods framed Gates's view of the future. Addressing a Las

the World Trade Organization met in Seattle in 1999, labor union and human rights proponents received national attention when they protested that international capital exploited workers and natural resources as mere commodities.

Vegas computer trade show as keynote speaker in 1994, Gates tied his company's prospects to the World Wide Web—the Internet that would do away with "middlemen" and "distributors" and create an "ultimate market" of "friction-free capitalism." This "world's central department store," he insisted, would include "digital wallets," videoconferencing, and global library browsing and would be a place to do business or just "hang out."

Gates announced in 1995 that every Microsoft division would refocus on products to access and browse the Internet. The following year he negotiated a partnership with NBC to create a cable television news channel and web site. In 1997 Microsoft revealed plans to develop "Web TV"—a product that would allow consumers to receive on-line services through home television monitors and thus would erase the need for expensive computer hardware. Having set software standards for 90 percent of the world's personal computers in a $100 billion industry, Gates prepared to expand Microsoft's presence in computerized banking, retailing, and telecommunications. His autobiography, *The Road Ahead* (1995), an instant best-seller, presented the blueprint for innovation on the "information highway."

"We're about making great software, that's our deal," explained Gates in 1996. Yet industry critics contended that Microsoft's market dominance resulted from monopolistic practices similar to those of nineteenth-century industrial robber barons. After the company included software for its own Internet services in Windows '95, federal prosecutors mounted an antitrust suit that resulted in a judge's finding of "monopoly power." Gates argued that the competitive basis of technological innovation did not give anyone "a lock." As Microsoft prepared for an extended series of court appeals, the multibillionaire who still used the word *cool* insisted that postindustrial capitalism offered limitless opportunities for creativity and profits.

Given society's disparities of income and privilege, race relations remained a central problem of U.S. life. Civil rights leaders insisted that racial discrimination continued to victimize Hispanics and people of color and accused police of "racial profiling," a technique by which nonwhites were singled out for

EXHIBIT **8-10**   **THE EIGHT LARGEST SOURCES OF LEGAL IMMIGRATION**
TO THE UNITED STATES IN FISCAL YEAR 1994
(IN ROUNDED FIGURES)

Mexico	111,000
Former Soviet Union	63,000
China/Taiwan	54,000
Philippines	54,000
Dominican Republic	51,000
Vietnam	41,000
India	35,000
Poland	28,000

Source: *Statistical Abstract of the United States* (1996).

unreasonable searches, arrest, or violence. In 1992 the most devastating race riot in U.S. history occurred in Los Angeles after an all-white jury acquitted several policemen of assault following the videotaped beating of black motorist Rodney King. Three years later, former athlete and African American media star O. J. Simpson was acquitted of a double murder when a predominantly black jury questioned L.A. police procedures and discounted the testimony of a white officer who had used racial slurs. Disturbed by racist images of African American men and seeking to renew black family cohesion, Nation of Islam minister Louis Farrakhan convened a "Million Man March" in Washington, D.C. Meanwhile, a federal report revealed that one-third of black men in their twenties were either in prison, on probation, or on parole.

As nonwhites and Hispanics came to comprise more than one-fourth of the U.S. population, racial perceptions assumed a prominent role in the nation's policy disputes. In 1993 the Supreme Court ruled that congressional districts could not be drawn solely on the basis of race. In California, where whites were a statistical minority by decade's end, the University of California abandoned affirmative action, and voters passed a ballot initiative ending bilingual instruction in public schools. Responding to conservative concerns about cultural unity and mastery of fundamentals, politicians of both political parties pushed for national testing of public school teachers and students.

As critics characterized affirmative action as special preference, the nation witnessed an outpouring of white supremacy and militant nationalism. In Texas, a resurgent Ku Klux Klan accused Vietnamese immigrants of taking over the Gulf shrimping industry and vowed to stop illegal immigration from Mexico. Rival Klansmen lynched a young African American man in Alabama, although a suit by civil rights activists forced the group to sell off its assets and cease operations. David Duke, a former Klansman, won election as a Louisiana state legislator and drew headlines in close races for public office. Meanwhile, activists such as Tom Metzger of White Aryan Resistance (WAR) organized gangs of young racist "skinheads" in major cities, particularly on the West Coast.

Arming themselves for race war and civil strife, "patriot" groups such as the Order, the Aryan Nation, and Christian Identity confronted government authorities over weapons violations and tax issues. At Ruby Ridge, the Idaho home of white supremacist leader Randy Weaver, a controversial shoot-out in 1992 killed Weaver's wife and son and a federal marshal. Another confrontation led to the murder-suicide of seventy-five adults and children near Waco, Texas, in 1993, when government agents ended a fifty-one-day siege by attacking the compound of the armed Branch Davidian sect. White supremacist and antigovernment views also dominated the independent militia movement, active in the western states. Federal prosecutors tied extreme radicalism to two men convicted of the murder of 165 people in the 1995 bombing of the federal building in Oklahoma City—the worst act of domestic terrorism in U.S. history. Responding to a rash of black church burnings and individual acts of racial violence, civil rights activists pressed for federal "hate crimes" legislation.

Reacting to such violent rhetoric and sensational crime, critics challenged the popular culture industries to curtail presentations of violence and sexuality. Cultural commentators also worried about the nihilistic messages of punk and grunge bands such as Pearl Jam and Nirvana. A series of grisly public school shootings between 1998 and 1999 prompted a national debate over the relative dangers of guns versus the impact of violent movies, video games, hip-hop lyrics, and cult web sites. By 2000, politicians in both parties were demanding that media and communications giants practice self-restraint or face government interference.

In a climate of affluence and cultural ferment, social conservatives desperately sought to bolster traditional values. As the twentieth century ended, nuclear families—married parents living with children—constituted only one-fourth of all households and were only slightly more numerous than those consisting of single people. Fifteen million families were headed by one parent, usually a woman. Conservatives focused on abortion as a symbol of rampant self-indulgence and persuaded the Republican Congress to ban "partial-birth" procedures. Clinton vetoed the bill because it failed to provide adequate provisions concerning the mother's health. More radical "right-to-life" groups such as Operation Rescue organized blockades of abortion centers. Following a series of clinic bombings and fatal shootings, however, Congress prohibited the use of force or intimidation against women entering abortion facilities, and the Supreme Court upheld the right of local authorities to regulate antiabortion protesters in 1997.

IMPEACHMENT AND A NEW CENTURY

Political and social divisions helped to shape the controversial impeachment of President Clinton. Following the 1996 election, both houses of Congress

Federico F. Pena (1947–   )

The rapid rise of Energy Secretary Federico Pena illustrated the ethnic dimension of the "New Democrat" political movement. A member of a prominent South Texas Hispanic family, Pena grew up in Brownsville. The son of a cotton broker who stressed discipline, he served as an altar

boy before attending the University of Texas at Austin. Pena joined protests against the Vietnam War before earning his law degree in 1972. He then moved to Denver, where he became a staff lawyer for the Mexican American Legal Defense and Educational Fund. Pena concentrated on police brutality and voting rights cases before signing on as legal advisor to the Chicano Education Project, which involved him in efforts to promote bilingual education.

At thirty-one, Pena began his political career with election to the Colorado legislature, where he was chosen as Democratic minority speaker. He built on these successes in 1983 by running for mayor of Denver against a fourteen-year incumbent and won the election. Yet in the mid-1980s an economic slump in the oil, mining, and high-tech industries produced high vacancy rates in downtown Denver offices. When Pena stood

investigated a series of Democratic campaign abuses, including the acceptance of illegal foreign contributions, improper solicitations by Vice President Gore, and the use of White House facilities for political fundraising. The administration responded to critics by insisting that it supported the campaign finance legislation proposed by Republican Senator John McCain and Democrat Russell D. Feingold. In 1998, however, the Republican Senate failed to stop a filibuster against the reformers' proposal to ban unregulated "soft money" donations to political parties. By that time, Clinton faced the greatest crisis of his political career.

In 1997 the Supreme Court ruled that an Arkansas woman could pursue a sexual harassment civil suit against former governor Clinton. Shortly after the president made history by testifying in the case, press reports alleged that he had conducted a sexual affair with a former White House intern and had

for reelection in 1987, he faced a 22-point deficit in the polls. Resorting to negative advertising, he portrayed his Republican opponent as a tool of big business and scored another close victory, which he used to gain public support for a convention center, a new airport, and a major-league baseball team.

Success at the local level permitted Pena to enter the national arena. Seeking to implement a campaign promise that executive appointments would reflect diversity, President Clinton opened his first cabinet to an unprecedented number of women, African Americans, and Hispanics and named Pena as secretary of transportation. The cabinet officer enforced strict fuel economy standards and encouraged the establishment of new airlines to compete with the major carriers. He also developed plans for environmentally protective high-speed trains and directed the investment of pension funds in the modernization of transportation systems.

Pena perfectly combined the virtues of urban professionalism with long-standing traditions of ethnic identity and urban politics. When a vacancy occurred in the Department of Energy in 1997, Clinton responded to the large Democratic vote among Hispanics by naming Pena to the high-profile post, a position he held for a year prior to returning to the private sector.

denied the relationship under oath. As rumors flew, Clinton used a television interview to emphatically deny involvement in an extramarital sexual relationship. Attorney General Janet Reno now permitted Special Whitewater Prosecutor Kenneth W. Starr to investigate whether the White House had encouraged the former intern to lie. Although the sexual harassment case was dismissed (Clinton ultimately settled it for $800,000), the president was compelled to appear before a federal grand jury in 1998.

Despite the fact that he had misled aides, family, and the public, Clinton insisted he had been "legally correct" in his original testimony before the civil court. Seeking to take advantage of the president's evasiveness, Republicans prevailed upon the House of Representatives to release the salacious details of Starr's report and to approve two articles of impeachment for perjury before the grand jury and obstruction of justice. Although Clinton's personal

American Beauty (1999)

Rejected by Hollywood's established studios, American Beauty *was produced by Steven Spielberg's Dreamworks at a modest cost of $15 million. The first motion picture feature of British director Sam Mendes and TV sit-com writer Alan Ball, this surprising film became a major commercial and critical hit, winning five Academy Awards, including best picture. As cultural conservatives and social progressives continued to clash over the state of the nuclear family,* American Beauty *offered a dark parody of the idealized life of the suburbs that depicted feelings of loneliness and rage with both humor and empathy.*

"I'm dead already," forty-two-year old narrator Lester Burnham announces at the beginning of the film. Kevin Spacey plays an upper-middle-class homeowner about to be fired from his hated job writing press releases for an advertising media magazine. Despite a life of affluence and relative comfort, Spacey confronts the unraveling of his entire existence. His wife Carolyn

© Douglas Slone/Corbis

(Annette Bening) is an ardent real estate broker who drives a sports utility vehicle, immerses herself in motivational audiotapes, and strives to couple up
with the hot realtor in town. Lester's daughter, Jane, barely talks to him.

Jane sees her father as a self-centered loser, disgusted that he lusts after
her best friend, a blonde and nubile high school cheerleader. Meanwhile, she
finds comfort with the next-door neighbor, the son of a rigid marine colonel
and depressive mother. While the colonel rages against the dangers of homosexuality, represented by two cheerful gay partners named Jim who live
down the street, his son survives by dealing marijuana and cherishing the
beauty of the "life behind things."

Liberated from his despised superiors at the magazine, Lester celebrates
his new role as a fast-food server, an exercise in downward mobility that mocks
the affluent pretensions of the booming 1990s. Reverting to adolescence, he
buys a red 1970 Pontiac Firebird and works out in his garage while listening to
Bob Dylan tapes and smoking dope supplied by his entrepreneurial neighbor.
As American Beauty moves toward a fated climax and an ironic commentary
on middle-class homophobia, it offers a sardonic approach to family life that
suggests that fantasy and violence offer the only escape from conventional existence—that normality itself is an illusion.

In a period in which the media focused on the horrors of school shootings
and other acts of random violence, audiences seemed to appreciate American
Beauty's attempt to delve beneath the surface of human motivation. None of
the characters in the movie "are quite what they seem," explained director
Mendes. Instead of stereotypes, the film provided a complex view of people
infused with ambiguity and pain, suggesting the potential for emotional
growth and self-understanding. "I feel like I've been in a coma for twenty
years and I'm just now waking up," confides Lester.

American Beauty's off-beat portraits of conventional morality, misplaced
affluence, and personal heroism defied the pieties of politicians and traditional
cultural authorities. The film revealed the public's fascination with fractured
families whose foibles were simultaneously sad and funny. Refreshed by the
movie's counterpoint to materialism and self-interest, critics praised Hollywood for telling a story that celebrated life's potential for surprise, beauty, and
transcendence.

approval ratings plummeted, most voters opposed removing him from office for nonpolitical offenses. As televised impeachment proceedings shifted to the Senate in 1999, a majority of senators failed to vote for conviction on either article, far short of the two-thirds margin required to replace a president.

At the end of a presidential term marked by unprecedented budget surpluses and the longest run of prosperity in U.S. history, the nation still struggled over its political identity. Arizona Senator McCain sought to make campaign finance reform the focal point of an insurgent run for the White House in 2000. Yet the Republican nomination went to Texas Governor George W. Bush, son of the former president. Offering himself as a "compassionate conservative" who emphasized the importance of inclusion, Bush promised to reinvigorate the nation's public education with a combined program of federal funding, performance standards, and vouchers for private schools. As the candidate called for less government and greater accountability from citizens, he proposed to place caps on civil suit settlements, enact across-the-board tax reduction and reform of the Internal Revenue Service, and privatize aspects of Social Security. To illustrate his commitment to military readiness and deployment of a missile protection system, Bush chose Dick Cheney, his father's defense secretary, as his running mate. The Republicans addressed conservative social issues by opposing affirmative action quotas and demanding prohibition of "partial birth" abortions.

Seeking to separate himself from Clinton's personal scandals without distancing himself from the administration's accomplishments, Democratic candidate Al Gore asked Connecticut Senator and Clinton critic Joseph I. Lieberman to be his vice presidential standard bearer, making Lieberman the first Jew to run for national office on a major party ticket. Gore supported McCain's campaign finance reforms, gun control, prescription drugs for all Medicare recipients, a children's health care bill, and managed health care reform. Calling for more federal aid for public schools, he offered carefully targeted tax cuts to compensate middle-class families for medical insurance, child care, and higher education expenses.

In a period in which the economy continued to boom but the public remained divided about the moral issues raised by Clinton's tenure, the election produced one of the closest and most bitterly contested presidential races in U.S. history. Green Party candidate Ralph Nader took 2.7 percent of the vote while minor party candidates captured another 1 percent. Nearly all the remaining ballots were split between the Republican and Democratic candidates. Gore won the popular tally by over 539,000 votes (0.3 percent of the total) and took the West Coast and most of the industrial states of the Northeast and Upper Middle West. In the evenly divided electoral college, the selection of president came down to the vote in Florida, where George Bush initially emerged with a miniscule plurality of several hundred votes.

When Democrats protested that antiquated voting machines had failed to register thousands of partially punched or indented ballots in their strongholds in south Florida, the state supreme court ordered officials to ignore an election certification deadline and accept the results of manual recounts from three counties. Yet Gore's attorneys contested the certification when only one of the three counties completed its tally before the court's new deadline. The Democrats suffered another blow when a state trial judge rejected the vice president's contest on legal and evidentiary grounds. Yet the Florida Supreme Court reversed the ruling, 4–3, in a surprising decision that ordered a statewide recount of all ballots showing no vote for president. Five weeks after the election, however, the saga came to a dramatic climax when the U.S. Supreme Court halted the recount by a 5–4 vote. In a controversial ruling, the Court concluded that the absence of statewide recount standards amounted to a violation of the "equal protection" clause of the Fourteenth Amendment. It also cited difficulties in completing the recount by deadlines established by state law.

As a result of the Court's intervention, Florida's twenty-five electoral votes were recorded for George W. Bush, who emerged with a narrow 271–266 victory in the electoral college. The evenly divided election also produced a 50–50 tie in the Senate when the Democrats picked up four seats. In the House, the Republican plurality was reduced to a mere ten votes. Having lost the popular vote in a bitter election marked by legal maneuvering on both sides, Bush promised to restore the luster of the presidency by pursuing a bipartisan agenda with muted acrimony. Yet as Democrats and Republicans competed for the ideological center, personal rancor and partisanship appeared to take on unprecedented dimensions in U.S. politics.

The 2000 election addressed many of the issues that had framed public discourse throughout the post–World War II era. What were the proper duties and limits of government? How was prosperity to be sustained? Could public policy play a role in enabling more citizens to share in the American Dream? What actions might contribute to erasing technological barriers to economic opportunity? Were social welfare programs financially viable without a more disciplined allotment of resources? Could national leaders facilitate social peace among the country's diverse ethnic and cultural groups? Was it possible to sustain nationwide cohesion and purpose without the unifying influence of a monolithic foreign enemy? Could life in the emerging century be reconciled to traditional moral values and continuity with the past?

As Americans looked to the future for assurances of greater affluence and security, they appeared to share the same hopes and fears that had inaugurated the atomic age in 1945. Accustomed to the persistent dangers of an unstable world and wary of the promises of politicians, they could only hope that national leaders would confront the awesome complexities and challenges of modern life with vision, courage, and integrity.

INFOTRAC COLLEGE EDITION

Using Keywords, enter the following search terms:

Berlin Wall, Fall
Gulf War, History
Clarence Thomas, Hearings
Bill Clinton, Presidency
Bill Clinton, Impeachment
Ross Perot
Boris Yeltsin
Newt Gingrich

RECOMMENDED READING

Alex Roberto Hybel, *Power over Rationality: The Bush Administration and the Gulf Crisis* (1993). A detailed monograph and survey covering the high point of Bush's presidency.

Stanley Allen Renshon, *High Hopes: The Clinton Presidency and the Politics of Ambition* (1996). This psychological biography provides an intriguing analysis of Clinton's personal strengths and weaknesses and offers a fitting preview to the impeachment crisis.

Theda Skocpol, *Boomerang: Clinton's Health Security Effort and the Turn Against Government in U.S. Politics* (1996). More than a eulogy on failed health care reform, this thoughtful analysis by a scholar and policy consultant addresses eroding faith in government in the post–Reagan era.

Michael Lind, *The Next American Nation: The New Nationalism and the Fourth American Revolution* (1995). An assessment of the way in which migration patterns have altered the ethnic and cultural mix of U.S. society.

Additional Reading

For overviews of the Bush administration, see John Robert Greene, *The Presidency of George Bush* (2000); Michael Duffy, *Marching in Place: The Status-Quo Presidency of George Bush* (1992); and Charles Kolb, *White House Daze: The Unmaking of Domestic Policy in the Bush Years* (1994). Ecological issues are the focus of the relevant segments of Robert A. Shanley, *Presidential Influence and Environmental Policy* (1992). Bush's economic and social policies are contextualized in the appropriate chapters of William C. Berman, *America's Right Turn: From Nixon to Bush* (1994), and of Alonzo L. Hamby, *Liberalism and Its Challengers: From F.D.R. to Bush* (rev. ed., 1992). See also Kitty Calavita et al., *Big Money Crimes: Fraud and Politics in the Savings and Loan Crisis* (1997).

The end of the Cold War stimulated an outpouring of scholarship. For the involvement of peace groups, see John Lofland, *Polite Protesters: The American Peace Movement of the 1980s* (1993), and David Cortright, *Peace Works: The Citizen's Role in Ending the Cold War* (1993). Overviews of the Cold War include H. W. Brands, *The Devil We Knew: Americans and the Cold War* (1993); Warren I. Cohen, *America in the Age of Soviet Power, 1945–1991* (1993); Michael J. Hogan, ed., *The End of the Cold War: Its Meaning and Implications* (1992); and Richard Ned Lebow and Janice Gross Stein, *We All Lost the Cold War* (1994).

Background to the Gulf War is provided in the relevant segments of Michael A. Palmer, *Guardians of the Gulf: A History of America's Expanding Role in the Persian Gulf, 1933–1992* (1992). See also Richard J. Barnet, *The Rockets' Red Glare: War, Politics, and the American Presidency* (1991). On foreign policy decision making, see the relevant portions of Harold Koh, *The National Security Constitution: Sharing Power After the Iran-Contra Affair* (1992), and of Louis Fisher, *Presidential War Powers* (1995).

Political journalists continue to monopolize the work on the Clinton administration. See Elizabeth Drew, *On the Edge: The Clinton Presidency* (1994). For policy making and politics, see Bob Woodward, *Inside the Clinton White House* (1994), and *The Choice* (1996). Another view can be found in James B. Stewart, *Blood Sport: The President and His Adversaries* (1996). For the president and first lady, see Roger Morris, *Partners in Power: The Clintons and Their America* (1996).

For the 1996 election, see John Hohenberg, *Reelecting Bill Clinton: Why America Chose a "New" Democrat* (1997). Clinton policies are discussed in Charles O. Jones, *Clinton and Congress, 1993–1996* (1999), and in Jacob S. Hacker, *The Road to Nowhere: The Genesis of President's Clinton's Plan for Health Security* (1997).

Political alienation is the topic of William Greider, *Who Will Tell the People: The Betrayal of American Democracy* (1992), and Stanley Greenberg, *Middle-Class Dreams: The Politics and Power of the New American Majority* (1996). See also Michael F. Spath, *Dangerous Delusions: America on the Brink* (1995).

For racial politics, see the last segments of Dan T. Carter, *From George Wallace to Newt Gingrich: Race in the Conservative Counterrevolution, 1963–1994* (1996), and George Lipsitz, *The Possessive Investment in Whiteness: How White People Profit From Identity Politics* (1998). See also Orlando Patterson, *The Ordeal of Integration: Progress and Resentment in America's "Racial" Crisis* (1997). Immigrant issues are explored in David M. Reimers, *Unwelcome Strangers: American Identity and the Turn Against Immigration* (1998). A useful case study can be found in Lisa Lowe, *Immigrant Acts: On Asian American Cultural Politics* (1996). For the patriot movement, see Michael Barkun, *Religion and the Racist Right: The Origins of the Christian Identity Movement* (1994).

Index

American Independent Party, 176, 184–185
American Indian Movement (AIM), 167, 199
American Indians, 103–104, 166–167, 182, 199, 260–261
American Psychiatric Society, 198
American Telephone and Telegraph (AT&T), 242
Americans for Democratic Action (ADA), 26
Amtrak railroad system, 296
Anaya, Rudolfo, 200
Anderson, John B., 240
Andrews, Dana, 4
Angelou, Maya, 261
Antiapartheid protests, 245, 277
Antibiotics, 12
Anticommunism (domestic targets)
and civil rights, 108, 192
and Eisenhower, 56–57, 68–71, 82
in 1950s, 47–50, 55–56, 68–73, 76–77, 81, 88, 107, 200
in 1940s, 8, 16–17, 31–33, 48, 57, 76–77, 99
after 1960, 138, 192, 236
and Nixon, 31, 32, 47, 188
and organized labor, 8, 75
and Reagan, 237
and Truman, 31, 33, 37, 57
Anticommunism (and foreign policy) 139, 200–201, 246–247, 286
and Carter, 232–234
and Clinton, 288–289
and Eisenhower, 61–65, 77, 82–86, 88–92, 114–117
and Johnson, 154–157, 161, 167–168, 175–176, 179
and Kennedy, 120, 122–125, 132–141
and Nixon and Ford, 189, 202, 204–206, 220–221
and Reagan and G. H. W. Bush, 237–238, 244–253, 289
and Truman, 20, 24–31, 33–36, 39–43, 47–48, 50–55
Antiimperialism, 165, 206
Antimonopoly, see Antitrust laws
Antisemitism, 99, 108, 277
Antitrust laws, 13, 66, 299
ANZUS treaty (1951), 55
Apartheid, 231, 233, 245, 277
Appalachia assistance program, 153
Apple Computer, 256, 298
Aquino, Corazon, 245
Arafat, Yasir, 290
Arbenz, Jacobo, 65
Area Development Agency, 125
Aristide, Jean-Bertrand, 289
Armas, Carlos, 65
Arms control, see Nuclear disarmament
Arms-for-hostages accord (1986), 247, 251
Armstrong, Neil A., 197
Army-McCarthy hearings (1954), 72, 78
Aryan Nation, 301
Asian Americans, see Immigrants
Asimov, Isaac, 11

Astronauts, 90, 124–127, 197, 267
Aswan Dam, 90
Atomic energy, 11, 12, 67, 218, 227
overseas, 25, 41, 63, 70, 209, 289
and power plants, 230–231
Atomic Energy Act (1946), 11, 67
Atomic Energy Commission (AEC), 11, 12, 42, 47, 67, 69–71, 90
Atomic weapons, 11, 12, 138
and Carter, 232–234
and Clinton, 288, 289, 297
and Eisenhower, 61–63, 67–69, 81, 82, 86–90, 116, 124
and Daniel Ellsberg, 210, 252
and internal security, 31, 41, 48–49, 69–71
and Kennedy and Johnson, 124, 135–140, 154
after 1980, 252–254, 279–280, 306
and Nixon, 209
public anxiety, 1950s, 55–56, 59, 88–89, 113, 138
public anxiety, 1940s, 11–12, 43, 47, 49
public anxiety, post-1960, 135, 138–139, 252
"Atoms for peace" proposal, 63, 116
Attica prison riot, 202
Atwater, Lee, 278
Automobiles, see Motor vehicles

"Baby boomers"
since 1980, 256, 295
between 1945 and 1960, 14–16, 18, 96–97, 100–101, 112
between 1960 and 1980, 142–143
Baez, Joan, 169
Baghdad Pact (1955), 90
Baker, Ella, 144
Baker v. Carr (1962), 76, 107
Bakke case (1978), 237
Bakker, Jim, 263
Baldwin, James, 111, 165
Ball, Alan, 304
Ball, George, 157
Bank of America arson, 206–207
Banking Act (1982), 242
Barnett, Ross, 130
Barrio, Raymond, 200
Barrow, Clyde, 172–173
Baruch, Bernard M., 25
Baseball, 99, 104, 303
Batista, Fulgencio, 115
Bay of Pigs invasion (1961), 133–134, 140
Beat generation, 113, 144, 170
Beatles, 142, 145, 170
Beatty, Warren, 173
Bebop, 112–113
BeeGees, 195
Begin, Menachem, 232
Beirut bombings (1982), 245
Bell, Daniel, 98
Bell Laboratories, 12
Bening, Annette, 305
Bennett, William J., 266